The First Knowledge Economy

Ever since the Industrial Revolution, debate has raged about the sources of the new, sustained Western prosperity. Margaret Jacob here argues persuasively for the critical importance of knowledge in Europe's economic transformation during the period from 1750 to 1850, first in Britain and then in selected parts of Northern and Western Europe. This is a new history of economic development in which minds, books, lectures, and education become central. She shows how, armed with knowledge and know-how and inspired by the desire to get rich, entrepreneurs emerged within an industrial culture wedded to scientific knowledge and technology. She charts how, across a series of industries and nations, innovative engineers and entrepreneurs sought to make sense and a profit out of the world around them. Skilled hands matched minds steeped in the knowledge systems new to the eighteenth century to transform the economic destiny of Western Europe.

MARGARET C. JACOB is Distinguished Professor of History at the University of California, Los Angeles.

The First Knowledge Economy

Human Capital and the European Economy, 1750–1850

Margaret C. Jacob

CAMBRIDGE
UNIVERSITY PRESS

CAMBRIDGE
UNIVERSITY PRESS

University Printing House, Cambridge CB2 8BS, United Kingdom

Published in the United States of America by Cambridge University Press, New York

Cambridge University Press is part of the University of Cambridge.

It furthers the University's mission by disseminating knowledge in the pursuit of education, learning, and research at the highest international levels of excellence.

www.cambridge.org
Information on this title: www.cambridge.org/9781107044012

First published 2014

Printed and bound in the United Kingdom by Clays, St Ives plc

A catalogue record for this publication is available from the British Library

Library of Congress Cataloguing in Publication data
Jacob, Margaret C., 1943–
The first knowledge economy : human capital and the European economy, 1750–1850 / Margaret C. Jacob.
pages cm
ISBN 978-1-107-04401-2 (hardback)
1. Industrialization – Europe – History. 2. Technological innovations – Economic aspects – Europe – History. 3. Economic development – Europe – History. I. Title.
HC240.J335 2014
330.94′0253–dc23
2013021430

ISBN 978-1-107-04401-2 Hardback
ISBN 978-1-107-61983-8 Paperback

Contents

Figures

Maps

Acknowledgements

Every chapter in this book owes a debt to a handful of contemporary scholars whose work has been read and absorbed, even if not always cited. In random order they are Larry Stewart (for his writings see www.industrialization.ats.ucla.edu), Joel Mokyr, Jack Goldstone, Deirdre McCloskey, Joyce Appleby, David Reid, Matt Kadane, and Ian Inkster. All have critiqued portions of this text, or its conference paper versions, and saved the author many an error. Equally important have been grants from the US National Science Foundation (NSF), and the National Endowment for the Humanities, which funded the above-mentioned website where the Marshall MSS at the Brotherton Library, Leeds can be read. That library's assistance and hospitality were matched by that of the North of England Institute of Mining and Mechanical Engineers, Newcastle, one of the finest archives in Britain for the study of the coal trade and early industrial development in general. Chapter 2 relies heavily on its riches. The Birmingham City Library possesses the extraordinary Boulton and Watt archives, central to Chapter 1 of this book, and, like the staffs of other British sites, its personnel have been immensely helpful.

Research for Chapters 3 and 7 was made possible by the NSF, and I must thank my post-doctoral fellow, Dorothee Sturkenboom, for the many weeks she spent in Belgian archives concerned with education. David Reid did the same for Manchester. The hard-working staff of the Archives nationales in Paris, and also various provincial French repositories, made Chapters 5 and 6 possible. A version of Chapter 3 appeared in the *Canadian Journal of History*, 2001, and one of Chapter 4 in *History of Science*, 2007. A portion of Chapter 1 appeared in *Scientific Culture and the Making of the Industrial West* (1997).

Now, as I enjoy the comforts of Los Angeles, I want to dedicate this book to special friends who make life so rich: Joyce Appleby, Scarlett Freund, and Teo Ruiz. My spouse, Lynn, is always in my mind and by my side, not least my most helpful critic.

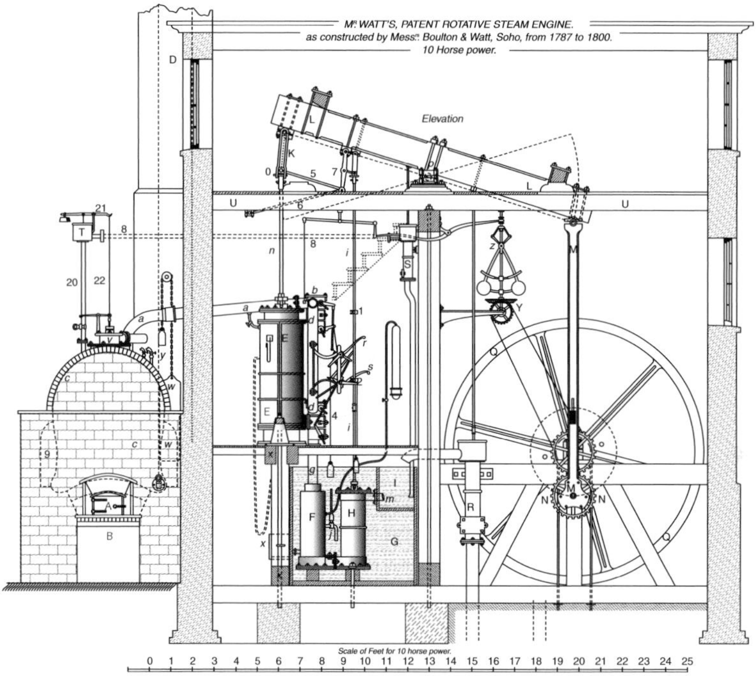

Figure 1 Steam engine

Introduction

Knowledge and industrial development: the stakes

By "the first knowledge economy" we refer to the era of the Industrial Revolution from roughly the 1760s to the 1850s, first in Britain and then in selected parts of Northern and Western Europe, with particular attention to Belgium. Only and first in this period did economic growth based upon technological innovation become continuous. There were ebbs and flows to be sure, recessions, even depressions, but still the wealth of the affected nations continued to grow, and, slowly, so too did per capita income of families. Put another way, the so-called Malthusian dictum, that prosperity would fuel population growth that would inevitably be stopped by food shortages, came undone. By the last quarter of the nineteenth century, real wages had risen, as had the population in general, and output in agriculture and manufacturing had also risen to meet the new demand.

Since that time the debate has raged as to how the dictum had been broken. What were the key factors that made sustained Western prosperity possible? The answer presented in this book focuses upon mechanical knowledge, derived largely but not exclusively from Newtonian science, and the theoretical underpinnings that it supplied to technological innovation in mining, manufacturing, and the application of steam power more generally. The new knowledge economy displayed many cultural elements – wider circulation of information, new teaching venues, and curricular reforms – more visible first in Britain than on the Continent. None of the elements was more important than the organized body of mechanical knowledge distilled in lectures, textbooks, and curricula. It was what French observers came to call industrial mechanics and it became crucial to technological innovation. When we speak in the present about our knowledge economy, it helps to know where and when an earlier version of it began.

Stories told by economic historians

The generalization presented here about the critical importance of knowledge in breaking the Malthusian dictum challenges existing assumptions beloved by some economic historians. For example, the literature in economic history simplistically argues that Britain industrialized first because it had abundant coal. It was there for the chiseling and hauling, so entrepreneurs seized upon it. One British historian tells us that the Industrial Revolution was not economic so much as it was "physical, chemical and biological . . . a means of escape was found, by happenstance rather than conscious design initially [leading to] a rising expenditure of energy." Willy-nilly, we are asked to believe, the British began to tap the energy capital that had been locked up in coal deposits 300 million years previously. Industries needed coal; hence it was extracted. Another version of the same argument about coal claims "the only limit on the expansion on [its] energy use is the capital accumulation required for that extraction."[1]

In the case of coal, the problem with the "capital brings success" argument rests on the inaccessibility of much of the coal, and the need for skilled engineers to figure out how to extract it from below the surface of a mine. As we will see in the chapters ahead, knowledge of basic mechanics and the running of steam engines played a decisive role in making the coal usable. In the course of the eighteenth century the tried and true methods for coal extraction were revolutionized. Skilled engineers were vital in the process, and detailed, small-scale problem-solving at mine after mine gradually expanded the tonnage extracted throughout the British Isles.[2]

Another commonplace in the economic history of the Industrial Revolution awards pride of place to semi-literate tinkerers, particularly in the vital manufacturing sector of cotton. In that older view, historians such as Pat Hudson believed "there was almost no exchange of ideas between scientists and industrial innovators. Scientific advance at the time lay mainly ... far removed from the sphere of major industrial advances."[3] The *personae* of the earliest British entrepreneurs have been described as deficient in "technical and commercial expertise," a condition remedied in time only by employing specialists.[4] This version of economic history

[1] E. A. Wrigley, "In Quest for the Industrial Revolution," *Proceedings of the British Academy*, 2003, Vol. 121, pp. 168–70. He softens this view in *Energy and the English Industrial Revolution* (Cambridge University Press, 2010), pp. 44–7. See P. Warde, "Energy and Natural Resource Dependency in Europe, 1600–1900," in C. A. Bayly *et al.*, *History, Historians and Development Policy. A Necessary Dialogue* (Manchester University Press, 2011), p. 233.

[2] As predicted in F. M. Scherer, *New Perspectives on Economic Growth and Technological Innovation* (Washington, DC: Brookings Institution Press, 1999), pp. 62–4. See also P. Hudson, *The Industrial Revolution* (New York: Edward Arnold, 1992), p. 24.

[3] Ibid.

[4] P. L. Payne, *British Entrepreneurship in the Nineteenth Century*, 2nd edn., 1988, and found in I. A. Clarkson, ed., *The Industrial Revolution. A Compendium*, Atlantic Highlands, NJ: Humanities Press, 1990, p. 70; now available from Humanity Books, Amherst, NY.

Figure 2 A spinning jenny still in use in Trowbridge, c. 1930 © Science Museum/Science & Society Picture Library.

caricatured early industrialists as primarily untutored artisans for whom invention by tinkering superseded abstract knowledge of scientific or technological principles.[5] "Practical knowledge," we are told, exists divorced from "theoretical" or "abstract" knowledge. The rigidity of this model neglects the fact that early industrialists in cotton could be both artisanal and machine savvy while being theoretically sophisticated. To be sure, making spinning jennies did not necessarily require a working knowledge of mechanical principles derived from science; connecting and maintaining multiple spinning machines to steam power did.

The records in Manchester tell a much more complicated story, and again, without dismissing the skilled hand worker, show the role played by the application of mechanical knowledge to the manufacturing of cotton cloth. Turning to Leeds and its linen industry reveals a similar pattern: scientifically informed entrepreneurs in league with engineers – all mindful hands – brought new technology to the factory floors.[6]

New evidence from early American industrialization also demonstrates that technical knowledge during the late eighteenth and nineteenth centuries consisted of multiple skills of varying degrees of abstractness.[7] A new "technical literacy" sprang up along with new manufacturing technologies and included, in addition to traditional alphabetical literacy, the ability to make mathematical calculations of increasing sophistication and to read and understand technical drawings and models.[8] The earlier evidence from Britain points to a similar configuration of mathematical calculation, trial and error experimentation, and the ability to follow the complexity of new machinery.

In much post-Second World War era scholarship, we got a list of reasons why England industrialized first, and by extension why the West industrialized first. Old School economic historians told how just about everything except education and knowledge – i.e., culture – held the key to

[5] See P. Mathias, "Who Unbound Prometheus?" in P. Mathias, ed., *Science and Society 1600–1900* (Cambridge University Press, 1972).

[6] For a relevant account of the skilled tinkerer, see J. Smail, "Innovation and Invention in the Yorkshire Wool Textile Industry: A Miller's Tale," in L. Hilaire-Pérez and A.-F. Garçon, eds., *Les chemins de la nouveauté: innover, inventer au regard de d'histoire* (Paris: Éditions du CTHS, 2003), pp. 313–29. For a good description of the millwright of the mid eighteenth century see D. T. Jenkins, *The West Riding Wool Textile Industry 1770–1835* (Edington: Pasold Research Fund Ltd., 1975), pp. 101–2, quoting Fairbairn. And see P. Hudson, *The Industrial Revolution* (London: Edward Arnold, 1992), p. 24.

[7] E. W. Stevens, Jr., *The Grammar of the Machine: Technical Literacy and Early Industrial Expansion in the United States* (New Haven, CT: Yale University Press, 1995). See R. Thomson, *Structures of Change in the Mechanical Age. Technological Innovation in the United States 1790–1865* (Baltimore, MD: The Johns Hopkins University Press, 2009).

[8] Stevens, 1995, pp. 2–4. On the pedagogical and epistemological problems associated with graphical representation, see Chapter 2.

industrial development: access to coal, cheap labor, surplus population leading to increased division of labor, the slave trade, or abundant capital, or consumerism creating large domestic markets. A mono-causal determinism has dominated the debate, a universalizing discourse that basically says to the rest of the world: my way or the highway. Taking culture seriously, as it pertains to education and the inculcation of knowledge, means acknowledging complexity in history, the multiple avenues by which to escape the misery of poverty, or, more broadly, the Malthusian dictum.[9] It also valorizes the universally present human ability to know new things and to put that knowledge to work always within specific historical contexts.

One further example of determinism current early in the twenty-first century needs to be given. Contemporary economist Robert Allen argues that in Britain labor was dear and coal was cheap; hence people produced machines that saved on the first and accessed the second. The argument would seem to ignore a basic rule in economic life: for people out to make a profit, all inputs and expenditures are equally scarce. If the economists have not gotten us thoroughly confused, there is more. Other economic historians tell us that the wage data required to test the suggestion are simply not available.[10]

As we will see in Chapter 2, even though the records are spotty for the eighteenth and early nineteenth centuries, wage rates exist for coal mining. It is possible to compare wages in British coal mines with other costs incurred, and, just as important, with wages at roughly the same time in France. The comparative method employed for just one industrial site –

[9] A good start for learning about the practitioners of these economic schools and their disagreements would be R. Brenner and C. Isett, "England's Divergence from China's Yangzi Delta: Property Relations, Microeconomics, and Patterns of Development," *The Journal of Asian Studies*, 61, May 2002, pp. 609–62, taking issue with K. Pomeranz, *The Great Divergence: Europe, China, and the Making of the Modern World Economy* (Princeton University Press, 2002), who is a proponent of the demography view of economic development. Brenner and Isett emphasize property relations, free markets and consumption. These are sophisticated historiographical traditions that require careful attention. They just do not admit culture into the discussion. For a theoretical approach to culture and sharing my view of its relationship to economic life, see E. L. Jones, "Culture and Its Relationship to Economic Change," *Journal of Institutional and Theoretical Economics*, 151, 2, June 1995, pp. 269–85. On the value of admitting differences, and the tortured history of universalizing generalizations, see the entire Roundtable "Historians and the Question of Modernity," *American Historical Review*, 116, 3, June 2011, pp. 631–751, with essays by Zvi Ben-Dor Benite, Gurminder K. Bhambra, Dipesh Chakrabarty, Carol Gluck, Mark Roseman, Dorothy Ross, Carol Symes, Lynn M. Thomas, and Richard Wolin.

[10] For the claim that we cannot know wages with any certainty, see R. Fox, ed., *Technological Change. Methods and Themes in the History of Technology* (Amsterdam: Harwood Academic Publishers, 1996), p. 162. For the high wage argument, see R. C. Allen, *The Industrial Revolution in Global Perspective* (Cambridge University Press, 2009).

the coal mines of Northumberland – calls into question the high-wage argument. So, too, does the fact that wages were also high in the Dutch Republic, but industrialization occurred there nearly two generations after it did in Britain and Belgium.[11] Finally, there is overwhelming evidence that the cost of keeping workhorses proved more of a drag on profit than the wages of the miners.

Another reason for diverting attention from knowledge derives from what little we know about formal education, particularly in Britain. Part of the reason for this myopia about formal and informal education may derive from the appalling state of British educational records prior to about 1850. Making education a local matter may have many virtues, but leaving behind a paper trail is not one of them. We do know that grammar schools in places such as Manchester and Newcastle turned toward technical education after 1750, and that all over the North efforts were made to create schools. Students had to find schools generally near a manufacturing town before they could find one that would teach some science and math.[12] Yet the teachers of Latin took a dim view of anything that might displace its kingly status. It has been thought for some time that education stagnated in Britain after 1750, although that view is now widely contested.[13]

[11] The classic study on this topic is J. Mokyr, *Industrialization in the Low Countries, 1795–1850* (New Haven, CT: Yale University Press, 1976), pp. 168–89, and 218.

[12] See P. Elliott, "The Birth of Public Science in the English Provinces: Natural Philosophy in Derby, 1690–1760," *Annals of Science*, Vol. 57, 2000, pp. 61–100. And see John Rylands Library, Manchester, John Seddon MSS, Box 1/1–16, f. 12, March 7, 1756, Rev. Seddens to James Nicholson. Seddens is going up and down the country raising subscriptions to set up academies, e.g. Birmingham and Bristol. Nicholson is a merchant in Liverpool. He is distributing Locke on *Human Understanding* but also volumes of sermons; Folder #4 Rev. Holland to James Nicholson on school Holland runs in Bolton; charges 20 guineas a year exclusive of washing and ½ guinea entrance fee. Those destined for the counting house have emphasis placed on the English authors, geography, history, and math. His son will then go on to the Warrington academy after time at this school; and see Benson MSS, MS B1/26 Caleb Rotheram of Kendal to George Benson; December 24, 1733 from Kendal, "we are in need desperately of academies in the north; miserable Scots men fill in here and there because no one would employ them at home." March 6, 1734/5 he is being offered a living in Durham but wants to hear from London about his future as a tutor and the prospect of setting up an academy there in Kendal. He stays in Kendal and by 1753 he is teaching natural philosophy (see #9, November 25, 1753 same to same). In f. 10, 1735, we learn that he is teaching mathematics – "I have a distinct consideration for that branch of Instruction" – from letter to Mr. Blackstock, September 13, 1735. And for having to leave a grammar school to find one near Sheffield that taught some science, see G. Hinchliffe, *A History of King James's Grammar School in Almondbury* (Huddersfield: The Advertiser Press Ltd., 1963), p. 91. Academies or grammar schools were forms of what Americans call secondary education.

[13] See D. Mitch, "The Role of Education and Skill in the British Industrial Revolution," in J. Mokyr, ed., *The British Industrial Revolution. An Economic Perspective*, 2nd edn.

Culture and education in the new economic history

Recently reformed economic historians, led by Joel Mokyr, have come to recognize that "a small group of at most a few thousand people . . . formed a creative community based on the exchange of knowledge" and they became the "main actors" who ushered in the Industrial Revolution in the West. "Engineers, mechanics, chemists, physicians, and natural philosophers formed circles in which access to knowledge was the primary objective." Mokyr and others now recognize that rates of general literacy, while to be applauded, tell us little about the few thousand who made up the community inventing or accessing an industrial knowledge base. Those men are central to the story this book is telling. By the mid eighteenth century in Britain schoolmasters appeared in manufacturing areas offering to teach the usual subjects but also mathematics and mechanics. Some of their pupils who remain nameless and recordless may nevertheless belong to this book's cast of characters.[14]

Historians have recognized the remarkable role played by educational institutions run by British Dissenters (non-Anglican Protestants) and especially Quakers. They have also argued that the child-rearing practices of Dissenters maximized self-reliance and the desire to achieve. In the pages ahead, educational and religious backgrounds can be documented in some British cases, and, not surprisingly, Unitarians, Presbyterians, and Quakers will figure prominently, although by no means exclusively.

Nothing compares to the educational records preserved by the French state and hence we know a great deal about what the secondary schools

(Boulder, CO: Westview Press, 1999), pp. 241–79. For the defenders of Latin, see J. A. Graham and B. A. Phythian (eds.), *The Manchester Grammar School, 1515–1965* (Manchester University Press, 1965).

[14] J. Mokyr, *The Gifts of Athena. Historical Origins of the Knowledge Economy* (Princeton University Press, 2002), p. 66. For British education, see CGEH Working Paper Series "The Role of Human Capital in the Process of Economic Development: The Case of England, 1307–1900," A. M. de Pleijt, Utrecht University, November 2011, Working Paper No. 21, www.cgeh.nl/working-paper-series/, accessed September 4, 2012. For an older view, no longer compatible with the evidence, see W. B. Stephens, *Education in Britain, 1750–1914* (New York: St. Martin's Press, 1998), Chapter 4. For how difficult knowing about literacy can be, see D. Vincent, "The End of Literacy: The Growth and Measurement of British Public Education since the Early Nineteenth Century," in C. A. Bayly *et al.*, *History, Historians and Development Policy*, pp. 177–92. For one such school, see P. Lord, "History of Education in Oldham" (M.Ed. thesis, University of Manchester, 1938). (Found at John Rylands University Library, Main: Thesis 7328), pp. 49–50. James Wolfenden taught school in Oldham during the eighteenth century and an advertisement for his school announced: "James Wolfenden – Private Teacher of Mathematics in Manchester and its vicinity, respectfully informs the public, that he can, at present engage a few more pupils who may be instructed in Arithmetic, Geography, and the Use of the Globes, as well as higher branches of Mathematics and their application to Mechanics."

taught in the period 1750 to 1850 in France and the Low Countries. Continental education in France and Belgium (under French control from 1795 to 1815) became a largely secular affair after 1795, and the role of Catholicism is difficult to assess in the period up to 1815.[15] In Britain, meanwhile, we can demonstrate the presence of mechanical knowledge in coal mining, in textile factories, at canals and harbors, in committees of the House of Lords, and not be able to prove where it was learned. On the Continent it is possible to access abundant educational records, and the knowledge offered in the schools can be described in detail. The last three chapters focus on these Continental sources and the mixed story that they tell about the deployment of scientific knowledge.

Armed with knowledge and know-how, inspired as much by the desire to get rich as by any other motive, entrepreneurs emerged within an industrial culture wedded to scientific knowledge and technology as the means to an unprecedented end: profit from power-driven productivity from inorganic sources. The transformation from organic to inorganic power was gradual, and in many places water and wind power remained vital well into the nineteenth century. Nowhere did the transformation in forms of energy production occur as rapidly as it did in Britain after 1750.

Now, as we sense the dangers to the global environment brought about by the gases and heat released by industrial energy, we may come to see the Industrial Revolution as an event of greater complexity than simply a means to escape abject poverty.[16] Yet given what we now know about the role of culture and education in making industrial economies, may we not also presume that knowledge will foster the creation of green economies?

Development studies and thinking outside the box of traditional economic history

At present, some experts focused on under-development believe they know what makes technological innovation happen, and emphasize its inextricable connection to science in both formal and informal sites of learning. Something else is also reasonably assumed to be certain, even if we do not agree on how it works: over the long term, knowledge and technological progress reduce poverty. When the United Nations or various economists focus on the least developed nations, they want to

15 For child-rearing practices, see Flinn, *The Origins of the Industrial Revolution* (London: Longman, 1966), pp. 87–90.

16 See F. A. Jonsson, "The Industrial Revolution in the Anthropocene," *The Journal of Modern History*, 84, 3, September 2012, pp. 679–96. On knowledge in relation to economic development, see Scherer, 1999, pp. 32–42.

know, among many things, what policies they employ to promote scientific and technological knowledge leading to innovation. They ask for reports about whether or not Bangladesh (or Cambodia, or Haiti, or Uganda, among over forty other nations) gives priority to science and technology. Has it developed initiatives for both in the educational system from primary and secondary to higher education? Does industrial and engineering research pay attention to technological issues; does technical and vocational training do the same?[17]

The UN asks questions in the present about the present that, despite the benefits and dangers of hindsight, we should be asking about the past. What knowledge was needed in the First Industrial Revolution, and how was it acquired, and sometimes simultaneously applied?

Not everyone asking these questions, or advising the least developed nations, has a workable understanding of how knowledge is transmitted. They adopt a mechanistic perspective on science, technology, and contemporary poverty. They tell developing nations just to take what they can get from more technologically advanced markets or nations, and assume that access to foreign technology is equivalent to its effective use. Information, knowledge, and learning, regardless of their source or cultural context, translate into productivity. This top-down conception of knowledge ignores the fundamentally dynamic character and plural contours shaping its production and generation. The mechanistic perspective assumes that knowledge is socially disembodied and universally transferable. It ignores the

[17] M. Mackintosh, J. Chataway, and M. Wuyts, "Promoting Innovation, Productivity and Industrial Growth and Reducing Poverty: Bridging the Policy Gap," *Special Issue of The European Journal of Development Research*, 19, 1, 2007. See *The Least Developed Countries Report, 2007. Knowledge, Technological Learning and Innovation for Development*, United Nations Publications, Autumn 2007; for a copy see http://unctad.org/en/docs/ldc2007_en.pdf, accessed December 4, 2012.

For the recent statistics where a least developed country is defined as having a gross national income per capita of above $900 and less than $1,086, see United Nations Conference on Trade and Development, *The Least Developed Countries. Report 2009. The State and Development Governance* (New York: United Nations, 2009), and see p. 163, "the modern form of industrial policy is indispensable for articulating the links between science, technology and economic activities, through networking, collaboration, and fine-tuning and learning components (learning by doing, adaptive R&D, and labor training.)" In 2008 the lower threshold income was $750. For the experts, see R. G. Lipsey *et al.*, *Economic Transformations. General Purpose Technologies and Long Term Economic Growth* (New York: Oxford University Press, 2005); Mokyr, 2002; J. Horn, *The Path Not Taken. French Industrialization in the Age of Revolution 1750–1830* (Cambridge, MA: MIT Press, 2006); H. Nowotny, ed., *Cultures of Technology and the Quest for Innovation* (New York: Berghahn Books, 2006); and the essay by H. U. Vogel, "The Mining Industry in Traditional China: Intra- and Intercultural Comparisons," pp. 167–90. See also M. C. Jacob, "Mechanical Science on the Factory Floor: The Early Industrial Revolution in Leeds," *History of Science*, 45, 148, 2007, pp. 197–221. This issue of the journal is devoted entirely to a discussion of Mokyr's *The Gifts of Athena*.

values, components, and processes, such as literacy rates or access to printing, that shape its generation; it also ignores history. Knowledge becomes human capital when we "own" it, and that happens through bottom-up education, formal, informal, on the shop floor, in the home – whatever works. Historical research tells us that Britain experienced a sustained increase in primary and secondary (what it called grammar) schooling around 1750. It was also the first Western nation to industrialize.[18]

Such a cultural inquiry into innovation has its critics. An historian of India finds this kind of analysis, with its emphasis on applied science, inherently Eurocentric. Many who do not understand the approach may say the same. By highlighting industrial mechanics we denigrate the scientific fertility of other parts of the world, or so the argument runs. If areas outside of Western Europe lacked such expertise, then we must be arguing that they were somehow inferior, that something went wrong and the science that was practiced in India or China or the Ottoman Empire can be ignored or devalued. To make the case that historians of Western science are Eurocentric and mean-spirited about the rest of the world, a caricature of Western science around 1750 has to be invented. Western science must be rarefied. Rather, it should be seen as a mélange of various interventions into nature, as indigenous and bottom-up – not, as was the case in India, the work of rulers and their courtiers. Prasannan Parthasarathi argues incorrectly that Western science was everywhere controlled by government administrators or experts who were rigorously mathematical, experimental, and above all rational (whatever that means). The complexity of science, as distilled by textbooks, technical hands-on knowledge, and technological innovation, disappears in his account.

Parthasarathi accuses those who study science and the Industrial Revolution of denigrating the inventiveness of the non-Western. Botanical innovations from India, medical procedures from China, modern surveying techniques from South Asia, Sanskrit texts (some yet to be deciphered), Indian astronomy, mathematics, military technology, European and Asian interactions – Parthasarathi argues – made non-European science just as vital as what existed in the West. This author is not denying the vitality of non-Western scientific traditions; they just do not explain the role of the first knowledge economy in Western industrial development. Knowing about non-Western innovativeness does not, however, help to explain why industrial mechanics and unprecedented economic development appeared first

[18] F. Machlup, *The Economics of Information and Human Capital* (Princeton University Press, 1984), pp. 430–52. Flinn argues that the lack of capital and technical skill, plus an unwillingness to accept "the social disruption which inevitably accompanies" new technology, can explain its failure in underdeveloped countries; see Flinn, 1966, p. 69.

in Birmingham, or Leeds, or Manchester, or in various other sites within Western Europe.[19] Similarly, valorizing science as the key to Western "superiority" is itself a form of reductionism that imagines science as an entity floating separately from all other historical factors.[20]

Steam engines

Advocating bottom-up education does not mean that foreign technology should be spurned: quite the reverse. Once imported, however, it must be naturalized and the principles employed in its creation understood and made capable of being deployed creatively. A key technological item of the eighteenth century that had to be mastered, the steam engine, required knowledge of basic mechanical principles – what contemporary observers called "industrial mechanics." This knowledge enabled an engine to be made and, just as important, to be repaired or improved upon. With steam we have one of the first general-purpose technologies (computers are ours), and the principal source of power technology, inorganic because it was not based primarily on the labor of humans, or animals, or even the flow of water or wind. It was recognized as early as the 1780s that although expensive, steam was the best method for generating energy.[21]

Entrepreneurs jealously guarded their technological knowledge, as did other innovators. Imagine a place where any of the new devices central to early industrial development – steam engines, spinning jennies – had never been seen, and there we find the temptation to make secret detailed drawings of the equipment with the intention of selling it. When that

[19] Parthasarathi, 2011, Chapter 7. See also W. J. Ashworth, 2007, pp. 349–78, an essay that makes valuable points but mistakenly identifies this author with arguments that rely on cultural superiority.

[20] Such is the approach in Niall Ferguson, *Civilization: The West and the Rest* (New York: Penguin, 2011), Chapter 2.

[21] R. Beatson, *An Essay on the Comparative Advantages of Vertical and Horizontal Windmills: Containing a Description of a Horizontal Windmill and Water Mill, upon a New Construction* (London and Edinburgh, 1798), pp. 3–4. See also P. M. Litton, ed., *The Journals of Sarah Mayo Parkes, 1815 and 1818, Publications of the Thoresby Society*, Second Series, Vol. 13 (Miscellany), 2003, p. 3, where a water wheel is used to move a hammer in Sheffield; p. 4 to dye blue woolen cloth at Wakefield, "most of the moveable apparatus is conducted by steam"; pp. 5–6 for an extensive description of the Wormald and Gott factory where the steam engine "is the great moving power in this extensive factory" that employed machines to mix the wool with oil, to spin its thread by steam-driven machines (she claims that one man can do the work of 80); fulling "is very simple: the cloth is merely put into a wooden trough, to which two heavy wooden hammers are attached, that just fit into it, and each hammer works . . . all the vats for dyeing the cloth are boiled by steam, which save much expense and labor." In Leeds (p. 13), she sees coal carriages moved by steam; p. 16 on woolen cloth dressed by machinery moved by steam.

happened the police were called in, the workman's home searched and the drawings confiscated. Needless to say, in almost every country intellectual property theft led to dismissal or prosecution at the very least.[22]

Who were the innovators?

In this book we examine how, from roughly 1750 to 1850, some people in Western Europe came to own the knowledge necessary to deploy steam and a host of other technological innovations that became central to industrial development. These innovators affected nearly every industry, and the bulk of these inventions came from skilled men who had once been apprentices and were overwhelmingly literate. Sometimes they published their findings; at other times they jealously guarded them. Only a few of the people in this book were never apprenticed.[23]

We begin with two famous industrial innovators: James Watt and Matthew Boulton, of steam engine fame. We examine their relationship, their politics, and especially their grasp of applicable knowledge. No other members of the first generation of industrialists, on either side of the Channel, left records as deep and broad: family correspondence, letters to and from buyers of their engine, notes on what needed to be known in order to run the engines, details of scientific work and contacts, accounts of travel in France – an archival treasure trove. These records permit us to examine in depth their knowledge base and interactions between themselves, their competitors, their confidants, their wives and children. The Boulton and Watt relationship offers a paradigm that was independently replicated in industrial partnerships in many countries, except that most of those did not leave such complete records. These two steam men, based in Birmingham, allow us to put a face on the human capital that went into the new industrial economy, and we will meet their like in Chapter 3 about Manchester and Chapter 4 about Leeds, among other places.

[22] For just such an event see Stadsarchief, Ghent, Fonds Napoleon de Pauw, James Farrar to Lieven Bauwens, April 15, 1800, "the designs and files which we found are now in my possession and I think he has been employed by some person or other ... But hope we shall be able to find all this out. ..." Farrar made spinning mules at 65 Louis d'ors with 216 spindles; they are 14½ inch long and 1 inch in diameter in the front. Farrar is English.

[23] NBER Working Paper Series, National Bureau of Economic Research, Cambridge, MA, April 2011,"The Rate and Direction of Invention in the British Industrial Revolution," by R. Meisenzahl and J. Mokyr, Working Paper 16993, accessed December 4, 2012 at www.nber.org/papers/w16993; and see B. De Munck, S. L. Kaplan, and H. Soly, eds., *Learning on the Shop Floor. Historical Perspectives on Apprenticeship* (New York: Berghahn Books, 2007), Chapter 1 by De Munck and Soly. On the widespread practice of apprenticeship in Britain, see P. Wallis, "Labor, Law, and Training in Early Modern London: Apprenticeship and the City's Institutions," *Journal of British Studies*, 51, 4, 2012, pp. 791–819.

Boulton and Watt also illustrate the local conditions that pushed science in a mechanical and applied direction. Whether in Birmingham, or Leeds, or Newcastle and Manchester, everything – capitalist competition, formal and informal education, attitudes toward work, a sufficient food supply to fuel hard labor, religious convictions – played a role that was specific to time and place. An older generation of historians once recognized that no clear border marks off economic life from politics, religion, science, and education, and we will encounter all of these aspects of human life. But we do lay emphasis on knowledge and the means by which it was acquired and deployed.[24]

Case studies

In this book we will begin with case studies drawn from British records. The opening study, centered largely in Birmingham and its archival treasure trove, is followed by studies on the coal industry around Newcastle upon Tyne, the cotton industry in Manchester, and linen in Leeds. All these studies are heavily based on family and firm records, generally of one company or partnership. They have been chosen for particular reasons, not least because their records were saved. Each seeks to address problems and disputes about the way historians have understood industrialization.

The case study has both strengths and weaknesses. Every locality is unique, so how can generalizations be made? By multiplying the localities and finding similar results in all places – that is, the presence of industrial mechanics and its application among industrializing entrepreneurs – generalizations acquire a degree of authenticity not easily accomplished by any other method. The studies reveal that mechanical knowledge bled circularly into factory practices just as machines in turn demanded new skills and innovative approaches. And the evidence continues to mount. These case studies complement earlier examples of scientific knowledge at work in the House of Lords committee that had to approve canal bills, in the refurbishing of Bristol's harbor, and in the application of steam engines to lead mining in Derbyshire.[25]

[24] On the food supply, see C. Muldrew, *Food, Energy and the Creation of Industriousness: Work and Material Culture in Agrarian England, 1550–1780* (Cambridge University Press, 2011). For evidence that the Dutch had a similarly high caloric intake, see A. E. C. McCants, *Civic Charity in a Golden Age: Orphan Care in Early Modern Amsterdam* (Chicago: University of Illinois Press, 1997), pp. 41–6, 213–16. The older generation lies in the work of G. N. Clark, *The Wealth of England from 1496 to 1760* (New York: Oxford University Press, 1946), p. 190.

[25] J.-C. Passeron, J. Revel, and S. W. Wormbs, eds., *Penser par cas* (Paris: École des Hautes Études en Sciences Sociales, 2005), pp. 9–44. For an attempt to describe these interactions in the twentieth century, see D. Edgerton, "'The Linear Model' Did Not Exist:

A comparative approach

There was nothing automatic about technological innovations and applications. They occurred in an historical process full of supporters and opponents, accidents and failures. As a lead mine owner said when he contemplated the installation of a steam engine: "How this may answer no one can say; so much depending on accidents." In all places, governmental policies played vital roles – on the Continental especially in educational matters – and continue to do so.[26] In eighteenth-century Britain the state fostered economic development indirectly and education was entirely in the hands of localities. There were no subsidies for patents and few monetary rewards for industrial inventions, but there were legal institutions that protected patents, permitted canal and road building, and tried to stop industrial espionage, especially by foreign spies. The French state went further and actually provided subsidies to entrepreneurs, or used the state corps of engineers to improve harbors or dig canals.[27] Yet as contemporary critics were the first to note, France lagged behind Britain in industrial development until well into the nineteenth century. The comparison between and among France, the Dutch Republic, and Belgium is even more complicated, as we will see in the final chapters.

Comparison among countries within the geographic quadrangle of Edinburgh, London, Amsterdam, Rouen, and Paris appears reasonable because of a number of factors. The majority of the population in all these cities was Christian, with Britain and the Dutch Republic essentially Protestant, and Belgium and France essentially Catholic. In the case of the Low Countries the borders were malleable, with migration back and forth – between Flemish-speaking Belgium and the Dutch Republic, and between southern, French-speaking Belgium and the north of France – fairly

Reflections on the History and Historiography of Science and Research in Industry in the Twentieth Century," in K. Grandin and N. Wormbs, eds., *The Science–Industry Nexus: History, Policy, and Implications* (New York: Watson, 2004), pp. 1–36. For Bristol, the House of Lords, etc., see M. Jacob, *Scientific Culture and the Making of the Industrial West* (New York: Oxford University Press, 1997), Chapter 9.

26 D. E. Drew, *Stem the Tide: Reforming Science, Technology, Engineering, and Math Education in America* (Baltimore, MD: The Johns Hopkins University Press, 2011). For the lead mine, see Sheffield City Library, Bagshawe Collection, MS 494, John Barker's Letter Book, 1765–1811, entry for September 30, 1794, on a mine subject to a great deal of flooding.

27 Birmingham Central Library, JWP 4/14 Letters from Aimé Argand, Paris to Watt, August 4, 1785, on the financial difficulties of the Périer brothers, "all their resources being quite exhausted, when the Controleur Gl. took pity on them, came to the engine, saw it with admiration and thought it his duty to support so great and so useful an undertaking. He then immediately lent them 1,200,000 livres with 50.000 pounds st. with which they paid all their bills, the king took 100 actions; and little after the actions rose to 150 pounds where they are now."

common. The scientific communities in all four countries traded information through letters, journals, and personal contacts, and had available – even if contested by religious authorities, among others – the new mechanical science of Descartes and especially Newton. In addition, contemporaries in all four countries watched and commented upon their neighbors and occasionally sought to import new inventions, particularly from Britain. By 1750 censorship of books without religious content and offering no threat to church or state was virtually non-existent, and scientific and technical knowledge in print had become public and accessible to the reasonably literate. The commentators and importers accessed public knowledge – abstract, practical, and hands on – that made invention, or an understanding of new industrial practices, possible.

Contemporaries knew a thing or two

We congratulate ourselves for having brought scientific knowledge back into the story of Western industrialization. Yet nothing about the conclusions of recent scholarship would have surprised the French revolutionaries or the first generation of British or Continental European industrial pioneers, however lowly. Listen to what a British maker of spindles for cotton jennies, Mr. D. Clark, could imagine. In the first decade of the nineteenth century he had migrated to Belgium, where opportunity beckoned, and he searched for investors in what he believed was "a simple method [I have discovered] . . . I can make spindles more round, more straight and more all of one size than was ever done in England." He knew that the best spindles for cotton spinning were hand made in Paris, but at twice the cost. He also knew competition was scarce on the Continent: "where could be found a clock maker sufficient to make spindles [?]" Clark had found a method of duplicating a more perfect spindle: "The secret lies here that as soon as one is finished some thousands are finished likewise." He was also writing to a technologically savvy entrepreneur in cotton manufactures who could understand what he was saying.[28]

Then this spindle maker forecast the meaning and future of industrial manufacturing: "Everyone that makes mule jennies ought to support my interest, for it is for their credit I have labored, for as they enlarge their machines, the spindles should be made better & better, & what is the grand difficulty is this, to be cheaper & cheaper . . . for one machine will

[28] For the importance of clockmakers in early machine making, see G. Cookson, "The West Yorkshire Textile Engineering Industry, 1780–1850," submitted for the degree of D. Phil., University of York, Department of Economics and Related Studies, July 1994, p. 51 *et. seq.*

supply all France, and other countries if it was necessary ... These spindles I mean to sell under the title of Clark's Mathematical Spindles, for muslin, etc." His vision may be reasonably called modern in its expectation of limitless progress and profit, even nascently imperial.

Clark signals to the prospective investor his familiarity with mathematics, and also, in the case of steam, with the applied science of mechanics. Both required some education, probably of a formal sort. He explains that for power in his factory he will use water and not horses, as they are too dear; or if possible a steam engine might be found or, better still, made by him. There were imponderables to be sure: the cost of coal, wages (always to be as little as possible, "for the offenders to work and ... there will be but very little to pay them"), capital – yet to be found. The key to success, however, lay in the knowledge and skill Mr. Clark believed he possessed – and the increase in productivity would be infinite. All the elements of the First Industrial Revolution were present in his account: with his knowledge he was innovating for profit, but he told himself and a would-be investor that ultimately everyone would benefit – improvement upon improvement would follow. Not least, he viewed workers for wages as "offenders" to be paid as little as possible.[29]

Clark believed in a future dominated by technological improvements and ever increasing profits. We have no way of knowing whether he had read the great theorists of the eighteenth century, Adam Smith on free market economics or Condorcet on the improvement of the human condition. Perhaps by 1812 when Clark wrote, their ideas were just part of the cultural landscape. Certainly by 1795, in the new central schools introduced first in France and then in Belgium, the professors of physics and chemistry had taught that elementary experiments could be applied to all the objects one might have in hand. More important, they believed that a less expensive and more perfect industrial machine depended upon the success and elegance of observation or physical experience.[30] Ordinary men with training and hands-on experience of nature and its principles could work industrial wonders. As Brett Steele has taught us, the French administrators had learned the hard way that knowledge of Newtonian

[29] See Stadsarchief, Ghent, Fonds du Napoleon de Pauw, MS 3285, D. Clark, writing from Mons, to James Farrar, whom he wants to intervene with the leading cotton industrialist in Ghent, Lieven Bauwens, 6 Messidor, 1812. All quoted material appears in this letter.

[30] Archives nationales, Paris, F 17 1344/1, report by M. P. Buyts, writing from the central school in the Département de la Lys, 24 Fructidor, year 6, to the Ministry of the Interior, Paris. "Quant à la partie expérimentale élémentaire je leur apprends à multiplier journalièrement leurs expériences et à y appliquer tout objet que se trouve pour ainsi dire habituellement sous leurs mains, je leur fait seuler que c'est moins de la cherté et de la perfection d'une machine que de l'industrie de celui qui l'emploie que dépend le succès et l'élégance d'une observation ou d'une expérience physique."

mechanics could help to win wars, and thus they had reason for wanting it spread far and wide.[31]

How not to use the cultural argument

The cultural argument has been put to nefarious uses. Here the culture of applied science is being referenced, not in the first instance religion, or national ethos, or work habits. These may be factors, as discussed in Chapters 2 and 3 on the religiosity of Birmingham's early industrialists and Manchester's cotton barons, but as yet ethos or habits are poorly understood, particularly at their origins, and often have been used to blame the victims of poverty. Nothing about the argument advanced here should be taken as normative with regard to the rest of the world, or even parts of Europe such as Spain where industrialization came very late. The absence of a culture of applied science tells us nothing useful about a nation or tribe except that we are asking questions about it that were irrelevant to its dominant concerns.[32]

The literature about culture and industrial development has also been burdened by wrong-headed understandings of eighteenth-century science. Modern twentieth-century notions of what constituted science have been applied back to the eighteenth century, and Newtonian physics was said to have had nothing to do with industrial development. It was the work of tinkerers with little more skill than the ability to carve wood for a better spindle. Even the skilled tinkerer trained in mechanical applications, like Mr. Clark, mattered little in this now obsolete account. The engineers' grasp of economic issues, or the mechanics needed to build a steam engine, seemed of little importance. Until about twenty years ago, almost no one interested in the question of early Western industrial development circa 1750 to 1850 looked at what constituted education in science, whether in English, French, or Dutch. The specific scientific culture cultivated first in England, then adopted by the French revolutionaries, never – until recently – made it onto the radar screens of historians.[33]

[31] B. D. Steele, "Muskets and Pendulums: Benjamin Robins, Leonhard Euler, and the Ballistics Revolution," *Technology and Culture*, 35, 2 (April 1994), pp. 348–82.

[32] Here I agree with Daron Acemoglu and James A. Robinson, *Why Nations Fail: The Origins of Power, Prosperity and Poverty* (New York: Crown, 2012), Chapter 2. It is a pity that the authors did not address the nature of scientific culture.

[33] For the early interventions, see A. E. Musson and E. Robinson, *Science and Technology in the Industrial Revolution* (with Foreword to the Second Printing, Margaret C. Jacob) (Reading: Gordon and Breach, 1989, first printing 1969). Margaret C. Jacob, *The Cultural Meaning of the Scientific Revolution* (New York: Alfred Knopf, 1987) and *Scientific Culture and the Making of the Industrial West* (New York: Oxford University Press, 1997).

Suddenly the interpretive tide has turned, partly under the impact of cultural history and partly because our "new economy," with its knowledge base in information technology, suggests that what is in people's minds just might be important. Here I am augmenting my initial contribution to this discussion, made in 1987, and presenting new evidence that culture belongs high on the list of a small cluster of key variables. Being comparative, using Britain, Belgium, France, and the Dutch Republic as test cases, permits us to explore the area of North-Western Europe with a set of questions not generally asked of it.[34] With Western eyes we have asked other parts of the globe to explain their deviations from modernity without – for whatever reason – being comparative about the historicity of what went on in North-Western Europe.

There is no single sufficient cause

Being comparative about major industrial settings shows that a particular scientific culture emerged in those places co-terminally with industrial development, or, in some of its educational elements, in advance of it. Let us be clear: we are not arguing that this culture is *the key, the sufficient cause.* If it were, its primary educational promoters on the Continent, the French – not the Belgians – sleekly and elegantly would have made French cotton and coal king. Beginning in 1795, French central schools had united basic physics with industrial machinery in ways previously unimagined. In places that were the back of beyond, professors launched ambitious courses in physics that began with a definition of the subject, moved on to bodies and motion, explained universal gravity by using pendula, and ended many months later with detailed descriptions of pumps that used air pressure to do their work in mines or factories.[35]

[34] For previous interventions see the above cited works and Jacob and L. Stewart, *Practical Matter: Newton's Science in the Service of Industry and Empire, 1687 to 1851* (Cambridge, MA: Harvard University Press, 2004); in article format, M. C. Jacob, "Mechanical Science on the Factory Floor: The Industrial Revolution in Leeds," *History of Science*, 45, 148, June, 2007, pp. 197–221; "Scientific Culture and the Origins of the First Industrial Revolution," *História e Economia – Revista Interdisciplinar*, 2, 1–2, 2006, pp. 55–70; "Technical Knowledge and the Mental Universe of Manchester's Cotton Manufacturers" (with D. Reid), *Canadian Journal of History*, 36, 2, 2001, pp. 283–304; and in French translation, "Culture et culture technique des premiers fabricants de coton de Manchester," *Revue d'histoire moderne et contemporaine*, 50, 2003, pp. 133–55.
See also http://industrialization.ats.ucla.edu/ accessed September 4, 2012.

[35] See AN, F 17 1344/1 Cahiers 1, 2, and 3 sent to the Ministry of the Interior by Sartre, professor of physics and chemistry at Laval in the department of the Mayenne. Similar lesson plans survive for the Lot, Amiens, the Gard, the Charente, the Meuse, etc.

In the same vein of eschewing the sufficient cause, economic explanations devoid of culture just do not work. If capital were the key, the Dutch would have led the way in Europe. If high wages forced the hand of miners and manufacturers to look for alternative sources of power, then once again the Dutch would have beat everyone, even the British, in manufacturing with new sources of power. If we take the first knowledge economy seriously, we do so not to laud the West but to learn from it.

1 A portrait of early industrial lives

The Watts and Boultons, science and entrepreneurship

Sometimes the lives of two men and their families open a previously obscured history and point toward the human capital expended, the striving and achievement at the heart of early industrial development. James Watt (b. 1736) of steam engine fame, and his partner, a manufacturer of metal objects, Matthew Boulton (b. 1728), need little introduction. The nature of their partnership does. It offers a paradigmatic example of the human qualities and shared values that propelled early industrial growth. Their partnership embodied a marriage between business sense and mechanical knowledge that together made possible the application of power technology to the mining and manufacturing process. Boulton did not simply supply the capital and Watt the know-how, as has been assumed. In the mid 1770s, Boulton and Watt established a partnership that rested on trust, thrift, mechanical knowledge, technical skill, and market experience.

Almost every successful partnership visible in the first generation of industrialists, from the 1780s to the 1820s, independently replicates the Boulton–Watt relationship. Sometimes the business acumen and mechanical knowledge rested in the same mind; most times it did not, as we shall see in the partnerships at work in textile manufacturing and coal mining. Mr. Clark, whom we met in the introduction, sought to bring his technical skills into contact with Lieven Bauwens, a Belgian but British-trained capitalist with a deep knowledge of the mechanization of cotton manufacturing.

Indeed, jealous contemporaries knew, however vaguely, that men like Boulton and Watt had special advantages. As they prospered they were envied, despised, and imitated as monopolists. They shielded their pride by imagining themselves as having an accurate reputation only among men of science. They knew that other men of business, as Watt said, "hate me more as a monopolist than they admire me as a mechanic."[1] The partners were,

[1] Birmingham Central Library (unless otherwise noted all references to Watt and Boulton manuscripts in this chapter are from the BCL), MS LB/1 Watt to Robison, 10/30 1783: "I

Figure 3 James Watt, engineer, 1801

Engraving by C. Picarte after a painting by Sir William Beechy (1753–1839) of James Watt (1736–1819)

am almost unknown except among a very few men of science." On the many facets of Boulton's career, see the essays in S. Mason, ed., *Matthew Boulton: Selling What All the World Desires* (Birmingham City Council in association with Yale University Press, 2009). On the nature of their friendship, see, for instance, Letter Book, #62, Boulton to Watt, Soho July 1776, on Watt's money matters, marriage, engines to be sold, etc.

however, thoroughly capable of striking back. The desire to establish a monopoly in any business venture was never far from their thinking.[2]

Middling men and politics

Mechanical knowledge was the least of what little men like James Watt were required to have. In Britain, innovations meant patents, and patents meant politics. Private bills in Parliament, through which patents could be secured, also required lobbying – licking "some great man's arse" was the way one of Watt's philosopher-friends put it. Or, as Lord Cochrane coyly said, when he wrote to Watt with the good news from Parliament: "I wish you all the success you could wish, notwithstanding that we coal masters, have no reason to rejoice at any improvement that diminishes the consumptions of fuel." Nonetheless, with Watt's patent for an engine with a separate condenser secured, Cochrane ordered one for his new Scottish mines. So, too, did the President of the Royal Society, who had mines on his estates.[3] Soon textile manufacturers in Manchester would also be ordering the engine equipped with a rotating device that Watt invented to modify its up-and-down stroke and to power the machines in their factories.[4] Long used to operating Newcomen steam engines, numerous coal mines followed suit, as did mining works in copper, tin, and lead. Within a decade the partners' engine spread from Cornwall to Northumberland, and to selected sites in North-Western Europe, especially in Belgium.

Conceived as early as 1768, Watt's innovation with the separate condenser also aimed at economy and profit; it was claimed it allowed his engine to do as much as five times the work for the same quantity of coal as

[2] Cornish Mining World Heritage, www.cornishmining.net/story/bwpapers.htm, AD 1583/3/51, Watt to Wilson, November 8, 1788. For statistics on the various counties and the diffusion of the engine, see Nuvolari *et al.*, "The Early Diffusion of the Steam Engine in Britain, 1700–1800: A Reappraisal," Working Paper Series, January 2011/03, pp. 1–35, at www.lem.sssup.it/.

[3] James Watt Papers, 4/76, Edinburgh, March 13, 1775, Cochrane to Watt. See also James Hutton to Watt in 1774 on approaching Parliament: "Your friends are trying to do something for you what success will attend their endeavours time only will show – every application for publick employment is considered as a job and to be carried into execution requires nothing but a passage thru the proper channels; it is then a well digested plan; the honestest endeavour must to succeed put on the face of roguery but what signifies the dress of a rogue unless you have the address of a wise man; come and lick some great man's arse and be damned to you." See J. Gascoigne, *Joseph Banks and the English Enlightenment: Useful Knowledge and Polite Culture* (New York: Cambridge University Press, 1994), pp. 211–12.

[4] James Watt Papers, W/6; see, for example, letter of March 13, 1791, Manchester, from James Watt Jr. to his father on orders of his engine and competitors at work in the town. See MS C2/10 item 3, list of all Watt engines at work in Manchester in 1797.

Figure 4 Swainson Birley cotton mill near Preston, Lancashire, 1834
Drawing by Thomas Allom

did the older Newcomen engine. When he was sure of his engine, Watt then applied to Parliament and the House of Lords for an act to secure his patent, and a parliamentary committee took testimony on the authenticity of his discovery. Such testimony required a reasonable knowledge of mechanics by the members of Parliament who oversaw private bills or patents. Their questioning could range from an examination of the novelty of a device to the hydrostatics involved in canal building and water diversion.[5]

Testifying before the Lords also required political savvy on the part of engineers and inventors. No understanding of British industrial development that downplays the importance of the state and state policies can begin to address what happened in the late eighteenth century. Indeed, contestation with the state over regulation and quality further induced

[5] For Watt's earliest drawing of the double condenser, see C. Fox, *The Arts of Industry in the Age of Enlightenment* (New Haven, CT: Yale University Press, 2009), pp. 101–5. These details are drawn from that report; James Watt Papers, 4/53, April 11, 1775, "Committee on . . . Mr. Watt's Engine Bill." On why he chose to go before Parliament, see C. MacLeod, *Inventing the Industrial Revolution: The English Patent System, 1660–1800* (New York: Cambridge University Press, 1988), p. 73. For testimony before the House of Lords by engineers and canal companies, see Jacob, 1987.

"manufacturing experts [to be] typically educated in some aspect of natural philosophy."[6]

Never imagine that, in the first decades of their partnership, Boulton and Watt received encouragement from the larger society or were easily rewarded for their ingenuity. Business and lobbying success notwithstanding, Watt and his associates responded by taking a dim view of all the imagined official protectors of the public interest.[7] In his letters to his second wife, Annie, written when he was trying to renew the patent to his engine, he was blunt: "We go to the House of Commons with no hope of victory. . . . I am held out as an extortioner, as a . . . man who claims rights to the inventions made by others before my day's begun. It may so be deemed but if it is, I hope to live to see the end of a corrupt aristocracy that has not the gratitude to protect its supporters, nor the sense to uphold its own decrees." Boulton and Watt saw themselves as men of the middling classes ruled over by a parliament controlled by the landed. They turned to the scientific community in London for assistance. Watt explained to Annie that he would "go to the Royal Society in the evening in hopes of meeting some friends who can be of use to us in Parliament."[8]

Enemies lurked in every corner. We may see the virtues of the vibrant public sphere that from the mid seventeenth century took an interest in experiments and scientific publications, but Watt could not wait to get away from "an ungrateful public."[9] He never stopped worrying that someone, somewhere, out among the knowledgeable public, would infringe his patent, or that it would be revoked. Even when he had made £3,000 profit from his engine, he lamented to Josiah Wedgwood, another innovative entrepreneur with scientific know-how, that "we have got so many pretenders now that I fear they will make us little people if we let them."[10] When Watt wrote to Boulton to express his fears, he said that his enemies would cynically argue that the breach of patent would be "for the good of the public." We may see public science as the great innovation of the age;

[6] W. J. Ashworth, "Intersection of Industry and the State," in L. Roberts *et al.*, *The Mindful Hand. Inquiry and Invention from the Late Renaissance to Early Industrialisation* (Amsterdam: Koninklijke Nederlandse Akademie van Wetenschappen, 2007), pp. 349–78; and reinforcing the point, J. Hoppit, "The Nation, the State, and the First Industrial Revolution," *Journal of British Studies*, 50, 2, 2011, 307–31. For the quotation about contestation and expertise in natural philosophy, see W. J. Ashworth, "Quality and the Roots of Manufacturing 'Expertise' in Eighteenth-Century Britain," in *Expertise: Practical Knowledge and the Early Modern State*, ed. E. H. Ash, Vol. 25, *Osiris*, Second Series (University of Chicago Press, 2010), p. 252.

[7] Boulton and Watt Papers, James to Annie Watt, House of Commons, April 3, 1792.

[8] Boulton and Watt MSS, London, February 1, 1792.

[9] Boulton and Watt MSS, MII/4/4/28, James to Annie, February 28, 1792.

[10] James Watt Papers, LB/1, May, 1782 Watt to Wedgwood.

Watt had little confidence in any aspect of the so-called public. His fears also alert us to the presence of numerous potential competitors who looked to knowledge of the new power technology as a way to make a substantial living. To compete effectively they, too, would have to understand the mechanics and physics involved in making steam engines work. Watt drew enormous self-confidence in the face of less scientifically knowledgeable rivals; "his presumption will meet a check from Dame Nature who is confoundedly obstinate with those who do not understand her ways."[11]

Business partners in science and engineering

A common body of technical knowledge, much of it derived from the application of Newtonian mechanics, permitted technical communication between Boulton and Watt. Their partnership of knowledge flourished within the framework created by voluntary association in the Lunar Society of Birmingham, at whose meetings scientific pursuits were the order of the day (the first day of the full moon each month). The dozen or so members also shared a moral economy of values and attitudes best described as simultaneously self-aggrandizing, disciplining, and enlightened. All these commitments allowed the Boulton–Watt partnership to grow into a deep friendship between the families, that continued into the lives of their sons. The trust rested upon candor, honest dealings, and a healthy pride in their growing wealth and achievements.

These were men of very different backgrounds. Boulton inherited his father's business and was something of a dandy, an Anglican who understood higher finance and the manufacturing of everything metal, from buttons and buckles to coins and watch chains. He loved fame, married well, and used his wife's capital as he needed it. While his firm struggled for many years and was overextended in debts before the success of the steam engine business, Boulton became a man of elegant tastes and social grace, more at home in courtly society than on the workshop floor.[12] However, his social graces did not prevent him from designing

[11] BCL, James Watt Letters, LB/1, Watt to Wedgwood, September 1782; written about a rival in his own workshop.

[12] E. Hopkins, "Boulton before Watt: The Earlier Career Re-considered," *Midland History*, 9, 1984, pp. 43–58. For background, see L. Davidoff and C. Hall, *Family Fortunes: Men and Women of the English Middle Class, 1780–1850* (London: Hutchinson, 1987), pp. 247–52. It is not the case that Watt Jr. served no apprenticeship: he was sent to work with Manchester manufacturers but did not last long with them.

mechanical modifications to the early engines produced in the new partners' Soho factory near Birmingham, and he remained conversant with the mathematical and technical knowledge needed to build new engines.[13]

By contrast we think of Watt as an engineer and inventor. In fact, he was also an entrepreneur, almost entirely self-made, a dour and provincial Scot, inward looking, repressive of himself and his family – all had little regard for "the aristocratical." His confidence in money matters easily faltered and he was pleased to have Boulton as confidant and advisor. Nonetheless, in private the Watts laughed playfully at Boulton's excesses, his eating and drinking, his conspicuous consumption of everything from coaches to garden chairs. Watt was also a compulsive saver, and as a result he and his family left one of the largest archives ever assembled by a single family and business. The Watt family, and by extension the Boultons (also with a rich archive), are irresistible for any history focused on early industrial knowledge, culture, and mores. Their engine was "arguably the single most important technical advance of the whole industrial

[13] Letter Book #57, Boulton to Watt, February 24, 1776: "I forget the specific gravity of one metal, but I fear it is so light as to rise above the center of this wheel and so run out at ye 3 steam pipes; at least you'll be confined to work with a weak steam but that defect may be remedied by making the pipes bent thus hence the fluid metal may rise if necessary as high as A, the steam pipe S may be continued by the side of ye wheel up to A and then turn toward ye Axis." www.cornishmining.net/story/bwpapers.htm. AD 1583/5/69, Boulton to Wilson, November 28, 1792: "They say they have Erected at Tin Croft a Wonderful Engine, the Ne Plus Ultra of all Engineering I therefore think it proper to strike before they have erected others which perhaps may be better, because they are larger, & because they may correct some of their Errors & copy us Closer than they have done: but as they have now an Engine that is come to the extent of its power, & we have had a full proof of its effects from a light load to the extent of its Powers; I think this opportunity should not be lost in accepting of their Challenge. I have therefore sent you a sketch for your consideration & I have sent a copy of it, for Mr. Westons consideration. I have chose to propose a 27 In[ch] Cylinder[e]r with an 8 feet Stroke in it & a 6 feet in the pump because the Cylinder in Tin Croft in which 4/5 of the power is produced is 27 In[ch] Diam[ete]r & an 8 f[ee]t Stroke – The area of 27 is = 1 to 572,555 [here is given a square symbol] In[ches] x by 28 lb [pounds] is = 16031 pounds weight for the Load of a double 27 with ye Beam divided as 6 is to 8 & that is more than 3 times the present Load of Tin Croft, for I confine my offer to Tin Croft under all its present Circumstances such an Engine may be contrived so as to work Single or double & though it will have more power than they want at present, yet as you say they have cut a new Vein of Water & their mine being Rich I am persuaded they will in a few Years want all the power of a Double 27 – But you say it will be attended with a great expence. It will be full 900£ but not 1000£ & if we furnish that mine with a new Engine they ought to pay for it on Condition we take the savings for it after the rate of a single 27. And if it was my affair solely I would be at the whole of the Expence & thereby give them a Death Blow rather than live to be tormented by their Lyes & those of their ignorant friends." A drawing is supplied. For recent revisions to the notion of the entrepreneur, see C. S. Mishra and R. K. Zachary, "Revisiting, Reexamining and Reinterpreting Schumpeter's Original Theory of Entrepreneurship," *Entrepreneurship Research Journal*, 1, 2011, Article 2. Available online at www.bepress.com/erj/vol1/iss1/2.

revolution period."[14] Partly through their efforts, late in the century Birmingham came to be seen by the French as the site of unprecedented manufacturing skill.[15]

Nevertheless, however ingenious their innovations, British entrepreneurs still had to raise capital. Not being readily able to form joint stock companies, they resorted to partnerships. Together the dandy and the Scot created a business in steam that made their engine, and its Soho company, paradigmatic of the profound change at the heart of the First Industrial Revolution. They marketed the first general-purpose power technology capable of replacing organic labor – men, horses, and water – and they died rich men. By 1800 they and their heirs – like the textile barons and mine owners we will meet in the pages that follow – were key players in an emerging industrial elite that had been unimagined a mere generation earlier. Toward the end of his life, Watt, now famous, was even hailed by some as the Newton of his age. Certainly by the 1790s French scientists eagerly sought his scientific acumen and invited him to contribute to their journals.[16]

Armed with a fierce work ethic, James Watt had no intention of remaining the lowly apprentice he was in London during the 1750s when we first get a substantial look at his life. Before that he had had some formal education, but applied science and mechanical craft were his ticket to a

[14] On money matters, see Watt to Boulton, July 8, 1776, letter book #60: "I am afraid I shall otherwise make a very bad bargain in money matters, which wise men like you esteem the most important part." Far greater detail about the partnership and Watt's life can be found in Rev. Dr. R. L. Hills, *James Watt*, Vols. 1 & 2 (Ashbourne: Landmark Publishing, 2002–5). Volume 3 appeared in 2006. For the importance of their engine, see Wrigley, 2010, p. 44. The Boulton family archive is also at the Birmingham Central Library. See also BCL, James Watt Papers, MS 3/69, where the young Watt is using trigonometry to try to estimate the volume of Loch Ness. A similar portrait of Watt appears in B. Marsden and C. Smith, *Engineering Empires: A Cultural History of Technology in Nineteenth-Century Britain* (New York: Palgrave, 2005), Chapter 2.

[15] Guilliaud, Mémoire au Directoire Exécutif, 11 Prairial, an 4, Archives Departmentales, Loire L 930, manufacturer at Saint-Étienne to the government" "Je suis convainçu moi-même, d'après les connaissances que m'a données l'expérience, que le seul moyen de perfectionner la marine, en ce qui touche la partie que je vais traiter, et de raviver en même-temps le Commerce et les Manufactures de quincailleries, est de former un établisement de forges et de fonderies nationales, qui réponde à la majesté du Peuple Français, qui rivalise, par son utilité, tout ce que Birmingham a offert d'honorable à la nation Anglaise; de le placer sur un sol désigné par la nature, habité par des hommes industrieux, et dans lequel on pourrait fabriquer avec des avantages incalculables, et que ne peuvent pas présenter les établissements qui existent en ce genre."

[16] BCL, James Watt Papers, W/11 1787–1790, Letter from Berthollet, December 28, 1788. Mostly concerned with the development of chemical characters – Watt is working on this and Hassenfratz in France and he is told that they have formed "une société" to publish every three months a volume of "annales chimiques" – Morveau, Lavoisier, Monge, Hassenfratz, Adet and myself. Asking him to communicate anything to us that might be useful – they would be happy to receive even work that is contrary to their opinions. "Nous voulons avoir l'impartialité, et la gravité qui conviennent aux sciences."

better future. Although nowhere as well off as Boulton, when they first met Watt was not without resources. His prosperous father, James Watt of Greenock (1698–1782), was a merchant and outfitter of ships who knew about mathematical instruments and navigational devices (as did his brother, John, and their father, who taught mathematics). Watt's father was also an elder in the local Presbyterian kirk, with connections to the university in Glasgow.

In keeping with these university connections young James supplied the Professor of Chemistry, Dr. Black, with cinnamon from one of his father's shipments. Clearly James aspired to higher things, as well as practical knowledge, and when his preserved letters begin, he is in London learning as much as possible about machines. He cut out numbers and letters in the shop of a clockmaker. He bought telescopes, compasses, and needles for his father and his father's friends; he learned how to make quadrants, mathematical and musical instruments, organs, and flutes; he made globes; he was tutored by a schoolmaster, probably in mathematics; he taught drawing and map-making, became a skilled draughtsman, and within two years he was hiring his own workers.

By 1773 Watt's first wife was addressing her letters to "James Watt, Engineer" and he was in the field surveying terrain intended for commercially useful canals. By then he could assess the economics of a building venture as well as the hydraulics, discussing the projected savings to shippers in terms of time, insurance money, and the value to investors as the result of profits to be made from the reduced cost of coal shipping.[17] When he first returned to Glasgow after his London apprenticeship, Watt's artisanal skill was such that he could work as a mechanic-instrument maker for its College where he was allowed to receive his mail.

By the mid 1760s Watt had turned his attention to the most sophisticated mechanical devices of the day, to the cutting-edge power technology of steam and electricity.[18] He may not then have grasped the principle of latent heat upon which Joseph Black, Professor of Chemistry at Glasgow, demonstrated that his engine depended, but he understood the effect of gravity or the force of inertia on its strokes.[19] Watt, like engine makers Newcomen and Savery before him, also understood the novel and counter-intuitive concept of a vacuum, derived as it was from the new science of the seventeenth century. Some time in his youth he also came to

[17] James Watt Papers, 3/69, report dated 1774 to the Lords of the Police for Scotland.

[18] MS 4/11, letter of October 8, 1765 to his father; MS C1/15 correspondence with Lind on his electrical machine.

[19] James Watt Papers, MS 3/18, and letter of February 16, 1782 to Boulton: "I am certain that with proper loads such an engine can easily make 30 strokes per minute when not impeded by vis inertia or gravity."

know about the properties of steam as an "elastic fluid" and the necessary geometry, as well as practical mechanics, needed for his engine.[20] He used geometry and trigonometry in surveying, and had studied the Newtonian mechanical textbooks of Desaguliers and 's Gravesande, the latter especially difficult mathematically. In 1763 Watt made, with the manual dexterity of a skilled craftsman, his own steam engines of both the Savery and Newcomen kind.[21] So when asked to repair a Newcomen engine, he knew the mechanical principles at work as well as the strengths and deficiencies, and he knew how to work in wood and metal. Contemporary engineers recommended a similar working knowledge, and the engineer Robert Beighton said, "The affairs of the world could never be carried forward without the help of Science."[22]

Watt's repair job turned into his life's work; he never stopped trying to improve his already vastly improved version of the steam engine. He did all of this without ever spending a day in a university classroom or a Dissenting academy where men of his religious background invariably went, Oxford and Cambridge being unavailable to non-Anglican Protestants. Over time his mechanical and mathematical learning – easily documented in his voluminous correspondence and notes – put him in touch with industrialists throughout Britain as well as with some of the finest Continental scientists of the era. As Josiah Wedgwood told Watt when he struggled to have his patent renewed, "I am happy that you are at liberty to confound your enemies. Invention is so rare and so useful a quality that it ought to be protected and encouraged to the utmost. It is a misfortune to your cause that it is to be determined not by men of science or by men of business but by lawyers." All such sentiments reinforced his self-definition as a man of science and business.[23]

In the late 1760s Watt perfected the separate condenser that kept the engine's steam at a constant temperature and pressure and permitted the

[20] Watt to Boulton, February 9, 1782, MS 3/18, on a competitor: "As his theories are all abstract and run only on the commonly known properties of steam as an elastic fluid I cannot conceive anything wherein he can surpass us particularly as he seems to be greatly divested of geometrical principles." This is followed by a long mechanical discussion. See MS 3/69, his report dated 1774, where he has used trigonometry to try to estimate the volume of Loch Ness.

[21] To Mr. Robison, October 30, 1783, JWP, Letter Book. On the science involved, see H. Floris Cohen, "Inside Newcomen's Fire Engine, or: The Scientific Revolution and the Rise of the Modern World," *History of Technology*, 25, 2004, 118–19.

[22] West Yorkshire Archive Service, Wakefield, MS C482/1, June 19, 1778, Beighton writing to William Martin, also with a discussion of Priestley's views.

[23] BCL, Boulton and Watt MSS, letters between the Wedgwood and Watt families largely from the 1790s and this one from Josiah W., Jr., dated Etruria, April 2, 1795. See also John Rylands Library, Manchester, James Jr. to Josiah Jr., January 26, 1799, announcing success after seven years of struggle to re-secure the patent on the steam engine.

engine's cooling and condensation to occur in the condenser without affecting the steam in the cylinder. The condensation, then the refilling, of the steam in the condenser – not simply the external air atmosphere or the vacuum – lowered or raised the piston of the engine without the other parts ever having to be cooled. Older engines such as Newcomen's with one cylinder had to have the steam (and hence its metal container) cooled by a spray of cold water, and the parts had in turn to be reheated by the next infusion of steam. Watt's innovation was elegant and brilliant. It drew upon his exceptional talents as an instrument maker and his knowledge of drawing and mathematical exactness. His earlier work with clocks, watches, steel springs, levers, iron braces, brass fittings, and mathematical instruments gave him habits of precision and exact fitting that proved critical for making his complex engine work. By 1778 a French prospective buyer, who had been to England, reported that the Boulton and Watt firm had installed twenty-seven engines in Britain – and then made a list of every one of them and their use.[24]

Intelligence, hard work, and dedication to science infused the lives of Watt and Boulton. All cemented the camaraderie and moral values of both men and those of their entire circle. Although not as harsh on himself and others as Watt, Matthew Boulton, a chemist in his own right, put the relationship between virtue and science succinctly: "A man will never make a good Chymist unless he acquires a dexterity, & neatness in making experiments, even down to pulverising in a Mortar, or blowing the Bellows, distinctness, order, regularity, neatness, exactness, & cleanliness are necessary in the laboratory, in the manufactory, & in the counting house."[25] The virtues needed for science were of a piece with those needed by industrial entrepreneurs such as Boulton and Watt. Boulton was so proficient as a chemist that his discoveries were valued by the most original British chemist of the age, Joseph Priestley.[26]

[24] James Watt Papers, 6/46; list of his tools in a letter to his father, from London, June 19, 1756. In 1784, when he advised a friend what her son needed to know to become an engineer, Watt put drawing first, then geometry, algebra, arithmetic, and the elements of mechanics; see same collection, Letter Book, May 30, 1784 to May. On his invention, see B. J. Hunt, *Pursuing Power and Light: Technology and Physics from James Watt to Albert Einstein* (Baltimore, MD: The Johns Hopkins University Press, 2010), pp. 4–13. On the twenty-seven engines, see Archives Nationales, Paris, Marine MS G 110, f. 178, and at work at an iron forge, a bog mine, leather works, salt works, etc.

[25] Quoted in Musson and Robinson, 1989, pp. 210–11, Boulton to his son, 1787.

[26] R. E. Schofield, *The Enlightened Joseph Priestley: A Study of His Life and Work from 1773 to 1804* (University Park, PA: The Pennsylvania State University Press, 2004), p. 104. And see J. Insley, "James Watt's Cookbook Chemistry," *Notes and Records of the Royal Society* 65 (September 20, 2011), pp. 301–8.

Watt, too, shared a deep interest in chemistry, as did his second wife. Annie Watt came from a bleaching family and had her own serious scientific and intellectual interests. She and her father were experimenters in bleaching techniques, and in the 1780s worked with a newly discovered substance, chlorine, about which the French chemist Berthollet wrote at length to Watt. The marriage partnership of James and Annie allowed them to discuss her experiments. More prosaically, she never hesitated to scold her husband or to lecture him affectionately on everything from his health to the curtain fabric he should buy on his travels. She also understood his business, both financial and technical, and he could write to her for engine parts and be sure she knew precisely what he was describing.

Boulton and Watt's success in engines and business reinforced their conviction that they, too, were scientists. Watt thought himself to be as smart as the French chemist, Lavoisier, about whom he wrote, "Mr. L[avoisier] having heard some imperfect account of the paper I wrote in the spring has run away with the idea and made up a Memoir without any satisfactory proofs. . . . If you will read the 47 and 48 pages of Mr. de la Place and his memoir on heat you will be convinced that they had no such ideas thus, as they speak clearly of the nitrous acid being converted into air."

Watt worried that no one would believe him because he was not, like Lavoisier, an academician and a financier.[27] As far as Watt was concerned they were in the same league, although as hindsight would show, Watt, like Priestley, failed to see the significance of Lavoisier's discovery of oxygen and his dismissal of phlogiston.

Both Watt and Boulton, despite such disagreements, maintained an active communication with French scientists. On a journey to Paris, where Boulton and Watt conversed at ease with their hosts, Boulton's notes mention his dinner companions. All were men of science or engineers, the Périers, Bertholet, Monge, Vandermonde, Lavoisier, de Luc, and friends. The same was true of Boulton's time in the Dutch Republic.[28] Scientific communications within Britain, and with the Continent, were a constant part of Boulton and Watt's intellectual life. Predictably, when they went to Paris they looked for technical proficiency and scientific learning; they were two sides of the same coin.

[27] JWP Letter Book November 30 [1783] to Mr. de Luc.

[28] MS 3782/12/108/49, f. 24. He arrived in Paris on November 18, 1786; MS 3782/12/108/17 in Holland, where Boulton met with Steenstra, Van Lienden, May. Boulton spelled Périers as "Perriers." In 1792, a course in physics and chemistry is being given at the Jardin des plantes in Paris, see AN, Paris, F17 1344/1; see the description of his previous activities by Laportal, year 7.

Britain and France: the comparative dimension

Like other British industrialists, Boulton and Watt knew that their achievements had to be measured from an international perspective. By the late eighteenth century British–French rivalry was as much economic as it was military, and market share meant being able to compete effectively at home as well as abroad. Yet the why and the how of Britain's growing economic domination in Europe and the Atlantic puzzled contemporaries as much as it challenges historical explanation. Every conceivable economic argument has been advanced by way of explanation. Boulton and Watt saw the rivalry and the comparison not in economic but in cultural terms.

Perhaps the most curious and helpful observations made by the many British visitors to France in the 1780s reside in the notes taken by none other than Boulton (who was accompanied for all or part of the time by Watt).[29] Indeed, they were the guests of the French king and received contracts for work at Versailles.[30] Boulton arrived with a comparative agenda in mind, one he in turn recommended to others. He made lists of all the mechanical and chemical arts, especially those found in France but not seen in England.[31]

As it happens, Boulton was asking the very questions that a comparative historian would pose when trying to understand the roots of French industrial retardation. Boulton had many motives, not least among them gaining access to a quantitative understanding of the energy used, and still needed, in various French hydraulic projects where one of his steam engines might find a place.[32] He especially wanted to know how much it would cost to import coal from England and concluded, "France ought to seek to work her coals and not depend on wood only." Before this trip

[29] Papers of Matthew Boulton, MS 3782/12/107/14, 1786. Watt is there in January 1787 at Calais. See www.cornishmining.net/story/bwpapers.htm and Cornwall Record Office, AD1583/2/27Letter, Ann Watt to Wilson, December 4, 1786: "I received yours of the 11th this morning with the account for November I also received the account for Oct[obe]r I am very happy to hear everything remains quiet in Cornwall – Last Saturday I received a letter from Mr Watt tho he wishes much to be at home he says nothing of his leaving France he says from the kind reception they have meet with they have neither time to write nor almost to think that they are kept constantly engaged."

[30] Ibid. D1583/2/33 Letter, Boulton to Wilson regarding Baron Stein, and of work proposed for the King of France, January 27, 1787.

[31] BCL, MS 3782/12/107/28, dated 1800, ff. 15–16, in this instance possibly a request he made to his French visitors, Mr. and Mrs. Gautier and de Luc.

[32] BCL, MS 3782/12/108/49, 1786–7, f. 9 notes on the water supply of Paris with assistance from M. Deparceux, f. 18 on the cost of coal imported from Swansea or Newcastle, £1.3.0 per ton with extensive notes and measurements of the water works at Marly and Challiot.

Boulton also had experience with French bureaucracy and had been willing to have his engine tested on the polders near Dunkirk, but not in Paris where he claimed nothing comparable could be seen.[33]

Perhaps in Paris Boulton and Watt were looking for men like themselves. Boulton wanted to know about "all publick meetings and schools for the promotion of human knowledge and arts."[34] Most helpfully for us, he made a list that included the Royal Academy of Sciences, the Society of Agriculture and Economical Arts, schools for millers, bakers, metallurgy, public medicine, surgery, design and painting, as well as chemistry, architecture (where drawing, geometry, and mathematics were taught), the King's library, the Royal School of Hydrostatics, and a *lycée* in the Palais Royale where twice a day lectures could be heard "in all the sciences." In addition there were ten different free private lectures open every day. Boulton was looking for the Paris version of public science and he found it easily without the benefit of independent or unlicensed newspapers. The *Journal de Paris* regularly listed lectures in the city. Boulton also noted schools for the deaf, dumb, and blind, for recreations such as riding and fencing, and multiple near-university-level colleges.

Boulton discovered that all sorts of science could be found in the French capital (the provinces were a different matter), but what did this translate into, in terms of improved manufacturing?[35] Again, Boulton made his lists. He found French inns to be inferior (in part because they did not serve tea); tables, chairs, and pottery were inferior; and in general he determined that "the riches of the country seem to be all applied to the use of the king." Some of Boulton's observations were fairly stereotypical of English reactions to Gallic customs. Then Boulton got serious and found significant French superiority in jewelry, watches, clocks, vases ("far superior"), wine, snuff boxes, fine silk and velvet, wooden shoes, bleaching of linen and silk, better presses for cutting, coining money, better rolling of lead pipes, and the superiority of just about all the artisanal goods coming from Lyons.[36] Boulton also

[33] AN, Marine, MS G 110, ff. 171–2. [34] Ibid., ff. 18–24.

[35] BCL, MS 3782/12/108/49, ff. 32–3. For science in the French capital, see essays by M. R. Lynn and L. Roberts in *Science and Spectacle in the European Enlightenment*, ed. B. Bensaude-Vincent and C. Blondel (Aldershot: Ashgate, 2008), pp. 65–74, 129–40.

[36] L. Perez, "Silk Fabrics in Eighteenth-Century Lyon," in *Guilds, Innovation and the European Economy, 1400–1800*, ed. S. R. Epstein and M. Prak (Cambridge University Press, 2008), pp. 232–63. For some confirmation of what Boulton saw in Paris, see A. Guillerme, *La naissance de l'industrie à Paris. Entre sueurs et vapeurs: 1780–1830* (Seyssel: Champ Vallon, 2007), pp. 312–16.

assessed where he thought English superiority lay: optical, mathematical, and philosophical instruments, coaches, chaises, and all carriages, "all useful things in iron, steel, doors, lathes, tables and drawers and tables." In sum, the common people back home lived better and English life in general was more convenient, with greater neatness and cleanliness in evidence. Watt, meanwhile, had nothing but praise for the quality of metalworking used in French cylinders intended for the steam engine of the Périers.[37]

Decades later, Mr. Clark would note the fine craftsmanship in expensive French cotton spindles. But just as in cotton textiles, French artisanal work could also be twice as expensive as British-made items. At precisely this moment a French commentator on the crisis in the cotton industry brought about by English competition observed "that it is very difficult to introduce in France and in the space of a few months all *les Méchaniques* that are in vogue in Great Britain, and whose actual perfection is the fruit of more than fifteen years of constant work." The crisis originated from the less expensive British cottons flooding the market.[38] Boulton would have been well aware of the parlous state of the French cotton industry.

Allowing for bias and provincialism in Boulton's and Watt's assessments, what can we extract from them that hints at the industrial gaps that, as we shall see, would open between France and England in the period after 1800? Boulton noted a gap in general prosperity that other observers of France also recorded. He tells about French artisanal superiority in a variety of consumer goods and time-keeping devices, and in linen and silk. But when describing "cloth" – we may assume cotton and wool – Boulton put it in the plus column for England.[39] Add to the mix the means of transportation, iron and steel production, and instruments to teach applied mechanics, and therein the English, he believed, excelled.

In the 1780s, we can see through Boulton's eyes what the French revolutionaries sought to correct but a few years later through a new industrial and educational policy implemented in the mid 1790s.

37 www.cornishmining.net/story/bwpapers.htm, MS D1583/2/31, Letter, Ann Watt to Wilson, January 9, 1787: "I had the pleasure of receiving yours of the 5th this morning inclosing the account for Dec[embe]r which is sent to Mr Pearson I am very sorry to hear of the three Engines you mention as it may be the cause of some quarreling but the Cornish gen[tleme]n need give themselves no trouble to prevent Engines being sent out of the Kingdom Mr watt wrote me that he saw Cylinders cast & bored by Mr Perrier better done than any of Mr Wilkinsons & that all the noise that was made about the tool bill was to no purpose for he was sorry to say that many of our Artists might learn from France more than the French now can learn of us that their late improvements were immense."

38 AN, Paris, F 12 658 A, 1788–9.

39 BCL, MS 3782/12/108/49, f. 36. This notebook contains these important comparisons.

Curiously, Boulton had also identified elements now increasingly thought to be critical for early industrial development: mechanical knowledge focused on application, machines made of iron and steel, productivity in coal extraction, improved transportation, a general prosperity that made surplus capital more readily available. When we focus on the issue of French "retardation" we should remember Boulton's analysis.[40]

Inheritable knowledge and skills

Boulton and Watt's vision of what was needed for success in the business of power technology informed the education they insisted upon for their sons. Despite his own debt to artisanal practice, Watt demanded that they have an even more rigorous and formal scientific and mathematical education than was available to him – although it did include bookkeeping. Along with good morals, James Jr.'s (b. 1769) schooling, both in England and on the Continent, was meant to provide him with a career either as an independent mechanical engineer or a merchant, depending upon the direction his talents took.[41] Of these Watt took a harsh and dim view, and indeed James Jr. admitted that he had little mechanical skill, and hence as late as the 1790s he could do little to assist his father with a malfunctioning engine that he was supposed to examine.[42] Nevertheless, the education Watt gave James imparted enough of the necessary business skill, entrepreneurial spirit, and international contacts that he eventually inherited the business and did well enough at it. As *pater* Watt explained to his son, "you should procure some system of mechanics which is more full than 's Gravesande on Mechanics, hydrostaticks and the doctrines of motion which are the parts of natural philosophy which will be most use to you."[43]

Parts of what both the Watts and the Boultons did for their sons was to ensure that they received a Continental education and were conversant with a wider cultural and intellectual universe than Birmingham or its environs. Although they were quintessentially entrepreneurs, both Boulton and Watt in their way became cosmopolitans. Throughout the

[40] For a detailed treatment of these factors and many more, see J. Mokyr, *The Enlightened Economy: An Economic History of Britain 1700–1850* (New Haven, CT: Yale University Press, 2009).

[41] On James Jr.'s education, see Musson and Robinson, 1989, Chapter 5.

[42] BCL, W/6 James Jr. to father, November 5, 1793.

[43] LB/1 private letter book, March 27, 1785, James Jr. is in Geneva. And see 3/13 85 to same, "be only with men of science; industry and application require method and regularity without these the latter do not do . . . never lose sight of Christian precept do unto others as you would have them do unto you. I am your true friend."

Figure 5 James Watt, Jr., son of James Watt, c. 1800

world of science they had international correspondents from the 1770s onward. Watt received requests to purchase his copying machine – yet another invention, that allowed the writer to copy a letter as it was being written – from as far away as India. Closer to home, friends asked for his chemical assistance in finding truer pigments for their water coloring. The

Boulton and Watt sons inherited those business and intellectual contacts and both families came to value sophistication and politeness – the skills imparted by formal and informal education.[44]

Yet there were important differences in emphasis between what these very different men valued for their male children. In young Boulton's case the education was self-consciously genteel; Boulton had large pretensions both for himself and his son. But Watt attended little to the elegance of the setting and was much more concerned that James Jr. learn science and mathematics and not waste his time on theater or novels. Annie Watt saw much greater value in cultural pursuits, in travel, poetry, and rhetoric. She begged her son Gregory (b. 1777) to show her his writings and to be her friend. Despite their varied social aspirations, first and foremost both the Boulton and Watt families instilled science in their sons. It was the key to personal and business success.

Lurking radicalism

In matters political and intellectual the Watt peas did not fall far from their pod. Watt's son by his first marriage, James Jr., inherited his father's distrust of other people's interests, although he, like his father's circle of friends, had his idealistic and utopian side. However difficult their strivings, early industrialists could act as loyal subjects while longing for political influence and looking with admiration at the American and French revolutions. At Glasgow in the 1790s, given the opportunity for a university education, predictably Watt's second son Gregory learned science and specialized in geology. Indeed, the Scottish universities of Edinburgh and Glasgow taught a full array of the most contemporary science. Industrialist families thus favored them, and by the 1790s Watt's engine was being explained to university students in Edinburgh. North-country entrepreneurs like the Strutts chose Scottish universities for their children precisely because they inculcated applied science. At this same time Oxford, in reaction to the French Revolution, turned away from science and embraced Aristotle as the source of natural knowledge.[45]

44 For the letter from India, see BCL, James Watt Letter book, J. Robison, 1797 and for water coloring, W. Withering to Watt, October 1, 1790.

45 Accessed September 13, 2012, http://digital2.library.ucla.edu/viewItem.do?ark=21198%2Fzz0019rp5j&viewType=3; the student notes of Lovell Edgeworth at Edinburgh in the 1790s. For Oxford, see Heather Ellis, "'A Manly and Generous Discipline?': Classical Studies and Generational Conflict in Eighteenth and Early Nineteenth Century Oxford," *History of Universities*, 25, 2, 2011, 143–72. For the Strutts, see Fitzwilliam Museum, Cambridge, MS 48–1947, by Joseph Strutt, "On the relative advantages and disadvantages of the English and Scottish Universities," dated 1808.

At Glasgow the ethos of practical science intended for progress and industry could also have a political analogue. Gregory did Greek and rhetoric while learning, as his college notebooks tell us, that wealth and power produce "a crowd of servile sycophants" and that there are societies where "the haughty tyrant seated on his gorgeous throne ... dreaded and obeyed by an abject people is for the time considered ... at the zenith of human glory. The hand of death cuts him short in his career; he perishes in the midst of his splendor."[46]

These were dangerous teachings that harkened back to the seventeenth-century English revolution and were hardly appropriate for young men destined for prosperity and business.[47] Presumably such sentiments were seen as acceptable by the Watts, at least for the intellectually gifted Gregory. For their part, James and Annie Watt were outwardly as cautious and conformist as they needed to be, with Watt even advising James Jr., who was given to radicalism, to be submissive and respectful to powerful men.[48] In 1791 Watt told his friend, the radical chemist Joseph Priestley, that "while Great Britain enjoys an unprecedented degree of prosperity" and other countries are in the throes of revolution, it would be folly to risk "the overturn of all good government."[49]

During the Birmingham riots against Priestley and other Dissenters who supported the French Revolution, the Watts were protected by their workmen (whom they generally regarded as worthless), and after the riots they were very careful and somewhat withdrawn politically. Indeed, Watt was repeatedly convinced that their home and factory had been targeted. By 1793 he laid great emphasis upon his loyalism, but there is no evidence that he began to treat his workers any differently or better.[50] Boulton

46 James Watt Papers, Gregory's exercise book, C4/C18A.

47 For the survival of revolutionary sentiments, see K. Wilson, "A Dissident Legacy: Eighteenth Century Popular Politics and the Glorious Revolution," in *Liberty Secured? Britain before and after 1688*, ed. J. R. Jones (Stanford University Press, 1992), pp. 299–334. For the education in science available at Edinburgh in the 1790s, see also East Riding of Yorkshire Archive Service, Arthur Clifford's "Journal of my Studies," MS DDCC/150/276, passim. For Edinburgh education in mathematics and science in the period after 1658, see R. H. Houston, "Literacy, Education and the Culture of Print in Enlightenment Edinburgh," *History*, 78, October 1993, p. 385.

48 James Watt Papers, BCL, LB/1, Watt to James Jr., January 16, 1784.

49 James Watt Papers C1/20 letter of July 8, 1791, a draft letter written just six days before the Birmingham riots. For the hint of a class element in the riots, see P. Langford, *Public Life and Propertied Englishmen 1689–1798* (New York: Oxford University Press, 1991), p. 245.

50 www.cornishmining.net/story/bwpapers.htm, AD1583/4/69, Watt to Wilson, July 20, 1791: "We have had an effective Mob here none of your shilly shally Cornish Mobs, You will see by the papers some of the execution they have done, We have luckily escaped, though we have no doubt we were objects of their fury, On Sunday we packed up some of our Cloaths & valuables expecting a visit on Monday, but some Military arrived on

remained convinced that at any time the rioters would once again take aim at their business and persons.[51]

The Watts were far from content with the social hierarchy that rendered them middling. By the 1780s James and Annie had the time to follow contemporary national and international politics avidly, and politics must have been a subject of household conversation. In that period Watt railed against excessive taxation and saw few common interests between the landed who controlled Parliament and middling men of commerce and industry like him. Threatened with the imposition of a tax on coal, Watt let drop his belief that such an injustice would "breed rebellion." When frustrated in Parliament he fumed to Annie against "aristocratic scoundrels" and threatened that "a little more of this will make me an enemy to corrupt p.s [parliaments] and a democrat if democracy were a less evil."[52] He also helped to procure witnesses "to the cruelties practiced by the slave traders." Boulton went further and actually engaged in lobbying the prime minister about the government's "ruinous" taxation proposals.[53] Watt

Sunday night which prevented them. At Soho we were armed, our men promised to stand by us & would have given them a warm reception but we could scarcely have defended our houses. We are worn out with anxiety & fatigue therefore shall not answer any of your letters, indeed I cannot think upon business, till matters subside, the mischief done is very great, above £100000 Some of the rioters are taken & many more known, but the infernal instigators are still behind the screen. It seems originally to have been a plot to exterminate all dissenters, but soon became one to demolish every house where plunder was to be had. The soveraignty of the people was established for 3 days & 3 nights without constraint but I assure you we did not like their Majesties Government."

51 AD 1583/5/6, February 15, 1792, Boulton to Wilson in Cornwall: "Workmen are paradeing the Streets, with Cockaids in their Hats & assembled by Beat of Drum Headed by Ignorance & Envy with their Eyes turnd towards Soho. I follow no business but what I have been the Father of, & have done much more for the Birm [in] g [ha] m Manufactures than any other individual. I have declined the paltry trade of White metal Buttons, which is the article that is so much affected by the rise of Metals, & that in which Rioters are employd. I mix with no Clubs, attend no publick meetings, am of no Party, nor a zealot in Religion: neither do I hold any conversation with any Birm [in] g [ha] m persons & therefore I know no Grounds but what may be suggested by Wicked & Enveyous hearts for supposing me to be the cause of the late rise of copper. However I am well guarded by Justice, by Law, by Men, & arms. Pray write me p [e] r return . . . Yours sincerely Matt[he]w Boulton."

52 Boulton and Watt MSS MII/4/4/10, March 1792, James to Annie. On the slave traders, same folder, letter of March 30, 1792.

53 www.cornishmining.net/story/bwpapers.htm, AD1583/1 Correspondence, Volume 1, Watt to Mr Thomas Wilson, Chacewater, Truro, Cornwall, via Bristol, Birmingham, July 11, 1784: "The Coal Tax would have proved ruinsome to us & to the manufacturers of this country but I hear that it is laid aside & wisely other wise it would have bred rebellion." And see AD1583/1/47, Letter, Boulton to Wilson, February 10, 1785: "Yours of ye 31st Ul[ti]mo the post did not deliver until this minute so that it hath been ten days in coming. Mr Watt went to London with Mr Wilkinson on Tuesday even [in] g and as I have had two summons's from Mr Pitt I shall set out tomorrow even [in] g upon the subjects of the Iron Trade, the Irish trade, & many of the late taxes, which the Commercial part of this Country are unanimous & Violent against. I refer you to the news papers for our resolves at the Quarterly meeting of ye Iron Masters at Stourbridge [Worcestershire]

remained convinced that their options were dwindling down to loss of trade, emigration, or civil war.[54]

Watt's vision of the political process, like that of many other industrialists, was intensely social. Men of birth were the problem: "I hear a Society is formed at Freemasons Hall for shortening the duration of parliaments, but as the leaders are noblemen & gentlemen of great property, & I believe aristocratic there is no danger of their acting upon republican principles." Such principles, he said, "struck great terror into the supporters of the present corrupt system."[55] By the same token Watt said that he had nothing to do with reform societies. He was never clear about what alterations he would put in place of the existing system, but his outward loyalism masked a deeper anger.

Science, industry, and reliance on family and kin made the Boultons and Watts of the world harder, not easier, to govern. The diversion provided by work and profit did, however, keep them relatively passive. Even as they were horrified by the violent turn taken by the French Revolution, the Watts had no illusions about the power and pretensions of kings and aristocrats. When the French army threatened Italy, Watt said that "if they spare the monuments of the arts the rest is only the retribution of divine justice on an execrable government."[56]

His hatred of tyranny and superstition is best illustrated by the willingness of James and Annie to send Gregory to Glasgow with its hardly moderate political climate.[57] Not surprisingly, the attitudes learned in

which I attended, & likewise the Resolves of ye Birm [in] g [ha] m committee w [hi] ch will be pub [lishe] d in a day or two. You are too tranquil in Cornwall to enter into the spirit of these sort of politicks but tis necessary somebody should & that even the whole manufacturing & Commercial part of the Kingdom should be unanimous in correcting the erronious principles w [hic] h our Government hath adopted in laying taxes, perhaps you will feel when I say dont tax Mines nor the means of getting rich but tax Riches when got & the expenditure of them." Boulton instructed Wilson to burn the letter.

54 Cornish Record Office, AD1583/1/53 Letter, Watt to Wilson, April 16, 1785: "I have it on good Grounds that a tax is proposed to be laid on the exportation of Copper & on Tin, It having been represented to the minister that the former is sold £10 p [e] r ton cheaper abroad than in England and that they can get the latter from no other quarter. The Minister has shewn a degree of obstinacy and faculty of manœuvring in the Irish business and in the Excise Laws that nobody thought him capable of – And at present he seems likely to carry his points in the house of Commons, at least, the consequences of which will be dreadfull unless the higher powers side with the people. Loss of trade Emigration or civil war is what we are threatened with. I mention this to make you put your neighbours on their guard, for if the Minister subsists & thinks proper to tax copper, he will not be foiled nor persuaded out of it."

55 BCL, MII/4/4/27, James to Annie, April 26, 1792.

56 Boulton and Watt MSS MII/4/4/1–51; letter from Watt to Annie, November 10, 1792; see letter of November 5 on the retribution of divine justice.

57 James Watt Papers, MS 6/14 November 20, 1794, Annie Watt to Gregory; same to same late 1794 on burning an effigy of Thomas Paine.

Glasgow took hold. When travelling in Austria, Gregory wrote to James Jr. that it was a land of "aristocracy, gluttony and imbecility. . . . Every wholesome regulation of poor Joseph [II] has been annulled and Austria sunk a half century into Barbarism."[58] The mindset of early industrialists and entrepreneurs displayed piety, discipline, striving, and science, but also a proud going-against-the grain attitude toward established and landed authority. In their values, attitudes, and educational aspirations lies the making of the English middle class who may rightly be described as the bourgeoisie.

Little wonder, then, that when the French Revolution broke out, James Jr. sided against "crimes of tyrants" and in defiance of his father marched in the streets of Paris and supported the revolution right into the Terror. He told his father firmly that the monarchs of Europe "are in general so despicable that they are not worth attending to ... by an enlightened age."[59] In his youth, James Jr. displayed another version of the going-against-the-grain radicalism that appeared from time to time in the family. He quarreled with his father, lectured him on politics, told him not to trust stories born of "aristocratical malice that only make me smile," and mourned the revolution's turn toward violence – but as someone who continued to believe in its principles. By 1794 James Jr. was in the thick of English Jacobin circles, had been denounced on the floor of Parliament by Edmund Burke, and feared returning to England. He did so only after the radical Thomas Walker was acquitted by the courts.

By late 1794 James Jr. thought "the revolution will remain more a terror to the friends of the people perhaps than to their enemies." Despite the disappointments brought by the French Revolution, he continued to expect and welcome profound change. James Jr. deeply believed that the changes in industry as they accelerated in the 1790s would "result in strange things. . . . I have repeatedly said to father now that the machine is set in motion we may wait quietly the result."[60] Perhaps that prospect, plus the hope of inheriting his father's business, kept him from fulfilling his plan to expatriate to America with Priestley and his radical utopian friends of the early 1790s.[61] Certainly the expansion of Boulton and

[58] James Watt Papers, C2/12, Gregory to James Watt, Jr., August 3, 1802.

[59] James Watt Papers, MS W/6, Nantes, October 17, 1792, James Jr. to his father.

[60] James Watt Papers, BCL, James Watt, Jr. private letter book; letter to Cooper, no date on the machine set in motion; September 16, 1794 to Stephen Delesart [?], on the revolution. For an example of the spin-off from Watt's engine, see L. Tomory, "Building the First Gas Network, 1812–1820," *Technology and Culture*, 52, 1, January 2011, pp. 75–102.

[61] James Watt Papers, MS W/6, James Jr. to his father, from Naples, May 8, 1793. See John Money, *Experience and Identity: Birmingham and the West Midlands, 1760–1800* (Montreal: McGill-Queen's University Press, 1977), Chapter 9.

Watt's engine business could leave its heirs expecting a continuously upward trajectory of profit.[62]

While we know a great deal about the politics of James Jr. and his brother, Gregory, Watt Sr. played his political cards close to his chest. In his youth, while trying to set his machine in motion, if Watt ever thought about politics he kept his views to himself, never even confiding them in extant letters to his first wife or his father. Only infrequently, especially when his interests were threatened, did he vent his spleen against the great and wellborn. In the 1790s his letters abroad became moderate and loyalist, but then he knew that spying was commonplace and that the authorities were opening the mail of men in his circle, especially the known friends of Priestley.[63]

In the end, above all else, both the Boulton and Watt families coveted a place in a world that would make room for their interests and success. As Watt said to his wife when Parliament saved his patent and thus served his interests: "That two poor Mechanicks & the justice of their cause have more interest in his house [of Commons] than an Aristocrat, so be it always."[64] When his interests were placated and he could get on with being a scientific entrepreneur, then Watt was a loyalist. In his mind the world was divided between men of science, practice, industry, and merit, and everybody else, great and lowly. Any one of them could thwart the progress of one's industry.

Striving, virtue, and the Protestant entrepreneurial life

The sources of the entrepreneurial spirit have been the subject of much discussion. Over a century ago the German sociologist Max Weber said that the worldly asceticism induced by Protestantism held the key to unlocking the new personae of the seventeenth and eighteenth centuries.[65] He found the new entrepreneurs most notably among Watt's associates, and even used Benjamin Franklin, a distant and elderly colonial correspondent of Watt's intellectual circle in Birmingham, as the prime exemplar of the early spirit of capitalism. Certainly Watt and Franklin

[62] For an example of that trajectory, see The Brotherton Library, Leeds, The Marshall MSS, MS 200/26 f. 38, which says that the Boulton–Watt engine bought in 1792 was 20 horsepower; it was replaced in 1821 by 40 hp at Mill A; in 1795 Mill B had a 28-hp engine, which was replaced in 1814 by 56 hp; the 1797 mill was built at Shrewsbury with a 56-hp engine.

[63] For background, see I. R. Christie, *Wars and Revolutions: Britain, 1760–1815* (Cambridge, MA: Harvard University Press, 1982), pp. 215–29.

[64] Boulton and Watt Papers, James to Annie, April 6, 1792.

[65] See M. Weber, *The Protestant Ethic and the Spirit of Capitalism* (New York: Scribner's, 1953).

were evenly matched when it came to frugality, obsessive saving, caution with regard to frivolity and luxury – all ascetic characteristics, Weber argued, of the self-made entrepreneur.

Extreme champions as well as detractors of Weber's thesis have written much nonsense about it. Among the errors has been the assumption that in naming Protestants as good capitalists, Weber meant to exclude Catholics or Jews. But Weber need not be read as having created "ideal types" trapped by their theology rather than molded by time and circumstances. Weber's point should be seen as an historical one: Protestantism with its emphasis upon predestination induced a permanent uncertainty about salvation. If doubt did not lead to despair, it induced the Protestant ethic that was slightly more conducive to worldly asceticism, to an almost mindless striving among larger numbers of literate non-nobles who were generally attracted to reformed religion in the first place.

From the sixteenth century onward Protestants were most commonly found in cities and towns where heresy was harder to eradicate. They had access to printing presses, and in urban settings were better able to practice artisanal and commercial crafts. The other major and older forms of Western religiosity carried with them historical baggage and associations with corporate or hierarchical or ghettoized life that restricted individual freedom, or frowned upon aggressive expressions of self-interest coupled with risk taking – thus tending toward enforced savings. With Catholicism, an independent-minded clergy, responsive by custom and law to bishops and kings, meant that it was harder to get the new values of self-made men preached from the pulpit. Where Protestants were in the ascendancy – as was the case in England, the Dutch Republic, Geneva, and parts of Scotland – not surprisingly mercantile life flourished. None of this means that Catholics could not or would not excel at business, but it does suggest that Protestantism succeeded more easily and effectively at creating a capitalist ethos. Nor does it suggest that in the eighteenth century Protestants would turn effortlessly from mercantile to industrial capitalism. Many complex factors – among them market size, access to coal or water power, patterns of consumption, attitudes of elites, access to science and civic associations – had to be in place before, for example, the British, and not the Dutch, industrialized first. On the Continent, Belgium, with its largely Catholic population, industrialized before its neighbors.

The Protestant ethic – habits of striving, disciplined labor, and self-examination – within a moral code framed by piety and science can be seen in the Watt family as early as 1690. The surviving papers of John Watt, James's uncle, attest to the family's Protestantism of a Calvinist variety, its interest in science, its diligence at artisanal craft of a mechanical and mathematical sort. Even the hints we have of the family's politics at that time suggest a debt to Puritanism with radical digressions into Quakerism, Whiggery, and possibly revolutionary sentiments that looked back with affection to the English republic of the 1650s.[66]

James Watt inherited all these cultural debts. As a young man he kept his Bible with him wherever he went; he also always carefully maintained his accounts. He advised his son (even when he was in Calvinist Geneva) to spend his Sundays in Bible reading. In his youth Watt saw an Anglican service in the great cathedral at York and he found it "ridiculous" for its ostentation. The talking of prebends and canons during the service shocked him.[67] A few decades later Watt briefly became something of a religious seeker, and departed from the Presbyterianism commonplace to a Scottish childhood. Off in Cornwall surveying coal mines where his engine could be installed, he even attended Anabaptist services – much to the chagrin of his second wife.[68] Work, however, was always front and center in his life.

Earlier, working as a journeyman apprentice to a London carpenter, and despite "rheumatism," he worked ten, twelve or more hours a day – so hard that his hands shook with exhaustion.[69] He kept meticulous records of his expenditures and was held accountable by his father, who acted as his creditor, banks being seen as a court of last resort turned to only when a career or business was foundering.[70] First and foremost this was a family in the business of getting ahead.

[66] For the Protestant ethic in Watt's lifetime and within Dissenting circles, see M. Jacob and M. Kadane, "Missing Now Found in the Eighteenth Century: Weber's Protestant Capitalist," *American Historical Review* 108, 1, February 2003, 20–49.

[67] James Watt Papers, James to his father in Scotland, June 12, 1755, arrives in York ("thank God") and visits the Cathedral; the one in Durham "Magnificent;" "ridiculous manner of worship of Prebends and canons" who were laughing at the time they "were addressing the most high." He is quite shocked. He likes England but thinks the people are "very sharp."

[68] Papers of Matthew Boulton, Box 357, September 1, 1777, Annie Watt to Mrs. Boulton; Annie to Matthew Boulton on Watt's depression, April 15, 1781.

[69] James Watt Papers, James Watt to his father, July 21, 1755: "My hand is shaking after working." On the life of the London apprentice, see P. Earle, *The Making of the English Middle Class: Business, Society and Family Life in London, 1660–1730* (London: Methuen, 1989), pp. 100–5.

[70] The preceding and following paragraphs draw details from James Watt Papers, MS 4/11 letters to father, 1754–74, October 1756, James now back in Glasgow; has got some instruments from Jamaica. He is getting mail at the College. Young Watt is working on the foundations of the observatory. The uncle, John, is in straits for money and had to draw from a bank. Sorry to hear that his brother Jockey has not got employment, January 9, 1758: "You should not give any fee with him as one of his age that understands book-keeping ought rather to be getting." See letter of May 31, 1758; Jockey wants to go abroad after he has served his time, "a foolish notion," his brother James tells their father. See bill

Like fathers and sons, wives and husbands made partnerships based upon worldly striving. Watt's first wife, Margaret (Peggy) Miller, who was barely literate, still worked in his instrument shop with him as a replacement for two of his "lads," and ran his business when he was in the field working as a civil engineer and surveyor. In the 1760s, in the critical period of Watt's inventiveness, Peggy's uncle loaned Watt money on the guarantee of his merchant father.[71] When Peggy died, the widower and father Watt was once again aided by his father and family, who looked after his children. When he remarried, to Annie MacGrigor, in 1775, she was significantly more literate and learned than Peggy had been, as befit the wife of an engineer and inventor.

Before the more spacious times that came with prosperity, when the Watt family could indulge in politics or send their son to university or their children to the Continent and wider learning, there was much work to be done. From the time of Watt's uncle John, if not before, the Watts were fiercely intent upon upward mobility. They were quick to indict any family member who could not or would not work. The rigor can be seen in Watt's father and it passed from generation to generation as well as laterally within each generation, only softening between siblings of the later eighteenth century. By then prosperity and the cult of sensibility encouraged kindness between brothers, but especially between sisters and brothers. In the 1750s, Watt's father harshly judged his sons; young Watt in turn despised his brother, Jockey, when he had no work, and urged his father to give him not a farthing.

Watt in turn raised his own son by his first marriage with a similar harshness.[72] When Jamie wrote from the Continent to show his father his ability in French, Watt could not fault the grammar so he attacked his style and penmanship. He sent his son mechanical problems from the Newtonian textbook by 's Gravesande while chiding him for using too much paper. His unaccountable harshness toward the daughter of his first marriage, Peggy – after her mother died and he was settled in his second – extended to Watt's refusal to attend her wedding, and he disdained James Jr. for wasting his time with sentimental journeys to see his sister. As distinct from the affectionate, even pleading tone of some of his letters

of 1762 detailing Watt's debts to his father. See MS C4/A7 for his father's account books for 1748–9. On the slow development of banking among the middling sorts, see Davidoff and Hall, 1987, pp. 245–6.

71 James Watt Papers, BCL, MS 4/11. Letter in 1766; at the time they are selling flutes. On the rediscovery of women's role in enterprise see Davidoff and Hall, 1987, p. 279.

72 James Watt Papers, BCL, W/6, July 7, 1791, Manchester, James Watt, Jr. to his father: "Upon a revision of the motives which gave rise to my journey to Scotland [to see his sister], I cannot find anything deserving of the severe reprehension you bestow upon it, and although deeply hurt by the severity of your remarks..."

to his two wives and theirs to him, Watt wrote to his daughter on the eve of her marriage: "It is his province to order and yours to obey nor are you ever to dispute his will even in indifferent matters." He regarded her as "very dull and far from being accomplished."[73]

So much striving and harsh judgment did, however, take its toll. Inside Watt, anxiety and depression walked hand in hand; he struggled with depression and severe headaches for his entire adult life. Even as a young instrument maker and surveyor he was terrified by the risks he was taking, and success did nothing to alleviate his dark brooding.[74] The fierce competition ate at him. The debts he incurred launching the steam engine business made him "prey to the most cutting anxiety."[75] Even when he had become successful, his son and heir of the same name begged him to "treat with the contempt they merit ... the malignant cavils of your competitors in trade and the envious suggestions of the rivals of your abilities and reputation." Such was human nature that "in every age and country the wisest and best men have always suffered most by the petty calumny of those who had no other means to make themselves conspicuous."[76] Annie Watt turned to the Boultons to express her deep concern about her husband's unhappiness.

All the Watts suffered from various mental and physical ailments; indeed, tuberculosis claimed two of the children. The experience led Watt into experiments with inhalable gases and to participation in the circle around the chemists Thomas Beddoes and Humphry Davy. Watt said that only science saved him from depression and the languor it induced. Boulton, by contrast, was ever ebullient and sympathized with his partner-friend's afflictions to the point of taking his pulse when he was ill. In general, Boulton displayed – earlier than Watt – a secularism that would become commonplace in nineteenth-century industrial circles.[77]

A greater familiarity with the early industrial circles of Birmingham, Manchester, and elsewhere suggests that Weber missed two other, equally important, ostensibly "secular" forces found distinctively in their midst:

[73] MS LB/2, April 25, 1791, to Peggy; LB, May 30, 1784, on Peggy as dull.

[74] James Watt Papers, W/6, James Watt, Jr. to his father, April 19, 1791, Manchester: "I am extremely concerned to see by your letter ... the low state of spirits that your late misfortunes in business have thrown you into. I wish you could treat them with more indifference and rather look forward to future prospects, than suffer your mind to be depressed by reflecting on the past." As early as 1762 Watt suffers from depression, as shown by a letter from his fiancée, Margaret Miller (MS 4/4, 1762, signed "Miss Millar").

[75] James Watt Papers, LB/1 July 11, 1782, Watt to Wedgwood.

[76] Ibid. James Jr. to James Watt, April 19, 1791.

[77] James Watt Papers, MS L/B1, Watt to de Luc, October 8, 1786; Boulton to James Watt, Jr., London, May 18, 1795: "I have just seen your Father and felt his pulse which is 90. He has certainly a bad cold which keeps him down in both body and mind."

the new scientific culture and its religious stepchild, Unitarianism. It had roots in the sixteenth-century heresy of Socinianism, an equally new variety of Protestantism that rejected the doctrine of the Trinity and also eventually came to rebel against Calvin's doctrine of specific predestination. By the eighteenth century Unitarians laid emphasis upon the search for universal principles acceptable to people of good will. Unitarianism matured into congregations and chapels in England during Newton's lifetime (he died in 1727) and partially under the impact of his science. Newtonian science and Unitarianism were seen decades later by Joseph Priestley, the intellectual leader among non-Anglican Dissenters like the Watts, as integral to true religiosity, marks of a distinctive and worldly asceticism at work in lives dedicated to invention and the profit that comes from striving.[78]

Weber gave us a sketchy map and a rich vocabulary for understanding first commercial, then early industrial capitalists. If we walk through the north-country English terrain where the latter were most numerous, while using a post-Weberian historical sensibility, their values come more sharply into focus. Weber's analysis makes such a journey possible, but with him alone paths would be missed. The trail carved out by a scientific religiosity made possible the turn toward a specifically more advanced form of Western capitalism, toward the industrial.

The particular form of Protestantism remarkably commonplace among mid to late eighteenth-century British manufacturers and entrepreneurs was a strange hybrid of Christianity, ancient heresy, and rationalism. This Unitarianism informed the lives of the Watts and the Wedgwoods – the Boultons ostensibly remained Anglicans – just as it was "strongly over represented" among Lancashire and Manchester cotton manufacturers or coal engineers like John Buddle.[79] The witty Erasmus Darwin may have been right when he said that this anti-Trinitarian faith provided "a feather with which to catch a falling Christian." But the feather may also supply a missing link. Weber struggled to explain the long-scale transmutation by which the doctrine of predestination led to striving and not to despair.[80]

[78] Quoting A. Howe, *The Cotton Masters, 1830–1860* (Oxford: Clarendon Press, 1984), p. 61. See also H. W. Wach, "Religion and Social Morality," *Journal of Modern History*, 63, 1991, 425–56; D. C. M'Connel, *Facts and Traditions Collected for a Family Record* (Edinburgh: printed by Ballantine and Co. for private circulation, 1861). Manchester Central Library, Social Science Reference, Q929.2 M76.

[79] Weber, 1953, pp. 108–15.

[80] See the comments of Thomas Amyot to William Pattison, November 25, 1794, P. J. Corfield and C. Evans, *Youth and Revolution in the 1790s: Letters of William Pattison, Thomas Amyot and Henry Crabb Robinson* (Gloucestershire: Alan Sutton Publishing, 1996), p. 93.

The eighteenth-century version of Protestantism that most effortlessly linked Protestantism to a comfortable, worldly morality was Unitarianism. It offered the conviction that a rational God – and not Calvin's inscrutable and judgmental one – would reward and replenish. Late eighteenth-century preachers of the anti-Trinitarian creed even on occasion eschewed doctrinal expositions and dwelt chiefly on the issues presented by everyday moral issues. Morality in turn rested upon the rationality of the deity as it had been revealed by the new science. Science as symbol and its laws as reality – with Newton's achievements at its pinnacle – offered a unique psychological resource and identity to British industrial actors. Science may have been as important as – and inseparable from – their religious or normative convictions. More than in any of the other varieties of late eighteenth-century Protestantism, science, more aptly physico-theology, had been woven into the Unitarian credo.[81]

Science meant more than simply knowledge about nature, although being a man of science meant having a special relationship with nature.[82] The lifetime practice of scientific experimentation, however derivative, denoted a particular kind of person, generally but not exclusively a man whose life was governed by orderliness, probity, and self-confidence, combined with a willingness to go against the grain and a belief in the possibility of limitless progress. That belief rested on the bedrock of order and harmony decreed in the universe by Newtonian science. As Larry Stewart has shown, Unitarianism received philosophical coherence and sophistication from Newtonian concepts of absolute space and Newton's matter theory. As Priestley put it, "if there were no general laws of nature . . . there would be no exercise for the wisdom and understanding of intelligent beings . . . and no man could lay a scheme with a prospect of accomplishing it." The laws discovered by science literally made projects doable and

[81] BCL, JWP, 3/18 Watt Sr. to Boulton, 1782 (no month or day given): "It is as if Nature had taken up an adversion to Monopolies and put some things into several peoples heads at once to prevent them, and I begin to fear that she has given over inspiring me as it is with the utmost difficulty I can hatch anything new."

[82] J. T. Rutt, ed., *The Theological and Miscellaneous Works of Joseph Priestley* (London: Smallfield, 1817), Vol. 2, *Institutes of Natural and Revealed Religion* (originally published and intended for the young in three volumes, 1772–4), p. 11. Hereafter cited as Rutt. Also see Vol. IV, p. 168 from *Appendix*, containing *A farther Consideration of the Objection to the Doctrine of Necessity, as favouring indolence and vice.* And see L. Stewart, "Samuel Clarke, Newtonianism, and the Factions of Post-Revolutionary England," *Journal of the History of Ideas*, 42, 1, 1981, pp. 53–72, especially pp. 58–61. See also M'Connel, 1861, p. 149: 'M raised in the Church of Scotland, but while in Chowbent he became a Unitarian, which he remained for the rest of his life. Attended the Unitarian chapel in Mosley Street, at the corner of Marble Street. . . . He was a devout man. I remember, as one instance, how constantly, in watching the progress of events which led to the downfall of Napoleon I., he attributed those events to a superintending Providence."

accomplishments possible. They affirmed that everything in nature possessed "an indissolubly connected chain of *causes and effects*." By analogy, the laws of nature made striving seem appropriate and goals attainable, particularly in a world where industrialists could imagine themselves as envied and put-upon. The providence that oversaw events worked benevolently. In the Unitarian credo, rational economic activity, to use Weber's phrase, owed more to Newton's God than it did to Calvin's.[83]

One figure acted as a lightning rod for Unitarian convictions. The sermons and writings of Joseph Priestley merit brief attention, not for what they can tell us about Unitarianism *per se* but about the psychological undergirding of the first Western industrialists. In so many of his sermons and writings, Priestley reveals the sources of the magnetism he enjoyed in these circles. His values were theirs, and that began with science.

Imagine for a moment the Birmingham congregation that Priestley stood up to address for the first time on the last day of 1780. This congregation sought a set of ethical standards for living, a purified Christianity that laid emphasis upon life's immediate needs. It had started out as Presbyterian but like so many chapels evolved into Unitarianism. When the trustees of the Meeting House brought Priestley to the town to be their minister, his Unitarianism was widely known, indeed could only have been one of the reasons that they employed him.

In hindsight we may legitimately describe Birmingham at this moment as the epicenter of the nascent Industrial Revolution. Boulton and Watt's Soho factory lay on the outskirts of the town and over the next decade or so

[83] Rutt, Vol. 15, *A Sermon preached December 31, 1780, at The New Meeting, in Birmingham on Undertaking the Pastoral Office in that Place.* First published in 1781, especially p. 39n where Priestley alludes to his predecessor, who "distinguished himself by his zeal against the doctrine that are generally termed *Calvinistical*, and by his firmness in encountering great opposition from the bigotry of his time." On the chapel, see BCL, MS C 1174, f. 42. For the speed with which people walked, see the diary of Malesherbes, "Voyage en Angleterre, 1785," American Philosophical Society, Philadelphia, MS B/M 291. Consider G. E. Cherry, *Birmingham: A Study in Geography, History and Planning* (New York: Wiley & Sons, 1994), Chapter 3; and for manufacturing activity, see K. J. Smith, ed., *Warwickshire Apprentices and Their Masters, 1710–1760* (Oxford: Dugdale Society, 1975) and M. Berg, "Product Innovation in Core Consumer Industries in Eighteenth-Century Britain," in *Technological Revolutions in Europe: Historical Perspectives*, ed. M. Berg and K. Bruland (Cheltenham: Edward Elgar, 1998), pp. 138–40. On Reynolds' factory, see National Library, Ireland, MS 13176(4), April 23, 1799 Frances Edgeworth to HB. On Watt and the chapel, BCL, JWP, W/13, October 21, 1791. In a letter of July 19, 1791 to Dr. de Luc, Watt claimed: "Though our principles which are well known as friends to the established government and enemies to republican principles should have been our protection from a mob whose watch word was Church and King yet our safety was principally owing to most of the dissenters living in the south of the town, for after the first moments, they did not seem over nice in their discriminations of religion or principles, I among others was pointed out as a presbyterian though I never was in a meeting-house in Birmingham and Mr B. is well known as a Churchman."

it sent twenty-seven steam engines to Manchester alone. A French visitor in 1785 remarked on the pace of the town's day, how in Birmingham the people walked with a remarkable alacrity. We should conjure up in our mind's eye a town that possessed dozens of small workshops producing "toys" (any small metal object) in abundance as well as pistons and cylinders in the manner of Wilkinson, who bored there for Boulton and Watt. A few years earlier Adam Smith had thought its luxury trade worthy of mention in *The Wealth of Nations*. A visitor in 1799 and a friend of the Watts described, perhaps with some exaggeration, a "manufactory of *White Lead*" that employed 6,000 workmen with engines that burned 500 tons of coal daily. A Mr Reynolds owned it, and his wife was a Quaker. Dissenters were remarkably well represented in the ranks of the master craftsmen and owners, and to complete the scene we may imagine them packing the Meeting House to get a good look at their new and nationally known minister. When the Dissenters were endangered in 1791, Watt claimed that he had never been in a meeting house in Birmingham, but we know that he and his sons were close to Priestley. To complete our imaginary journey, let us place the Watt family in the pews on December 31, 1780.[84]

Having set this scene and even conjured up the ghost of Max Weber, we may want Priestley to endorse self-interest, or detail the meaning of a generalized predestination, or to demand from everyone a calling. Indirectly all those themes were present that day and on many others, but uppermost in Priestley's mind lay the character of the world and of the Unitarian Dissenter in it. Like himself, who had been persecuted for his views, such a man possessed fortitude and patience. He was accustomed to going against the grain and staying the course. In time the beliefs of such people would prevail, he believed, and "be generally received by Christians." Priestley noted that while being their minister, he would pursue his philosophical, that is, natural philosophical, interests, as well as his pastoral and theological chores, as "they are perfectly harmonious with, and promote each other." He would be an exemplar, a man of science diligent in all his callings.

First and foremost Priestley saw himself as a Christian, and true to timeworn Christian themes he rose that first day to address the subject "that this world is not our home." The otherworldliness of the Christian, he admonished, must come first, but he then added "riches, honors and pleasures ... are but *secondary* things for us. We are to receive them thankfully, and above all, to improve them properly, if, in the course of

[84] Rutt, Vol. 15, Preface to A Sermon ... December 31, 1780, pp. 29–33.

Divine Providence, they fall to our lot." Accumulation and its enjoyment have an ethically acceptable place in the life of this congregation, provided they do not "come in competition with our duty, and our obedience to the commands of Christ." If they do, members of this congregation must renounce their riches. Priestley wanted his worshipers to perceive that they lived more "in an openly hostile, than ... in a seemingly friendly world." In an oppositional condition they will realize that there is "no state of enjoyment or repose to be looked for here." Being a Unitarian meant striving continuously in the face of adversity.[85] If they were listening, the Watts would have approved.

Priestley assured his congregation that business and Godliness were compatible. There was nothing wrong in "mixing with the world, and sharing the emoluments of it [and becoming] attached to them ... this is unavoidable, and not amiss." The purpose of their mutual sociability lay in preparing the Unitarian to face "the frowns or the smiles of the world ... Thus are we striving for the *bread that perishes*," and, at the same time, more earnestly still for "that which endureth to everlasting life (John vi, 27)." The whole point of their fellowship was that they, and not the minister, "being too often entirely dependent upon his people," must play the role of admonishing one another to stay firm in their principles. By far the most important of which is the doctrine of the Divine Unity and the humanity of Christ; "all other matters are of far inferior consequence." Only equal in importance to those doctrines stand the uses to which Christian societies should be put, that is, they are "a means of preserving purity of manners." Manners re-enforce doctrinal purity, and all are maintained by socializing with one's own kind.[86]

Priestley pared Christianity down for people involved with commerce and industry. He made clear its doctrinal essence and then laid emphasis upon the psychology of seeing one's self as different and the role of the congregation in enforcing a purity of manners. He openly accepted that "a great number of the Unitarians of the present age be only men of good sense, and without much practical religion ... there is in them a greater apparent conformity to the world than is observable in the others [that is, the most zealous Trinitarians]." The implications of his congregation's worldliness were largely confined to the necessity to educate their children in proper Unitarian doctrine, a task that Priestley set for himself in imitation of the education of youths that he had observed among Continental

[85] Rutt, pp. 34–45.

[86] Rutt, Vol. 15, A Sermon preached at the New Meeting in Birmingham, November 3, 1782, pp. 49–51; Rutt, Vol. 2, Institutes of Natural and Revealed Religion (originally 1772–4), pp. 39–40.

Lutherans and Calvinists. He accepted that "the amassing of money must be allowed to be reasonable, or at least *excusable*, provided there be a probability that a man may live to enjoy it, or that it may be of use to his posterity." Error lay in pursuing money as an end, or for its own sake, and not at all as a means to anything further. "If a man really intends nothing but the good of others, while he is amassing riches, he is actuated by the principle of benevolence." To a limited but remarkable degree Priestley endorsed the pursuit of gain by Godly men who maintained a stance of opposition to the establishment and probity in their manners. Philanthropy and the care of the next generation's commitment to the faith were the trade-off required from those who amass riches.[87]

Science and its laws, as interpreted by Unitarians such as Priestley, permitted a step away from predestination with no concomitant relaxation in the necessity for striving. The religious ideology to be found at the epicenter of early British industrialization does not quite fit what Weber imagined would be there. By the eighteenth century the worldly asceticism about which Weber was so right owed much to science and liberal Protestantism. Worldly asceticism has to be seen as becoming pervasive precisely during the eighteenth century because by then there existed the framework of a law-bound, rational universe where causes lead inexorably to effects. The universe laid out essentially in the *Principia* provided the foundation for the confidence of the industrialist, the sense that he and his family could accumulate and enjoy because they were marching to the beat of a time-bound, law-like improvement instilled into a rational universe. It justified and made guiltless their prosperity, their relative happiness over that of their workers. A universe governed by laws framed the daily negotiation and competition by which industrialists could in turn maintain the purity of manners, the moderation, and the service to the greater good that made them special in a hostile world. In the face of an established Church and landed wealth, men of commerce, industry, Unitarianism, and science possessed a self-awareness that naturalized and made acceptable, even socially benevolent, what might have been construed, then and now, as greed and rapaciousness.

The secular and enlightened

In addition to Unitarianism, other factors have generally been left out of the Protestantism/capitalism paradigm, and most important was the transformation toward the secular within European cultures during the

[87] L. Hunt and M. Jacob, "The Affective Revolution in 1790s Britain," *Eighteenth Century Studies*, 34 (2001), 491–521, on Gregory Watt and his circle.

eighteenth century. We assign the term "Enlightenment" to this larger cultural shift and it had certain key components: dedication to experimental science generally of a Newtonian variety; an emphasis on the reform of existing institutions, with a particularly cold eye cast upon religious practices described as superstitious; and a glorification of print culture, sociability, toleration, utility, and merit.

The enlightened voice was a universalizing one in that it resembled the Christian or clerical voice. But after that, the resemblance diverged. In the most extreme case the man or woman of the Enlightenment could live entirely for this world, dispensing with Bible reading, fear of damnation, hope for salvation, church or chapel attending, and almsgiving. Charity, benevolence, sensibility, passions and interests, consumption and comfort, even luxury, as well as politeness in society, could preoccupy the life of the new secularist. Most devotees of the secular in Protestant countries, where the clergy had been subjected to lay authority, never went to the extreme of atheism or pantheism. They quietly shifted from Bible reading to the newspaper and drifted away from church-going, except perhaps on special family occasions.

Something like that odyssey seems to have occurred in the lifetime of James Watt and his family, especially his two male children of his first and second marriages. Gradually *pater* Watt's letters say less and less about Bible reading, or invoke God, or even send Christmas greetings. Annie Watt will send such greetings occasionally, but they are highly secular in tone, even to her adored son, Gregory. Her greatest desire was for his longevity and their mutual friendship. His father counseled him to express disapprobation if "any of your companions expresses sentiments that are immoral or irreligious." But Watt did not spell out what those sentiments might be, and if the scatological letters Gregory received from some of his friends are any indication, the advice went unheeded.[88]

Gradually Watt evolved from his Dissenting Protestant roots with their fundamentalist associations and legal disabilities into a secularist, a man of the Enlightenment. Even before him, Boulton arrived at the same place. Annie Watt also worshipped self-improvement – as she told Gregory, "you know we live but to improve" – but in that parental relationship her character softened, as did James Watt's, toward a sickly but talented son who would die at the age of twenty-seven. In 1800 the elderly Watt even wrote to this favored son about the beauty of the sea coast and "its most

[88] For Gregory, see James Watt Papers, MS C2/15, which also provide a good account of Watt's total assets in 1804. Consider J. Golinski, *Science as Public Culture: Chemistry and Enlightenment in Britain, 1760–1820* (New York: Cambridge University Press, 1992), pp. 176–94.

romantic forms." In wealth and then retirement James and Annie Watt changed and mellowed, but only slightly. He became a true gentleman of science, branched out into chemistry and machines for medical treatment of lung and breathing disorders, took up an international scientific correspondence, and espoused a version of the moderate Enlightenment. She carried on an intense friendship with Gregory and included her opinions on what he should study and the virtues he must cultivate.

Even in profound sorrow at the deaths of their daughter and Gregory, neither parent has much to say about the will of God or eternal salvation. In general, Watt's letters of a Sunday (his letter-writing day) make no mention of sermons heard or pieties felt. The same was not true for science or business.

He and Annie never hesitated to use Erasmus Darwin as physician to the family, and his reputation for irreligion was well established. Gregory's will, recorded hastily at his death in 1804, left nothing to church or chapel; Watt himself made the same omission in 1819. James Jr. became so thorough a Jacobin with democratic tendencies that his letters barely deserve scrutiny for religious sentiments. None so far has been found, and the radicalism of his circle was a scandal in its time.[89]

Similarly, Gregory Watt had serious scientific interests and understood his father's business. Although in constant ill health, Gregory also had a taste for the libertine – at least as found in letters from his male correspondents. When on the Continent he bought an ample cross-section of books by the eighteenth-century French *philosophes*, the widely regarded leaders of the Enlightenment. James Jr.'s political reading was also almost entirely radical or republican, and when not voraciously scientific, he added a goodly mixture of canonical texts cherished by the Enlightenment: Bacon, Locke, Hartley, Hume, Newtonian works, Voltaire, and Mirabeau. He did own a Bible and a Church of England prayer book.

Unfortunately we know less about father Watt's reading habits. Somewhere between the Cornish coal mines and the successes of the Birmingham years, James became an anti-Trinitarian, possibly under the influence of Joseph Priestley. When Priestley took up his clerical living in Birmingham among Dissenters originally of Presbyterian identity, he sought to rationalize all religiosity around the unitary Godhead. Priestley also preached constantly about the virtues of comfort and prosperity, provided the mind's eye kept glancing at the deity. Unitarians, lecturing at the same time in Manchester, made similar points.

[89] See A. Stott, "Evangelicalism and Enlightenment: The Educational Agenda of Hannah More," in *Educating the Child in Enlightenment Britain: Beliefs, Cultures, Practices*, ed. M. Hilton and J. Shefrin (Aldershot: Ashgate, 2009), pp. 41–55.

Although never as radical as his errant son, somewhere along the way Watt became more a man of the Enlightenment than simply a non-Anglican Protestant. In that journey he precisely resembles Benjamin Franklin. The secular face of early capitalism Weber somehow missed. Neither Franklin nor Watt was an original thinker in matters religious as they were voiced in various intellectual circles criss-crossing the Atlantic. They simply chose values that expressed how they saw the world, and clearly little about it invited supernatural explanations.

The point about this search of the souls of various Watts is to try to assess what the progressive and universalist spirit of the Enlightenment might have contributed to the mentality of early industrialists and entrepreneurs on both sides of the Channel. The emphasis placed here on the secular should correct an excessive reliance on Protestantism, or religion in general, as the single cultural wellspring of the industrial spirit. Practical, applied, utilitarian, innovative scientific culture – plus more and better science – became a credo in enlightened circles to which industrialists such as Boulton and Watt belonged.

Enlightened industrialists may have been monopolists to their competitors, or exploiters to their workers, but among themselves they could appear to be thoroughly secular, modern men. By contrast, some Evangelical Protestants of the period evinced the kind of hostility toward the Enlightenment that seized the Catholic opponents of the French Revolution – with educational consequences that in France resulted in an outright hostility toward science.

The Enlightenment permitted British industrialists to imagine that their industry had universal meaning. Enlightened thought validated them as improvers and progressives; it put a polished veneer on their unrelenting self-interest. Just as much as, if not more than, their Protestantism, enlightened values inspired and legitimated their striving. In time, mechanized industry and the culture that spawned it would indeed come to be seen throughout the Western world as vehicles for progress, as forces dependent upon deeply secular values that could be universally propagated. The moderate Enlightenment found throughout the Northern and Western hemisphere from the 1720s onward belongs in the cultural history of the Industrial Revolution, both in England and on the Continent. The Watts as entrepreneurs and scientific people lived that Enlightenment just as much as any French *philosophe* lived his.

The success of Boulton and Watt's engine would have been unthinkable without the growing pool of mechanically knowledgeable entrepreneurs and civil engineers visible by the second half of the eighteenth century. Their skills and knowledge criss-crossed the country, carried by traveling lecturers, teachers of mathematics, and self-organized study groups that explained and examined the mechanics of Newton. Members of the House of Lords relied on such mechanical knowledge when questioning engineers. Cotton manufacturers such as the M'Connels and Kennedys of Manchester, and linen manufacturers such as the Marshalls of Leeds, employed the mechanical lingua franca when negotiating about a new engine or attending scientific lectures.

The "enlightened economy" that rested upon the skills of working engineers may be seen at mines, factories, canals, and refurbished harbors, and nowhere were the steam engines of the eighteenth century more important than in mining. Watt wrote some of his most detailed instructions about what needed to be known in order to install and run a steam engine for a Cornish copper mine. More so perhaps than any other area of Britain, the North East, the Northumberland and Durham coal mines, with Newcastle upon Tyne as their commercial and shipping center, supplied the fuel that first made Newcomen's and then Watt's engines run. It is hard to imagine the new power technology without supplies of relatively inexpensive coal. Some have even said that without coal England would never have been the first to industrialize. But would that quantity of coal have been available if not for the steam engine?

2 The knowledge economy and coal

How technological change happened

Boulton and Watt knew that their steam engines, and those that preceded them, were vital for coal extraction, but history has forgotten just how important. Everyone agrees – then and now – that coal was essential in the early stages of what came to be called the Industrial Revolution. By the mid eighteenth century, even foreign observers sensed the growing importance of coal in Britain. In the 1750s French ministers charged with the task of overseeing industry and commerce devoted time and personal energy to assessing the state of manufacturing in both England and France. After seeing for themselves what was happening in England, they reported nervously on the great usage of coal in dyeing, cooking, and heating. Owners of mines can exploit the mines freely; indeed, the French ministers claimed that both owners and workers enjoy a greater freedom in Britain.[1]

How did the British come to tap into the locked-up energy of coal? To answer the question we need look no further than the coal fields of Northumberland. When reading the records of early eighteenth-century mines there, it is routine to find computations made by viewers, as coal engineers were known, explaining how much coal *cannot* be accessed: "Both these seams in an acre, (to take half and leave half) will yield . . . 87000 tons at 12 s ten pence rent [and] will amount to £52,000. Little can be expected from a second working, because of fire & the water that lies above which will be let down by working the walls."[2] Again, the mine of Bowers and Rogers in Northumberland "has in it low and bad top coal, main coal must be won by a pumping Engine & ¾ of coal not worth working . . . main coal being cast down 7 or 8 fathoms & therefore cannot be wrought without drawing water." In the same vicinity the viewer

[1] For the comparison of French and English manufacturing, see the report by Holker, Inspector General, at Archives nationales, Paris (hereafter AN), MS F12 13100, first folder.

[2] In 18th-century British money, a pound (£) was worth 20 shillings, and a shilling (s) consisted of 12 pence (d); a guinea was worth 21 s.

reported that "the seam at Monkcaton is 5 quarters & the coal exceeding good and clear, but not winnable, without a fire engine." In 1749 an eighty-five-year-old miner recalled how it was not possible to get down to the coal in a mine "on account of the water which there was then no other way of drawing but by horses and coals not being so valuable then as now." Another old-timer recalled "there being no way then for drawing it but by horses which would have been too great a charge."[3]

The observation about the high cost of horses raises yet another wrinkle in the puzzle of the relative speed of industrialization in various European countries. Their cost remained high throughout the period of rapid mechanization in mining, as Mr Clark noted in 1812 when he remarked that the labor of horses was too expensive and water or steam had to be used. Indeed, engineers reported in 1753 that a steam engine with a 42 inch cylinder could do three times the work in an hour of a horse-driven engine. By the early nineteenth century at Benwell Colliery a small traveling engine cost £5 10 s a week to do in the same time the work of six horses (£8 8 s) and six men (£6), a substantial saving.

Note that the horses, including their wear and tear (an extra £1 2 s per week), were considerably more expensive than the weekly salaries of the wagon-men. French records tell the same story. In the same period before 1820, French administrators writing for internal consumption proclaimed "the economic superiority" of the steam engine and measured the savings by saying that for the cost of one franc it replaced the labor of one horse. They also estimated that forty-eight engines were at work in France.[4]

In Paris, French engineer Jacques Périer applied for a *brevet*, or patent, to protect his steam engine, and he made clear that its main value, when applied to coal mining, lay in the savings accrued by reducing the use of horses. His application of 1791 makes no reference to other engines at

[3] North of England Institute of Mining and Mechanical Engineers (hereafter NEIMME); the quotation about water and fire comes from MS GA/2, 1727, ff. 1–2; f. 15 for Bowers and Rogers; f. 10 installing an engine came to £1910 in 1728; f. 6 where we learn that in the same period working a ton of coal would cost 58 shillings and 49½ pence. On Monkscaton, see f. 26. See f. 37 for the size and number of engines that might be needed in 1737 at Gateshead Colliery, with the total cost estimated at £1500 over two years, and f. 38 where viewers were given comparative costs of different methods of accessing the coal, with the fire engine option coming in at £1600 more than a method of gears and shafts; see f. 99 for the cost of keeping an engine running for one week. The elder John Barnes seems involved in many of these negotiations. See Brown/1/92, where "we can now perceive it was a great error in our neighbours that they did not putt theirs [engine] lower down and by increasing their bad contrivance the men works mid leg deep in water." For the reminiscence of miners, see BUD/14/223, and BUD/14/225 for expense of horses.

[4] Archives nationales, Paris, MS F 12 2200, box labeled "Inventions diverses" on an engine built or provided by Mr. Edwards, April 8, 1817; list of forty-eight engines in same dossier.

work in the coal mines of France, although there may have been about a dozen steam engines in the whole country.

The consumption of horses, as opposed to the wages of mine workers, could not have varied much from country to country. Yet the British were faster than their French or Belgian counterparts when it came to installing engines.[5] Where steam engines had to be used, eventually their costs did not exceed what would normally be paid out as salaries for workers or in the maintenance of horses. For another example, around 1800 in the Dutch Republic the same power when supplied by horses or windmills far exceeded the cost of installing and maintaining the engines.[6]

The economics of bringing more and more coal or water to the surface centered on the cost of the alternative method and not on the cost of wages. It involved decisions where technical expertise, particularly in the expensive engines for lifting water, played a critical role. There was little room for error if money was to be made. Viewers had to estimate the size of a needed engine cylinder, the number of engines, and the overall cost. They also had to break down the costs involved with keeping an engine running for a week when in 1735 two men cost £1 7 s, while the repair and maintenance of the engine's boiler and all gear came to £2 13 s. Indeed, sometimes in the short run the engines themselves cost more than the immediate profit their work could hope to generate; in time, savings would offset the cost of installation. Every engine had to have its worth calculated: "The N.W. engine having a 60" cylinder and one 14 and a 12 foot boiler lifts 61½ tons with 12 inch pumps and made a 6¾ foot strike

[5] NEIMME, MS BRO/1 (letter book), f. 152, June 29, 1753, Leonard Hartley and William Brown to client in Throckley: "By a calculation I find an engine whose cylinder is 42 inches will work three set of pumps of 12 inch diameters and 12 fathom deep and at a moderate way of working will draw about 1200 hogs head of water wine (sic) measure in an hour which is full 3 times as much as your horse engine can draw when the horses go a pretty good pace. If you think that will do for you could wish to have a regulating beam at least 30 inches deep and 24 inches thick and 30 feet long if possible to be got that length; my reason for having it so long is the design to make my stroke 2 foot longer than usual. [wants to know if he can get three trees]." Then he notes that "a cylinder of 42 inches large enough . . . will require about 20 bolls of coal a day," thus the daily expense of coals 18 s 9 d if the engine works constantly. See also J.-C. Périer, *Brevet d'invention. Établi par la loi du 7 Janvier 1791. Machine à vapeur, propre à monter le charbon des mines* (Paris: Baudouin, 1791), pp. 1–6; found at British Library, 936 f. 9/61. NEIMME, Watson/3/13, f. 120, circa 1813. See also, for more on costs, W. H. B. Court, "A Warwickshire Colliery in the Eighteenth Century," *The Economic History Review*, 7, 2, May 1937, pp. 221–8, where we learn that a 3-hp engine could draw sixty tons of coal in twelve hours from a depth of 114–120 yards and cost about £200 (p. 224). For grinding stones, see Stadsarchief, Ghent, Fonds Napoleon de Pauw, MS 3285, D. Clark, from Mons, 1812.

[6] H. W. Lintsen, "De vuurmachine van het droogdok in Hellevoetshuis" in M. L. Ten Horn-van Nisjen *et al.*, eds., *Wonderen der Techniek. Nederlandse ingenieurs en hun Kunstwerken* (Zutphen: Walburg Pers, 1994), p. 25.

and 9 in a minute." This engine burned 12½ cwt of coals, which made 17 coal bolls upon a strike. In addition, the engineers had to understand and be able to calculate the effects of air pressure: "[when calculating the pressure that would offset the weight of the water to be removed] to make an equilibrium to the weight [of water] above there will be 6844 lb counterpoise pressure of the atmosphere upon every square inch of the piston."[7]

When searching for someone to run and oversee an engine, owners and viewers said that he "must understand the theory and practical part of engines and [have] a complete mastery of his business." By 1800, mechanical handbooks existed that put in print what had to be understood conceptually and mathematically to make a steam engine work effectively. Given the skills needed, a viewer could earn £150 per annum, a respectable middle-class income, ten times what the average collier could earn in a year, and more than three times what a business accountant could earn.[8]

When decisions of great economic consequence had to be made, scientific knowledge accompanied economic information; they were woven seamlessly together. The British were not smarter than or superior to the French and the Belgians. They did, however, have more readily available a body of scientifically and technically informed knowledge that could

[7] NEIMME, for the weight of the atmosphere, see Bud/25/20, f. 111, dated April 29, 1769 and see ff. 114–15, December 23, 1774, for calculations of consumption of coals by Smeaton's engines, "experiments made at Long Benton Colliery."

[8] For a handbook, see T. Fenwick, *Four Essays on Practical Mechanics* (Newcastle upon Tyne: printed for the author by S. Hodgson, 1802), 2nd edn., and second essay. And for the economics of steam, see NEIMME, Bud/25/20 from 1745, where two engines must be shut down "if the engines are kept going the colliery cannot be carried on without considerable loss." For the comment about an engine man with theory and practice, see Tyne and Wear Archives, Newcastle, MS DX198/1, 1824, f. 15 from William Stewart. See in BCL, JWP/4/69, Boultons Anwr v. Hornblowers Answr, "Points necessary to be known by a Steam Engineer," 1st: "The Laws of Mechanics as a Science," 2nd: "Their usual practical Application to the Construction of Machinery including the subsidiary Contrivance of catches & detents &c. 3rd: "The means of making & constructing the various Parts of Machines in Wood Iron Brass & other Materials." 4th: "The Laws of Hydraulics & Hydrostatics, by which the Pressure of Columns of Fluids as well as their statical Weights are to be estimated; also the Quantities of any given Fluid or Liquid – which will pass thro' any given Aperture or Pipe in a given Time." For the mathematics that a steam engineer had to comprehend, see W. Pryce, *Mineralogia cornubiensis, a treatise on minerals, mines, and mining: containing the theory and natural history of strata, fissures, and lodes. To which is added, an explanation of the terms and idioms of miners* (London: printed for the author, 1778), p. 155. For salary of a viewer, see NEIMME, Buddle/3/103, Hebburn colliery, in 1810. On an accountant's salary, see John Rylands University Library, Deansgate, Botfield Papers (1758–1873), August 19, 1789 – Robert Dumkey of Malinslee [?] agrees to serve Thos. Botfield as a Bookkeeper to keep his Accounts for the Term of seven years, to keep the Accounts "just, true & secret or forfeit 40 pounds." To be paid 40 pounds per year Wages & paid that Quarterly & paid all Travelling expenses upon Business.

assist profit seekers in coal. We routinely ask, why Britain first? To get an answer, we might just as profitably ask, why Northumberland first? The region was among the very first to apply power technology, not primarily to manufacturing but to mining.

Some understanding of how owners and engineers accessed technological inventiveness must be present if we are to understand what made coal one of the key elements in the new power technology at the heart of early industrial development. On the cultural side I am here – in relation to the growth in access to coal – filling in the story of what needed to be known in order to achieve growth. Knowledge and skills had to be in place before the vast expansion of mineable coal became possible. Such skills belonged to a cadre of viewers who consulted with owners "respecting their own concerns" in a partnership that played a critical role in mining just as it did in manufacturing. Increasingly, economists, economic historians and historians of science and technology are joining in the assertion that applied science and technology played a key role in industrialization. It also applies to the extraction of coal.[9]

Economic determinism

Some economic historians, following an interpretation developed several decades ago by H. J. Habakkuk, argue that the key to launching the Industrial Revolution lies in a train of economic developments, most precisely in high wages and cheap energy. Without these factors that made Britain's wage and price environment distinctive, no amount of technical and scientific knowledge would have become relevant. It's allegedly simple: economic necessity makes inventions happen and necessity determines success in application.

One contemporary economist argues that labor was dear and coal cheap in Britain; hence people produced machines that saved on the first and accessed the second. Even though the records are spotty, some eighteenth-century and nineteenth-century wage facts exist for coal mining and it is possible to compare wages in British coal mines with other costs incurred, and, just as important, with wages at roughly the same time in France. By addressing the factual basis for the wage argument, at least when it comes to coal, we put to one side the rationale for arguing that only economic incentive is needed to account for innovation. In the 1720s, wages at the mines for key workers were on average a shilling and a half a day, and they barely rose for decades. In the

[9] NEIMME, the phrase "about concerns" comes from MSS of John Buddle, book 21, f. 220, "October 29th 1808 Exposition of the State of Benwell Colliery."

same period, a stonemason earned 2 s a day. There is little evidence in addition that wages inhibited profits. In 1785, the labor of eight men working the coal brought, after their wages were paid, a clear profit of £6 5 s per week. The labor of twelve men produced a profit of £10 8 s and they were paid approximately £1 1 s per week. If workmen were sick or maimed, 1 s and 1½ pence (sic) was allocated for them *annually* in 1786. For decades there was little upward pressure on mining wages, yet the use of steam engines grew exponentially.[10]

Wages in Northumberland, 1730s and 1750s

Date	Wages for overman
1727	1 s 1½ d per day
1734	1 s 1½ d per day
1739	1 s 2 d per day
1740	1 s 2 d per day to 1 s 3 d
1741	1 s 2 d
1743	1 s 1½ d per day
1758	1 s 5½ d

If we move to the late eighteenth and the early nineteenth centuries, when international industrial competition began in earnest, we know that a

[10] For the claim that we cannot know wages with any certainty, see Fox, 1996, p. 162. For wages, begin with NEIMME, FOR/1/5/1–48 for the 1720s and earlier in the century. And see NEIMME, wages per day: FOR/1/5/10, in 1727 overman; FOR/1/4/17 in 1734; FOR/1/4//18, 1735; FOR/1/4/36 in 1739; FOR/1/4/53 in 1740; FOR/1/4/55 in 1740. This colliery is installing two engines with 42-inch cylinders at a cost of £3,600 (FOR/1/4/54); FOR/1/4/64 in 1741 at Gosforth colliery; in 1743 (FOR/1/4/89a); FOR/1/4/54 for 1747; f. 179 for 1758. Many of these records are in the hand of Amos Barnes. For 1785, see NEIMME, JOHN/2, "Views and Estimates (J. Johnson), 1738–1786," the entire volume with detailed viewings from the 1730s to the 1780s; f. 136 where in 1785 an overman makes 2s 9d with most wages in that range, going to as low as 2s 6d for trap door keepers. In 1765, at Whitehaven, a hewer earned 1s 6d to 1s 8d per day for a nine- or ten-hour day; the minimum wage being paid was 1s; see O. Wood, "A Cumberland Colliery during the Napoleonic War," *Economica*, New Series, 21, 8, 1954, p. 60. In 1812, when there was a shortage of workers, a pitman who brought up about sixteen corves earned 4 shillings a day; see shelf 17/ca, NEIMME East/3a, f. 8 Mathias Dunn, "Sundry Memoranda of his own transactions in 1812." In 1849, a back-overman received 21 s a week; a general overman, it is said, should receive between 26 s and 28 s per week; see *Glossary of Terms used in the Coal Trade*, Newcastle, 1849 and found in collection entitled "History of Coal Mining," #125, ff. 5–64, a collection of unbound pamphlets and newspaper cuttings at NEIMME. See Tyne and Wear Archives, Newcastle, MS GU/MA/2/2, f. 19, in 1737 a newly freed apprentice was admitted to the Merchants Adventurers Company for the sum of £25. In the same archive, MS GU/MS/2/8, records of the masons' company, a working mason earned 2 s for a day of work in 1728 and in 1735; in 1734 a mason paid £5 for admission to the company.

pitman in a British mine could earn 4 s a day, that is, about £1 for five days of work, and that wages in a French mine in the same period ranged generally from 1.3 to 3 francs a day, with the pound trading at roughly 21 to 25 francs. There is also evidence that in 1785 British wages were about the same, 20 or 21 shillings a week. Where we can find the total costs of labor, week by week in 1809, including casual labor from blacksmiths, etc., a mine that put out weekly coals valued at £60 6 s to £64 9 s could run a weekly profit of between £19 18 s and 22 pounds 22 shillings. Obviously there were fluctuations and all labor costs in a week could range from £40 10 s dipping down into lows of £31, but the profits do not correlate with the ratio to wages. Wage costs could be as low as £31 7 s and profits could still be as low as £19 6 s.[11]

By the early nineteenth century, the relationship between British and French wages had changed. In 1812 an anonymous coalman visited the regions around the Loire valley where one third of all the coal mines in France, he claimed, were located. The quality of the coal was as fine as, if not finer, he said, than what could be seen anywhere, including England. He observed work habits, machines, wages and prices, horses, hand pumping devices, right down to noting that "a great many of the small coals are consumed in the manufacturing of nails in the district." He criticized the French custom of having men carry out the coals on their backs and said it "should be exploded from every well conducted mine for it is so dangerous having to scale ladders with this load." He recorded that seventy-three French mines worth more than 2 million francs in stock and machinery produced 2,923,781 quintals of coal (multiply by 220 lb for English weight), and this was accomplished by 1,402 workers, 356 horses, and 11 steam engines.

French wages offered the surprise: carriers of coal made between 1 franc and 50 centimes and 2 f 25 c a day; the best-paid workmen made 1 f 75 c to 3 f for piecework. In short, wages ranged from an overman's salary of 5–8 francs a day to the lowest for ordinary workers such as carriers, putters, and laborers, who managed 2–2.5 a day to, at best, 3 f 50 c. In 1814, a British overman (not necessarily with the same tasks, despite the name), along with a few less well-paid boys, averaged their wages at 8 s 3 d for a week of work; in 1824, an English overman made 3 s a day, and an on-setter, who put full tubs into the cage and took them out, once emptied, made even less. In 1833, an overman made the princely sum of £1 6 s a week. In short, French wages in coal mining were comparable to what was paid in Britain. Or at best, French wages were higher but not by much. On either side of the

[11] NEIMME, Wat/1/6/36, statistics from Heverhill Colliery from March 21, 1808 to March 25, 1809.

Channel the addition of just one worker would tip the cost differential between a French or British pit.[12]

Generally the tasks and titles of British mine workers can be correlated with those of French miners, with the exception of the overman, who is paid more highly in francs than his counterpart in shillings. What counts is the highest wage, regardless of the title of the worker. Where wage data can be accessed, and just as important compared, in both Britain and France during the period from 1799 to 1820 a much more nuanced account of wage differentials becomes possible. Even allowing for the fluctuations in exchange rates brought about by revolution and then war – in 1799, 25 f 76 c bought 21 s, and in February 1812 £1 equaled 17.46 f, while in 1816 the franc was back to 25.3 francs to the pound – with one or two years of exception, there the exchange rate remained for some decades. Wages in both places were remarkably comparable.

In a North Country colliery that was struggling, in 1802 wages for a hewer could be as low as 1 s 10 d per day. As profits improved, hewers could earn 3.6 s a day while the highest paid man in the pit, the overman, earned a guinea or 21 s a week, and that sum had been in place since the 1790s. In 1803, there were other mines where hewers could earn anywhere from 3 s 9 d a day to 5 s. These wages rose slightly in response to a war-induced labor shortage. Where once it had been possible to bind a man to a mine for a few shillings, in 1805 hewers were being bound for £5 5 s, although it is not clear how much of that would actually have to be paid out at the end of three years. Absenteeism lowered the pay-off, even for missing a day. By 1811 and 1816, at the same mine hewing and putting fetched 3 s 6 d a day, with an extra 6 d for carrying more than the normal yards. Recall that in this period the highest-paid French mine worker could earn up to

[12] AN, Paris, F/14/4250 1805, Statistique du departement du Mont-Blanc – daily wages of miner 1.30 F; mitre foudeur 2.50; maitre forgeron 3.00; maneurre 1.10 F, signed Leliver, dated circa 1811. In the year 8 (which began in September 1799), a guinea, i.e., 21 shillings, was trading for 25 francs and 76 centimes; see *Journal du soir*, N. 502, 13 vendemaire, year 8, p. 4. For the anonymous visitor to the Loire, see NEIMME, FOR/1/13/106–127; wage is at bottom of ff. 118–19; English wages ff. 188–9. Wages in 1814 – a bad year – for an overman including screening, wailing, banking, and drawing came to 16 shillings and 3 pence for a fortnight of work. See also AN, Paris, F 14/1316, Direction General des Mines, dated May 6, 1811, says there are 544 mines in the country for coal, with 33,923 workers and having a value of Fr. 22,223,728.30; there are 659 mines in the country, including metals and iron. For British wages in 1833, see NEIMME, Bud/24/66. See the wages argument in R. C. Allen, *The Industrial Revolution in Global Perspective* (Cambridge University Press, 2009). On any given day more or less could be earned depending on the amount of coal extracted; see R. Colls, *The Pitmen of the Northern Coalfield. Work, Culture and Protest, 1790–1850* (Manchester University Press, 1987), pp. 48–51.

8 f a day.[13] The French wage structure cannot explain why in the entire Loire region in 1819 there were only eleven steam engines to be found at seventy-three working mines.

Of course, the determinist wage argument conveniently ignores the Low Countries, where from Mons to Maastricht coal was available (either from the area or shipped across the North Sea from Newcastle), and where from Middelburg to Amsterdam wages were exceptionally high. In contrast to the British model, in the course of the seventeenth century Dutch guilds for workers grew in strength and numbers. By 1700 70 percent of Amsterdam's workforce belonged to a guild that in turn protected wages. Yet the Dutch did not industrialize until well into the nineteenth century.[14]

Finally, the assertion that labor was uniquely dear in Britain, one made by carefully excluding the Dutch Republic, is a presentist and internationally comparative perspective unavailable to British coal operators of the eighteenth and early nineteenth centuries. To make matters worse, all the calculations about British wages assume a male breadwinner, and the caloric intake of his family is rendered considerably below what could sustain an energetic life for men, women, and children. Wages may be deemed high when their recipients have enough to eat. By European standards most English hand workers and their families lived at best at a subsistence level precisely in the period when industrialization began in earnest.

One further comparison seems in order. In Scotland, serfdom existed until 1775 and partially until 1799; could the labor of serfs be more expensive than that of free wage earners? Historians see the Scottish mines as technologically backward right into the early nineteenth century.

13 NEIMME, Northumberland Record Office (NRO), 3410/Wat/1/6/3 written by Watson to Mr. Sadler, April 27, 1802 and the hewer was the highest paid worker. In the same series, see 6/6, "Morpeth Banks Colliery Memorandum Book 1804", figures for April 1, 1811. For wages in 1794, see Humbleworth pit pay in Watson/1/13/10 May 29, 1794. For the wages of hewers in 1803, see Buddle/13/1/39–53, 59, for 1801, see ff. 76–7 where the rate varies from 3 s 5 ½ d to 4 s 11 d over a dozen mines included. The engine man made less than 3 s.

14 For Dutch wages, see P. Lourens and J. Lucassen, "Ambachtsgilden in Nederland: een eerste inventarisatie," *NEHA-JAARBOEK voor economische, bedrijfs- en techniekgeschiedenis* 57, 1994, pp. 34–62 for an overview of guilds in the Netherlands, and idem, "Ambachtsgilden binnen een handelskapitalistische stad: aanzetten voor een analyse van Amsterdam circa 1700," *NEHA-JAARBOEK voor economische, bedrijfs- en techniekgeschiedenis* 61, 1998, pp. 121–62 for guilds in Amsterdam. See also C. Lesger, "Merchants in Charge: The Self-Perception of Amsterdam Merchants, ca. 1550–1700," Chapter 3 in M. C. Jacob and C. Secretan, eds., *The Self-Perception of Early Modern Capitalists* (New York: Palgrave-Macmillan, 2006). For a critique of the gender bias in Allen's account, see J. Humphries, "The Lure of Aggregates and the Pitfalls of the Patriarchal Perspective: A Critique of the High Wage Economy Interpretation of the British Industrial Revolution," July 2011, Nuffield College, Oxford, and found at http://d.repec.org/n?u=RePEc:nuf:esohwp:_091&r=his.

But they contradict the high wages argument and declare that the depressed state of wages and low status of mining made it harder for a professional and technically skilled managerial class to emerge. When late in the eighteenth century wage rates in Scotland became higher than those in England, professional managers possessed of engineering skills, with a vast practical knowledge and a respect for scientific inquiry, were still in short supply. Wages, low or high, did not drive the supply side, the complex factors that made technical skill available. Indeed, low wages could lead to greater profits and hence more capital to invest in innovation. That did not happen in Scotland.[15]

One piece of the economic argument needs to be taken very seriously: everywhere coal could be found, Newcomen engines were cheaper to run than engines drawn by horses. They were also an improvement on water power, but initially only to an extent of a saving of about 5 percent. In both textiles and mining, water technologies remained important. Yet as Donald Cardwell told us some years ago, "the first great mills were not driven by traditional draft-made wheels but by accurately designed machines based on new scientific ideas."[16]

Winning the coal

Ultimately the best way to lay high-wage arguments to rest – once and for all when it comes to coal – requires taking a close look at how coal was "won," at the new, science-inspired technology, particularly as found in the vital eighteenth century. Surface coal, as well as its shafts, had been mined in Britain from at least the fourteenth century. For all of the period up to the first decade of the eighteenth century, the winning of coal had been entirely dependent upon organic energy, the labor of men, water wheels, windmills, and horses. They would remain important into the nineteenth century. But in the second decade of the eighteenth century a new source of energy appeared in the form of the Newcomen steam or fire engine. It had been preceded by the less efficient Savery fire engine.[17]

[15] B. F. Duckham, "The Emergence of the Professional Manager in the Scottish Coal Industry, 1760–1815," *Business History Review*, 43, 1, 1969, pp. 30–6.

[16] D. S. L. Cardwell, "Power Technologies and the Advance of Science, 1700–1825," *Technology and Culture*, 6, 1965, p. 192.

[17] See J. Conyers, *The Complete Collier: or the Whole Art of Sinking, Getting, and Working Coal-Mines etc. as Is Now Used in the Northern Parts Especially about Sunderland and Newcastle* (London: G. Conyers, 1708, reprinted Newcastle, 1846), where it is clear that only human or horse labor is available; found at NEIMME, Tract 29. The author is one John Conyers, see E. Clavering, "The Coal Mills of Northeast England: The Use of Waterwheels for Draining Coal Mines, 1600–1750," *Technology and Culture*, 36, 1995, p. 214. See F. Nixon, "The Early Steam Engine in Derbyshire," *Transactions of the*

Figure 6 View of Newcastle upon Tyne, 1783

Figure 7 The Collier, 1814

Newcomen Society, 31, 1957–8 and 1958–9; E. Hughes, "The First Steam Engines in the Durham Coalfield," *Archaeologia Aeliana or Miscellaneous Tracts Relating to Antiquity*, Fourth Series, No. 27, Newcastle, 1949, pp. 29–45.

With Newcastle as their urban hub, the landed estates in the region of Northumberland developed early in the eighteenth century as sites of distinctively mechanized systems, first for the raising of water, then for coal. Throughout much of the century Newcastle possessed a population between 25,000 and 33,000, and in the period from the 1620s to 1800 more than ninety publishers, booksellers, and printers could be found in the town. The installation of steam engines, although not their day-to-day maintenance, was uniformly the work of the highly literate.[18]

The region's coal engineering and colliery records are also uniquely broad and deep. They tell about prices and wages, installation costs, tons of extracted coal, the relations between engineers and owners. They also tell in passing – by their silence – that unlike the situation in France, English coal owners or leasers received no subsidy from the crown "for the damages" they incurred by their efforts to exploit the resources of the mine. When costs were cited as prohibitive, salaries are seldom mentioned. Even later, during the Napoleonic wars, labor was in short supply and access to Continental markets had become more expensive. Yet in this setting, wages still went unmentioned and "the increased price of working, from the great advance on timber, iron, ropes, horse corn, etc.," i.e., commodities, appeared determining.[19]

[18] C. J. Hunt, *The Book Trade in Northumberland and Durham to 1860. A Biographical Dictionary of Printers, Engravers...Booksellers, Publishers* (Newcastle upon Tyne: Thorne's Students' Bookshop, 1975), pp. 105–6. See also anonymous ms notes in *The Newcastle Memorandum-Book: or Pocket-Journal for the year MDCCLV* (Newcastle upon Tyne: Thomas Slack, 1755), *inter alia*, showing owner exchanging Voltaire, Montesquieu, Pope's Essay, Derham, Pope's Homer, Moliere, Hudibras, Locke on education, works in physico-theology, Telemachus, Addison's Poems, etc. Given the quantity of exchanges, this may be the record book of a bookseller, indeed the journal's publisher, as there is a loose promissory note from him enfolded in the volume (found at BL c. 142.dd.28). For some 5,500 books available in the town, largely in English but also in French and Italian, in all fields including natural philosophy, chemistry and medicine, see *A Catalogue of R. Fisher's Circulating Library, in the High-Bridge, Newcastle* (Newcastle upon Tyne: M. Angus, 1791). For books printed in the town, see *Archaeologia Aeliana*, Third Series, Vol. 3, 1907, pp. 91–102.

[19] For French subsidies and protection, see AN, Paris, E 2660 2a, f. 25 June 18, 1765, damages awarded to Jean Pierre Nivolty, etc. In same ms, f. 34, see damages being awarded to Simon Jarry of Nantes for "un grand nombre de bâtiments et de machines nécessaires pour donner à son exploitation toute la perfection dont elle étroit susceptible, 13 Nov. 1765." Joseph Jary is his son (f. 35v). The family is given a second privilege; they have been working at these mines for twenty-five years and before them the region had to rely on English coal. The privilege of thirty years is being renewed as of 1766. On costs during the war, see NEIMME, BUD/23/40–43, July 15, 1808 Buddle to Surtees. In 1807, a foot of wood (of unknown width or depth) sold for 2 s 6 d per foot; see *The Newcastle Memorandum-Book or a Methodical Pocket-Journal for the year MDCCCVII* (Newcastle upon Tyne: S. Hodgson, 1897), anonymous manuscript accounts, see costs for March 9 at BL call #1607/3837.

Throughout the eighteenth century, when Northumberland viewers were asked to assess the economic viability of a colliery, high wages *never* appear as a factor, but the enormous expense associated with the engines, their installation, and maintenance became a *leitmotif*. Mine overseers were as vigilant about costs as their manufacturing counterparts. They broke down costs on a daily basis and assessed the expense of items as dear as engines or as cheap as the boys who hauled coals. In the very early application of the steam or atmospheric engine invented by Thomas Newcomen, the engine rented from £2.18.0 to £4 per week while the lowest-paid men working the coal pit received 1 s 6 d per day, and the highest 20 s or £1 per week. There is no indication that bringing in the engine reduced the number of necessary workers.[20]

If there was any single cost that made doing the business of coal prohibitive in Northumberland, and elsewhere, it was precisely the expense of installing new engines, whether at ground level or 300 feet down at the upper stratum of the mine. Entrepreneurs worried about those costs, even in a setting where coal to run the engines was as cheap as it was ever going to be, and they are silent on the cost of workers' wages. It was clear from as early as 1722, if not before, that the engine could extract water from mines more cheaply than horses. In the second decade of the century an engineer who was also a teacher of mathematics installed the first fire engine on the banks of the River Tyne. Elsewhere in the same decade the earliest Newcomen engines were rented, presumably because the cost of outright purchase must have been

[20] See NEIMME, East/3a/48–49, 1812 memorandum by Matthias Dunn, with list of wages where waste men are paid 20 s per week; single putters 6 d a day, masons 3 s 8 d per day, etc; see f. 72 note that binding money, up to £2 2 s, also had to be put up, although not if there was a surplus of labor; f. 107, April where overman is paid 12 p a day. See also NEIMME, John/2, the entire volume with detailed viewings from the 1730s to the 1780s. Occasionally it is recommended that more men or boys be hired. See also Wolverhampton Archives, Edward Short's notebook, on leasing for the second decade of the eighteenth century, MS DX-840/2, f. 4; f. 59, in 1717 one John Compson is paying £4 per week for engines clearly being used in mining. BL MSS 44, 799, f. 136, a graph showing amount and prices of coal since 1871 to 1888, with a separate graph (in black) showing wages at collieries in south-west Lancashire, indicating that highest wages for the entire period were reached only in 1873–4, with a subsequent depression for the remaining years coinciding roughly with selling prices obtained in the same period at a Wigan colliery. The markers on the left column suggest that in the 1870s wages ran from 4½ s to the high in 1873 (only) of 7½ s, a rate never again obtained in the period recorded. In 1799, millwrights managed to raise their pay to 4 s 6 d per day "both at home and abroad." See BL MSS ADD 38355, f. 169. For the care about costs taken by manufacturers, see J. Uglow, "Vase Mania," in M. Berg and E. Eger, eds., *Luxury in the Eighteenth Century: Debates, Desires and Delectable Goods* (New York: Palgrave, 2003), pp. 156–8.

prohibitive. In the 1740s, installing a Newcomen engine cost approximately £667. Faced with such costs, engineers of the 1740s told colliery owners: "At least two engines more must be erected there to draw these feeders at so great an expense that in our opinion the colliery cannot work to profit." In 1752, another pit was also deemed useless because a "fire engine ... will cost £400 yearly ... and that will cast them no profit." By that time textbooks were available that described the Newcomen engine and its workings.[21]

As early as 1720 mine owners were being advised that if they wanted to make otherwise shallow, unprofitable coal mines usable they needed to buy a fire engine. That sort of advice came generally from viewers or overseers, mine engineers hired to oversee a mine or mines. The actual owners of the mines, who could be landed aristocrats, the church, or genteel heirs, seldom knew much about the mines from which they profited. This is not to imagine for a second that they were uninterested in profit, but rather to point out that the proprietors were passive players in the physical accessing of their coal. In 1828, out of a list of forty-one mine owners on the Tyne, only five actually worked their own mines. Two years later, after forty years of experience as a viewer or mine engineer, John Buddle told a parliamentary inquiry that he knew of only five proprietors who actually worked mines

[21] NEIMME, MS Watson/2/4/15, on the cost of erecting an engine in 1747; and in MS 3410/brown/1 (letter book) 29; June 1753 Leonard Hartley and William Brown, overseers or viewers, wrote to a client in Throckley: "By a calculation I find an engine whose cylinder is 42 inches will work three set of pumps of 12 inch diameters and 12 fathom deep and at a moderate way of working will draw about 1200 hogs head of water win measure in an hour which is full 3 times as much as your horse engine can draw when the horses goes a pretty good pace." Having clearly determined mathematically that the fire engine was superior to the horse, the writers went on: "If you think that will do for you could wish to have a regulating beam at least 30 inches deep and 24 inches thick and 30 feet long if possible to be got that length; my reason for having it so long is the design to make my stroke 2 foot longer than usual." The wooden cylinder of 42 inches "would be large enough a boiler to serve such a cylinder – it will require about 20 bolls of coal a day – daily expense of coals 18 s 9 d." The next letter corrects the first and says that after consulting with our best workmen we think a cylinder of 40 inches or less would do it. On knowledge available in 1722, and the savings to be had from steam engines replacing horses, see J. Brand, *The History and Antiquities of Newcastle upon Tyne* (London: B. White and Son, 1789), Vol. 2, p. 685, note b and p. 686 for the teacher of mathematics and Emerson's book on mechanics of 1754. For an early nineteenth-century description of going down into one of these mines and placing engines and horses, see [The Publishers], *A Historical and Descriptive View of the County of Northumberland and of the Town and County of Newcastle upon Tyne* (Newcastle upon Tyne: Mackenzie & Dent, 1811), Vol. 1, pp. 126–7. NEIMME, MS John/2/107, April 15, 1745 among the signatories Amos Barnes; John/2/111 dated June 4, 1752, and concerning the Clover and Lucky pits; John/2/ 6–12, May 1, 1745; and John/4 Statements and Reports as to Willington Colliery and East and Little Benton, New Winning 1774–86 f. 94; September 8–22, 1786 – a typical period expenses and maintaining the engine the single largest expense.

in the Durham and Northumberland region. More so than in manufacturing, engineers were key players in mining decisions.[22]

In the previous hundred years knowledge of mechanics and steam engines had become increasingly essential and the overseers possessed both. Again in 1830 Buddle could inform Parliament that the introduction of steam and the science-inspired safety lamp permitted twice as much coal to be extracted than would have been possible without them. Engines were used primarily for pumping water and winding coal out of mines, and only in the mid to late nineteenth century for hauling and cutting into seams. The safety lamp highlighted the ever-present danger from noxious gases, saving many lives but also permitting all involved to know what seams were dangerous and to search for other routes for extraction.

Given the stakes, truly knowledgeable engineers had to advise on the feasibility of an engine, its desired size, the time required to erect it, etc. They also performed exact observations down to the minute, recording the number of strokes an engine completed over a measured period of time. They translated speed and time into profits, provided the leasers could follow their calculations. They could tell when a boiler needed replacing, or when building an engine for a pit at the cost of £3,846 was the only feasible way of "winning the coal." They also traveled the countryside inspecting engines owned by others in order to determine whether "the saving will be very considerable." By the mid eighteenth century workers themselves noticed if a viewer was a "poor scholar" or "not much learned." By 1800, the leading viewer of the region had developed an intimate knowledge of steam engines and could specify exactly what the engine should do while shopping among Boulton and Watt's competitors for the best deal. In Northumberland – in just one county – by 1769 there were probably one hundred pre-Watt steam engines working, a remarkable amount of horse power from a non-organic source. Nothing comparable can be found in any Continental setting; in 1816, the French government counted forty-eight engines at work in the entire country.[23]

[22] Watson/1/6/19 letter of October 25, 1802 to John Watson on the Duke of Portland's coal fields advising him to put in a new steam engine. For the 1828 list, see C. E. Hiskey, "John Buddle (1773–1843). Agent and Entrepreneur in the North-East Coal Trade," Thesis for the degree of M. Litt., University of Durham, 1978, Vol. I, pp. 30–1.

[23] For the French engines in 1816, see AN, Paris, MS F 12 2200, list dated April 8, 1817; and for engines in Northumberland, see NEIMME, MS East/3b, Matthias Dunn, "History of the Viewers," f. 47. For engineers and scholars at work in the country, see NEIMME, Wat/3/13/120, circa 1813. See also Court, 1937, pp. 221–8, where we learn that a 3-hp engine could draw sixty tons of coal in twelve hours from a depth of 114–120 yards and cost about £200 (p. 224); for exact calculations, see MS 3410/brown/1 (letter book) 29; and same letter of July 14, 1753, where we also learn that "after consultation

As late as the 1830s English mechanics with a knowledge of steam engines, by then being used in rail locomotion, applied for employment in France precisely because they had been trained and worked in Britain. Indeed, in 1840 we estimate that 34,000 hp from steam could be found in France and 350,000 hp in Britain. The gap existed despite the efforts undertaken by the Ministry of the Interior under Napoleon and beyond to encourage innovation in "machines hydrauliques." By the 1850s, inquiries were being made to the British consul in China about the possibility of procuring coal there. Such was the demand.[24]

By the early nineteenth century the great international rivalry between Britain and France was being measured as much by industrial development as by wars won or lost. By that time in France an ideology was firmly in place in liberal circles that valorized science and mathematics as the key to technological innovation. At the same time in Prussia we now know that educational improvements played an important role in facilitating its push to catch up with British industrial prowess, only this occurred well after 1800.[25]

All this progress in power technology came at a price. It initiated a quantum leap in the costs of improving and maintaining a profitable pit. In the 1720s, costs and profits for pits could be measured in the hundreds of pounds; within twenty years, from the 1720s to the 1740s, both were beginning to be measured in the thousands. The costs of the necessary engines would render some mines no longer profitable to work and new sites would be needed if the owner's profits were to be maintained. The technologically informed viewers or engineers were often making business

with our best workmen," we think a cylinder of 40 inches or less would do it. See BUD/23/54–55, letter of January 17, 1809 from John Buddle to Butterly Iron Co of Derbyshire on the size and type of engine required with comparison to Boulton and Watt's design.

24 Désert *et al.*, *De l'hydraulique à la vapeur XVIIIe–XIXe siècles* (Caen: Cahier des Annales de Normandie, No. 25, 1993), p. 10. An applicant for a position at the *École des arts et métiers* (AN, F 12 4897, dossier M. de al Borne) wrote in 1830 to explain his qualifications: "d'étude d'une manière approfondie, dans les meilleurs ouvrages français et anglais, les procéder perfectionné de la culture moderne, et d'en pratique des applications." For an English prisoner being released because of his knowledge of mechanized cotton production, see AN, MS f 12 4897 June 17, 1812, the case of Mr. Schmit. For the diffusion of the engine in eighteenth-century America and Europe, see C. W. Pursell, Jr., *Early Stationary Engines in America: A Study in the Migration of a Technology* (Washington, DC: Smithsonian Institution Press, 1969). For an English applicant for work in France, see Archives nationales, Paris, F12 4809, "place d'emploi ... M. Crosland," writing from Paris, 1738. For China, UCLA, MSS Collection #722, the papers of John Bowring, Box 1, Charles Villiers to Bowring, September 23, 1853.

25 Consider Fox, 1996, p. 162; Becker *et al.*, "Catch Me If You Can: Education and Catch-up in the Industrial Revolution," *Stirling Economics Discussion Paper 2009–19*, p. 162. Available online at http://d.repec.org/n?u=RePEc:stl:stledp:2009–19&r=his. Accessed September 27, 2012.

or economic decisions, and they could be of "the opinion that the profits will not be equal to the extraordinary expense attending to the surcharge of water." If the impulse set in to lower the expense of wages, the steam engine's installation may have been a precipitating factor – and not vice versa. In the 1760s, when a Newcomen engine was installed in Mons in the Austrian Netherlands, the owners also installed a clock. The engine was so expensive that every minute of labor had to be accounted for.[26]

In the Newcastle area, Newcomen engines came into use between 1714 and 1721, but were only commonplace in the 1740s. By that time the cost of keeping an engine running per week was in the vicinity of £15, and despite the expense of the initial installation, engineers could on occasion advise that the engine be shut down in order to maintain profitability in the short term. At one colliery the existing engines could not draw up all the water that had to be extracted, and the pit was deemed not profitable enough to support another engine. The performance of the engines determined how much coal could be extracted. It was that simple, and yet that complicated.

Not surprisingly, as early as 1724 the London-based committee that held the rights to the Newcomen engine had a representative at work in Newcastle. By 1769 all the engines were of the Newcomen style, soon to be followed by engines designed by John Smeaton and then, in the 1780s, by James Watt. Thus, in about fifty years, mining in Northumberland had moved from quarrying at the surface, then to bell-pit mining, and finally to in-depth extraction that would increase in depths and quantities steadily – in large measure because of what the engines could do to extract first water and then the coal itself. In Northumberland mining, the steam engines excelled because they could run on the scrap coal available on site, thus making the source of energy self-contained economically and requiring no negotiation with neighbors over water rights and usage.

The entrepreneurs' greatest problems lay in energy lost through friction, and we should hardly be surprised to see viewers and engineers working relentlessly on the problem. The pattern of constant attention to perennial mechanical problems promoted innovation. By the 1790s, courts, lawyers, engineers, and imitators agreed that Watt's engine needed a specifically mechanical knowledge base. They then spent time and capital arguing about whether Watt's specification for his 1769 patent on his engine had been sufficient to allow others to imitate it once the

[26] NEIMME, FOR/1/5/1–48, for the 1720s and earlier in the century. There were exceptions, e.g., in 1713, costs of pulling down sinking pits could rise to £5,000. In the 1720s, workers were paid 1 s and 2 d a day; see f. 28. Also, for costs in the 1740s, see NEIMME/BUD/25/1–5 on the need to replace a boiler in 1744. See BUD/25/7–10 on the need to close down mines. There was a parliamentary inquiry in 1739 on the state of the coal trade. For Mons, see Archives d'état, MS A.E.M. Charbonnages Bois du Luc, ff. 51–87.

patent lapsed.[27] All this trial and error added up to making British coal engineers universally sought after by the first decade of the nineteenth century. They found employment for high wages in France, Spain, Portugal, and as far away as Australia. Owners in Russia, Virginia, and Nova Scotia also sought advice from the leading viewer of the Tyne and Wear region, John Buddle. When he in turn wanted to prepare his nephew to become a colliery viewer he sent him to London to study chemistry and mechanics. By the 1790s, the intellectual elite of Newcastle formed a Literary and Philosophical Society that listed first among its objectives gaining access to the knowledge accumulated by "the ingenious persons who are employed as viewers." The improvements introduced and the profits realized in the coal industry occupied the attention of the society for much of its early nineteenth-century history.

By the middle of the nineteenth century it was recognized across Europe that even working miners needed "to be taught the principles of certain sciences," especially if they aspired "to become captains and agents." Also by the 1830s, Durham University brought Buddle in as a consultant for a course on mining and civil engineering. Once again in mining engineering we can see the complex interaction of rational mechanics with practical trial and error, what, as we saw, the French theorist G. J Christian called industrial mechanics. In mining, however, nothing substituted for going down in the pits.[28]

[27] For expenses with engines, see NEIMME, BUD/25/6 from April 15, 1745; signed by a number of inspectors, including Amos Barnes; BUD/25/14–15 on closing down collieries where the water cannot be controlled, same folder, f. 21 where engines can be found that were installed in 1745 and still working in 1815. For bell-pit mining, where a shaft was driven down into the coal and it was scooped out in all directions, see R. S. Smith, *Early Coal-Mining around Nottingham 1500–1650* (University of Nottingham, 1989), pp. 4–5; R. L. Galloway, *A History of Coal Mining in Great Britain* (Newton Abbot: David and Charles, 1969 reprint of the edition of 1882), p. 82, an economic fact about friction known in Desaguliers' time (d. 1744). Clavering, 1995, pp. 229–31. NEIMME, Bell/3/327–333, a copy of John Curr, *An Account of an Improved Method of Drawing Coals and Extracting Ores, &c. from Mines* (Newcastle: S. Hodgson, 1789), where principles of friction are addressed by extra wheels.

[28] Hiskey, 1978, pp. 15–19; foreign consultations, 91–2; Buddle educated by his father, also a viewer, p. 5; on the various ways of educating a viewer, pp. 13–15. Buddle's father wrote *Practical Methods of Approximating the Equilibrium Power of an Overshot Water Wheel*, advertised in 1780, see Bell/3/387; I have been unable to locate a copy. See also NCBI/JB/2261–2271, correspondence on technical problems at Sheriff Hill colliery. R. S. Watson, *The History of the Literary and Philosophical Society of Newcastle-upon-Tyne (1793–1896)* (London: Walter Scott, 1897), pp. 36–45. See NEIMME, FOR/1/5 date 1733, on winning the south end of Heaton Colliery by using a fire engine, total cost would be £1,240, with £700 going into the engine; also using a bobb gin, £364.5, with erecting the bobb gin costing £150, as calculated by Amos Barnes. In 1740, fire engines were running at £1,000 each, possibly reflecting their supply and demand or the need for larger engines; see FOR/1/5/56–57 engine to be removed so as to save on costs, see f. 6 on

Access to technical knowledge needed for the pits had become necessary decades earlier. From at least the 1730s the most expensive item that a colliery would have to purchase was its steam or fire engine. A new breed of viewer/engineer who understood engines, their installation, power, and maintenance offered written promise of previously unimagined savings. It is also clear that from decade to decade in the course of the eighteenth century, colliery after colliery turned to steam as the most efficient agent for working deeper and deeper mines. In turn, the viewers came to have their labor divided such that by the 1830s a 45-hp engine had its own engineman, with an annual salary of £54 12 s. Yet in the century or more that low-pressure steam engines came to dominate the coal fields, their price, adjusted for inflation, actually fell. In the 1730s, a fire engine with a 30 inch cylinder could be bought and installed for £800 and maintained for about £200 per annum; one with a 42 inch cylinder could be bought and installed for about £1,500; in the 1740s, a standard engine with a 32 inch cylinder went for about £1,200, while in 1832 a vastly more powerful Watt-style engine with 45 hp sold for £1,500. In the same period a single-cylinder 34 inch engine fetched £850. What is clear is that engines were becoming cheaper.[29]

The long-term importance of steam is hard to overestimate. It produced a new era and put every coal field, once thought lost, within the grasp of its owner's exploitation. By the 1720s in the most important British coal fields found in the Durham and Northumberland region, steam engines were visibly present. They relied upon two important discoveries we associate with the new science of the seventeenth century: the existence of a vacuum and air pressure, or as it was known then, the measurable weight of the air. A generation ago, the historian of

Jesmond colliery; ibid. f. 12, Amos Barnes and George Claughton asserting that they can win the colliery "at least 1600 cheaper than any other person from the new engine which is erected at Dent's Hole."

29 NEIMME, BUD/24/61, on 45-hp engine for the Jane pit for drawing wagons on railways; size of cylinder not clear, price £1,500; this entire volume is an excellent source for the cost of many engines, wagons, barrels, buckets, pumps, etc. by various manufacturers from 1800 to 1841. For the 1730s, see NEIMME/GA/2/37–38. And see John Rylands Library, M'Connel and Kennedy, MCK/2/1/3 Letters Received, 1797 (MCK/2/1/3/1 A-F; /2 G-R, /3 S-Z) from John Southern writing for Boulton and Watt, May 16, 1797. They have received M'Connel and Kennedy's inquiry of May 12 about a 14-hp steam engine. Will not be able to deliver by early September. Will require at least 6–7 months since 14-hp engines are unusual and will require some new patterns for the cylinder, piston, etc. A 12- or 16-hp engine, however, can be delivered in about five months. Lists costs for the engines and labor: 14-hp engine, £777.5.0; wood frame, cistern, iron work, £90.0.0; putting together, £60.0.0; Total: £927.5.0. A 16-hp engine will cost £831.2.0. A 12-hp engine will cost £621. £80 will be deducted from engine cost if M&K supply the boiler. "All these are exclusive of suction & plain pipes of cold water pump if they be necessary." B&W also think that M&K's plans for heating the factory are reasonable, but will mean a greater consumption in fuel for the engine. This will be cheaper than running a separate heating system. [There is a variety of calculations of price for the different engine types, probably done by M&K.]

technology A. P. Usher put it nicely: "The concept of the Newcomen engine brought to a close a long sequence of studies of the vacuum that is represented in science by the work of Galileo, Torricelli, Pascal, von Guericke, Boyle, and Papin; and on the empirical side by de Caus, Worcester, Savery, and Papin."[30]

Contemporaries in extraction understood such scientific principles at work as early as Savery's engine, an invention of the late seventeenth century. An anonymous engineer working in Northumberland explained that by condensing the steam a "vacuum [is] effected . . . the pressure of the atmosphere on the surface of water . . . and so water is raised from the mine." He supplied a detailed drawing of the engine and how it worked, "without," he added, "going into the minute particulars for if such be wanted . . . Bowmes's book called 'Steam Engine' had better be obtained."[31]

By the second decade of the eighteenth century, aside from books, scientific lectures on mechanics, optics, and hydrostatics were given in Newcastle and the surrounding area, and those topics appear in lectures throughout the eighteenth century. The Newtonian James Jurin lectured there before moving on to Cambridge and so too did the Presbyterian minister John Horsley. Both had links to the Newcastle Grammar School and both employed scientific apparatus in their lectures. Wherever they were given, and however well demonstrated, lectures had to match the needs of their listeners, and in some places they just skipped "experiments relating to the mechanical powers which as they did not much engage my attention I pass them by."[32] Lecturers were creatures of the market and got paid to explain what their customers wanted to hear.

[30] For the quotation, see A. P. Usher, "The Industrialization of Modern Britain," *Technology and Culture*, 1, 1960, p. 115.

[31] For the drawing of the Savery engine (patented in 1698) in Northumberland, and detailed instructions on how it works, see NEIMME, WKS/16/33. For the growing use of steam engines at mid century, see Galloway, 1969, Chapter 26. For images of some of these engines, see T. H. Hair, *A Series of Views of the Collieries in the Counties of Northumberland and Durham* (London: James Madden, 1844); in 1770, the export of coal caldrons was 213,645; in 1790, 298,077; in 1800, 573,793 coast wide and 47,487 foreign; in 1805, 552,827 coast wide, and this is just from Newcastle. In a parliamentary document the coals from Newcastle are reckoned in tons in 1837 as 2,385,192, which rose by 100,000 the following year. A caldron is just short of 3,000 lb. In 1837, Newcastle sent 471,150 tons to foreign places. See M. Dunn, *An Historical, Geological, and Descriptive View of the Coal Trade of the North of England; Comprehending its Rise, Progress, Present State, and Future Prospects* (Newcastle upon Tyne: Pattison and Ross, 1844), pp. 22–3; claims that by 1721 steam engines were in common use in this district for the purpose of drawing water. Bowmes's book is yet to be located.

[32] Quoted from set of lecture notes, "Some Account of the Philosophical Lectures and Experiments: Read and Explained at Whitby in February 1760" by J. Arden, found at the Whitby Literary and Philosophical Society Library, Pannett Park, Whitby, unfoliated, under Lecture the Fourth.

The industrial development of coal mining entwined with technological advances in other sectors of the British economy. One example should suffice. From his experience with steam engines in the factories of Marshall in Leeds, Matthew Murray began to build his own steam engines and to advise Newcastle coal owners as to the type and size of the engine that would work best in the setting of a mine. Skills developed for growth in one area of mechanized industry could be transferred to another, creating synergy that could be imitated by other industrializing areas in the Western world.

Successful technological decision making required a knowledge base. Again an example: in 1715, James Cunninghame inherited a Scottish mine, and having no experience, he hired an overseer. He in turn advised buying a fire engine. A member of the consortium with economic interests in Cunninghame's mine was duly dispatched to London to purchase a Newcomen engine and an engineer to install it. As was all too easy to imagine, the owners purchased an engine that proved to be without sufficient power to drain the water-sodden mine. In 1732, a more efficient engine had to be bought, at the cost of £239, and with it Cunninghame's mine began to turn a serious profit. If access to cheap coal and the prevalence of high wages are the key variables, and ingenuity appears when profit calls, why was the wrong engine purchased? What explains the long wait to improve this particular engine? What explains the evidence that some regions rich in coal, such as Scotland, can be described as being technologically backward into the 1840s? Perhaps a few more examples will provide some illumination as to the factors at work in technological trial and error with direct economic consequences.[33]

The first elements that had to be present if the correct engine were to be installed were numeracy and an understanding of the relationship between the structure of the engine and the work it could deliver. In June 1753, Leonard Hartley and William Brown, overseers or viewers, wrote to a client in Throckley: "By a calculation I find an engine whose cylinder is 42 inches will work three set of pumps of 12 inch diameters and 12 fathom deep and at a moderate way of working will draw about 1200 hogs head of water ... in an hour which is full 3 times as much as your horse engine can draw when the horses go a pretty good pace." Having clearly determined mathematically that the fire engine was superior to the horse, the writers went on: "If you think that will do for you could wish to have a regulating beam at least 30 inches deep and 24 inches thick and 30 feet long if possible to be got that length; my reason for having it so long is

[33] Hughson *et. al*, *The Auchenarire Colliery: An Early History* (Ochiltree: Shenlake, 1996), pp. 12–13.

the design to make my stroke 2 foot longer than usual." The cylinder of 42 inches would be a large enough boiler to serve such a beam; it would require about twenty bolls of coal a day and a daily expense of coals, 18 s 9 d. The next letter corrects the first and says that after consulting with their best workmen, they think a cylinder of 40 inches or less would do it.[34]

Overseers, as well as skilled craftsmen, knew enough about profit and measurement to present the owners with economic costs and choices. The relationship between good engineering practices and profit had been spelled out in print only in 1744, in Desaguliers' *A Course of Experimental Philosophy*. To lower expenses, the owners of coal mines, he admonished, "need to find a philosopher to come and find a means to bring down the end of the beam [of a water pump] without men or horses." His experimental course became the textbook of early industrial development, introduced into the curriculum of French schools as late as the 1790s. There are reasons why the great engineers of the eighteenth century (who thought of themselves as natural philosophers) need to be factored into the story of industrial development. It will not do to simply say, well someone – anyone – would have done it eventually. It asks us to imagine an industrial revolution without Thomas Newcomen, Desaguliers, John Smeaton, John Buddle, or James Watt.[35]

Their steam engines forced a change in economic thinking about inventions and work as early as the 1740s. Before 1742, applications for patents for new inventions routinely proclaimed "introducing and improving such new Arts and Inventions as will employ great Numbers of our Poor, keep our money at home, and increase ... the exportation of our own Manufactures." Only in 1742 did the steam engineer John Tuite receive praise and a patent for his "Labour and Expense, invented and brought to Perfection, a Water Engine, by which he can, with the Force of less than one Man's Labour, raise One hundred Tons of Water to the Height of Twenty-Five Feet in One Hour." The poor and the cost of their labor had not changed in the intervening ten years. What had changed? The obvious economic benefits to be derived from the labor of one less man.[36]

[34] NEIMME, BRO/1/29 (letter book); on Brown's career, see Dunn, 1844, p. 41. J. Desaguliers, *A Course of Experimental Philosophy* (London: W. Innys *et al.*, 1744), Vol. II, p. 468. See June 11, 1731, "A Bill for Preserving and Encouraging a New Invention in England by Sir Thomas Lombe, and granting him a further Term of Years for the Sole Making and Using of his Three Italian Engines," read March 7, 1732; to be seen at http://parlipapers.chadwyck.com/. For the older view of mining as a way of employing people, see Conyers, 1708. Engraving of early coal mine, n.d. but almost certainly from early in the eighteenth century, found in NEIMME, MS BELL/3/265.

[35] Desaguliers, 1744, Vol. 2, p. 468.

[36] *An Act for Vesting, for a certain Term therein mentioned, in John Tuite, his Executors, Administrators and Assigns, the Sole Property of a Water Engine by him invented.* Harper

Calculations around money and machines became part and parcel of everyday industrial life. In 1761, John Smeaton calculated that the effective power of the best pumping engines was 7 lb per inch, and that when the cylinder was about 18 inches, ten 6 feet strokes per minute might be achieved. He calculated that a 24 inch cylinder could be worked by one bushel of Newcastle coals per hour. Once Smeaton had done the heavy mental lifting required to come up with a rule, other engineers found their work made a lot easier. By the end of the century it made good economic sense to open mathematical schools in the major coal mining regions. The skills needed were in constant demand. As we will see in Chapter 6, well into the 1820s the French scientist and school inspector André-Marie Ampère pleaded with the ministry in charge of education to reform it by adding more mathematics, physics, chemistry, and mechanics useful for industry.[37]

Atomic theory also played a role when, by the 1760s, coal was subjected to microscopic inspection in an effort to discover what we would call its molecular structure. Engineers took note of such examinations and kept references to them. They also came up with formulas that attempted to predict the amount, the quantity of coal that a site might yield. By 1800, the calculations had become even finer and one engineer could write to a client:

> On calculation if I am correct I find that the rope wheel must make 22 revo [lutions] with a 6 inch rope to draw 2 corves at a pull in 2 minutes which according to the sizes of the spin and nut wheels will require the engine to perform at 12 to 32 feet strokes in that time and consequently the piston will move with a velocity of 250¼ feet a second. And allowing 2 minutes for landing the 2 corves the mach [ine] will deliver 48 corves an hour, but as 10 hours out of 12 can at most be allowed for drawing coals. The engine will deliver 24 corves in that time.[38]

Coal engineers gave the owners educated choices: "Now I submit to your consideration whether this is not too great a speed for the engine to travel, as

Collection of Private Bills, 1695–1814, 1742–4; can be seen at http://parlipapers.chadwyck.com/fulltext.do?id=harper-001066&DurUrl=Yes. He is given a term patent of twenty-one years as of June 24, 1742. In 1732, Sir Thomas Lombe was given patent for three Italian engines, one "to wind the finest silk, another to spin and the other to twist" and it will "employ great numbers of the poor."

37 Dunn, 1844, p. 23 for Smeaton; for Ampère, see: www.ampere.cnrs.fr/ms-ampere-302-89-1.5.html, manuscript from about 1830. NEIMME, Bell/387 announcement of 1799, on William Casson opening a school for mathematics in the town.

38 NEIMME, Bell MS/3/337 printed notice from 1769 on the microscopic examination of coal to establish, if possible, the shape of what we would call its molecules. Taken from *The Universal Magazine*. NEIMME, WAT/2/4, Extracts from the Journals of John Watson commonly known in the coal trade as "his honor Watson." Journal covers the period 1745 to 1754; entry for 1746: an acre of coal that lies under an acre of land in a six foot seam will produce 143 tons of coal at 22 wagons with ten 19 bolls to a wagon, with 36 gal to a boll according to the best computation.

I am apprehensive that by its alternating so quick, too great a strain will be paid upon the moving parts and even going at this pace it will not draw the coals sufficiently quick, as the 2 corves ought to be drawn and landed in 2 minutes." Mining required educating, and if the owners did not follow a description they were told the Newtonian principle needed: "With this difference that the weight which two shafts of equal diameter or squares will bear to each other, is in the inverse proportion of their lengths. You will however find that your principle of calculation is erroneous if you refer to Emerson's *Mechanics* 4 to 5th edition prop.73 where problem is demonstrated." By the 1790s viewers had also become familiar with chemistry and routinely consulted texts such as Watson's *Chemical Essays.*[39]

Eighteenth-century engineers who became overseers or viewers had not necessarily been trained in coal mining before they came into the business. As early as the 1740s the viewer John Watson, who had done an apprenticeship with his cousin, another viewer, still found that he needed to make a "dictionary to explain the hard words & terms of art used in working coal mines." In the next generation, also working throughout the Northumberland region, John Buddle had to make a dictionary for himself that literally translated coal-mining terminology. Much of it of medieval origin and used daily by workers at the site, words such as whim (an old word for a gin), trouble, bob gin, kibble (a wooden bucket on a rope), corf (a coal basket that would hold 10–30 pecks), and not least a ten (usually 440 bolls of eight pecks) needed to be explained to him. Such handbooks in printed form became a torrent in the generation after Buddle as more and more men involved themselves in the intricacies of coal mining and did so with no family experience in the mines. The words had once belonged to a centuries-old oral tradition that now had to be printed and translated in order to be understood. The words worked well enough in the entire age of organic power, from roughly the fourteenth century to the 1720s and 1730s, and then new, more skilled, technically trained men had to be imported into what had once been a relatively closed universe inhabited by generations of miners and their overseers.[40]

[39] NEIMME, MS Watson/2/4/ ff. 1–12; MS 3410/Wat/2/4 Extracts from the journals of John Watson; the journal covers the period 1745 to 1754; entry for 1746: an acre of coal that lies under an acre of land in a six foot seam will produce 143 tons of coal; on Newtonian mechanics, Bud/15/21–22, letter of 12 June 1803 Bundle Jr. to Curr.

[40] NEIMME, for the beginning of Watson's dictionary see WAT/2/4/94, 1749. For a modern-day list to assist readers, see B. R. Mitchell, *Economic Development of the British Coal Industry 1800–1914* (Cambridge University Press, 1984), pp. xiii–xiv. See also J. Trotter Brockett, *A Glossary of North Country Words*, 3rd edn.; [Anon.] *Provincial Words Used in Teesdale in the County of Durham* (London: J.R. Smith, 1849); G. Clementson Greenwell, *A Glossary of Terms Used in the Coal Trade of Northumberland and Durham* (Newcastle upon Tyne: John Bell, 1849); W. Hooson, *The Miners Dictionary.*

One characteristic lingered on among the scientifically informed viewers and engineers. The world of coal was still somewhat closed in on itself and identity came from competence and not social place, birth, or breeding. Take one index of social mixing that was commonplace to the age and examine where viewers and engineers fitted in, if they did. Masonic lodges dotted the English urban scene throughout much of the eighteenth century. By 1800, thousands of British men organized some, if not all, of their leisure activity around the lodge meetings. The first Grand Lodge records from Newcastle that give members' names and occupations date from 1805. While the Literary and Philosophical Society associated itself publicly with the Grand Lodge, the evidence from the Provincial Grand Lodge of Northumberland membership list shows very few viewers or engineers in its earliest years. Its ranks were filled by commercial agents, corn merchants, cloth manufacturers, excise officers, builders, farmers, even hand workers like masons, tailors, and grocers, but only one viewer and one mine owner. It is not until the 1850s that viewers and engineers become commonplace, indeed the latter occupation only appears in the Masonic records at that time. Membership could not have been determined by social class exclusively considering that tradesmen and hand workers are quite visible in the Grand Lodge.[41]

The fraternal absence of coal men suggests that their social universe was shaped by their knowledge and interests. Not least, the owners tried wherever possible to unify their practices and to withhold coal if prices for shipment or purchase were not to their liking. They expected their agents and viewers to assist in those closed-door negotiations, as the correspondence of John Buddle richly documents. Such cartel-like behavior, occasionally secret, would only have reinforced a common identity and set of interests, and concessions won "entirely resulted from the firmness, and unanimity of the coal owners." So united they could induce "fear and trembling . . . [among] ship owners and Clubbists" whom they regarded as "enemies."[42]

Explaining Not Only the Terms Used by Miners but also Containing the Theory and Practice of that Most Useful Art of Mineing, More Especially of Lead-Mines (Ilkley: Scolar Press, 1979); facsimile of the edition published at Wrexham in 1747. W. E. Nicholson, *A Glossary of Terms Used in the Coal Trade of Northumberland and Durham* (Newcastle upon Tyne, 1888).

41 For the ties between the leadership of the Lit-Phil and freemasons, see NRO SANT/DRA/ 2/9/2/14/ A and B, plate copying the stone laid by Lit-Phil and head of the Grand Lodge. Newcastle, Neville House, MS Register Provincial Grand Lodge of Northumberland, f. 5 shows in 1814–15 one viewer and one "coal owner," although not every name at this date has an occupation listed. Where occupations are uniformly provided we find in the 1840s only two viewers.

42 NEIMME, Papers of John Buddle, book #23, ff. 1–23, from 1808; on secrecy, see f. 97; ff. 64–5, Buddle to William Ord, March 20, 1809 and f. 87 Buddle to Ellison, May 15, 1809 on their enemies.

Where we see viewers and coal men clubbing outside of the world of mining, science figures prominently in the experience. Buddle (d. 1843), the most important and quite wealthy viewer of the early nineteenth century, collaborated with the London-based chemist, Humphry Davy. Their common interests began with science and extended into technical innovations for which Davy – and not Buddle – became famous. Chemical knowledge and experimentation enabled Davy to invent one of the most important devices ever found in mines, the safety lamp.

Safety lamps

Davy's invention of the first safety lamp depended upon his experimental work: "The fire damp I find, by chemical analysis is, as it has been always supposed, a hydro-carbonate ... in proportion of 4 in weight of hydrogen to 1 ½ of charcoal ... it will not explode unless mixed with six times its volume of atmospherical air ... Again the gas mixed in any proportion with common air, I have discovered, will not explode in a small tube, a diameter of which is less than ⅛ of an inch (or even a large tube), if there is a mechanical force urging the gas through this ... the discovery of these curious and unexpected properties of the gas, leads to several practical methods of lighting the mines without any danger of explosion." Davy did this work while in direct contact with John Buddle, who asked for his assistance and who fully expected that he could follow the technical and chemical description of Davy's experiments.[43]

In 1815, Davy's scientific friends in Newcastle supplied him with "bottles of fire damp" from Hebburn Colliery and these became the basis for the experiments that led to the safety lamp. Its importance and Davy's priority as innovator were in turn examined and confirmed by Buddle and his colleagues at a general meeting of coal owners in Newcastle late in 1815. The ever-vain Davy in turn saw to it that his discovery came before the Royal Society, and its *Philosophical Transactions* published the first authentic account in 1816. Buddle and his associates in Newcastle in turn conducted their own "experiments" with the working models of lamps supplied by Davy. He regarded other

[43] Northumberland Record Office, SANT/BEQ/18/11/13/ff. 175–80, Davy to the Rev. John Hodgson, October 18, 1815 and ff. 187–93. Almost all of the 600 ff. in this manuscript are devoted to Davy's invention, Buddle's role, etc. For Buddle's assessment of it, see NEIMME, FOR/1/13/72–73 dated 1816.

claimants to his invention as committing "piracy," but there is good evidence to suggest that George Stephenson, independently of Davy, had also experimented with hydrogen and had as early as October 1815 brought one version of a safety lamp into the mines where he was a viewer.[44]

Newcastle's Literary and Philosophical Society got into the dispute and brought the lamps back to the same colliery from which the inflammable gas had been drawn, and vouched for the safety and originality of Davy's invention. Stephenson was the son of a pitman and proud of it, and although illiterate until his eighteenth year, he learned the mechanics needed for steam as a colliery engineman. Also of humble birth, Davy rose socially by virtue of his industrialist friends, the Watts who discovered him, and certainly by his ingenuity in science. For all those reasons, and as a consequence of his commanding position at London's Royal Institution, Davy won the credit. The ensuing controversy about priority tells us more about the sociology of early nineteenth-century science than it does about the available science to be deployed indigenously in an industrial setting. The point of the episode with Stephenson concerns the wide availability of the knowledge base upon which Britain's coal resources were employed in industrial development.[45]

Perhaps we can now better understand what contemporaries saw when they attempted to imitate the British relationship between industrial activity, science, and technology. The French created the *École polytechnique* to do just that, and it was imitated throughout Continental Europe. When US manufacturers, artisans, or engineers looked across the Atlantic, they turned what had once been friendly or charitable societies into institutes for science and mechanics where lectures could be offered "on principles of science applicable to manufactures and the mechanic arts." In the 1820s they sought to imitate the societies for the arts found in London, Glasgow, and Paris that "have contributed to human invention in the last half century." Even New Yorkers recognized that something unique had occurred first in British towns such as Newcastle upon Tyne, Birmingham, Leeds, and

[44] Ibid., ff. 197–229. Sir Humphry Davy, *On the Fire-Damp of Coal Mines. From the Philosophical Transactions of the Royal Society*, London, 1816; NRO, SANT/BEQ/18/11/13/ ff. 286–98.

[45] J. Smith, "George Stephenson and the Miner's Lamp Controversy," *North East History*, 34, 2001, pp. 113–36. See R. Colls, "Remembering George Stephenson," in R. Colls and B. Lancaster, eds., *Newcastle upon Tyne: A Modern History* (Chichester: Phillimore & Co, 2001), pp. 272–5.

Manchester. They wanted to promote the acquisition of useful knowledge "among the working classes" broadly defined. By the 1860s, the scientific culture that originated in Britain could be found in the United States and throughout large parts of Northern and Western Europe.[46]

[46] The General Society of Mechanics and Tradesmen became New York Mechanic and Scientific Institution, MS Minutes, Charters and By-Laws, November 27, 1822; for Glasgow, London, and Paris, see Minutes, February 15, 1824.

3 Technical knowledge and making cotton king

The story about the need for technical knowledge to access coal in Northumberland's deep mines has an analogue in the manufacturing of cotton. For decades, in both industries, we have been told that learned knowledge – as distinct from practice – had nothing to do with the First Industrial Revolution, that skilled artisans who seldom cracked a book held the key to British industrial prowess in cotton. In the production of cotton cloth, emphasis has been laid upon water power as distinct from steam, and thus the knowledge of mechanics – the science of local motion – needed to employ power technology has been neglected.[1]

As with Boulton and Watt, two leaders in mechanized cotton production will have to stand in for the first generation of cotton manufacturers. As a leading cotton baron and one of the subjects of this chapter, John Kennedy (b. 1769) eventually became a wealthy man. In order to assemble his factory Kennedy had to understand different rates of velocity and the impact that a steam engine would have on spinning. Just as important, he had to understand and approve – or alter – plans for the mechanization of his cotton factory drawn up by civil engineers, in this case Boulton and Watt.[2] Eventually Kennedy, in partnership with

[1] Research for this chapter made possible by NSF grant number 9906044. For the downplaying of steam prior to 1820, see S. D. Chapman, *The Cotton Industry in the Industrial Revolution* (New Jersey: Humanities Press, 1990), reprinting essays from 1972 to 1989. But by 1802 as much as £1 million may have been invested in steam; see J. Tann, "Fixed Capital Formation in Steam Power 1775–1825: A Case Study of the Boulton and Watt Engine," in *Studies in Capital Formation in the United Kingdom 1750–1920*, ed. Charles H. Feinstein and Sidney Pollard (Oxford: Clarendon Press, 1988), p. 179.

[2] John Kennedy, *A Brief Memoir of Samuel Crompton; With a Description of His Machine Called the Mule, and of the Subsequent Improvement of the Machine by Others* (Manchester: printed by Henry Smith, 1830), pp. 24–9. Accessed at UCLA Management Library, Goldsmiths'-Kress Collection Microfilm, H31 G57, film no. 26180: "The rollers, according to the fineness of the thread, would only admit of a certain velocity per minute, for instance, with 200ds, the rollers could only go at the rate of 25 or 26 per minute, and the spindle about 1,200. But when the rollers ceased to move, then the spindle was accelerated by the spinner to nearly double its former speed. In what manner the acceleration of the speed of the spindle might be effected by machinery without the aid of the spinner, was suggested to me,

Figure 8 John Kennedy, cotton spinner and textile machine maker

by observing in Mr. Watt's steam engine, that one revolution of the beam (if I may use the expression) acting upon the fly wheel by means of the sun and planet wheel produced a double velocity. The difficulty however of making the necessary apparatus at that time, induced me to use the more complicated method of four wheels of unequal sizes for producing the same effect."

James M'Connel (b. 1762), figured out how to use the Watt engine effectively, and together they became among the leading cotton industrialists of Manchester.

The making of two Manchester cotton barons

Born and raised in rural Scotland from whence they migrated to Lancashire, M'Connel and Kennedy became – within fifteen years of the establishment of their partnership in Manchester in 1795 – members of the region's elite sociocultural institutions. We know about the economic factors that contributed to the growth of M'Connel, Kennedy, & Co.[3] The secular knowledge and the religious values underpinning the partners' style of business practice have largely been left unexamined. We turn first to their gradual acquisition of knowledge in state-of-the-art mechanics, then to what we know about their religious commitments.

Somehow M'Connel and Kennedy acquired mechanical sophistication. As with so many early industrialists, we cannot document exactly where or when the acquisition occurred, but we can demonstrate its existence. Nothing in their background suggested that it would be there. The lack of educational opportunities in Kirkudbrightshire, where M'Connel and Kennedy lived until early adolescence, meant that even basic instruction in reading, writing, and arithmetic required considerable effort.[4] M'Connel family memory had it that James hiked the four or five miles from his home to New Galloway in order to study at the parish school.[5] Although both the Kennedys and the M'Connels were small-time farmers and landowners, Kennedy appears to have come from a more distinguished and formally educated ancestry. Kennedy's grandfather had been a shopkeeper and a "Baillie of the Borough of New Galloway," and his father, Robert, had studied at the University of Edinburgh before taking up farming on the family land. Kennedy also claimed that his mother was well educated. Yet Kennedy and his siblings

[3] For extensive information on M'Connel, see the memoir written by his son, David C. M'Connel, *Facts and Traditions Collected for a Family Record.* A copy is available in the collections of the Manchester Central Library. John Kennedy, "Brief Notice of My Early Recollections, in a Letter to My Children," in J. Kennedy, *Miscellaneous Papers on Subjects Connected with the Manufactures of Lancashire reprinted from the Memoirs of the Literary and Philosophical Society of Manchester.* Privately printed, 1849, pp. 1–18.

[4] Kennedy, "Brief Notice," p. 4.

[5] D. C. M'Connel, *Facts and Traditions Collected for a Family Record*, p. 132. Chapter 7 reproduces a letter that James M'Connel, Jr. wrote to his brother detailing what James knew about their father's life. The letter is dated January 1861 and often reflects uncertain memories about M'Connel and particulars that the brothers had learned from their parents and other relatives.

recalled distinct "short comings in the way of education."[6] He claimed that he "had little inducement to acquire much beyond reading the Testament and saying our Catechism and writing our names."[7] Kennedy got lucky when, just before leaving for England, he encountered a young teacher who "opened my mind to the beauty of mechanical pursuits, and gave me some ideas of connecting a few causes together to produce a desired result."[8] Significantly, Kennedy also attended the natural philosophy lectures of John Banks, who was then offering a course in Preston.[9] Neither M'Connel nor Kennedy ever pursued natural philosophy as an avocation – as manufacturers such as Boulton and Watt or John Marshall in Leeds did – yet they were able to take advantage of the burgeoning interest in technological innovation. Later in life the breadth of interests Kennedy displayed in the essays he wrote for the Manchester Literary and Philosophical Society indicates that he thought as deeply about the social effects of technology as about the technology itself.[10]

In their youth, necessity stimulated a search for alternatives. The Kennedys' farm had not provided a lucrative source of income. M'Connel's father also had not prospered, not even to the degree previously enjoyed by his own father.[11] M'Connel's maternal uncle suggested in 1779 that he be trained as a carpenter under the tutelage of another uncle, William Cannon, who worked as a machine maker in Chowbent, Lancashire. He was willing to take the young M'Connel as an apprentice.[12] Along with his partner James Smith, William was part of a growing Scottish immigrant community that had made Chowbent a center of expatriate Scottish life.[13] Indeed, soon after taking M'Connel as an apprentice, Cannon and his partner accepted four more youngsters from the New Galloway region – the brothers Adam and George Murray, Alexander Smith, and, significantly for this story, John Kennedy.[14]

Like M'Connel, the young Kennedy faced limited opportunities in the region, and at the same time desired "to know and see something beyond the still valley and the blue mountains that surrounded the place of my birth."[15] In addition, his mother taught him the need for practical and skilled education. "My mother," Kennedy recalled in his memoirs:

[6] Kennedy, "Brief Notice," p. 4. [7] Ibid., p. 5. [8] Ibid., pp. 4–5. [9] Ibid., p. 14.

[10] Towards the end of Kennedy's life these papers were collected and published as *Miscellaneous Papers*.

[11] D. C. M'Connel, *Facts and Traditions Collected for a Family Record*, p. 133. [12] Ibid.

[13] Kennedy, "Brief Notice," pp. 14–15.

[14] D. C. M'Connel, *Facts and Traditions Collected for a Family Record*, p. 133.

[15] Kennedy, "Brief Notice," p. 6.

was a strict disciplinarian, and maintained, that to work and learn a trade was the way to become independent, and that with some mechanical skill we should find employment in every part of the world, and stand a chance of getting forward in the world, if we would pay attention and improve ourselves, and have always a strict regard for honour and integrity: for the rich would always be glad to give employment to such a description of people; and if we showed any talent we should have a chance of being promoted and should make advance in business.[16]

The emphasis on technical skill was reiterated again and again in the Kennedy household: "Hearing this advice so constantly repeated by my mother, that we must learn to work with our hands, and seeing also how difficult it would be with our slender means to get on in the world, I at last screwed up my courage to say, I would leave home and become an apprentice to some handicraft business."[17] Kennedy took the message of application and virtue to heart and throughout his life remained concerned not only about the state of his own knowledge but also that of the laboring classes. At this stage in their development both Kennedy and M'Connel might be described as literate tinkerers.[18]

Long before fortune, the skills of manufacturing and trade first had to be acquired. What Kennedy and M'Connel learned during their seven or eight years working for William Cannon helped establish the foundations of their industrial careers. While we know that both apprenticed with the intention of learning carpentry, the exact nature of Cannon's business is not known. It appears that he was a carpenter and machine manufacturer, but we do not know what kinds of machines Cannon made. M'Connel's son David claimed that Cannon was a clockmaker, and that M'Connel learned about the cotton trade from other sources.[19] Kennedy, meanwhile, remarked in his memoirs that Cannon had trained as a carpenter and "had made a carding engine and [a Hargreaves] spinning jenny" for spinners in Carlisle.[20] As we learned from Mr. Clark's letter, clockmakers made spindles, and it is likely that Cannon worked on both clocks and

[16] Ibid., p. 5. [17] Ibid., p. 6.

[18] See the breadth of topics covered in Kennedy, *Miscellaneous Papers*, which includes articles on manufacturing, the poor laws, and the effect of technology on the working classes. For the firm's relations with its workers, see M. Huberman, "Industrial Relations and the Industrial Revolution: Evidence from M'Connel and Kennedy, 1810–1840," *The Business History Review*, 65, Summer 1991, pp. 345–78.

[19] D. C. M'Connel, *Facts and Traditions Collected for a Family Record*, p. 134.

[20] Kennedy, "Brief Notice," pp. 9, 13. C. H. Lee corroborates Kennedy's memory, claiming that Kennedy had apprenticed with Cannon "to learn the construction of carding engines, jennies and water frames." See C. H. Lee, *A Cotton Enterprise: 1795–1840: A History of M'Connel & Kennedy, Fine Cotton Spinners* (Manchester University Press, 1972), p. 10.

cotton-spinning engines. Since spinning machines were in large part constructed from often quite finely worked wooden parts, much of the machine maker's knowledge lay in woodworking. Furthermore, it was not uncommon for inventors to hire clockmakers when looking to build prototypes of new engine designs.[21]

In 1767, Richard Arkwright turned to the Warrington clockmaker John Kay to "bend him some wires, and turn him some pieces of brass" for the spinning machine that he was in the process of constructing. Later, when the job of building Arkwright's spinning machine proved to be too complex for Arkwright and Kay, the machinist Peter Atherton agreed to lend them a smith and a "watch-tool" maker to complete the work.[22] Recall, too, that James Watt began his career apprenticed to a clockmaker.

Clockmakers brought to the machine business finely tuned skills in metal and woodwork and the use of precision tools. It would not be surprising if Cannon had moved either from carpentry into clockmaking or vice versa. From the correspondence of the M'Connel and Kennedy firm, we do know that Cannon ordered machine parts and was probably involved in the manufacture of spinning machines.[23] Most of Cannon's apprentices went on to create very successful cotton manufacturing businesses. Indeed, Adam and George Murray, although lifelong friends of M'Connel and Kennedy, were also two of their most persistent rivals.[24] After seven or eight years with Cannon, M'Connel moved to Manchester in 1788, while Kennedy moved in 1791. Given how quickly their business achieved success, we might surmise that they were well served by their time under Cannon.[25] Kennedy knew enough to assume control of the machine-making department of

[21] John Rylands University Library, Deansgate, Manchester, M'Connel and Kennedy papers, MCK/2/1/5 Letters Received 1799, Salvin Bros. to M&K, November 22, 1799: "We have sent you three Muslin warps which please to sell for us." Also ordered six gallows pulleys and six iron jaws 10 inches long. "In sending mules you will send complete sets of wheels, as it does not suit us to employ a Clock maker." Hereafter all MCK papers are from the Rylands.

[22] E. Baines, Jr., *History of the Cotton Manufacture in Great Britain* (London: Fisher, Fisher & Jackson, 1835), p. 148.

[23] See, for instance, William Cannon to James M'Connel and John Kennedy, July 21, 1797 and August 28, 1797, MCK/2/1/3.

[24] D. C. M'Connel, *Facts and Traditions Collected for a Family Record*, p. 133. On the friendship and rivalry between M'Connel and Kennedy and the Murrays, see Lee, 1972, pp. 12–13, 27, and 153.

[25] For an overview of the developments of cotton-spinning machine technology in the eighteenth and nineteenth centuries, see G. Timmins, "Technological Change," in *The Lancashire Cotton Industry: A History since 1700*, ed. Mary B. Rose (Preston: Lancashire County Books, 1996), pp. 29–62.

the company and later contributed his own innovations to the improvement of the mule.[26]

After a short partnership with fustian merchants that ended in 1795, M'Connel and Kennedy turned the £816 they had each taken in profits into a new partnership and sought to increase production through the use of steam power.[27] Company letters suggest that they were well aware of the impact steam was having in the Manchester area. They also knew where to go for ideas and advice. They first contacted the company of Boulton and Watt in May 1797 and thereby began a relationship that was to last for almost half a century. They indicated their interest in purchasing a new steam engine and requested specific advice about the right engine and how it would fit within the new factory being built alongside the Rochdale ship canal in the Ancoats region of Manchester. Fuel efficiency was uppermost in their minds and they hoped to have the new engine heat the factory as well as run its machines – all at minimal cost.[28] They also consulted with James Lawson, the Boulton and Watt engineer already working in the area. Highly technical discussions ensued, and the steam engineers wrote: "Respecting the precise length for the rotative shaft and whether the engine will be connected to the machinery by spur wheels upon the middle part of the shaft between the bearing, or whether the power would be required to be transmitted thro' the outer gudgeon.

[26] W. Fairbairn, *A Brief Memoir of the Late John Kennedy, Esq.* (Manchester: Charles Simms & Co., 1861), pp. 4–8.

[27] For what was needed to install and run an engine in the way of technical knowledge see Birmingham Central Library (BCL), James Watt Papers, 4/69: "Boultons Anwr v. Hornblowers Answr:" "Points necessary to be known by a Steam Engineer" [Emphasis is on the principles of pneumatics and heat transfer.] 1st: "The Laws of Mechanics as a Science." 2nd: "Their usual practical Application to the Construction of Machinery including the subsidiary Contrivance of catches & detents &c." 3rd: "The means of making & constructing the various Parts of Machines in Wood Iron Brass & other Materials." 4th: "The Laws of Hydraulics & Hydrostatics, by which the Pressure of Columns of Fluids as well as their statical Weights are to be estimated; also the Quantities of any given Fluid or Liquid – which will pass thro' any given Aperture or Pipe in a given Time. The Resistance to motion or Aperture or Viz. Inertia of Matter whether solid or fluid, & in the latter Case, how it is likely to be affected by the Form of the Channel or Pipe which conveys it &c. &c." 5th: "The Doctrine of Heat & Cold, the relative Quantities of Heat imbibed by different Bodies in acquiring an equal Number of Degrees of sensible Heat. The conducting Power of different Bodies in Respect to Heat and Cold. The Quantity of Fuel necessary to heat a given Quantity of Water to the boiling Point." 6th: "The Bulk of various Liquids especially Water when converted into Steam under given Pressure. N. This is easily ascertained with sufficient Accuracy, by any Person having a common Engine by measuring how many Fills of the Cylinder of Steam, the Boiler could yield per Minute when no Injection Water was used & measuring the Quantity of Water evaporated in that Time." 7th: "The best practical Method of constructing Furnaces + seating Boilers so as to receive the proper Quantity of Heat from the Fuel."

[28] James M'Connel and John Kennedy to Boulton and Watt, May 12, 1797, draft and second version, MCK/2/2/2.

This information will be necessary for us in regulating the proportions of the shaft."[29] Suddenly more knowledge than tinkering was required.

As M'Connel and Kennedy moved from machine making into the business of cotton spinning by means of power technology, they had to enter into working relationships with mechanically trained engineers. They were not alone. In 1796, increased competition in the marketplace drove the cotton manufacturer Samuel Greg to establish a partnership with the technically trained engineer Peter Ewart, who had previously apprenticed under a civil engineer and had worked for Boulton and Watt and the Manchester cotton spinner Samuel Oldknow.[30] Continuing developments in engine technology put pressure on manufacturers to keep up with the changes in order to remain competitive in the market, and trained engineers like Ewart became key players, working side by side with local manufacturers, installing new engines, and training the manufacturers to maintain and make efficient use of them.[31] Being able to talk to the engineers as peers was the only way to insure that technological decisions with significant economic implications remained firmly in the hands of the entrepreneurs. As with mining, installing the wrong-sized engine could spell financial disaster.

The combination of new buildings and new steam engines committed M'Connel and Kennedy to a substantial financial outlay, and they also quickly realized that the demands of the new technology required a deeper understanding of the principles and mechanics of their operation. The engines and spinning machines, as well as the power trains that connected them all, required specialized knowledge about their precision parts and movements. As efficiency became an increasing concern, the knowledge of precise gear ratios and the methods of manufacturing by the exact interlocking parts became equally pressing.[32] Parts for engines, including planet wheels and plummer blocks for the rotative shaft, as well as pins and links, had to be understood.[33] The growing complexity of the

[29] M'Connel and Kennedy Archive (1795–1888), MCK/2/1/3 Letters Received, 1797 (MCK/2/1/3/1 A–F; /2 G–R, /3 S–Z), from Robinson Boulton for B&W, undated, but after July 1, 1797 and before September 12 that year.

[30] W. C. Henry, "A Biographical Notice of the Late Peter Ewart, Esq.," *Memoirs of the Manchester Literary and Philosophical Society*, Second Series, No. 7 (1846), pp. 113–36, esp. 114, 120–1, 125. Also M. B. Rose, *The Gregs of Quarry Bank Mill: The Rise and Decline of a Family Firm, 1750–1914* (Cambridge University Press, 1986), pp. 22–3.

[31] The correspondence of Boulton and Watt includes numerous letters to their engineers in the field and indicates the range of activities in which the engineers were involved. See, in particular, outgoing letters from Boulton and Watt to Peter Ewart, James Lawson, William and James Murdock, and John Rennie in the Boulton and Watt Collection, BCL.

[32] See Baines, 1835, Chapters 9–11; R. Guest, *A Compendious History of the Cotton Manufacture* (1823; reprint, London: Frank Cass & Co. Ltd., 1968).

[33] BCL, J. Lodge for B&W to M&K, October 26, 1798.

machinery, in turn, demanded greater degrees of "technical literacy" on the part of its makers and its users. The ability to read technical drawings, make precise measurements, and manufacture parts became essential to further innovation in machine technologies.[34] Other manufacturers wrote to M'Connel and Kennedy asking to inspect their works, "to . . . see how your Principal Movements are that we may make a light Calculation for proper speed [of the water wheel] – as well as the Manner of your Shafts for turning the Mules and the Dimensions of Your Chimney to fix a Stove to throw the hot Air into your Rooms."[35]

M'Connel and Kennedy took it upon themselves to learn as much as they could about mechanics and the new technology and to associate with those who had technical expertise. They also got to know every part of the steam engine's construction and oversaw its maintenance.[36] When, for instance, an engineer from Boulton and Watt's steam engine firm explained how the rotative shaft would connect to the beam of the engine, he was asking them to understand how the vertical motion of the engine would be translated into the circular needed to power jennies. M'Connel and Kennedy had to understand and respond, even correct the following:

You have here with a plan & elevation of the Engine, nearly according with [the] sketch made by Mr. Henry Creighton [from Boulton and Watt in Birmingham] when he called of you. . . . The supports for the P. Blocks of the Main Gudgeon cannot be cast in one piece with the entablature beam, & must therefore be screwed to it. We have drawn the latter under the spring beams, but if you wish to have it without the feather on its underside, it may be placed on the upper side,

[34] Stevens, 1995, p. 2. In Stevens' words: "Technical literacy required mastery of four notational systems and their related vocabularies and grammars: alphabetic expression, scientific notation, mathematical notation, and spatial-graphic representation."

[35] George Clayton, Bamber Bridge, Lancaster to M&K, September 1, 1798.

[36] MCK/2/2/2; [54] to Boulton and Watt, July 1, 1797; responding to letter of May 26; they will take only one boiler rather than two. "It is recommended to us by some of our experienced friends to have the boiler made larger and stronger than you commonly do for that power; Although it costs more we mention this that you may not be limited, when there appears to be an advantage;" [101] to Boulton and Watt, October 5, 1798: "We have got the Cylinder and base here today and are now very much in want of cement to put them together with. Please to Forward a Box of it by the first Coach if possible – have likewise got a Beam." [103] to Boulton and Watt, October 17, 1798: "We find the Planet wheel is so much damaged that [it] may break when the Engine is Set to work. Therefore please to send one as soon as possible with the pin fitted to it that was ordered for the Double Link." [111] to Boulton and Watt, January 16, 1799: "Having had some conversation with some of the Partners in the Underwood Spinning Comp., Paisley Respecting our Cylinder & Piston &c. that lay here which they have no objection to take for their Engine if you think they are as good as new. Shall be very Glad if you can bring it in the Price we leave to you. We believe the[y] are as good as can be made." [312] to Boulton and Watt, June 21, 1802, Requesting B&W to send as soon as possible the "Crank & Shafts & Fly Wheel Shaft with the wheels belong'g as our millwrights are nearly at a stand for want of them."

or let into them, and the pillar reaches up to it. The cross beams will be much farther asunder than . . . [the] sketch shewed them, but in the present drawings they are as we suppose you intend them: viz the present cross beam to remain where it now is, say 8 feet horizontally from the rotative shaft, and as the cylinder is removed 3.9 – the new cross beam will be 7.6 from the old one, from middle to middle. The cross plate might have wings to reach as far as the beams, but query if this be necessary. Or the supports of the P. blocks, might have their base-plate to extend to them, as represented in pencil on the elevation, but we think it looks too much of a thing. [*Then came the request that makes the point.*] We shall follow your instructions in this respect as also in any other you may point out, as differing from our sketch.[37]

While cotton manufacturers such as M'Connel and Kennedy ultimately relied upon engineers such as Creighton sent from Soho to install the machine, they then had to care for and service it.[38] Most important, they had to make technological decisions with immediate economic consequences.

In 1797, the first major decision M'Connel and Kennedy had to make – before even ordering their new engine – concerned its size. In their initial letter to Boulton and Watt, they began by expressing interest in a 14-hp engine, but John Southern, the Boulton and Watt representative who replied to their initial inquiries, explained that the 12- and 16-hp engines were more common and less expensive to build, since new patterns did not have to be created. Although M'Connel and Kennedy could have gone with their first-choice engine, they decided to order the larger 16-hp engine instead. While the initial cost of the 16-hp engine (£831.2.0) was less than that of the 14-hp engine (£927.5.0), this could not have been their only consideration. More powerful engines required on a daily basis more coal and hence were more expensive to run and maintain. If business deteriorated and the ability to buy fuel was seriously curtailed, it could mean disaster for the company that could not run the engine at maximum efficiency, or even run it at all. The cost of the 16-hp engine exceeded that of the 12-hp engine by more than £200, but the weaker engine may not have been adequate both to run spinning machines and heat the factory. The caution that M'Connel and Kennedy brought to other business decisions suggests that they would have carefully weighed their options in regard to a purchase as large as a steam engine. Together with the costs of the new factory building, the firm committed itself to £6,074.2.7, a

[37] John Southern for Boulton and Watt to M'Connel and Kennedy, November 30, 1804, MCK/2/1/10 Letters Received.

[38] MCK/2/2/2 Letters Sent, June 2, 1796–June 14, 1805; [103] to Boulton and Watt, October 17, 1798: "We find the Planet wheel is so much damaged that [it] may break when the Engine is Set to work. Therefore please to send one as soon as possible with the pin fitted to it that was ordered for the Double Link."

debt that could have fatal consequences if business fell for a considerable length of time. Fortunately for the partners, the firm secured adequate outlets for its cotton cloth and was able to afford further expansions in the early years of the nineteenth century, despite frequent downturns in the market. They began work on a new factory building in 1801 and a year later, a mere five years after the first engine came on site, they sought to purchase a 45-hp engine from Boulton and Watt. By 1800, Manchester came to be seen by French observers as the state-of-the-art place to manufacture cotton cloth.[39]

The process of integrating steam-engine technology into cotton manufacturing involved a reconceptualization of the relationship between architecture and technology as well as a new understanding of the connection between motive power and the spinning machinery itself.[40] During the installation of the first engine in 1797, the size of the engine room and the depth of the pipes with respect to the canal running outside the factory were of primary concern, and it was largely up to the Boulton and Watt engineers to decide how to proceed with the installation. With the new 45-hp engine the engineers relied upon M'Connel and Kennedy to make more of their own design decisions, although a process of ongoing negotiations continued.[41] By this point, M'Connel and Kennedy had become well versed in the material construction of their buildings as well as the technical diagrams supplied by the engineers.

The success M'Connel and Kennedy enjoyed, their expertise in making spinning machines, as well as in their actual use, meant that the company

[39] The engine alone cost £2,178. M'Connel and Kennedy also installed fire-extinguishing apparatus at this time at a cost of £426. Lee, 1972, p. 105. For foreign opinion, see Archives Départementales Seine, Amiens, MS 80003, Mémoire des officiers municipaux de la commune d'Amiens relatif aux diverses questions du gouvernement sur l'état des manufactures et du commerce de ce canton avant et depuis la Révolution et aux moyens d'amélioration de l'industrie et d'augmentation des debouchés, 22 Prairial, an VI; "Cet établissement mérite toutes sortes de considerations et donnera lieux par ses succès à la formation de plusieurs autres ce à quoi les rivières de ce département se prêtent avanteusement on peut même observer qu'il n'en est point en France sur lesquelles on puisse établir un si grand nombre de moulins dans un espace moins étendu puis quelles ont presque toutes une chute de 100 à 140 pieds depuis leurs sources jusqu'à la mer sur un cours de 15 à 30 lieux de sorte que ce département sensible destiné à rivaliser un jour les manufactures de Manchester qui entretient plus de 100 mille ouvriers et fait pour 80 à 90 millions d'affaires en étoffes de coton."

[40] R. Boulton for B&W, undated but after July 1, 1797; requesting the precise length for the rotative shaft and whether the engine will be connected to the machinery by "spur wheels upon the middle part of the shaft between the bearing, or whether the power would be required to be transmitted thro' the outer gudgeon. This information will be necessary for us in regulating the proportions of the shaft."

[41] See, for instance, John Southern for Boulton and Watt to M'Connel and Kennedy, November 30, 1804, MCK/2/1/10 Letters Received.

was worth emulating. As early as April 1797, John McNaught, a Scottish machine maker from Paisley, approached them with a long list of questions about the operational needs of the spinning equipment and the costs of hiring labor.[42] Although a machine maker by trade, McNaught was impressed with the operation of local spinners using new spinning jennies with up to 120 spindles and had decided to abandon machine making entirely. He wanted the transformation of his business to be completed by the end of May and was therefore eager to receive M'Connel and Kennedy's response. In August 1798, George Clayton of Bamber Bridge, Lancashire, also visited the company to investigate its operations and use of steam power. From that visit he decided to set up his own manufactory and requested that the partners allow a millwright to drop by to make calculations. Again, witness the growing importance of numerical literacy associated with the integration of new power and spinning technology. As we well know, the creation of this community of manufacturers and local engineers also hugely benefitted engine makers such as Boulton and Watt.[43] While steam appeared in Manchester by 1785, it was 1810 before the first steam engine made its appearance at the cotton factories across the Channel in Rouen.

For M'Connel and Kennedy, the installation of their first steam engine only began their relationship with the rapidly developing technology. In 1806, the partners considered the advantages of installing a system of gas lighting. Actual installation did not occur until 1810 (again Boulton and Watt did the work), but it is apparent that M'Connel and Kennedy seldom let developments in technological innovation pass them by.[44] In the first decade of the nineteenth century, fire prevention also began to preoccupy their attention, and they quickly turned to new technology for a possible solution. A boiler explosion in October 1798 dramatically demonstrated the vulnerability of the factory.[45] Such events grew more commonplace as steam engines appeared at factory sites.

That one experience convinced M'Connel and Kennedy: fireproofing the buildings had to be a priority, and they quickly looked to new pumping technologies to provide the work. In 1802, the company contacted no less than three London manufacturers of firefighting engines to request

[42] J. M. McNaught to M'Connel and Kennedy, April 11, 1797 and August 20, 1797, MCK/2/1/3 Letters Received. While in machine making, McNaught had made machine parts for M'Connel and Kennedy.

[43] Musson and Robinson, 1989.

[44] D. C. M'Connel, *Facts and Traditions Collected for a Family Record*, pp. 144–6.

[45] Robert Kennedy to M'Connel and Kennedy, October 20, 1798, MCK/2/1/4, Letters Received.

information regarding costs and installation.[46] At issue was the water pressure needed to effectively move water to the upper floors of their factory, a height of about 30 yards. More explicitly, M'Connel and Kennedy wanted an answer to a hydrostatics question: how much water could be pumped per minute, and what was the maximum height that the most powerful engines available could attain?[47] In reply, engine makers offered several options of variously sized engines with different designs. Additionally, they invited M'Connel and Kennedy to visit and inspect firefighting engines that had been constructed in the Manchester region.[48] Although M'Connel and Kennedy eventually purchased their engine from their old friends Boulton and Watt, they made the decision only after surveying the field of options. They understood trial and error and the relationship of profits to both. As Kennedy put it: "Whenever [and wherever] machinery is ... introduced ... people ... will immediately become acquainted with its use and principles. It is impossible to work machinery without having at hand people competent to its repair and management."[49] Profit and improvement motivated their acquisition of the requisite knowledge of machines and the principles behind them. Having it became crucial to success.

Manchester

Innovation requires seedbed conditions, a matrix of sociocultural facilities, knowledge and educational infrastructure, financial and capital support – in short, what has been called an "incubation milieu." In the late eighteenth century, cities such as Manchester – or in coal mining, Newcastle – played a strategic role in the creation and diffusion of innovation in cotton manufacturing.[50] The factory may have rested by a bucolic river, but the men who built it socialized and networked in chapels and societies found in the alleys and byways of the town. Out of scientific societies and religious communities came networks based upon values

46 M'Connel and Kennedy to Rowntree & Co., Engine Makers, October 7, 1802; M'Connel and Kennedy to J. Bramah [Patent engine &c. manufacturers], November 26, 1802; M'Connel and Kennedy to Phillips & Hopwood [engine makers], November 26, 1802. All are in MCK/2/2/2 Letters Sent.

47 M'Connel and Kennedy to Rowntree & Co., October 7, 1802. Identical information was requested of J. Bramah and Phillips & Hopwood.

48 Lee, 1972, pp. 103–5.

49 J. Kennedy, *On the Exportation of Machinery: A Letter Addressed to the Hon. E.G. Stanley, M.P.* (London: Hurst & Co., 1824), p. 16.

50 See Bertuglia *et al.*, *Innovative Behavior in Space and Time* (Berlin: Springer, 2000), pp. 4 and 18–19.

and knowledge, and therein lay the seeds of innovation in cotton manufacturing.

The cotton industry of Manchester displayed a distinctive religious diversity. Within the industry, non-Anglican Protestants notably exceeded the percentage that they constituted in the general population. More precisely, Unitarians, along with Quakers, were strongly over-represented among the textile masters. As we have seen, Unitarians professed a shared value system that endorsed scientific and abstract learning. This dedication to science belonged distinctively to the legacy articulated most forcefully by the Birmingham-based Unitarian minister and scientist Joseph Priestley.[51] Studies of cotton masters after 1820 have mentioned that they valued science and mechanical knowledge, yet as early as the 1790s such knowledge also fostered industrial innovation.[52]

Like so many early manufacturers in both Europe and America, M'Connel and Kennedy recommended the science of mechanics as the antidote to the high cost of labor or as the means for entrepreneurial advancement.[53] They were not alone. By 1800, educational reformers tied to Birmingham industrial circles, such as the Edgeworths, argued that practical, technical, and mechanical knowledge should be taught to children destined for work – at whatever level – in commerce and manufacturing.[54] We can now see that these educational prescriptions grew out of lived experience, out of what manufacturers such as M'Connel and Kennedy knew to be necessary for success in industrial ventures. Scientific knowledge and practical skills, each infusing the other, became the cornerstones of an ideology about science and industry that bore relation to practical reality, to how early entrepreneurs approached decision making. They had to be able to read plans and make decisions about a variety of sophisticated machines for weaving, for fire extinguishing, and,

[51] M. C. Jacob, "Commerce, Industry and the Laws of Newtonian Science: Weber Revisited and Revised," *Canadian Journal of History*, 35, August 2000, pp. 275–92.

[52] For science, see Howe, 1984, p. 59.

[53] For New World preaching on the subject, see Z. Allen, *The Science of Mechanics*, (Providence: 1829), preface; and D. Drake, *An Anniversary Discourse on the State and Prospects of the Western Museum Society* (Cincinnati, OH: 1820), pp. 32–3 on the superiority of English engineers during the American Revolution and the necessity to compete; kindly supplied by Joyce Appleby. Note that "only after 1815 was the first significant generation of American civil engineers educated and trained." See D. H. Stapleton, *The Transfer of Early Industrial Technologies to America* (Philadelphia, PA: American Philosophical Society, 1987), p. 126.

[54] M. Edgeworth and R. L. Edgeworth, *Practical Education*, 3 vols. (London, 1801: reprint, Poole: Woodstock Books, 1996); in particular Vol. 2, largely written by Richard. On what is needed to be known by workers: *Report of the Committee of the Birmingham Mechanics' Institution, Read at the Ninth Anniversary Meeting, Held Friday, January 2, 1835, in the Lecture Room, Cannon-Street* (Birmingham: printed by J. W. Showell, 1835).

most important, for steam.[55] In effect, those who mechanized manufacturing and applied power technology to it had to become proficient as civil engineers of sorts, and their clustering in cities such as Manchester and Birmingham made that proficiency more easily attainable.[56] The power achieved by early industrial capitalists such as M'Connel and Kennedy can be better understood if we conceive of them as knowledgeable, and not simply as striving. Kennedy was seen to be so knowledgeable that Parliament questioned him about the differences between English and French steam-engine builders, and asked him to explain the superiority of the former.[57]

As they prospered, these same industrialists became elite members of Manchester society. In a township that had grown to about 70,000 people by 1800, they used their social network to further promote technological knowledge at large. First their scientific and technical culture enabled their entrepreneurial development, aiding and abetting their wealth. Then that same culture made them genteel. The families of M'Connel and Kennedy, in particular, became deeply involved in the activities of some of Manchester's most important cultural institutions, especially the Manchester Literary and Philosophical Society and the Manchester Mechanics' Institute, both of which advanced the social image, prestige, and applicability of science and technology. M'Connel was also prominent in the Unitarian chapel life of the city, in particular the energetic chapel at Cross Street. It laid down a cultural foundation in Manchester that wedded science to economic efficiency – and both to Liberal, at times

[55] MCK/2/1/8 Letters Received, 1803 (MCK/2/1/8/1 A–H; /2 K–N; /3 O-W and unidentified); twelve letters from Boulton and Watt to M&K: James Lodge for B&W, to M&K, January 1, January 6, and February 26, 1803. Reporting of shipment of parts for extinguishing apparatus; John Southern for B&W, April 11, 1803, sends a plan designed by Mr. Creighton for the extinguishing apparatus. Actual drawing of plan is on the last page; five of the twelve letters from S. Lodge are dated 1802 (May 31, June 26, August 16, August 23, and August 26) and report the shipment of parts for a new steam engine – the parts are listed in detail. This engine seems to be separate from the extinguisher reported in the above letters; MCK/2/1/10 Letters Received, 1804 John Southern for B&W to M&K, November 30, 1804.

[56] MCK/2/1/12, Letters Received, 1806, Robertson Buchanan, Glasgow, to M&K, 15 April [1806] RB has "withdrawn" from cotton spinning and intends to return to civil engineering. "And I mark there is an extensive field open in that species of Engineering which relates to manufactures. I could hardly presume to offer my services to those who are so much masters of the subject as yourselves, but I presume many in your neighbourhood might save money by employing a person to arrange their plans for them and put them on paper as well in writing as drawing. Much might be done in the saving of fuel &c. and in the proper arrangement & construction of building machinery." For extensive information on M'Connel, see D. C. M'Connel, *Facts and Traditions Collected for a Family Record.*

[57] Chamber of Commerce, *Enquête faite par ordre du Parlement d'Angleterre pour constater les progrès de l'industrie en France* (Paris: Boudouin, 1825), pp. 137–61.

radical, politics. By the 1840s, Manchester had come to be dominated by cotton manufacturers generally of Unitarian affiliation. The preponderance of Unitarians among the wealthiest Britons far exceeded – nearly tenfold – their numbers in the larger population.[58]

In the next generation the scientific legacy of the city spawned James Prescott Joule, who "with his hard-headed upbringing in commercial, industrial Manchester ... quite explicitly adopted the language and concerns of the economist and the engineer," and who as a result pioneered the use of electro-magnetism for replacing steam in propelling machinery.[59] At the same time the Tory oligarchy that had dominated the town went down in defeat to a coalition of Liberals, "many of whom were still drawn from the network of Unitarian families whose political interests had been first defined in the 1790s."[60]

The Unitarian ethos

As we saw with Boulton and Watt, the Weber thesis about the relationship between Protestantism and capitalism requires considerable modification and fine-tuning. Among circles of industrialists, the Enlightenment served to secularize the striving impulse and to wed science irretrievably to it. The marriage of enlightened piety and science-based rationalism can be seen concretely in the ethos of Unitarianism. Its accommodation to worldly success is particularly striking, as is the zeal with which Unitarians reinforced the adoration of science and its application. Manchester's Unitarians provide a convenient example. At the 1786 opening of the Dissenting academy attached to the Cross Street chapel, its prominent minister, Ralph Harrison, explained to his congregation that it should never "hastily ... censure any scientific pursuit as frivolous and unimportant. Such is the affinity and connection between the sciences, that few are without eminent use; and it is not easy to understand any one, without some acquaintance with the rest. ... will not the character of the merchant, and the manufacturer become far more respectable and useful when adorned with the valuable accomplishments of science?"[61] In the

[58] See M. R. Watts, *The Dissenters,* Vol. II, *The Expansion of Evangelical Nonconformity* (Oxford University Press, 1995), p. 332. I owe this reference to Matt Kadane.

[59] I. R. Morus, *Frankenstein's Children: Electricity, Exhibition, and Experiment in Early-Nineteenth-Century London* (Princeton University Press, 1998), p. 189.

[60] D. Fraser, ed., *Municipal Reform and the Industrial City* (Leicester University Press, 1982), p. 23.

[61] R. Harrison, *A Sermon preached at the Dissenting Chapel in Cross-Street, Manchester, March 26th, 1786 on the occasion of the Establishment of an academy in that Town bound with A Discourse ... at the public commencement of the Manchester Academy, Warrington*, p. 10.

pews at Cross Street Lancashire and Manchester, cotton manufacturers were "strongly over represented."[62]

Indeed, the general Unitarian outlook encouraged the merging of theoretical and practical interests and did much to apply the resulting ideology to a brand of social morality.[63] In the late eighteenth century no one spoke more eloquently or forcefully for the Unitarian stance in the world than Joseph Priestley. Being a Unitarian meant striving continuously in the face of adversity while allowing that thankfulness was an appropriate response to riches.

In Manchester during the 1780s Ralph Harrison echoed similar themes. He would routinely explain how "Religious wisdom hath the promise of temporal prosperity and enjoyment." He further explained that knowledge also informs commerce and enhances success.[64] He spoke to a congregation that by the 1770s had become overwhelmingly commercial and industrial, including among its members manufacturers, a reed maker, a shoemaker, a warehouseman, physicians, plumbers, a velvet dresser, pin makers, shoe makers, and a yarn merchant.[65] Such mingling may also have created a window of opportunity for ambitious workers with a bent for mechanical learning. While Unitarians were not the only ones to become industrial and entrepreneurial innovators or social leaders, their predominance in Manchester society and cotton manufacturing in general leads us to ask what set of shared values made their influence possible. The cotton-spinning firm of James M'Connel and John Kennedy, two of the area's most successful cotton industrialists, provides some answers to the question.

[62] Quoting Howe, 1984, p. 61. See Wach, 1991, pp. 425–56. See also J. Seed, "Unitarianism, Political Economy, and the Antinomies of Liberal Culture in Manchester, 1830–50," *Social History*, 7, 1982, pp. 1–25; and D. C. M'Connel, *Facts and Traditions Collected for a Family Record.*

[63] Seed, 1982. Chapter 4 of R. Eckersley's "The Drum Major of Sedition: The Life and Political Career of John Cartwright, 1740–1824" (Ph.D. dissertation, University of Manchester, 1999) also investigates the connections between Unitarian beliefs and Cartwright's personal views on parliamentary reform and the abolition of slavery.

[64] Harrison, *A Sermon preached at the Dissenting Chapel in Cross-Street, Manchester, March 26th, 1786*, pp. 4 and 7–8; knowledge "renders them subservient to our use, and extends the sphere of human action . . . [knowledge] is the natural road to preferment and wealth, and challenges as its right the most important stations in society" and it is "friendly to the interests of commerce, and that whilst it banishes the fears of superstition and the madness of enthusiasm."

[65] The records of the Cross Street Chapel begin in 1646 when the congregation was identified as the United Brethren. See the Records of Cross St. Chapel (no other call number), John Rylands Library, Deansgate, Manchester; see esp. f. 240 and beyond for membership. And see R. Wade, *The Rise of Nonconformity in Manchester with a Brief Sketch of the History of Cross Street Chapel* (Manchester: Johnson and Rawson, 1880); p. 26 chapel building begun in 1693.

Neither M'Connel nor Kennedy wrote much regarding religious beliefs. Both were raised in the Church of Scotland, and in this Presbyterian context they developed their concern for practical skill and social utility. Distinctively, Kennedy also learned toleration. The political sympathies of his mother appear to have been with the Catholic Pretender (the last of the Jacobite kings descended from James II exiled in 1689). As a youngster she arrived in the south-west of Scotland "in the suite of some of the Pretender's friends," and in 1784 she supported attempts to extend rights of toleration to Catholics. She taught her son: "'Always conform to the Presbyterian chapel if there is one where you are going, but remember ... [that] Catholic and all other religions are alike good if you will act up to their precepts, and they are all equally efficacious to salvation.'"[66] This liberality of spirit served Kennedy well in Manchester. There many of his colleagues and friends, including his business partner, were Unitarians.[67] His mother's expressions of tolerance and devotion enabled him to be at ease amid the heterodoxy found in the town.[68]

A similar attitude of religious toleration appears to have been instilled in the M'Connel household, and it allowed James the freedom to explore and eventually adopt anti-Trinitarian beliefs. According to M'Connel family lore, they had dissenting roots and had probably suffered repression during the seventeenth century.[69] Once settled in south-west Scotland, the family became devout members of the Scottish Kirk, and it was in this environment that M'Connel was raised. Once in Lancashire, however, he appears to have been persuaded by the Unitarian arguments of his uncle and master, David Cannon, who had also influenced others in the area. Later in life, M'Connel remembered that "[f]or these [Unitarian] views [his] ... uncle was much abused by his neighbors and fellow-townsmen."[70]

The posture of dissent, etched by the experience of intolerance, contributed to the developing self-identity of Rational Dissenters and augmented their persistent calls for the full legalization of Dissenting views, particularly anti-Trinitarianism, which until 1813 remained outlawed under the 1689 Act of Toleration. In effect, the ambiguous legal status

66 Kennedy, "Brief Memoirs," pp. 10–11.

67 For a discussion of Unitarianism in nineteenth-century Manchester, see Seed, 1982, pp. 1–25.

68 Kennedy himself does not discuss his religious affiliations during adulthood in either his memoirs or the articles he wrote for the Manchester Lit and Phil. Robert Carlson identifies Kennedy as a Quaker but does not offer evidence for this claim. R. E. Carlson, *The Liverpool and Manchester Railway Project, 1821–1831* (Newton Abbot: David & Charles, 1969), p. 50.

69 D. C. M'Connel, *Facts and Traditions Collected for a Family Record*, pp. 8, 102–5.

70 Ibid., p. 149.

of Unitarians made them outsiders without rendering them overtly hostile to the reigning political order. During the 1780s, when M'Connel turned to chapel life, a period of growth for English Unitarianism had commenced. An increasing number of Presbyterian ministers and their chapels "converted" to anti-Trinitarian beliefs.[71] Upon moving to Manchester after the completion of his apprenticeship, M'Connel fortuitously found himself in this energetic religious community that complemented a thriving commercial environment.[72] As the company he partnered with Kennedy grew and prospered, M'Connel's social activities expanded in ways common to Manchester Unitarians. He became a lifelong Whig, an improver who also became a member of the Manchester Commission on Roads and the Manchester Literary and Philosophical Society. In chapel and society, Unitarian industrialists solidified the social and cultural matrix of innovation.

The complex religious world that M'Connel and Kennedy entered had been in development since the 1770s, when it came to be led by Manchester Unitarians belonging to the congregations of Cross Street Chapel and the smaller, but more radical, Mosely Street Chapel.[73] M'Connel associated with both congregations (although he seems to have attended Mosely more regularly), and Kennedy maintained friendships and business contacts with members of each. The strong representation of Unitarians among the various cultural institutions of eighteenth- and nineteenth-century Manchester meant that medical doctors, ministers, manufacturers, merchants, engineers, and small-business artisans alike shared social spaces in which they could advance their business interests as well as discuss science and politics. M'Connel remained connected to Unitarianism for the rest of his life, eventually being buried in the grounds of the Upper Brook Street Chapel in Manchester.

As their business prospered, M'Connel and Kennedy soon found themselves among Manchester's wealthiest citizens. With this wealth came social responsibility. During the first decade of the nineteenth

71 M. R. Watts, *The Dissenters*, Vol. I, *From the Reformation to the French Revolution* (Oxford: Clarendon Press, 1986), pp. 464–71; J. Goring, "The Breakup of Old Dissent," in *The English Presbyterians: From Elizabethan Puritanism to Modern Unitarianism*, ed. Bolam *et al.* (London: George Allen & Unwin Ltd., 1968), pp. 175–218; R.K. Webb, "The Emergence of Rational Dissent," in *Enlightenment and Religion: Rational Dissent in Eighteenth-Century Britain*, ed. Knud Haakonssen (Cambridge University Press, 1996), pp. 12–41.

72 On Manchester in the latter part of the eighteenth century, see A. Thackray, "Natural Knowledge in Cultural Context: The Manchester Model," *American Historical Review*, 79, 1974, pp. 672–709.

73 On the Manchester Unitarians and their place in Manchester society and politics, see Seed, 1982, pp. 1–25.

century, both joined the Manchester Literary and Philosophical Society;[74] in 1803, they became inspectors of the Manchester Infirmary.[75] During the 1820s they donated money to and sat on the board of the Manchester Mechanics' Institute, an organization dedicated to spreading precisely the kind of knowledge employed by the partners.[76] Furthermore, Kennedy served as a commissioner on the Provisional Committee in charge of the Manchester/Liverpool railway project and as a judge in the Rainhill locomotive engine trials of 1829. M'Connel served as a commissioner on the building of roads.[77] Given the importance and authority of the positions they held, we can see that technical knowledge played two roles – it provided a means for increasing wealth, and it served as a form of cultural capital that industrialists held in common with engineers, physicians, and practicing natural philosophers.

Contacts M'Connel and Kennedy made within Manchester religious life could also translate into other social realms, for example as an entrée into the Literary and Philosophical Society. This first met in a back room of the Cross Street Chapel and included numerous prominent members of the congregation among its members.[78] Founded in 1781 by twenty-four members of Manchester's professional and religious elites, the Lit and Phil focused on art, natural philosophy, literature, and philosophy. At its founding the Society's membership included physicians, ministers (Anglican and Dissenting alike), lawyers, merchants, and manufacturers, many of whom took an active part in the literary life of the society, publishing papers and giving public lectures.[79] The published memoirs of the society include papers on natural, experimental, and moral philosophy, as well as literature, history, art, and education. Although the

[74] From time to time membership lists for the Lit and Phil appeared in the *Memoirs of the Literary and Philosophical Society of Manchester*. Dates of election are given in Vol. 6 of the Second Series (1842), but by this time only Kennedy (elected 1803) was still alive. M'Connel's name first appears in the list in Vol. 2 (1813), but we might assume that he joined the Society soon after Kennedy. James M'Connel, Jr. and his brother William were elected in 1829 and 1838 respectively. Interestingly, just before his death, Kennedy was the oldest living member of the Society. Fairbairn, 1861, p. 10.

[75] MCK/2/1/8/3 Printed circular from J. B. Stedman, secretary to the Board of the Manchester Infirmary and Lunatic Hospital, November 19, 1803.

[76] D. C. M'Connel, *Facts and Traditions Collected for a Family Record*, p. 148. Also see the lists of board members printed in the annual Report of the Directors of the Manchester Mechanics' Institution.

[77] For Kennedy's involvement in the Manchester/Liverpool railway, see Carlson, 1969, pp. 50, 62, 218–19.

[78] W. V. Farrar, *Chemistry and the Chemical Industry in the 19th Century: The Henrys of Manchester and Other Studies*, ed. R. L. Hills and W. H. Brock (Aldershot: Variorum, 1997), Vol. I, pp. 187–91.

[79] For the Society's membership between 1781 and 1852, see Thackray, 1974, table on p. 695.

"useful arts" were considered preeminent among the society's interests from the start, it was several years before topics related to manufacturing and technology stood with equal stature to the liberal arts. While the early, published memoirs primarily represented the interests of local religious figures and physicians, later volumes included the work of engineers, merchants, and industrialist/manufacturers such as Peter Ewart, a member of the Mosely Street Chapel, who presented on the mathematics of motion.[80] Out of the society sprang a College of Arts and Sciences. It lasted only a year or two but became something of a precursor for the Dissenting academy that opened in 1786, supported and operated by local Unitarians. Only after protest from non-Unitarian members of the nonsectarian Lit and Phil was the academy declared wholly independent of the society.[81]

Of the two partners, John Kennedy made the most out of his connections to the Lit and Phil. Between 1815 and 1830 Kennedy read at least four papers to the society, all of which were published in the society's proceedings. In them Kennedy addressed themes that had become central to industrial life: the development of the cotton industry; the effects that machinery was having on the working classes; the social consequences of the poor laws; innovations in cotton machinery and the economic implications of the exportation of British-made machinery to the Continent.[82] For the most part, Kennedy's intellectual development closely followed positions staked out by Manchester's liberal industrialists. For him, innovations in cotton machinery drove the growth of the industry and represented the diligent and creative work of its practitioners. Diligence and application also reflected the moral health of the new industrial class. Indeed, he argued that the rapid growth of industry in Lancashire was "chiefly to be ascribed to the great ingenuity and the persevering, skillful, laborious disposition of the people." "In these qualities," he continued,

80 E. Hodgkinson, "Some Account of the Late Mr. Ewart's Paper on the Measure of Moving Forces; and on the Recent Applications of the Principles of Living Forces to Estimate the Effects of Machines and Movers," *Memoirs of the Literary and Philosophical Society of Manchester*, Second Series, 7, 1846, pp. 137–56.

81 On the College of Arts and Sciences, see T. Barnes' articles in the first two volumes of the *Memoirs*. On the relationship between the Lit and Phil and the Dissenting academy known as Manchester College (now called Harris Manchester College, Oxford), see J. Raymond and J. V. Pickstone, "The Natural Sciences and the Learning of the English Unitarians," in *Truth, Liberty, Religion: Essays Celebrating Two Hundred Years of Manchester College*, ed. Barbara Smith (Oxford: Manchester College Oxford, 1986), pp. 127–64, 134–5.

82 In 1849 these four papers were collected and published as *Miscellaneous Papers on Subjects Connected with the Manufactures of Lancashire*. Several were also published as individual pamphlets. A fifth paper was not delivered at the Lit and Phil but was published separately: J. Kennedy, *On the Exportation of Machinery: A Letter Addressed to the Hon. E.G. Stanley, M.P.* (London: Longman, Hurst & Co. *et al.*, 1824).

"I believe they surpass the inhabitants of every other part of this island, or of the whole world."[83]

The Literary and Philosophical Society, and its offshoot, the Mechanics' Institute, offered both education and business opportunities. Within a few decades of their founding, they were places where industrialists could think globally and approach visiting imperial agents of the Crown, in one instance, for information about the market in China for locally produced cotton garments. With supreme self-confidence, Manchester manufacturers asked only for samples of Chinese garments, saying, in effect, that if we only know what they want then we will imitate their styles on our steam-powered looms.[84]

Armed with wealth, scientific knowledge, a conviction of one's social virtue, and the omnipresent signs of industrial progress, cotton barons became emboldened. In the wake of his success, John Kennedy, now a Liberal ideologue, defended the new factory system from its critics. "The frequent complaints, both in public and private, against the manufacturing system, certainly demand an impartial investigation," Kennedy declared in a paper read before the Lit and Phil in 1815, "and none are more called upon to take a part in such discussions than those who are interested in manufactures."[85] Kennedy argued that far from contributing to the deterioration of morals, the creation of large factories and regular work hours had "good effects on the habits of the people. Being obliged to be more regular in their attendance at their work, they became more orderly in their conduct, spent less time at the alehouse, and lived better at home. For some years they have been gradually improving in their domestic comforts and conveniences."[86] This public defense of industry paralleled concerns that M'Connel and Kennedy expressed in their business correspondence.[87] Robert Peel's attempts to investigate and regulate the conditions of workers in factories, for example, came under strong opposition from manufacturers such as M'Connel and Kennedy, who considered Peel's efforts "a very dangerous interference" and liable to have "consequences [that] may be very injurious to all large

[83] J. Kennedy, *Observations on the Rise and Progress of the Cotton Trade in Great Britain, Particularly in Lancashire and the Adjoining Counties* (Manchester: The Executors of the Late S. Russell, 1818), p. 20.

[84] UCLA, MSS Collection #722, the papers of John Bowring, Box 1, January 8, 1854, letter of Christopher Cross, describing Bowring's visit to Manchester. A consul in China, Bowring was speaking on conditions there.

[85] Kennedy, 1818, p. 3. [86] Ibid., pp. 17–18.

[87] See, in particular, M'Connel and Kennedy to John Bell & Co., Belfast, February 13, 1816 and March 29, 1816; M'Connel and Kennedy to Robert McGavind & Co., March 28, 1816; M'Connel and Kennedy to W. Sangford, May 23, 1816. MCK/2/2/5 Letters Sent.

Manufacturers of every description."[88] The Unitarian emphasis on personal freedom could cut in decidedly self-serving ways.

Participation in the Lit and Phil offered Kennedy opportunities to celebrate the new industry as well as defend it. Kennedy's memoir on the inventor and cotton spinner Samuel Crompton highlighted the spirit of technical ingenuity even as it sought to underscore the difficult financial and social situations in which inventors sometimes found themselves.[89] Crompton's spinning mule had integrated the processes of Hargreaves' spinning jenny and Arkwright's water frame, and thereby made it possible to spin dozens of spindles of cotton thread simultaneously. Subsequent improvements to the machine increased the number of spindles into the hundreds.[90] According to Kennedy's account, Crompton's eventual descent into poverty toward the end of his life was the tragic outcome of family problems and his unwillingness to pursue the development of his own inventions for personal profit. Thanks to the charitable efforts of Kennedy and other friends and neighbors, funds were raised to provide Crompton and his daughter with a life annuity that gave them an income on which to live.[91]

The Mechanics' Institute

For cotton masters such as M'Connel and Kennedy, membership in the Manchester Literary and Philosophical Society translated into politeness, gentility, and charity – all impulses that led in 1825 to the founding and operation of the Manchester Mechanics' Institute.[92] In addition to making substantial donations of around £600, both partners sat on the Institute's board of directors, which made decisions regarding Institute buildings, the purchase of experimental apparatus, the setting of the curriculum, and the hiring of tutors and lecturers.[93] A highly ambitious project, the Manchester Mechanics' Institute ran an elementary school for reading, writing, and arithmetic, and offered numerous lectures and courses devoted to topics in mechanics, chemistry, natural history, mechanical and architectural drawing, and geography. By appealing to

88 M'Connel and Kennedy to John Bell & Co., February 13, 1816.

89 John Kennedy, 1830. 90 Kennedy, 1830, pp. 10–18.

91 Kennedy, 1830, pp. 8–9.

92 For a general account of the Mechanics' Institutes in Britain, see I. Inkster, "The Social Context of an Educational Movement: A Revisionist Approach to the English Mechanics' Institutes, 1820–1850," in *Scientific Culture and Urbanisation in Industrialising Britain* (Aldershot: Ashgate, Variorum, 1997).

93 On M'Connel's monetary donation, see D. C. M'Connel, *Facts and Traditions Collected for a Family Record*, p. 148.

both the working and middle classes the Institute provided an important means for popularizing science and encouraging specialized knowledge among factory employees. Even when it was not the focus of a course as a whole, practical knowledge stood out as a major component of the curriculum. As stated in its published rules, the Institute's established goal was to enable "Mechanics and Artisans, of whatever trade they may be, to become acquainted with such branches of science as are of practical application in the exercise of that trade; that they may possess a more thorough knowledge of their business, acquire a greater degree of skill in the practice of it, and be qualified to make improvements and even new inventions in the Arts which they respectively profess."[94] As we shall see in the next chapter, the scientific learning found in Leeds in the same period enabled "mechanics and artisans" to become industrialists.

In the lecture courses on mechanics offered by the Manchester Institute, the lecturers covered the design and operation of gears (particularly with respect to their use in mills), the design of their teeth, their operation in couplings and governors, and their utility for equalizing motion. Other lectures dealt with the concept and application of force, wind and water mills, and steam engines.[95] In subsequent years the Institute offered courses and lectures ranging from Mr. Adcock's lectures on the "Elements of Mechanism, as applied more especially to the Construction of Steam Engines," Mr. Hewitt's eleven lectures on the "Geography of British India, China, Central Asia, Turkey, Egypt, Arabia, Isles of the Indian Ocean and Northern Regions," Mr. Sweetlove's "Philosophy of the atmosphere," Mr. Bally's course on "Plaster & Wax casting, modeling, etc.," to Mr. White's "Power-loom weaving."[96]

For M'Connel and Kennedy, and other prominent cotton and steam industrialists such as William Fairbairn and Peter Ewart, who also sat on the board of directors, the educational mission of the Institute rested on the importance they themselves had come to ascribe to mechanical knowledge and formal learning. In effect, the Institute also elevated the status of practical knowledge to that of natural science in general, both by including topics of practical importance in courses on natural science and by offering independent courses devoted to practical skills such as mechanical drawing and machine operation. The way M'Connel and Kennedy outfitted their own minds became a hallowed truth: technical and scientific

[94] Report of the Directors of the Manchester Mechanics' Institution, May 1828, with the Rules and Regulations of the Institution (Manchester: printed by R. Robinson, St. Ann's Place, 1828), p. 23.

[95] Report of the Directors (1828), p. 9.

[96] See, for instance, the reports for 1828 and 1834.

knowledge were mutually supporting and intertwined. Early in the nineteenth century Manchester Grammar School (in effect a high school) appointed the natural philosopher and leader in the Lit and Phil, John Dalton, to teach Newtonian science, mathematics, and the constitution of mixed gases, steam, and vapor.[97]

Although the degree of success varied widely from one Mechanics' Institute to another around the country, the Manchester one proved to be a resounding success for several decades, in large part because it attracted the participation of workers and manufacturers alike. To the working class it offered an opportunity to improve basic skills through the knowledge of "scientific principles," and to the industrialist it offered another opportunity to gain visibility as cultural and civic leaders. Neither was intended to change the social or economic place of workers. Yet technical learning offered mobility, as Kennedy and M'Connel would have been the first to tell them.

We have known for some time that scientific thought in early industrial settings could validate social status, and in that sense its social uses could be as important as its technical ones.[98] The lives of M'Connel and Kennedy tell us more than that: they also highlight the cultural and intellectual dimension in the story of early British industrialization. In essence, they demonstrate that both scientific and technical knowledge informed business and social relationships. At first the knowledge provided a common language that made possible the interaction of manufacturers and engine builders, who could then build and use machines of increasing sophistication and complexity. The knowledge also provided the veneer of gentility necessary so that manufacturers could meet with other professionals – especially medical men and religious leaders – who had risen to a significant place in elite society. Early British industrial development attains greater nuance and sophistication when technical knowledge, set in its social and applied milieu, becomes part of the story.

[97] For a similar conclusion, see R. Thomson, *Structures of Change*, pp. 182–3. On Fairbairn and his understanding of the technical knowledge needed to be a successful millwright, see J. Mokyr, "Entrepreneurship and the Industrial Revolution in Britain," in *The Invention of Enterprise: Entrepreneurship from Ancient Mesopotamia to Modern Times*, ed. D. S. Landes, J. Mokyr, and W. J. Baumol (Princeton University Press, 2010), p. 203n. And see A. A. Munford, *The Manchester Grammar School, 1515–1915: A Regional Study of the Advancement of Learning in Manchester since the Reformation* (London: Longmans and Green, 1919), p. 246. For Dalton on steam, see J. Dalton, *Experimental Essays. On the Constitution of mixed Gases; and the Force of Steam or Vapour from Water and other Liquids in different temperatures . . . read to Manchester Literary and Philosophical Society, October 2, 16, 20, 1801* (*Memoirs*, 1802).

[98] See the argument by Thackray, note 72.

4 Textiles in Leeds

Mechanical science on the factory floor

We think of mechanization in the early nineteenth century and we think cotton; we also need to think textiles. When considering the application of mechanics, pneumatics, and hydrostatics, we turn to steam engines in cotton factories, or engineering plans for canals or the dredging of harbors, or the raising of water from North Country coal mines or London's Thames.[1] We also associate all those applications of power technology with the scientific culture and experimental habits that took root in eighteenth-century Britain. We can also witness scientifically informed, factory-based experimentation being taken up in the woolen and linen industries.

The lives of textile industrialists, rather like M'Connel and Kennedy in cotton, allow us to document the debt early manufacturers in linen and woolen cloth owed to mechanical science and chemistry. Where new machines and new applications of existing machines became the goal, science and technology were closely intermingled, not hierarchically but

[1] This chapter was made possible by grant #RZ-50395–05 from the NEH for collaborative research on "The First Generation of British Industrialists: Scientific Culture and Civic Life, 1780–1832." See also Musson and Robinson, 1969; and note, "The associations of intellect and of technique were more widespread in 1851 than often thought, and acted as a solid base to the Great Exhibition of that year and to the subsequent twenty years of Golden Age machinofacture." Quoting from Ian Inkster, found in his edited volume, with Griffin *et al.*, *The Golden Age: Essays in British Social and Economic History, 1850–1870* (Aldershot: Ashgate, 2000), p. 171. See also Jacob and Stewart, 2004; L. Stewart, "A Meaning for Machines: Modernity, Utility, and the Eighteenth-Century British Public," *Journal of Modern History*, 70, June 1998, pp. 259–94; and L. Stewart, "The Boast of Matthew Boulton: Invention, Innovation and Projectors in the Industrial Revolution," *Economia e energia secc. XIII–XVIII.* Istituto Internazionale di Storia Economica "F. Datini" (Prato: Le Monnier, 2003), pp. 993–1010; in addition M. Jacob and D. Reid, "Technical Knowledge and the Mental Universe of Early Cotton Manufacturers, 1800–1830," *Canadian Journal of History*, 37, 2001, pp. 283–304; translated as "Culture et culture technique des premiers fabricants de coton de Manchester," *Revue d'Histoire Moderne et Contemporaine*, 50, avril–juin, 2003, pp. 133–55. The argument presented here builds upon Jacob, 1987, and 1997. Endorsing and vastly expanding on these arguments is Mokyr, 2002, p. 66. Note in *Happy Chance*, Jack Goldstone makes a similar argument. And see J. Horn, "Machine-breaking in England and France during the Age of Revolution," *Labour/Le Travail*, 55, spring 2005, pp. 143–66. And *The Path Not Taken: French Industrialization in the Age of Revolution, 1750–1830* (Cambridge, MA: MIT Press, 2006).

dynamically, never one and the same thing, but never far apart.[2] We may even describe the textile entrepreneurs as "hybrid savant-technologists."[3] By 1800 they and their Yorkshire factories provide yet another example of a distinctive form of scientific culture, sometimes called "techno-science," present far earlier than the twentieth-century associations of the term would suggest. In the critical first generation of mechanization that began in the 1780s, linen and wool manufacturers in Leeds – like their counterparts in Manchester cotton – deployed scientific knowledge of a mechanical sort, and chemistry, to assist in the invention of new industrial processes and forms of industrial life.[4]

Neither the technology nor the science should be imagined as reducible one to the other. Sometimes theories and calculations were invoked, other times innovative making and doing with machines consumed time and labor.[5] Yet, distinctively, science in the form of Newtonian mechanics (as well as the new chemistry) received application on the factory floor, and its theories and methods, both experimental and mathematical, were applied *inter alia* to bobbins, to the weight, friction, and velocity of wheels, to the

2 R. Laudan, "Natural Alliance or Forced Marriage? Changing Relations between the Histories of Science and Technology," *Technology and Culture*, 36, 2, Supplement, 1995, pp. S19–22, and I would endorse her conclusion that "it is now generally accepted that there is something distinctive about technological knowledge and that it is neither irremediably tacit nor simply applied science."

3 I am borrowing this useful phrase from Ursula Klein, "Techno-science avant la lettre," *Perspectives on Science*, 13, 2005, p. 228.

4 In the period from 1780 to 1800 new professions appeared for the first time in the town: cotton and fustian manufacturers, flax and worsted spinners, printers on cloth, machine makers, pattern makers, and potters; see W. G. Rimmer, "The Industrial Profile of Leeds, 1740–1840," *Publications of the Thoresby Society, Miscellany*, 14, part 2, 1967, p. 135. The Brotherton Library Special Collections, MS 18, notes made by W. Lindley on a "number of steam engines engaged in the different branches of manufacture in Leeds and its immediate vicinity," March 1824, describe engines (37) in the production of wool cloth, flax spinning (23), stuff manufacture (2), cotton (2), dyeing (25), crushing seed (12), machine making (14), manufacturing tobacco, paper making, potteries. See also P. M. Litton, 2003, p. 3, where a water wheel is used to move a hammer in Sheffield; p. 4 to dye blue woolen cloth at Wakefield, "most of the moveable apparatus is conducted by steam"; pp. 5–6 for an extensive description of the Wormald and Gott factory where the steam engine "is the great moving power in this extensive factory" that employed machines to mix the wool with oil, to spin thread by steam-driven machines (she claims that one man can do the work of eighty); fulling "is very simple: the cloth is merely put into a wooden trough, to which two heavy wooden hammers are attached, that just fit into it, and each hammer works . . . all the vats for dyeing the cloth are boiled by steam, which save much expense and labor." In Leeds (p. 13), she sees coal carriages moved by steam; p. 16 on woolen cloth dressed by machinery moved by steam.

5 W. Lefèvre, "Science as Labor," *Perspectives on Science*, 13, 2005, pp. 194–225, has some useful things to say about the relationship but his vision generally concerns nineteenth- and twentieth-century forms of techno-science. Writing in the same issue, Barry Barnes offers a useful discussion of the various meanings given to the term, "Elusive Memories of Techno-science," pp. 156–7.

gravity, elasticity, and combustibility of atmospheric air.[6] All this occurred before anyone had figured out exactly how to weave linen or wool by applying steam power.

The generation of the 1780s to the 1820s proved economically decisive in cities such as Leeds, Manchester, and Birmingham.[7] By the 1790s the front-runners in the industrial race knew that what they were experiencing

[6] The Brotherton Library, Leeds, Marshall MSS, MS200/42, contains this note: "Leslie on Heat 8 vol. 1804 communicate to air 1/750 part of the whole heat which it contains, & it will expand 1/250 part of its bulk; MS 200/57 Notebook c. 1790, f. 1, Steam Engine – gives a list of engines at work in the region with all of their specifics and continued on f. 27 . . . undated, including some engines in Manchester, f. 2 Wrigley says there is nothing gained by a crank instead of a water wheel because of the great weight they are obliged to use at the beam end. G.W. says the Boulton and Watt's crank engines are the only ones that will produce a motion sufficiently regular for spinning." This note undated but the one below it using a different pen is 1812; f. 17 labeled Speed "the greatest speed at which they can spin cotton is 15ft a min. or 12 feet a min the day through including stoppages." f. 23 entitled Boiler, "Wrigley says it should be 4 times diameter of cylinder," dated 1804; ff. 24–5 dated 1795 with these initials given "M.M. The teeth of two wheels working together must necessarily rub against one another over so much space as the difference of length of two radii meeting at the center of action of the two wheels & of two radii meeting at the thickness of a tooth from the center of action, which is the place where the teeth first begin to act. Consequently the finer the pitch & the less friction there will be upon the teeth. The best form of the teeth of wheels is that which is the strongest & at the same time admits no tooth to come into contact but that which is in action. The form of the tooth is therefore determined by the relative diameters of the wheels which are to work together. To find the true form of the teeth of two wheels of equal diameters draw the pitch line at half the depth of the teeth, & setting one leg of your compasses on the pitch line in the middle of one tooth draw the point of the next tooth with the other leg;" ff. 34–5 Bobbin "the relative length & diameter of a bobbin must be so proportioned that it will always be the same weight in proportion to the lever at which the thread is acting . . . the central force is increased as the square of the velocities, & the weight of the bobbin is increased to counteract the increased central force of the thread. In the latter case of reducing the diameter of the bobbin the stress upon the yarn would be the same as before at a velocity of 2000 revs. Because the central force & weight of bobbin would both continue the same, & the power required for giving motion to the spindle would continue the same. The central force being likewise in proportion to the quantity of matter, a bobbin of the size above described which would not spin 16 lea yarn at a greater velocity than 2000 revs. Would spin 36 lea yarn at a velocity of 3000 revs. A min. In that case the 36 lea ought to be of equal strength with the 16 lea, otherwise it would break the oftener;" f. 38 Wheels continued from f. 24, "Perhaps the best general rule for the depth of teeth is to make the depth of the acting part 3/4 of the pitch;" f. 38 on strength of wheels "Rule The square of the thickness of the tooth multiplied by its breadth will give the number of horse power that the wheel is adequate to work, if it move at a velocity of its surface of 2 ½ [?] feet p. second of time. If the velocity is greater or less, the power is proportionate – The best breadth of a tooth is six times its thickness." See Marshall MS 200/57, ff. 24–5 "Theory of Wheels." All Marshall manuscripts are at The Brotherton. See the British electronic archives, www.nationalarchives.gov.uk/a2a/records.aspx?cat=206-ms200&cid=41#41 where the incorrect date of 1750 still appears.

[7] H. Barker, "'Smoke Cities': Northern Industrial Towns in Late Georgian England," *Urban History*, 31, 2, 2004, pp. 175–276; and for the political spokesman for this rising industrial class in Leeds, see D. Thornton, "Edward Baines, Senior (1774–1848), Provincial Journalism and Political Philosophy in Early-Nineteenth-Century England," *Northern History*, 40, September 2003, pp. 277–97.

Figure 9 The Aire and Calder at Leeds, West Yorkshire, c. 1830

was unique and commented upon it extensively.[8] Leeds, with its canal to Liverpool, stood at the center of a North Country district experiencing rapid industrial development. The extant archives demonstrate the intellectual underpinnings of those economic developments at work among leading textile manufacturers who became central to Leeds' own, and marked, economic development. It was not the place, or the time, where we expect to find industrialists possessed of expanded knowledge about the physical processes fundamental to power technology.[9]

Both Leeds and Manchester, in the same period, reveal a remarkably similar scientific culture. The similarity lies not simply in the economic ingenuity evinced by manufacturers as they adapted power technology to their particular manufacturing needs, but also in the technical and

[8] Boulton and Watt MSS, BCL, Series I Part 3 for extensive lists of steam engines being installed in the county of York from the 1780s onward, P6; consider Series I, Part 7, Box 322, Reel 97, #79, Boulton in Leeds writing to Watt in Birmingham, April 24, 1802: "At Manchester the increase of Mills and Dwelling Houses is beyond all former times, not less than 8 to 10 thousand in the last two years. Everywhere full employment and great plenty. Hull is increasing rapidly, where they are beginning a new Dock. At York I do not observe the smallest change."

[9] For a good overview of the period, see E. J. Connell and M. Ward, "Industrial Development, 1780–1914," in Derek Fraser, ed., *A History of Modern Leeds* (Manchester University Press, 1980).

scientific knowledge base commonly possessed and facilitating adaptation. Textile manufacturers learned lessons from textbooks and lectures in natural philosophy – they learned science often cast in an applied direction – then they did something not often attempted by the scientific lecturers or writers, they approached their own factory floor with new manipulations of the machines and with new conceptual tools. In the process they adapted both to the particular needs of their industry.

The application of power technology, most dramatically in the form of the steam engine, led entrepreneurs to favor the factory as the most accommodating place for manufacturing, soon to be imitated by all competitors.[10] The mechanical knowledge was not simply grafted on to an existing set of social and economic conditions. It shaped those conditions – expensive engines made factories all the more necessary – just as the content and form of the discipline of mechanics became increasingly applied, routinized, and expanded upon in factory after factory.

By the 1830s the knowledge once promoted by natural philosophical lecturers and Newtonian textbooks would become the possession of the ubiquitous engineers who, for example in Leeds alone, by 1824 had installed 129 steam engines that, according to a contemporary witness, generated at least 2,318 units of hp.[11] Steam power could assist first in spinning (but not weaving) threads and its boiler used for a stage in the dyeing process. Wool could also be dressed by steam-driven machines.[12] By the 1830s the weavers and fullers who aspired to become overseers of engines, or mill owners themselves, came to see that the manufacturing world of the West Riding had been transformed by a mechanical knowledge that they, too, needed to possess.

[10] BCL, Boulton and Watt Papers, Box 322 Series 1, Part 7, Reel 97, Boulton to Watt, Leeds, January 28, 1794: "From the general success of Mess. Wormald & Co's great Engine – I have no doubt of several others being wanted here if business mends on a similar plan as they are endeavouring to manufacture from the wool to finished cloth in the one building – which has not yet been done to any great extent. It caused a great bustle among the cloth makers who wish if possible to prevent it as they say merchants is becoming manufacturers. The cloth makers are a large body of men who all bring their cloth to a common hall for sale – each cloth maker has workmen of their own and they in general have the wool [?] (i.e. carded) at one place, spun at the other . . . it is not the working men who are so much set against it as their masters."

[11] Leeds University, The Brotherton Library, Special Collections, MS 18, "Number of steam engines engaged in the different branches of manufacture in Leeds and its immediate vicinity, from a survey of them made by W. Lindley in March 1824." In 1851, at the Great Exhibition, Leeds sent 134 exhibitors, led only by Manchester with 191, and Birmingham put forward a huge 230.

[12] Litton, 2003, p. 16. The dressing involved drawing out any loose fibers from the cloth with teasles, a process that also raised the nap.

By that decade the publican James Kitson gives valuable evidence of what needed to be learned, in his case at a local Mechanics' Institute. He described what he did not know – before he attended the institute in Leeds – in the following terms: "I had obtained an ordinary day school education, as knowledge of the simple rules of arithmetic, but was completely ignorant of the simplest parts of philosophy. I knew that steam caused the steam engine to work, but I did not know how or why; I knew that the pump caused water to rise out of a well, but I also believed that it was through the agency of suction, and I thought its power was unlimited as to extent."[13] Through education, Kitson acquired a detailed knowledge of steam and mechanics in general, and went on to become a prosperous engineer and a political reformer in the Whig tradition. The libraries and technical apparatus owned by the Mechanics' Institutes attest to the importance awarded to learning mechanics and observing steam engines, air pumps, and, by the 1830s, electrical devices.[14]

Opponents of the new machinery sensed what they were up against. They described technology as critical, that the effort "to convert our wool into cloth . . . by mechanical contrivances, without the intervention of human labor" had become "a race amongst individuals." The private greed of industrialists put "the public good . . . out of the question. It is in reality, each one striving against the rest, by every possible means, to draw to himself a large proportion of the business . . . mechanical contrivances [are employed to accomplish this]; every one endeavouring to carry them farther than another for his own particular advantage."[15] By 1800 critics and entrepreneurs alike knew that more efficient machines were vital to economic success, that speed and efficiency equaled time and labor saved, profit earned. Perhaps their enemies did not know about the effort soon-to-be-wealthy technologists also spent studying mechanical science.

[13] Quoted in R.J. Morris, "The Rise of James Kitson: Trades Union and Mechanics Institution, Leeds, 1826–1851," *Publications of the Thoresby Society*, 15, 1972, pp. 185–6. See the original in F. Hill, *National Education: Its Present State and Prospects* Vol. 2, (London, 1836), pp. 220–1.

[14] See The Tenth Report of the Keighley Mechanics' Institution, for the year ending April 4, 1836 with a list of the members, a catalogue of the books and apparatus (Keighley: R. Aken, 1836); this printed catalogue turns up in The Brotherton Library, Leeds University, Special Collections, Marriner MS 65/1. The institute was founded in 1825 and at times struggled.

[15] [Anon], *Observations on Woollen Machinery* (Leeds: Edward Baines, 1803), p. 4; reproduced in *The Spread of Machinery: Five Pamphlets. 1793–1806* (New York: Arno Press, 1972).

The Marshalls

The engines deployed most notably by the Leeds manufacturers, John Marshall in flax and Benjamin Gott in wool, operated machinery involved in nearly every other aspect of the process by which both fibers were readied for weaving, or dyed or processed, once woven. As a consequence they became the wealthiest and most influential cloth makers in the town.[16] What they knew about mechanization, and applied in their factories, laid down a template for others to emulate or envy. Gradually they became civic and political leaders. By the 1830s power shifted away from the landed gentry and toward men like John Marshall who took their seats in Parliament. At his death in 1840 he was worth well over £2 million. He had built multiple flax-spinning mills, acquired a country estate, and, fortuitously for us, saved multiple notebooks that document his participation in the scientific culture of the late eighteenth and early nineteenth centuries and its application in the mechanization of his factories.

No one carried the mechanical contrivances for their own advantage – to paraphrase their critics – further than John Marshall and Benjamin Gott. In the 1790s both installed 40-hp Boulton and Watt engines in their factories, and by 1824 Marshall's various flax mills used five or more engines, with the largest producing 71 hp and made by his associates, Fenton & Co. Did he understand how these engines worked? From detailed notes taken by him at the time, we know that in 1790, at a large room in Hodgson's Academy, in Upper Head Row in Leeds, Marshall attended a set of fifteen lectures given by the itinerant scientific lecturer, Mr. Booth.[17] These dwelt extensively on mechanics, hydrostatics, pneumatics, chemistry, astronomy, optics, electricity, pumps, and, as we know

[16] Marshall's rise is ably chronicled in W. G. Rimmer, *Marshalls of Leeds, Flax-Spinners 1788–1886* (Cambridge University Press, 1960); and see H. Heaton, "Benjamin Gott and the Industrial Revolution in Yorkshire," *The Economic History Review*, 3, 1931–2, pp. 52–3. Rimmer did not see the linkage between the natural philosophical and chemical work undertaken by Marshall and his industrial practices; he also missed the date of the important 1790 notebook. The electronic version of the guide simply picks up the typing error in the original. For the complete Marshall manuscripts see http://industrialization.ats.ucla.edu/.

[17] *The Leeds Intelligencer*, 38, 1894, December 14, 1790 tells us that "Booth's course of lectures on natural and experimental philosophy, astronomy, chemistry ... illustrated by ... apparatus, which has cost upwards of four thousand pounds" will consist of fifteen lectures at the cost of one guinea, three lectures a week, will begin if forty subscribers can be found ... claims his apparatus weighs up to 7 tons ... he can only give one course as he has obligations in Birmingham ... subscriptions can be had from him or at the bookstore of Mr. Binns. There was a John Booth who also lectured in Yorkshire in this period but there is no evidence that he was a follower of Priestley, nor did he announce or advertise any lectures at precisely the time when Marshall attended them.

from Marshall's lecture notes, one was devoted entirely to the steam engine and other devices.[18]

Given the content of the chemical lectures, we can with reasonable confidence identify Mr. Booth as loosely a follower of Priestley's phlogiston theory. A "Mr. Booth" is mentioned in a letter of 1783 to Joseph Priestley where it is said that he is seeking a recommendation. This is most probably Benjamin Booth, a scientific lecturer of the period who was involved in the circles of the 1790s associated with support for the French Revolution.[19] The association of radicals and scientific circles was a commonplace of the time. Of course, from 1767 to 1773 Priestley was the minister at Mill Hill Chapel in Leeds, a Unitarian establishment that the young Marshall (b. 1762) attended.[20] We can only wonder if Priestley, by 1790 relocated to Birmingham, might have urged Booth to tackle Leeds, or recommended him to members of his old congregation. Perhaps someone from the Gott family was also present at his lectures as the family can be associated with such interests. One John Gott (d. 1793) – possibly related – appears on a membership list of a London dining club of engineers who from 1771 met around John Smeaton. Benjamin Gott's half-brother, William, left behind a notebook filled with engineering terms and their definitions. The Gotts, like the Watts, had scientific knowledge in the family.[21]

When advertising his upcoming lectures in the *Leeds Intelligencer* for December 1790, Booth claimed that he had invested more than

18 Marshall MSS, MS 200/42, "Philosophical Lectures and Extracts," Booth's Philosophical Lectures, December 1790, Lecture 14 Miscellany, "Some particulars relating to various subjects which were before omitted. Water Wheels Steam Engines."

19 See E. Robinson, "An English Jacobin: James Watt, Junior, 1769–1848," *Cambridge Historical Journal*, 11, 3, 1955, pp. 354–5, which mentions that Benjamin Booth, science lecturer, was also brought up on charges of sedition, as was Thomas Walker in 1792–3; Booth was later released.

20 *Analytical Proceedings*, December 1991, 28 p. 403, in article entitled "The Lunar Society and Midland Chemists" by D. Thorburn Burns, cites a letter by John Wyatt, London agent for Matthew Boulton, which notes in passing: "Mr. Booth applied to Mr. Parker from recommendation of Dr. Priestley." He in turn is citing an article by Eric Robinson on The Lunar Society that appeared in *Annals of Science*, 1957, 13, p. 1. On the family's association with Mill Hill, see Rimmer, 1960, p. 14. For background on this Unitarian link to science, see J. Raymond and J. V. Pickstone, "The Natural Sciences and the Learning of the English Unitarians," in B. Smith, ed., *Truth, Liberty, Religion: Essays Celebrating Two Hundred Years of Manchester College* (Oxford: Manchester College Oxford, 1986), pp. 127–64, 134–5. On Priestley in Leeds, see R. E. Schofield, *The Enlightenment of Joseph Priestley: A Study of His Life and Work from 1733 to 1773* (University Park, PA: The Pennsylvania State University Press, 1997), Chapters 7 to 11.

21 The Institution of Civil Engineers, London, MS Society of Civil Engineers, Treasurer's minutes and accounts, 1793–1821, meeting record of "Smeatonians"; and The Brotherton Library, Leeds University, Special Collections, MS 194/14. See also Jacob, 1997, Chapter 5.

£4,000 in his demonstration equipment and that, in aggregate, it weighed over 7 tons.[22] Even allowing for exaggeration, this was a formidable arsenal that must have included air pumps and orreries, levers, pulleys, hydrometers, electrical devices, and – here I am going to hypothesize – possibly a small steam engine, or its replica. Perhaps only something quite that big would have given Mr. Booth such substantial tonnage, even if it were exaggerated. We know that demonstration replicas existed because early in the next century instrument makers listed them in their catalogues, and two decades before Booth lectured, John Smeaton informed James Watt that he had gone home and built one so as to test out Watt's claims about the energy that his engine could deliver.[23] Detailed printed lectures on mechanics in this period also employed engravings that depicted all the parts of the engine.[24] In 1799, Adam Walker's natural philosophical lectures included a list of the machinery found in his Winter Lecture Room, in Conduit Street, Hanover Square, London, and it included "Boulton, Blakey, Smeaton's and the common fire or steam engine." He claimed that they could not be removed because of their size, and they were used to illustrate the lecture on mechanics.[25]

The possibility that Booth also displayed demonstration engines takes on additional plausibility when he tells the forty subscribers he seeks to enroll (at the cost of one guinea each) that he can give only one course of

[22] *The Leeds Intelligencer*, 38, December 14, 1790. This Mr. Booth would seem to be the same Benjamin Booth, possibly mislabeled as "a labourer" in J. Barrell, *Imagining the King's Death: Figurative Treason, Fantasies of Regicide 1793–96* (Oxford University Press, 2000), pp. 171–9. Booth, like his brother Charles, attended Manchester Grammar School.

[23] BCL, James Watt MSS, Smeaton to Boulton and Watt, February 5, 1778. Consider "A small working model of a steam-engine all in brass . . . £23 2s. 0d" and "A Complete copy of Boulton & Watts most improved engine with the boiler and apparatus complete," £100, found in *A Catalogue of Optical, Mathematical, and Philosophical Instruments*, made and sold by W. and S. Jones, Lower Holborn, London, 1837, p. 13; in BL copy bound with C. H. Wilkinson, *An Analysis of a Course of Lectures on the Principles of Natural Philosophy*, London, 1799. There is some suggestion that as early as the 1730s Desaguliers was building models at home; see L. Stewart, *The Rise of Public Science: Rhetoric, Technology, and Natural Philosophy in Newtonian Britain, 1660–1750* (Cambridge University Press, 1992), p. 229.

[24] T. Young, *A Course of Lectures on Natural Philosophy and the Mechanical Arts* (London: Joseph Johnson, 1807), plate 24.

[25] A. Walker, *Analysis of a Course of Lectures in Natural and Experimental Philosophy*, 11th edn. (London: William Thorne, [1799]). F. Hardie tells us that he, too, had apparatus at his experimental philosophic lecture room that could be seen for a shilling; F. Hardie, *Syllabus of a Course of Lectures . . . at his Experimental Philosophic Lecture Room and Theatre of Rational Amusement, Pantheon, Oxford St., London* (London: W. Burton, [1800]), statement from the title page. The advertisement on the back page for Adam Walker's lectures in March says that he will devote one lecture to hydrostatics and hydraulics, with the Boulton and Watt engine figuring prominently.

lectures in Leeds because he has obligations in Birmingham.[26] Although not, as far as we know, a member of the Lunar Society, Booth would seem to belong on its fringes.

By dwelling in some detail on Booth's lectures, as filtered through the notations made by Marshall, we can get closer to the scientific way of thinking that cloth entrepreneurs could imbibe. They augmented their knowledge by reading in scientific literature, and Marshall left his reading notes in the same notebook where he recorded Booth's lectures. Before turning to Marshall's detailed discussions of the many "experiments" – to use his word – which he undertook on his factory equipment and in dyeing – experiments that began in the late 1780s and continued into the next generation of Marshalls, who inherited the mills – we want to know what Marshall learned on those wintery afternoons or early evenings at Hodgson's Academy.[27]

[26] *The Leeds Intelligencer*, 38, 1894, December 14, 1790: "Booth's course of lectures on natural and experimental philosophy, astronomy, chemistry . . . illustrated by . . . apparatus, which has cost upwards of four thousand pounds" will consist of fifteen lectures at the cost of one guinea, three lectures a week, will begin if forty subscribers can be found . . . he claims his apparatus weighs up to 7 tons . . . he can only give one course as he has obligations in Birmingham . . . subscriptions can be had from him or at the bookstore of Mr. Binns. The same advertisement a week later . . . "he cannot do it for less than 40 people." On December 28 we are told that the lectures will commence in the ensuing week, two nights a week, in Mr. Hodgson's large room at the academy. The first week will be on pneumatics, then hydrostatics.

[27] Marshall MS 200/53: "Experiments on spinning tow from June to October 1788," number 1 to 17 no foliage; for example, "From the above experiment it appears that flax will not spin with rollers the common way because the fibers will not stick together so much as to hand forward from one roller to another especially at such distances as the length of the fiber requires them to be. It will be spun best from a sliver drawn from the heckle after the same manner as worsted if that be practicable." The trial-and-error work of Matthew Murray noted here throughout; MS 200/55 entitled Bleaching; Vol. 1 contains his notes of every major chemist of the day; Berthollet, *Encyclopédie méthodique*; Ainsworth, Lavoisier, 1800 Chaptal's account of vapor bleaching, f. 2 Berthollet's method of bleaching by oxygenated muriatic acid, translated in the Repertory of Arts from the *Annales de chimie*. . . . "when it has spent its power, it is common muriatic acid, the coloring particles having taken away its oxygen." For the next generation, see Marshall MS 200/31 (I) (someone has written that this appears to be in the hand of John Marshall) and II October 30, 1825: "Proposed experiments during James's absence." Notes on his reading found in MS 200/42 include notes on Scheele's Chemical Essays, p. 92; Waltin's Chemical Lectures 1804, also (could be Martin's) agriculture; a note on Stonehenge as an ancient observatory; from Leslie on Heat 8 vol. – 1804 "Light is heat in a state of emission." "The same portion of heat raises the temperature of ice 10 degrees, water 9, steam 572 [?]; Dr. Moyle's lectures 1805 on the atmosphere, lightning, rivers, the ocean; a section labeled geology, combustible fossils; a note stating that a grain of hydrogen explodes with a force of 500 TT? (tons); notes labeled Leslie on Heat 8 vol. 1804; then notes on various books about travel. Also present notes on an item in the *Phil. Trans.* on geology and archaeology of Lincolnshire; notes on the sea at the equator and its elevation; South America; Coal, Hutton's Theory on formation of peat, extensive notations, for

In a format typical of eighteenth-century scientific courses in the Newtonian tradition – from Hawksbee to Dalton – Booth began with the very structure and uniformity of matter.[28] Throughout, the quotations are from Marshall's notes: "On matter consisting of atoms not discernible by the eye nor glasses, not capable of being produced or annihilated . . . 5 properties of matter considered, its extension, solidity, divisibility, capability of motion & vis inertiae."[29] Although not noted by Marshall, almost certainly at this point Booth would have gone on to explicate universal gravitation and the laws of local motion. Certainly Marshall learned that "the different attractions of matter were considered the attraction of cohesion, of gravity, of electricity . . . & [Booth offered] a long dissertation with several experiments on elective attractions, the knowledge of which is of great importance to chemistry & mineralogy."[30]

In the same first lecture Booth mentioned phlogiston and described an experiment "made of burning a piece of iron wire in a bottle of pure air which being lighted at one end burnt entirely away melted & dropped down reduced to a perfect calyx." Immediately its industrial application follows, "which shows the wonderful effect that would be produced by blowing pure air into furnaces instead of common air for no furnace will melt wrought iron."[31] In the lecture on pneumatics, the weight of atmospheric air on a man [and hence on a machine] is given as the equivalent of 37 tons.[32]

The first lecture set the pattern of all the others. Theory mixed effortlessly with the most basic applications, science with technology, with explanations about how siphons and pumps worked, including one said to have been invented by Booth. The discussion of the best method for raising water is followed immediately by Newton on the tides. "Newton attributed the tide on the opposite side of the earth from the moon to the solid part of the earth being more attracted than the water on the opposite side & being as it were drawn away from it."[33]

example, further notes include on Bruce Vol. 3, Helm's travels in South America; 1809 Barrow's voyage to China; de Luc's *Elements of Geology* 1809; Cuvier as discussed in the *Edinburgh Review*, 1811.

[28] For a list of Dalton's lectures, see A. Thackray, *John Dalton: Critical Assessments of His Life and Science* (Cambridge, MA: Harvard University Press, 1972), pp. 108–12, which in 1805 were as follows: 1. & 2. On matter, motion and mechanic principles, 3. Hydrostatics, 4. & 5. Pneumatics, 6. Hydraulic and pneumatic instruments, 7. 8. & 9. Electricity and Galvinism, 10. Magnetism, 11. & 12. Optics, 13. & 14. On heat, 15. On the elements of bodies and their composition, 16. On mixed elastic fluids and the atmosphere, etc., ending with astronomy, the solar system, eclipses, laws of motion of the planets explained by the whirling table, tides, system of the universe.

[29] Marshall MSS, MS 200/42, "Philosophical Lectures and Extracts, Booth's Philosophical Lectures, December 1790," from Lecture 1.

[30] Ibid. This manuscript is not foliated. [31] Ibid. [32] Ibid., Lecture 2.

[33] Ibid., Lecture 5 on hydraulicks.

The detailed lecture in hydraulics discussed the commonplace errors in the construction of pumps, that is "placing the low valve too high ... it ought to be placed as near as possible to the surface of the water because there the water ascending acts with the greatest velocity and force," as well as making the windbore of a less diameter than the working bar when "they ought to be the same diameter." Booth then gave a demonstration of his model pump that moved water by a continuous circular motion.[34] Another pump, he told his audience, could "at a stroke drain water both by the piston's ascending and descending ... the piece of wood then falls to the bottom and raises a quantity of water equal to its own weight at the other end of a beam." On the very next page Marshall recounted Newton on the tides, then noted that another scientific lecturer of the period, James

[34] Ibid., Lecture 5, "3. In the clack or valve ... the very best possible construction is the mitre clack – a working model of Dr. Franklin's contrivance for drawing water by a hair rope was exhibited & proved not to answer – a model of a pump invented by Mr. Booth was shewn which pumped the water by a continued circular motion – the piston moving in a circular pipe communicating with the well below & the reservoir above there is a value in that part of the circle which is between the ascending & descending pipe & before the piston comes at that valve it touches a catch which raises the valve into the ascending pipe, the piston passes & immediately the valve is lowered to its old place. A model of a pump which made a stroke drained water both by the piston's ascending & descending – a model of a machine for raising a quantity of water 3 feet high by means of a small stream of water equal to 78 [?] of the water raised falling 30 feet ... the piece of wood then falls to the bottom & raises a quantity of water equal to its own weight at the other end of a beam" and on the next page "Newton attributed the tide on the opposite side of the earth from the moon to the solid part of the earth being more attracted than the water on the opposite side & being as it were drawn away from it. Ferguson ascribes it to the centrifugal force arising from the earth's moving round its common center of gravity with the moon. That center of gravity is about 2000 miles from the surface of the earth." In discussing the clack or valve of the pump he notes that vibration decreases velocity; best construction is a "mitered clack." Lecture 10 pneumatick chemistry – long discussion of phlogiston theory and its errors ... next paragraph "dephlogisticaled marine acid discharges all color from vegetable substances – this is the new invention for bleaching which whitens a piece of cloth in a few hours – it is procured by putting oil of vitriol on sea salt which separates the acid of salt – then by adding some blue shale or manganese so commonly used for cleaning we find it heavier & the air in which it was calcined diminished in quantity ... vital air & inflammable air together when deprived of a part of their fire constitute water." In the very paragraph, "Dr Priestley discovered that when air was rendered totally unfit for animal life it was purified by plants (which were exposed to the light) which absorbed the phlogisticated part of it & rendered it pure vital air – phlogisticated air he consider as the patrilum [?] or food of plants. This agreed with Mr. Bakewell's plans of Dishley who finds that his grass flourished the most when flooded with pure spring water without any mixture of mud or manure of any kind. Plants therefore decompose the water, the inflammable part of which serves for their nourishment & the vital air is thrown off." Eudiometer for ascertaining the purity of air was explained ... Lectures 11 and 12 electricity "electric matter is a fluid sui generis – it follows the law of all other fluids in endeavouring to keep up an equilibrium in all its parts – all bodies more or less contain a portion of this matter & that portion may be increased or diminished." Then Dr. Moyes on Electricity ... applications are discussed and these are entirely medical; also how to deploy lightning rods to protect a house, proper distance between them.

Ferguson, ascribed "the centrifugal force arising from the earth's moving round its common center of gravity with the moon. The center of gravity is about 2000 miles from the surface of the earth." It would seem in the next breath – or certainly in Marshall's next sentence – we are told that the pump's vibration decreases velocity, and the best valve or clack to use is a mitered one.[35] The same forces that acted on the pump acted on the tides.

After detailed lectures on astronomy, opticks, pneumatick chemistry and electricity, mechanics followed. As did so many of the natural philosophical lectures of the eighteenth century this lecture began with basics: the lever.

> There is only one power in mechanics viz the lever – all others are resolvable into this. The quantity of power gained is exactly equal to the time lost. The length of a crooked lever is to be measured by dropping a perpendicular from the fulcrum to the line of direction of the two powers – Friction is equal to the weight & velocity of the moving body, & does not at all depend upon its greater or smaller surface. This was proved by a piece of wood on an inclined plane which required the same weight to draw it up on its edge as on the flat side which had 5 times the surface. The pivots of wheels should be small because of having less velocity but long that they may not wear the steps by having too great a weight on a small surface.[36]

The next lecture, devoted entirely to water wheels and steam engines, is listed in Marshall's notes, but the details are not elaborated upon. Notes taken on a book about heat, some fifteen years later, detail Marshall's continuing interest in steam and its manipulation.[37]

The time has come to pass from Marshall's rich notes on Booth's scientific lectures – rare though the survival of such notes may be – and turn to the scientific mindset that Marshall brought to his early industrial and technological activities. Certainly Marshall's approach to mechanical problems did not derive directly or entirely from Booth. Making such a claim would impoverish the multiple sources available to the John Marshalls of the 1790s: conversations with engineers (many of which he recorded),[38] consultations with fellow entrepreneurs, even competitors,

[35] Ibid., Lecture 5 on hydraulicks. [36] Ibid., Lecture 13.

[37] Ibid., "From Leslie on Heat 8 vol. – 1804 Light is heat in a state of emission. The same portion of heat raises the temperature of ice 10 degrees, water 9, steam 572. [? Symbol unclear.]"

[38] MS 200/57 Notebook c. 1790, opening pages list all items alphabetically, f. 1 Steam Engine – gives a list of engines at work in the region with all of their specifics and continued on f. 27 … undated, including some engines in Manchester; f. 2 Wrigley says there is nothing gained by a crank instead of a water wheel because of the great weight they are obliged to use at the beam end. G. W. says the Boulton and Watt's crank engines are the only ones that will produce a motion sufficiently regular for spinning; f. 4 water wheel dimensions of various and Wrigley's comments; f. 6 lists names of Mechanicks, e.g., Joshua Wrigley, erector of Steam Engine & Cotton Machinery – Man (Manchester); then spindle makers, steel burners, roller makers.

the long hours spent tinkering and testing rollers, spindles, dyeing techniques – all were important. Scientific knowledge and methods – in both mechanics and chemistry – remarkably similar to what Mr. Booth, and numerous other natural philosophical lecturers displayed – informed the approach Marshall, and his engineer employee, Matthew Murray, took.

This was science on the shop floor, and without seeing its role we cannot see the distinct knowledge that went into the early Industrial Revolution. Nowhere else in Europe did this particularly applied version of mechanical science take hold so early and so decisively, and it contributed to making Leeds by the 1830s the foremost center for woolen cloth in the Western world. By the 1820s the city and the Marshall firm led the country in linen production.[39]

Newtonian bobbins and teeth

When Marshall experimented with his equipment in order to improve its efficiency he did so with mathematical precision and with reference to general laws.[40] He was also a consummate technologist, intensely interested in machines employed by others or in other industries, such as those used in cotton spinning.[41] With his own machinery friction was a matter of particular concern. This quotation from one of his experiment books dated 1795 demonstrates how calculation and generalization figured noticeably in his style:

> The teeth of two wheels working together must necessarily rub against one another over so much space as the difference of length of two radii meeting at the center of action of the two wheels & of two radii meeting at the thickness of a tooth from the center of action, which is the place where the teeth first begin to act. Consequently the finer the pitch & the less friction there will be upon the teeth. The best form of the teeth of wheels is that which is the strongest & at the same time admits no tooth to come into contact but that which is in action.[42]

[39] Rimmer, 1960, p. 125.

[40] Marshall MS 200/57 Notebook c. 1790, f. 38 labeled Strength of wheels, "To find the strength necessary for any given power – Rule The square of the thickness of the tooth multiplied by its breadth will give the number of horse power that the wheel is adequate to work, if it move at a velocity of its surface of 2½ [?] feet p. second of time. If the velocity is greater or less, the power is proportionate – The best breadth of a tooth is six times its thickness."

[41] Ibid., f. 17 labeled Speed "the greatest speed at which they can spin cotton is 15ft a min. or 12 feet a min the day through including stoppages."

[42] Marshall MS 500/57, Notebook c. 1790, ff. 24–5. See similar points being made by Rev. S. Vince, *A Plan of a Course of Lectures on the Principles of Natural Philosophy* (Cambridge: J. Archdeacon, 1793), p. 40: "The friction of a body does not continue the same when it has different surfaces applied to the plane on which it moves, but the smallest surface will have the least friction." Note in one British Library copy of this book, owned in 1800 by Thomas Barber of Cambridge (call number 1600/1154), the student's ms notes read in

The form of the tooth is therefore determined by the relative diameters of the wheels that are to work together. Marshall believed that friction occurred most at the exact point where the circumference of the tooth met the wheel. He continues: "To find the true form of the teeth of two wheels of equal diameters draw the pitch line at half the depth of the teeth, & setting one leg of your compasses on the pitch line in the middle of one tooth draw the point of the next tooth with the other leg." Understanding that friction was not a result of velocity but rather of contact points created the possibility of its more efficient reduction. Similarly, the action of the bobbins as they spun the linen was approached mechanically: "The relative length & diameter of a bobbin must be so proportioned that it will always be the same weight in proportion to the lever at which the thread is acting." In addition,

> In the first case the yarn between the flyer leg & the bobbin would have to bear a stress 2¼ times as great as at a speed of 2000 revs & the spindle would require 2¼ times as much power to give it motion, because the central force is increased as the square of the velocities, & the weight of the bobbin is increased to counteract the increased central force of the thread.[43]

In the latter case of reducing the diameter of the bobbin the stress upon the yarn would be the same as before at a velocity of 2,000 revs. Because the central force and weight of the bobbin would continue the same, "the power required for giving motion to the spindle would continue the same."[44] The Newtonian discussion of bobbins continued: "The central force being likewise in proportion to the quantity of matter, a bobbin of the size above described which would not spin 16 lea yarn at a greater velocity than 2000 revs. Would spin 36 lea yarn at a velocity of 3000 revs. a min. In that case the 36 lea ought to be of equal strength with the 16 lea, otherwise it would break the oftener."[45] Teeth and bobbins could be dissected mathematically, as in the rule, "The square of the thickness of the tooth multiplied by its breadth will give the number of horse power that the wheel is adequate to work, if it move at a velocity of its surface of 2½ feet

part: "Some Writers have asserted that Friction is increased in the same body if its velocity be increased, but this is not the case, as appears from Mr. Vince's Experiments," found in blank sheets after p. 44.

43 Marshall MS 200/57, ff. 34–5. Note in lectures remarkably similar to Booth's the following appears in the first lecture: "If any two weights balance each other when hung from a straight lever, they will be to each other inversely as their distances from the fulcrum." Found in Vince, 1793, p. 7. These lectures concerned in this order: mechanics, hydrostatics, optics, magnetism, and astronomy.

44 Vince, 1793, p. 9: "In a fixed pulley, the power is equal to the weight."

45 Marshall MS 200/57 Notebook, dated 1790, but notes continue, and this one on f. 36 is dated 1805.

per second of time. If the velocity is greater or less the power is proportionate. The best breadth of a tooth is 6 times its velocity." Year after year Marshall recorded the weight of bobbins when empty and full.[46]

How the techno-science worked that called for this application of Newtonian mechanics to bobbins included oftentimes the shop-floor presence of inventors with multiple skills. In the manuscript folio about "Theory of Wheels – 1795" where the bobbin is explicated appear the initials "M.M." In precisely this period Marshall was dependent upon the many innovations that his employee, the engineer Matthew Murray, effected in the weaving of linen thread. Fed up with the machines then operating throughout the north, Marshall in his experiment book dated 1788 tells us that "we gave over spinning and set Matt Murray to work on a new loom."[47] For the next five years they sought to find machines that would spin thread as fine as, if not finer than, could be done by hand. They investigated worsted and cotton factories to see what, if anything, could be borrowed from their techniques. The notes left by Marshall contain discussions of tow, slivers, rollers, and carding machines, and after three years of experiments, tell of success: "This plan answered every end we wished, the slivers was level and without patches, the fibers were taken off straight, and we thought it was carded as well as possible."[48]

The technical vocabulary of early industrialists

In comparing Marshall's manuscript notebook on Booth's natural philosophical lectures and the experiment book with the initials "M.M." next to the discussion of the central force and weight of bobbins, we begin to see a pattern. Engineers and entrepreneurs shared a vocabulary that was deeply technological just as it was scientifically informed. Theory and practice were inextricably entwined; the initials suggest that Matthew Murray at the least understood, or at the most explained, this bobbin principle to Marshall. Arguably Murray was to Marshall as Watt was to Boulton, entrepreneurial engineer to mechanically literate entrepreneur. Theirs was a shared vocabulary and its dictionary was both technical and scientific.

The engineer and entrepreneur spoke a language that could lead to enormous economic success, especially, as was the case with Marshall and Murray, when only one of them, namely Marshall, controlled the

46 Marshall MS 200/6/1/19, f. 38; also ff. 36–7, for year-by-year measurements.
47 Cited in Rimmer, 1960, p. 29. For a discussion of Murray, see G. Cookson, "Family Firms and Business Networks: Textile Engineering in Yorkshire, 1780–1830," *Business History*, 39, 1997, pp. 1–20.
48 Ibid., p. 32, from Marshall's ms notebook, "experiments." See also MS 200/53 "experiments on spinning tow from June to October 1788."

capital and the profit. Yet in technical matters theirs was a partnership, with Murray apparently more the engineer but also highly literate. For example, friction held one key to economic success, and when not worrying about carding and bobbins, the friction of wheels also occupied the attention of the firm. They wanted to find the best depth of the teeth that would impact the wheel with least friction and yet be deep and thick enough to offer durability. The approach was both experimental and geometrical.[49] Science taught them to generalize, to see the interconnectedness of centrifugal forces at work on the tides and on bobbins. The ability to conceptualize force, velocity, and weight combined with painstaking adjustments and innovations, with trials and errors made on shop-floor equipment. The ideas were no good without developing new equipment.

In the experiment books on dyeing and bleaching the same, interactive pattern between the science and the technology holds. Consistently reference is made to the latest experimental work. Marshall took chemical notes out of books by Lavoisier, Berthollet, Chaptal, and Ainsworth, among others. In passing Marshall applied atomic theory, noting that, when oxygenated, muriatic acid "has spent its power, it is common muriatic acid, the coloring particles having taken away its oxygen."[50] Marshall's notes on the *Encyclopédie méthodique* suggest that he read French chemistry without the aid of a translator and that he knew the latest works nearly as soon as they appeared, and diligently recorded a steady stream of chemical experiments.[51] Marshall and Murray knew how they could inform their shop-floor practices. It made perfectly good sense for Marshall to read among the cutting-edge chemists, or to adapt the boiler of his steam engine to steam cloth that he was attempting to dye.[52] It is we who have imposed contradictions, tinkerers vs. real scientists, trial and error vs. serious experimentation, and science vs. technology. Merging the one into the other also does not work, as it refuses to see the variety of skills at play. Both the lofty and the mundane lay at the heart of early industrial processes.

Once the engines had been installed and the machines made ever more efficient, less rigorous men could copy and improve. The notes taken in the experiment books of the next generation of Marshalls display the same dedication to trial and error but none of the theoretical sophistication seen in the jottings of Marshall with their bows to Murray's expertise. The sons

49 See note 6 for the best breadth of a tooth, citing MS 200/57, f. 38.

50 Marshall MSS 200/55, f. 2. For a similar discussion of oxygenated muriatic acid, see W. Nicholson, *A Dictionary of Chemistry* (London: G.G. and J Robinson, 1795), p. 209 entry under bleaching of linens.

51 MS 200/55, f. 21 March 1798: "We began to try experiments with the bleaching liquor . . . after procedures done first by Ainsworth working on cotton."

52 Marshall MSS 200/55, ff. 63–4.

noted how "rolling we have tried as an experiment and found its effect very similar to that of stamping ... there is more expense and more waste in freeing the flax from its matter and caked character before it can be heckled. It is fair to presume that if well managed, there would also be more advantage ... a third method may possibly be found in the agency of steam ... steam may carry away part of the glutinous matter from the fiber."[53] The next generation does not present the same record of restless examination, of interrogations of engineers about which engine, if any, will do the work, of an appeal to abstract principles. They were no longer needed; the basics of the factory were established and could be improved upon. Perhaps for the second generation science had become so naturalized in family and civic life that its presence on the shop floor could be assumed, or talented employees could be hired who possessed the requisite education in it.

The Gotts

The establishment of a cost-efficient factory took years of trial and error. Early in the 1790s, the Gott firm consulted with a variety of engineers on the best engine to install in its factory.[54] Already the leading woolen and worsted manufacturing firm, it accepted Boulton and Watt's offer to install a remarkable 40-hp steam engine, and Benjamin Gott, the most mechanically proficient partner in the firm, became a consultant in the region on engineering problems.[55] In an experimental notebook similar to those left behind by Marshall, Gott detailed how his factory manipulated steam engines with varying amounts of water, at varying temperatures, and discovered that "a pound of water therefore in the state of steam contains more caloric than a pound of boiling water in the proportion of 950 to 212. Q.E.D."[56] Gott also pioneered the use of steam in the process of wool dyeing.[57] As he told the inventor of a hydro-

[53] Marshall MS 200/31 (I), and (II), f. 15.

[54] The Brotherton Library, Leeds, Gott MSS, MS 193/2 letters from Boulton and Watt, Peter Ewart, James Lawson, John Rennie; MS 193/74–84 copies of letters from Boulton and Watt that are now housed at the Birmingham City Library and are also available on microfilm. The Gott MSS are in The Brotherton.

[55] Gott MSS 193/3 f. 98 letter of May 5, 1802, from Davison to Gott asking him if he would give him an opinion of his steam engine.

[56] Gott MSS/117 Bean Ing Mill Notebook of Prices and Processes [c. 108–125], "experiments made in the Dye house Park Mill, 9 Sept. 1800."

[57] Gott MS 193/3/f. 98 letter of Davison to Gott asking him if he would go with him to give his opinion of their steam engine to Goodwin, "but if you can't here are queries in writing," May 5, 1802. On the engine and its many uses for scribbling, carding, turning shafts and gearings, stones to grind dyewood, see H. Heaton, "Benjamin Gott and the Industrial Revolution in Yorkshire," *The Economic History Review*, 3, 1931–2, pp. 52–3.

mechanical press with which Gott was less than pleased, "we look after every operation of the work ourselves, and if we had experienced any advantage from the use of your press, we should have insisted on those men working it, or we should have appointed others in their places who would have been obedient."[58] Indeed, Gott became an expert on a hydro-mechanical press, a large and complex piece of equipment introduced late in the century, requiring an understanding of levers, weights, and pulleys, and used to imprint patterns on textiles.[59] He experimented to establish the relative merits of prototype machines offered by rival manufacturers of the device, and may have concluded that the press did not work as it should.[60]

The prestige that came with knowledge

The Gott firm and family, along with the Marshalls, became leaders in the civic and industrial life of Leeds. In fact, Gott's expertise was sought out by imitators and rivals alike.[61] Just like the Boultons and the Watts of Birmingham, the M'Connels and the Kennedys of Manchester, the Gotts and the Marshalls established themselves as leaders (or proprietary members as they were called) of a new Philosophical and Literary Society (first chaired by Gott). They and the other seventeen proprietors subscribed £100 for a building to house the society and put out £350 for scientific apparatus.[62] In 1821, the opening lecture valorized science, striving, and the industrial order: "The thirst for improvement gives an exaltation of character ... produce[s] the works of genius and the discoveries of science ... science, no longer confined to the closets of the learned, is

[58] Gott MSS 193/3 f. 97 Gott to Bramah, March 29, 1809.

[59] MS 193/ 3 f. 94. Note that tool making, unlike heat engines, water motors, bridge building, etc., received little guidance from scientific principles until the twentieth century; see R. B. Gordon, "Who Turned the Mechanical Ideal into Mechanical Reality?" *Technology and Culture*, 29, October 1988, pp. 744–78.

[60] Ibid., f. 97 Gott to Bramah from Leeds, March 29, 1809, on his hydro-mechanical press: "We have from your letter of the 25th instant that the sale and general adoption of your patent presses have been prevented by unfavorable representations respecting the merits & utility of the one you erected for us ... we must ... tell you that we look after every operation of the work ourselves, and if we had experienced any advantage from the use of your press, we should have insisted on those men working it, or we should have appointed others in their places who would have been obedient." See H. Heaton, *op. cit.*, p. 58, who takes a dimmer view of Gott's success in putting the machine to work.

[61] The Brotherton Library, University of Leeds, Gott MS 193/3/f. 98 letter of May 5, 1802, Davison to Gott, asking him to go with him to form an opinion of a local steam engine "but if you can't here are queries in writing."

[62] The Brotherton Library, Special Collections, MS Dep. 1975/1/6, May 7, 1819.

applied to the comforts and amelioration of mankind. Its influence is strikingly apparent alike in our houses and manufactories."[63]

The historical sources, on this occasion left by linen and woolen manufacturers in Leeds, present science and its methods as lying at the heart of a set of values, beliefs, deployed knowledge systems, in other words, of a new culture at work at the heart of early industrialization. The argument ultimately comes down to the realization that scientific acumen was not *just* cultural capital, it was also deployed. Leadership in the industrial cities passed to firms like Marshalls and Gotts in part because their knowledge base enabled them to invent or deploy mechanical contrivances that replaced human labor, to compete aggressively, and to imagine themselves as superior to the idle and landed of the countryside who still possessed access to political power.

None of these people should be imagined as provincials or self-described as inferiors. Their self-confidence was fueled by their success, and in the case of the Marshall family, social life included Dorothy and William Wordsworth. Mrs. Marshall and Dorothy had a friendship from their schoolgirl days and the two families visited and shared confidences in the Lake District. Never do we sense in their correspondence any hint of deference or awe on the Marshall side.

The Marshalls knew that their values and learning represented the future. When Marshall ventured forth into the countryside – he adored rural vistas and shimmering lakes – he lamented the backwardness of clergy and landlords alike. In Wartdale he said that, unlike his own firm that offered evening education to the children it employed, the local clergy were "too idle to put in a school when one is needed." In Swaledale he noted how the "Lords of the Manor" had failed to exploit their lead mines, "what a vast saving would the present state of knowledge in Mechanicks have made them. A steam engine that cost 600 pounds would have been put up in a few months . . . It is surprising that steam engines have not yet been applied to lead mines." In Whitehaven he complained how the great part of the town "pays a chief rent to Lord Lonsdale – he has some good houses here uninhabited & going to ruin."[64] In the world that John Marshall and Benjamin Gott wanted, nothing and no one were meant to be idle and that included the minds of engineers and entrepreneurs.

[63] C. Turner Thackrah, *An Introductory Discourse. Delivered to the Leeds Philosophical and Literary Society, April 6, 1821* (Leeds: Printed for the Philosophical and Literary Society by W. Gawtress, 1821), pp. 23–4.

[64] Marshall MSS 200/63, unfoliated. For their knowledge of the Lake District and the relationship between Jane Marshall and Dorothy Wordsworth, see E. de Selincourt, ed., *The Letters of William and Dorothy Wordsworth*, 2nd edn., revised by C. L. Shaver, Vol. 1. *The Early Years, 1787–1805* (Oxford: Clarendon Press, 1967).

Together they and countless other early industrialists brought the new science into places never imagined by its seventeenth-century progenitors. They knew that in combination with technology, science could make new worlds. One of them first emerged in their Leeds factories.

The conundrum of British education

There is more information about the factory floors of both Marshall and Gott than there is about their formal education. Neither can be associated with any certainty with the Leeds Grammar School, the main educational institution in the town that prepared men for Oxford or Cambridge. Generally the grammar, i.e. secondary, schools of England prepared boys for the clergy and offered a heavy dose of humanistic learning. Occasionally we can associate education in natural philosophy with one of the schools, or with a local Dissenting academy, when, for example, we know that John Dalton taught at New College in Manchester. Yet in Leeds, late in the eighteenth century, the grammar school headmaster opposed the teaching of anything that would detract from the learning of Latin, Greek, and the classics. We know that the town possessed boarding schools for boys – as early as 1769 – that offered accounting, arithmetic, geometry, trigonometry, and "the doctrine on mechanics with the theory and application of the mechanic powers." We know nothing more about them than that.[65]

Informal education in science can be found in Britain early in the eighteenth century, but can be documented largely by advertising for the courses, or by the textbooks eventually produced by the lecturers. As early as 1705 experimental demonstrators advertised events where instruments were used "to prove the Weight and Elasticity of the Air, its Pressure or Gravitation of Fluids upon each other: Also the new Doctrine of Lights and Colours, and several other matters relating to the same Subjects."[66] *Techne* and *scientia*, technology and science – while not one and the same thing – were close, indeed inseparable, in this tradition. In the 1730s, John Grundy, a land-surveyor and teacher of mathematics,

[65] See advertisements in the *Leeds Mercury*, January 3, 1769, January 16, 1770. There was a Commercial and Mathematical School on Boar Lane that taught natural philosophy in the late 1780s. In 1788, a Mr. Burton gave a course for men and women in natural and experimental philosophy endorsed by Joseph Priestley. There is a flyer for the course housed at the Education Library, Hillary Place, Leeds, and I wish to thank its librarian, Liz Lister, for this information.

[66] *Daily Courant*, Thursday, January 11, 1705, advertising the lectures and demonstrations of James Hodgson; cited in L. Stewart, "Science and the Eighteenth-century Public," in M. Fitzpatrick *et al.*, *The Enlightenment World* (New York: Routledge, 2004), p. 238.

proposed that every engineer should "understand Natural Philosophy in order to make his Enquiries just."[67] Shortly thereafter, John Desaguliers (Newton had been godfather to his son) declared in his published *Course of Experimental Philosophy* that natural philosophers were actually the only realistic guardians to prevent investors from being "impos'd upon by Engine-makers, that pretend to (and often fancy they can) by some new invented Engine out-do all others." The educational examples can be multiplied from almost every decade of the century.[68]

In the period from 1750 to 1850 British formal education at both the primary and secondary levels remained entirely decentralized. Schools could be sponsored by Dissenters such as Quakers or Unitarians, or paid for by local communities where families paid tuition and sometimes room and board. Grammar schools sprang up in earnest during the Henrican Reformation of the sixteenth century, but the histories of individual schools seldom contain detailed information on the curriculum, beyond the certainty that Latin and Greek were basic. After 1700 we can find isolated evidence for the teaching of Newtonian mechanics at the Dissenting Academies and occasionally in the notes of grammar school masters. At this time, of all boys roughly thirteen to eighteen, only about 10 percent received a formal secondary education – in Britain or anywhere else on the Continent.[69]

[67] John Grundy, Sr., *Chester Navigation consider'd* (n.d., ca. 1736). I owe this reference to Larry Stewart.

[68] Desaguliers, 1745, Vol. I, pp. 70, 138. On him, see A. T. Carpenter, *John Theophilus Desaguliers. A Natural Philosopher, Engineer and Freemason in Newtonian England* (London: Continuum, 2011). For the long-standing interest of the Royal Society in steam, see A. Smith, "'Engines Moved by Fire and Water': The Contributions of Fellows of the Royal Society to the Development of Steam Power," *The Newcomen Society for the Study of the History of Engineering and Technology. Transactions*, v. 63, 1991–2, pp. 229–30. See also R. Fox and A. Guagnini, *Laboratories, Workshops, and Sites: Concepts and Practices of Research in Industrial Europe, 1800–1914, Berkeley Papers in the History of Science*, Vol. 18 (Berkeley, CA: The Regents of the University of California, 1999); J. A. Goldstone, "Efflorescences and Economic Growth in World History: Rethinking the 'Rise of the West' and the Industrial Revolution," *Journal of World History*, 13, 2002, p. 334; Gordon, 1988, pp. 744–78; C. Griffin and I. Inkster, eds., *The Golden Age: Essays in British Social and Economic History, 1850–1870* (Aldershot: Ashgate, 2000); H. Heaton, "Benjamin Gott and the Industrial Revolution in Yorkshire," *The Economic History Review*, 3, 1931–2, pp. 50–65; and T. Levere and G. L'E. Turner, with contributions from J. Golinski and L. Stewart, *Discussing Chemistry and Steam. The Minutes of a Coffee House Philosophical Society 1780–1787* (New York: Oxford University Press, 2002). And as always invaluable, L. Stewart, "Science and the Eighteenth-century Public," in Fitzpatrick *et al.*, 2004.

[69] For the teaching in Bristol, see the diary of John White, Bristol Record Office, White MS, No. 08158, ff. 73–81; and David Reid, "A Science for Polite Society: British Dissent and the Teaching of Natural Philosophy in the Eighteenth Century," *History of Universities*, 21, 2, 2006, pp. 117–58.

The students at the Dissenting Academies were slightly older, university age being as early as fourteen, but could not – because they were not Anglicans – enroll in either Oxford or Cambridge. The Dissenting alternatives quickly established a reputation for teaching science and natural philosophy, as did the Scottish universities where non-Anglicans were in the majority. In addition, by 1800 the British popular publishers began to produce books with content on nature and its laws, aimed at children from roughly six to sixteen, and these taught anything from rudimentary geography, heliocentricity, or, in the more advanced cases, Newtonian definitions of matter and then the branches of mechanics, chemistry, and mineralogy. Also by the 1790s books aimed at the instruction of young men of the middle classes inculcated the value of mathematics and science.[70]

Beginning in the 1790s – and promoted by the French revolutionaries – Europeans became convinced that the British schools and public lectures offered an education more effective for industrial development than could be found on the Continent. In France, the gap in mechanical knowledge set in early in the century when Newtonian mechanics had to battle against either scholasticism or Cartesianism for a place in the curriculum of the colleges. Many of them were controlled by the Jesuits. They were expelled from France only in 1762. From the perspective of scientific knowledge and education of a mechanical sort, the English educated elite would appear at least a generation ahead of its Continental counterpart.[71]

[70] For an example, see J. Adkin, *Evenings at Home; Or, the Juvenile Budget Opened. Consisting of a Variety of Miscellaneous Pieces, for the Instruction and Amusement of Young Persons* (London: J. Johnson, 1794–8), Vol. 6 out of 6, pp. 130–6; and for more sophisticated science, see J. Joyce, *Scientific Dialogues* (London: 1800–3). See also J. R. Topham, "Publishing 'Popular Science' in Early Nineteenth-Century Britain," in A. Fyfe and B. Lightman, eds., *Science in the Marketplace: Nineteenth-Century Sites and Experiences* (University of Chicago Press, 2007), pp. 141–63. Books aimed at young people and their parents include S. Catlow, *Observations on a Course of Instruction for Young Persons in the Middle Classes of Life* (Sheffield: J. Gales for J. Johnson and T. Knott, 1793), where we learn the advantages of philosophy for commerce and the professions, pp. 34–40, and that such knowledge also helps "manufacturing and mercantile employments. Are not many of the former absolutely founded on that knowledge of nature and its laws, which philosophy contemplates, and are not numerous articles of trade prepared, or, at least accelerated in their preparation for the market, by such knowledge?" Claims that evidence of this is "innumerable."

[71] For a sophisticated statement of the lead, see G. Timmons, "Education and Technology in the Industrial Revolution," *History of Technology*, 8, 1983, pp. 135–49. For a clear statement of how the "new" economic history discounts the entrepreneur, see C. Trebilcock, *The Industrialization of the Continental Powers, 1780–1914* (London: Longman, 1981), p. 141; consider pp. 63–5 on the critical role of science and technology to late nineteenth-century German industrial development. See also L. W. B. Brockliss, *French Higher Education in the Seventeenth and Eighteenth Centuries: A Cultural History* (Oxford: Clarendon Press, 1987), p. 366.

Believing that to be so, from 1795 to 1815 the French transformed their secondary education and moved in the direction of schooling in applied science and technology for industry. Territories to which the French exported their Revolution by conquest, in particular the Low Countries, also saw their educational systems revamped in an industrial direction. The move toward applied mathematics and science, and the conviction that they lay at the heart of British industrial education, must have been based on anecdotal evidence, some of it culled by French spies.[72]

It could also have been based on the kind of evidence we have accumulated for the Boulton and Watt families, and for coal engineers in Northumberland, cotton, linen, and wool manufacturers in Manchester and Leeds, on the lone Mr. Clark in Mons. In every case we can demonstrate that the knowledge was present without being able to say with certainty where or how it was acquired.

Other situations or settings reveal further evidence of what could, or could not, be known by key British players in industrial development. The engineer John Smeaton, in the 1760s, when working with company directors who were financing a new canal, lamented their interference on technical matters: "The parties interfering *suppose themselves competent* to become Chief Engineers." Smeaton went on to say that they did not possess the degree of theoretical knowledge that they imagined themselves as having.[73]

In the last thirty years of the century canal building became something of a mania. To get the private land needed for the canals, bills had to be passed in the House of Lords, and its standing committees had to adjudicate disputes about how much water, needed for industry or agriculture, might be diverted. The records of these standing committees reveal that peers who served on them possessed the mechanical knowledge necessary to interrogate surveyors and engineers. In one such exchange the peers asked the surveyor: "Suppose two shutters of a mill of 4 feet each are elevated 17 inches with 4 feet over them. What quantity of water flows in a minute?" The reply: "278 tons per minute." The committee responded: "How do you ascertain it?" The reply: "By known hydrostatic principles." These same sorts of interrogations also reveal that some witnesses, in this

[72] AN, Roederer MSS, 29 AP 75 f. 395 – on the primary schools of England; there is no uniformity, especially in the grammar schools, which as a result of English prosperity have inadvertently improved the level of education and they have come to form the students for universities; on the subject of "calcul," a French reporter believed it to be the case: "C'est cette partie de l'enseignement qui a acquis la plus de perfection chez les Anglaises."

[73] W. Chapman, *Address to the Subscribers to the Canal from Carlisle to Fisher's Cross* (Newcastle upon Tyne: Edward Walker, 1823), pp. 2–3, 7. Emphasis inserted by Chapman.

case a mill foreman, had to tell the peers: "Upon my word, I do not know, for the power of a wheel is what I do not understand."[74] When testifying about the benefits to be derived from the Cromford and Birmingham canals, engineers asserted that they calculated "by known hydrostatic principles agreed to by all authors" and that they had consulted "with many who are scientific, and I have read most books upon the subject."[75]

Go to Bristol, the gateway to the Atlantic, but not a city we associate with industrial development. Newtonian mechanics were taught in its grammar school from mid century.[76] When in the 1780s and 1790s the issue arose of the necessity to improve its port, local civic leaders queried the engineer William Jessop as to the mechanical principles he applied and even managed to correct plans he had drawn up. They availed themselves of assistance from the Manchester Literary and Philosophical Society to which they sent copies of Jessop's engineering plans.[77] That sort of trading in mechanical knowledge was commonplace as merchants or factory owners knew, for example, that installing a steam engine that was too small or too large could spell economic disaster.[78] Derbyshire lead mine owners wrote anxiously to other owners: "Are there any very superior pumping engines to be seen at work in your country, if so I should like to see them – I mean engines that do a deal of work with a little fuel."[79] Knowledge correctly deployed could advance profits.

Economic necessity has been assumed to make the application of power technology essential, and this being so, the argument runs, application just happens. What may actually occur is that economic necessity makes the acquisition of knowledge essential, and the economic race is won by those who have luck, or sufficient literacy, or mental capacity, or governmental assistance, to acquire it. Certainly the successes of the Boultons and Watts, the Marshalls, M'Connels,

[74] House of Lords Record Office, London, Main Papers, May 26, 1789, evidence from Cromford Canal; May 19 and 20, 1809, Kennet and Avon Canal Bill, examination of John Rennie; May 19, 1809 Kennet and Avon Canal Bill. First discussed in Jacob, 1987, pp. 240–2.

[75] House of Lords Record Office, Main Papers, H.L., May 26, 1789 and May 24, 1791 on Birmingham Canal Bill.

[76] See note 69.

[77] Society of Merchant Venturers, Bristol, MS Letter Book, entry for July 17, 1792 to Mr. Faden, the London engraver who was to turn the engineer's drawing into a printed map.

[78] For a factory making steel that failed, see T. S. Ashton, *An Eighteenth Century Industrialist: Peter Stubs of Warrington 1756–1806* (Manchester University Press, 1939), p. 41.

[79] Sheffield City Library, Bagshawe Collection, MS 587 (30), f. 4, William Wyatt to Mr. Cope, Bakewell, January 31, 1837. Dr. N. Kirkham, "Steam Engines in Derbyshire Lead Mines," *Transactions of the Newcomen Society*, 38, 1965–6, pp. 72–3, 76–7, on Wyatt as an innovator. For an older orthodoxy about education, see W. B. Stephens, *Education in Britain, 1750–1914* (New York: St. Martin's Press, 1998), Chapter 4.

and Kennedys, and countless other manufacturers and mine owners, bred the desire on the part of others to emulate them. How better to do that – in a centralized state where it controlled education – than to put in place the requisite learning.

France before, during, and after its Revolution was by far the most centralized state in Western Europe, and by the late eighteenth century its industrial retardation relative to Britain was assumed and widely commented upon. It was an article of faith among the leaders of the French Revolution. They also believed in some form of democracy and that only an educated citizenry could participate in the new French republic. Beginning in the 1790s a set of bold experiments, particularly in secondary education, characterized the new reforms and high on the list stood education in science and mathematics with an applied focus. This was education aimed at industrial development and the inculcation of republican virtue. The French reforms spread along with the French army, particularly in the southern Low Countries. If we are to understand the interplay of knowledge and industrial development, the French reformers may further enlighten us.

5 The puzzle of French retardation I

Reform and its antecedents

"Retardation" is a mean word. Recently it has become impolite to apply it to people with disabilities or learning disorders, whatever their source. Perhaps national economies should also be exempt from such seemingly harsh judgment. Surely retardation in productivity can be understood only in relation to someone else's advance, and, of course, what we label as "retarded" may have seemed quite normal to contemporaries. How dare we arrogantly tumble into the past and pronounce a historical judgment?

We dare to do so in relation to France in the period from 1750 to 1850 precisely because the French at the time made similar observations, even if they politely shied away from using "retarded" when describing their anxieties about "our rival," England. It had become a mirror, and in it contemporaries saw a reflection of French deficiencies.[1] French observers sent by the government to Britain routinely remarked on how the English had vastly improved the use of coal in the manufacture of iron, thus achieving "a marked superiority ... over all other European countries." A French engineer hoped "that France will not remain always foreign to this new source of prosperity."[2] Aided by the hospitality of their engineering hosts, the engineers scurried about British coal fields making exact descriptions of the types and quantities of coal to be found. Competition did not preclude the fraternizing of men of science; lest we forget, there was still competition.[3]

1 L. Le Normand and J. G. V. de Moléon, *Description des expositions des produits de l'industrie française, faites a Paris depuis leur Origine jusqu'a celle de 1819 inclusivement* (Paris: Bachelier, 1824), Vol. I, p. 47 for "our rival." French accent marks unused in the original have not been added. On French retardation, see M. S. Smith, *The Emergence of Modern Business Enterprise in France, 1800–1930* (Cambridge, MA: Harvard University Press, 2006), pp. 3–9.

2 *Annales des mines*, second series (Paris: Treuttel et Wurtz, 1827), Vol. I, pp. 353–4; report by M. M. Dufrénoy and E. de Beaumont on the manufacturing of iron as observed in different coal-rich areas.

3 K. Chatzis, "Theory and Practice in the Education of French Engineers from the Middle of the 18th Century to the Present," *Archives internationales d'histoire des sciences* 60 (June 2010), pp. 43–78.

The custom of comparing relative progress between France and England was well in place by the second half of the eighteenth century. French spies routinely arrived in British towns and cities, prowling for information about innovations, or simply about the relative prices paid for items as varied as coal and cloth. Elaborate reports were then filed with the Ministry of the Interior in Paris, where officials watched nervously for signs of the British having made advantageous improvements. When introducing a new invention, in this instance for improving the sheen on silk, the inventor proudly noted his many trips to England and "the superiority of luster that the makers ... [there] apply to cottons, silk fabrics, and ribbons." He proclaimed that the same luster could now be obtained in France, thanks to his invention.[4] He was rewarded with a fifteen-year patent, free of charge. The inventor of a new pump for lifting water, who claimed that he had spent many years studying "the sciences" and "mechanical objects," assured the state that his pump delivered "a greater force than the English steam engine."[5]

Traffic in the direction from England to France also increased decade by decade, even into the revolutionary 1790s, when British radicals such as James Watt, Jr. – much to the annoyance of his father – marched with the Jacobins through the streets of Paris. His political ardor for French revolutionary politics did not prevent him from commenting extensively on factories and industrial processes observed, in one instance, in the cotton factories of Rouen. There the vast scale of the weaving operation of the Oberkampfs surprised him.

Young Watt, like the French themselves, had seen something important. In the first decade of the new century, during the reign of Napoleon, French officials charged with inspecting the secondary schools of Rouen insisted that the education given be tailored to the needs of industry, particularly in the city that was the most industrially advanced in France.[6] They built upon a set of educational innovations put in place

[4] Archives nationales, Paris [hereafter AN], F12 998, year 5, May 25, 1791, responding to the request by C. Bardel. The F series is entirely manuscript.

[5] AN, F 12 997, *dossier* Lainé and Justin de Varennes, 1792.

[6] Archives Départementales, Seine-Maritime, MS 1T 579: Collèges et Lycées, Affaires générales au sujet des écoles secondaires; AN Procès-verbal de la Visite des Écoles Secondaire de la Ville de Rouen, "... et dans les maisons d'Education dont les directeurs avaient sollicité, pour l'an 12, le titre de l'École Secondaire. Ils sont précédé à l'examen du mode d'enseignement suivi dans chacune, et ont interrogé les élèves depuis les premiers éléments de la langue jusqu'au degré d'instruction le plus élevé qu'offre chaque pensionnat. Observations Générales ... on a remarqué du Cn. Bricard, quelques élèves ont produit des dessins qui annoncent de véritable dispositions, et a cet égard on doit faire observer, qu'il est important de maintenir le goût ville qui est la plus forte de l'Industrie française, tous les sujets de cette industrie ont de plus ou moin loins, le Dessin pour Caze (?), si l'art

by the French revolutionaries, at a time when the war against Britain was taking an immense toll on industry. At the same time they believed that the English in their factories had discovered "the secret of mechanics. In this secret resides its industrial power."[7]

In the late 1780s, as we saw through the eyes of Boulton, French industry did not always compare favorably with what could be found in Britain. A few years later, the French revolutionaries thought that retardation was real and sought to correct it by a new industrial and educational policy implemented in the mid 1790s. They argued that French education in general needed to be turned in the service of "national industry, education in the arts and crafts," as was the case among France's competitors. They had help from the public. As early as 1791 a collection of wealthy Parisians sought to set up a new *lycée* that would have a cabinet of physics and chemistry; each gave 300 livres to the project. A few years later a petition by Parisian citizens called for education in descriptive and applied geometry, physical and chemical experiments, and elementary machinery.[8] From the perspective of scientific knowledge and education of a mechanical sort, literate Englishmen were probably at least a generation ahead of their European counterparts. Similarly, by the late eighteenth century, literate children had access to an explosion of popular books in English intended to teach them the basics of science.[9]

The Paris petitioners were on to something, or so a new generation of leaders believed. By the 1790s the leaders of the new regime – reacting against what they believed was a clerically induced backwardness –

du Dessin se perfectionne, les machines se multipliant, les procédés acquière plus de simplicité, les ouvrages manuels plus de commodité et de goût, et l'industrie nationale obtient une meilleur concurrence dans les marchés étrangers."

7 AN, Paris, F 12502, dated 1807. In the same box there is a report from the Prefecture of Police dated May 30, 1807 stating that "machinists" earn more than other workers, from three to five francs a day. See AN, F12 2467 1807–1811 on the "industrial crisis" affecting every French province.

8 For the 1791 project, see Bibliothèque historique de la ville de Paris, MS 772, f. 29. The petition is mentioned in the Parliamentary Archives, Vol. 64, pp. 233–9 in René Grevet, *L'avènement de l'école contemporaine en France, 1789–1835* (Villeneuve d'Ascq [Nord]: Presses universitaires du Septentrion, 2001), p. 300.

9 For a sophisticated statement of the lead, see Timmons, 1983. For a clear statement of how the "new" economic history discounts the entrepreneur, see Trebilcock, 1981, p. 141; consider pp. 63–5 on the critical role of science and technology to late nineteenth-century German industrial development. For the role of governments and the content of curricula, see http://epub.ub.unimuenchen.de/12691/1/Cantoni_Yuchtman_2011_Educational_Content_Educational_Institutions_and_Economic_Development_Lessons_from_History.pdf; D. Cantoni and N. Yuchtman, "Educational Content, Educational Institutions and Economic Development: Lessons from History," Munich Discussion Paper 2012–2, Department of Economics University of Munich.. And for scientific education for children. see Topham, 2007.

embraced with enthusiasm the Baconian vision of learning intended for industrial application. They wanted economic development, and the mechanical arts were at the center of their vision.[10] Their zeal was only fueled by spy reports that spoke of the technologically revolutionary qualities found in British industry.

The engineer and spy Le Turc wrote in 1794: "[When travelling in England] I saw with dismay that a revolution in the mechanical arts, the real precursor, the true and principal cause of political revolutions was developing in a manner frightening to the whole of Europe, and particularly to France, which would receive the severest blow from it."[11] Le Turc wrote to tell the revolutionary government about another, very different revolution that had become apparent even a full decade or more earlier. The British Industrial Revolution of which he spoke threatened to revolutionize the balance of power in Europe. From direct observation Le Turc described in detail British skill, and he spent serious sums from the French treasury trying to recruit English workers. Owing to reports such as these, as one expert on technology and economic development puts it, the French ministers of commerce nursed *un véritable obsession* about English competition.[12]

Indeed, in the 1790s French revolutionaries were so convinced of their insight into the culture of British science that they sought to foster and

[10] *Réimpression de l'Ancien Moniteur*, t. 29, 1847, pp. 402–3, #1, 1 Vendémiaire, Year VII, 26 Sept. 1798; François de Neufchâteau gave this speech at the festival: "Le flambeau de la liberté a lui, la république s'est assise sur des bases inébranlables; aussitôt l'industrie s'est élevée d'un vol rapide et la France a été couverte des résultats de ses efforts. Les agitations politiques, inséparables des circonstances, les guerres intérieures et extérieures, telles que les annales du monde n'en offrent point d'exemples, des fléaux et des obstacles de tous les genres, se sont en vain opposés à ses progrès; elle a triomphé des factions, des circonstances, de la guerre; elle a vaincu tous les obstacles, et le feu sacré de l'émulation a constamment agrandi la sphère de son activité. . . . Parmi les nations policées, les arts seuls peuvent consolider la victoire et assurer la paix. Les ennemis les plus acharnés de la république, vaincus et humiliés par la valeur de nos frères d'armes, se consolent quelquefois en se repaissant de la folle espérance de faire triompher leur industrie; c'est à vous de détruire ce prestige, par l'efficacité de vos efforts; c'est à vous de leur montrer que rien n'est impossible à des hommes libres et éclairées." See also François de Neufchâteau, *Circulaire aux Administration centrales de Départements et Commissaires du Directoire exécutif près de ces Administrations*, 9 Fructidor, Year VI, printed but found in AN, Paris, F12 985.

[11] Conservatoire des arts et métiers, Paris, MS U 216 Le Turc to Citoyen, 14 Nivoise An 3. Le Turc was born in 1748 and in the 1780s as an engineer and spy he had travelled extensively in England, describing techniques and recruiting workers. I owe this splendid quotation to the kindness of the late J. R. Harris.

[12] P. Minard, *L'inspection des manufactures en France, de Colbert à la Révolution* (Thèse de doctorat, Université de Paris-I, 1994), Vol. II, p. 467, referring to the correspondence from Trudaine to Tolozan. Between 1740 and 1789 the government spent 5.5 million livres on subventions for inventions (p. 475). On the early development of the division of labor in Britain, see Earle, 1989, pp. 18–34.

replicate it. They self-consciously imitated the conversation between entrepreneurs and engineers. First they had to invent the civil engineer – as opposed to the long-established and highly professionalized military engineer – and then they had to educate and favor technically competent entrepreneurs, sometimes embodied in the same person. The French even perceived the specifically Newtonian and mechanical mindset present in the ongoing technical conversation so necessary for the trial and error at the heart of successful technological invention. Describing British manufacturing prowess in 1807, worried Napoleonic ministers privately used this apt Newtonian metaphor: "The absolute necessity to create and sustain French industry is a problem that England has resolved for itself in a very decisive manner. It is with this powerful lever that she sustains the enormous mass of products. Their weight produces an overwhelming gravitation which pulls everything else into its orbit."[13] The French metaphor, perhaps unwittingly, pointed to one of the key elements in a new economic order: applied mechanics.

Before the revolution, British industrial success fueled French ministerial initiatives. The ministries of commerce and the marine, as well as the local *intendants* – the king's regional representatives – and local assemblies (or estates), were willing to give not only patents but also subsidies and prizes for inventions and pensions to their inventors.[14] Yet from the 1790s until today the verdict on all this activity has been in, and seldom modified: compared with Britain, by and large eighteenth-century France remained relatively backward in matters technological and industrial.

To this verdict the French revolutionaries supplied a cause. They systematically gave the old order a bad press for being obscurantist and interfering. One of the shibboleths in the historical literature about French industrialization in the eighteenth century is that everywhere "it was checked . . . by government interference."[15] It is true that the old-regime government was a more directly involved player in economic development than was its British or even Austrian (and absolutist) counterpart. In Belgium, the Austrians intervened in industry, granting permissions to

[13] AN, Paris, F12 502, a survey of French industry dated 1807. When the same administration tried to set up a school for public works to train engineers, its library began with the works of Newton. See the archives of the *École Nationale des Ponts et Chaussées* (hereafter ENPC), MS 3013, list of books coming from the Library of the Stadholder, beginning with mathematics and astronomy.

[14] For the day-to-day working of one such bureau, see H. T. Parker, *An Administrative Bureau during the Old Regime: The Bureau of Commerce and Its Relations to French Industry from May 1781 to November 1783* (Newark, NJ: University of Delaware Press, 1993). For a list of patents granted in 1791, see AN F17 1136.

[15] P. Langford and C. Harvie, *The Eighteenth Century and the Age of Industry*, Vol. IV in *The Oxford History of Britain* (New York: Oxford University Press, 1992), p. 78.

entrepreneurs to search for coal, subsidizing the cost of a steam engine, or demanding that they label and classify the coal extracted.[16]

Absolutism as a system of government could indeed promote development. The pre-1789 central archives of the French state, the ministries concerned with commerce, industry, and the marine, and the provincial archives as well, are rich with examples of efforts to drain harbors, develop the glass and chemical industries, and import British technology in silk and cotton manufacturing as well as in steam. The French crown was willing to give exclusive mining rights to entrepreneurs, sometimes for more than fifty years, especially to extract coal suitable for working with iron.[17] Or to cite but two building projects: efforts were made to improve the port at Havre and also at Calais, not with industry in mind but for their usefulness in a possible invasion of England. Numerous projects, some developed by foreign engineers and entrepreneurs, came to the attention of the old-regime government.[18]

Rather than being seen as the opponent of voluntarism and development, as the French revolutionaries and some modern economists believe, the pre-1789 French state should be seen as immensely interested in economic developments, in some cases eager to facilitate them. It was

[16] Archives générales du Royaume, Brussels, Conseil privé, A124, 1163, A-B-C, January 19, 1774 on labeling the coal; A124 1163 B, f. 95, January 14, 1771, on a subsidy; Conseil des Finances, MS 5052, giving permission to install a hydraulic machine in 1769 near Charleroi.

[17] Archives Départementales, Loire Atlantique, Nantes, MS C 129 Intendance de Bretagne, 1746 award to Simon Jarry, dating back to the 1730s and renewed in 1765.

[18] For archives, see AN, Paris, Marine G 106, on pumps, ff. 38–190; one of the earliest descriptions concerns a pump in a mine at Guadalcanal (Spain) done by an English company in 1731, f. 38. In the same archive a description of pumps installed in gardens in London by Newsham, 1743 (f. 42); f. 69 a pump of 1736 described as being able to elevate water in the English manner. By the 1770s (ff. 215–16, 253) it is overwhelmingly clear that English pumps are superior. See also Marine G 108 Mémoires et Projets, Machines, 1768–81, f. 87 on water supply for Paris compared with superior London system and discussion of higher cost of coal in Paris. On the silk industry in Lyon and John Badger, see AN, F12 1442 and letter of October 23, 1753 on trying to stay on the "good side" of Mr. Montigny from the Académie des Sciences; F12 993 on bringing English technology in cotton to Rouen; note report of 1747 from Mons on English techniques complete with a sample of cloth. As early as 1758, if not earlier, French ministers were in contact with English steam engineers and making inquiries about getting coal for the new engines; see AN, Marine G 110, f.133, London 1758 letter of T. Stephens to Mr. Kavanagh. Note also that according to one French report, the King of Prussia had an agent in London "to instruct the state on different manufactures"; see AN F12 657/9, dated 1776. For a general survey of changes after 1789, see *Scientifiques et sociétés pendant la Révolution et l'Empire. Actes du 114e Congrès national des sociétés savantes*, Paris, 3–9 avril 1989, Paris CTHS, 1990. Consider J. Payen, *Capital et machine à vapeur au XVIIIe siècle. Les frères Périer et l'introduction en France de la machine à vapeur de Watt* (Paris: Mouton & Co., 1969), p. 102n. See also H. A. de Ricouart d'Hérouville, "Le dessèchement des Moëres," *Revue de la Société Dunkerquoise d'Histoire et d'Archéologie*, 2, November 1985, pp. 68–75.

even willing to provide subsidized monopolies for technological innovation and it consulted the academicians as to the value of a project.[19] Not surprisingly, from the 1730s onward a steady stream of reports reached the government on a wide variety of mechanical subjects, from both home and foreign industries. Some of this information came from French academicians and engineers traveling abroad. By the 1780s the spy Le Turc was following on well-traversed paths.

That said, in 1793, at the height of the French Revolution, the radical Jacobin Convention (or parliament) abolished the French scientific academies inherited from the old order, both in Paris and in the provinces. With the demise of the Paris academy went the "jury" or bureau that had judged industrial innovations. The plan was to replace it with citizens trained in all genres of industry, in "the happy mélange of theory and practice which is absolutely necessary for making good judgments in the productive arts."[20] Two years later, it is true, the Paris academy was revitalized, reformed, and renamed, but with a quite different personnel, since many scientists had perished in the Terror. We may well ask how and why that happened, why a revolutionary government, however brutally or wrong-headedly, sought to abolish academies we associate with enlightened progress.

Ancien régime background

There can be no question that from the time of Colbert onward, the French monarchical government showed a marked interest in science and its application. In the 1750s, this interest focused on steam-powered boats, largely for military use; in the 1770s and 1780s, encouragement was given to the invention of mechanical devices for agricultural application.[21] Supported by the academies, the efforts to introduce "scientific farming"

[19] On this complex system of subsidies and grants, see L. Hilaire-Pérez, "Invention and the State in 18th-Century France," *Technology and Culture*, 32, 4, 1991, pp. 911–31. This article cites other secondary sources where it is claimed that French administrators "did not feel that English industry was much more advanced than their own, and other historians have said much the same thing." None of this research, however, has been actually comparative, and in addition there is a wealth of primary source material that contradicts the assessment. See David S. Landes's useful introduction in P. Higonnet *et al.*, *Favorites of Fortune: Technology, Growth, and Economic Development since the Industrial Revolution* (Cambridge, MA: Harvard University Press, 1998), p. 13: "Foreign contemporaries of the Industrial Revolution were anxiously aware that something momentous was going on in Britain that threatened to upset not only commercial relationships but the international order."

[20] AN, F12 1556, August 8, 1793.

[21] S. J. McCloy, *French Inventions of the Eighteenth Century* (Lexington, KY: University of Kentucky Press, 1952), pp. 30–1, 112–13.

were extensive and reflected the highest ideals of enlightened absolutism as found in the decades prior to the French Revolution.[22] Of course, it was precisely the linkage between the scientific academies and the interests of the crown that doomed their members in the eyes of the radical Jacobins.

The idealism behind the efforts of the academicians was partly Baconian and partly a reflection of the secular idealism so commonplace among the educated elites of the eighteenth century, both aristocratic and non-aristocratic. Both they and the royal ministers supported scientific inquiry chartered or licensed by the crown. One of the major *philosophes* of the 1770s even justified the linkage between absolutism and scientific inquiry. In urging the Spanish monarchy to institute an academy in its scientifically backward country, Condorcet, a leading philosopher of empiricism, explained that these academies are "an advantage for the monarchical state." His reasoning was as follows: "In a republic all citizens have the right to meddle in public affairs ... but it is not the same in a monarchy. Those whom the prince appoints have the sole right to meddle." But for men who have a need to agitate and therefore cannot abide the inactivity forced on them by the nature of the monarchical state, "the study of science can only represent ... an immense vocation with enough glory to content their pride and enough usefulness to give satisfaction to their spirit."[23] For such men academies of science are needed, or so the argument went.

The enthusiastic supporters of the state-sponsored French academies also routinely offered other arguments of a less overtly political nature. In 1781, the secretary of the Paris academy expressed both his nationalism and his enlightened liberalism when he presumed that the other European academies "owe almost all their existence to the noble emulation and mass of enlightenment that the work of the Paris Academy of Science has spread throughout Europe."[24] Had he just said "France," there might have been considerable truth to it. The Paris academy – which permitted only Parisians to join but excluded members of religious orders, such as the Jesuits – maintained a very high standard of original scientific inquiry throughout the century.[25]

[22] R. Rappaport, "Government Patronage of Science in Eighteenth Century France," *History of Science*, 8, 1969, pp. 119–36.

[23] J. E. McClellan, "Un Manuscrit inédit de Condorcet: Sur l'utilité des académies," *Revue d'histoire des sciences*, 30, 1977, pp. 247–8; consider K. Baker, *Condorcet* (University of Chicago Press, 1975), pp. 2–28, 401. For science in eighteenth-century Spain, see D. Goodman, "Science and the Clergy in the Spanish Enlightenment," *History of Science*, 21, 1983, pp. 111–40.

[24] J. McClellan III, *Science Reorganized: Scientific Societies in the Eighteenth Century* (New York: Columbia University Press, 1985), pp. 9–10.

[25] J. Heilbron, *Electricity in the Seventeenth and Eighteenth Centuries* (Berkeley, CA: University of California Press, 1979), pp. 115–17.

Many of the French provincial academies sought to imitate it. Their membership was overwhelmingly dominated by nobles, lawyers (many of whom worked with the nobility "of the robe," who were judges), and high clerics, who in the decades prior to 1789 met together "in search of prestige ... believing that progress would result from their collective reflection on new ideas."[26] They did everything from sponsoring public lectures to becoming increasingly interested in technology, agriculture, and commerce.

Yet in 1793 the revolutionary government took its vengeance on the academies, not on their ideals or on science *per se*, but on their personnel. The Paris Academy of Sciences lost nearly one half of its members as a result of the Terror; the provincial *noblesse* was equally detested, if not persecuted. Before the Revolution the academies had made many enemies precisely because of their power to approve or reject projects as diverse as the installation of a pump on a river or a new method of weaving. The resentment is palpable in the many letters left by disappointed applicants, who blamed the academicians for knowing nothing about industry or invention.[27]

Prior to the Revolution the extent of public interest in science could not be accommodated by the elite academies. A new populist science with mystical overtones captured the attention of men and women from high society to the poor. Some devotees dabbled in electrical cures performed by magician-like healers. They searched for medical improvements that would benefit all of society. In that search we can see a profound disillusionment with establishment science, with the austere and rationalistic academicians and their private pursuit of scientific inquiry. The leader of the movement was one Anton Mesmer, a Viennese doctor with Masonic connections, more quick-witted than profound. Mesmerism attracted men and women in large numbers, and as one woman saw it, the progress she had made in her own health augured a general cure for the ills of society.[28] In the 1780s, French social tensions engulfed science and pitted reformers against the entrenched academicians.

Yet at the Revolution, the science that triumphed more closely resembled engineering than it did magic.[29] *L'École polytechnique* founded

[26] D. Roche, *Le Siècle des lumières en province* (Paris: Mouton, 1978), Vol. I, p. 329.

[27] For examples of dislike of the academicians, see AN, Microfilm 13 5–7, letters of July 10, 1783, July 14, 1783; on the fate of the academy, see D. Outram, "The Ordeal of Vocation: The Paris Academy of Sciences and the Terror, 1793–95," *History of Science*, 21, 1983, pp. 254–5.

[28] Library of the University, Strasbourg, MS 1432, 1785; consider M. C. Jacob, *Living the Enlightenment: Freemasonry and Politics in Eighteenth Century Europe* (New York: Oxford University Press, 1991), pp. 199–202.

[29] J. H. Weiss, *The Making of Technological Man: The Social Origins of French Engineering Education* (Cambridge, MA: MIT Press, 1982), pp. 13–24.

in 1794 embodied the ideals of a revolutionary vision of science, of its "power to change the world."[30] Its founders wanted nothing less than a school for the science of the revolution.[31] They ignored the universities, which they regarded as moribund; they closed the academies and sought instead to reeducate teachers and hence the young. A generation after his English counterpart of the 1760s and 1770s, the French civil engineer came into his own, not to displace his military counterpart (science in this period never abandoned the war-making needs of the state) but to complement him in the new national state created by the Revolution.

In this abrupt turn toward industrialization, the utilitarian aspect of Enlightenment ideals took preeminence over all others. Among the Parisian *philosophes* there had been a marked interest in applied mechanics of the sort popularized by Desaguliers and the abbé Nollet. Decades earlier, Nollet learned his techniques of demonstration from 's Gravesande and the Dutch Newtonians. His focus concentrated on application and his career illustrates the side of enlightened scientific progress that looks most directly toward the industrial era. Indeed, lessons with Nollet led the Périer brothers to assemble their own cabinet of machines, and they in turn became the leading steam engineers from the 1780s onward.[32]

In the 1730s, Nollet opened his "cours de physique" in Paris, a lecture series that he eventually took to the French provinces, the Low Countries, and Italy. This series was perhaps the most popular ever given on the Continent, and Nollet's fame came to rest partly on his electrical experiments, which astonished and delighted his audiences. Indeed, popular enthusiasm for electrical effects cannot be ignored as one of the stimulants that enticed the eighteenth-century general public's interest in the new science. Not least, it was believed that electricity possessed medicinal value and could cure everything from tumors to the gout. Yet for all of Nollet's importance and originality –surpassed only by Benjamin Franklin as an electrical experimenter – his course of physics was grounded firmly in the practical uses of the new science.

Like his British counterparts, Nollet had to know the interests and limitations of his audience. He eschewed complicated mathematical applications, provided a glossary of terms for his readers, and in general avoided metaphysical or physico-theological questions in favor of practical examples to illustrate the "mechanism of the universe." In this last aspect his lectures

[30] J. Dhombres, "L'enseignement des mathématiques par la 'méthode révolutionnaire.' Les leçons de Laplace à l'École normale de l'an III," *Revue d'histoire des sciences*, 33, 1980, pp. 315–48.

[31] J. Langins, "Sur la première organisation de l'École polytechnique. Texte de arrêté du 6 frimaire an III," *Revue d'histoire des sciences*, 33, 1980, pp. 289–313.

[32] Bibliothèque historique de la ville de Paris, N.A. MS 147, ff. 446–69.

were representative of the general turn away from constant attention to religious questions, a shift clearly visible in scientific lectures given from the 1720s on both sides of the Channel. In concentrating on the useful, Nollet claimed that he was catering to public taste, and to accommodate it he used machines to illustrate the general principles of the new physics.[33] Nollet also concentrated on basic chemistry: how to dissolve metals, such as gold coins, how to use glues in porcelain making, how to use nitric acid to dissolve iron filings, the techniques of dyeing cloth and paper – in short, the chemistry useful in trade and hand manufacturing.[34] The general laws of physics, such as inertia and resistance, were explicated verbally as well as illustrated by the impact of moving balls of lesser and greater size. Once these general principles were established, the mechanical lectures embarked upon explanations of how the laws might be employed "to the greatest advantage."[35] Nollet made much of windmills for grinding, pumps that raise water "for our use or for the decoration of our gardens," vehicles for transportation, and levers and pulleys for architecture and navigation – all to be constructed not by simple "machinists" but by true mechanical philosophers. That such sophisticated machines can replace human labor and consequently save money was openly discussed. The approach taken by Nollet in his lectures could be described as proto-industrial rather than directly industrial, in that little is made of the actual uses of mechanical devices in coal mining, water engineering, or manufacturing. Nollet's lectures were so well known that they reached Philadelphia, where Benjamin Franklin's early work benefitted from his writings. In the Dutch Republic, the scientific lecturer Benjamin Bosma modeled his courses for women on those of Nollet.[36]

What is important to realize about the lectures of Nollet, and the other French popularizers of the new science in the old regime, is that they provided the French elite with an alternative to the relative scientific backwardness of the colleges and the University of Paris. Cartesianism was accepted in Paris only in the 1690s, although it remained controversial in the eyes of the church (and the state) well into the 1720s. The first Newtonian lectures at the university were in the 1740s, and Nollet himself

[33] Abbé Nollet, *Leçons de Physique expérimentale* (Amsterdam and Leipzig: Arksteé & Merkus, 1754), Vol. 1, preface, pp. xxii–xxv.
[34] Ibid. Vol. 1, p. 44. [35] Ibid. Vol. 3, pp. 1–5.
[36] See J. Delbourgo, *A Most Amazing Scene of Wonders: Electricity and Enlightenment in Early America* (Cambridge, MA: Harvard University Press, 2006). And see B. Bosma, *Redenvoering over de Orde en derzelver zigtbaarheid onder de Schepselen* (Amsterdam: 1765), second treatise; K. van Berkel, *In het voetspoor van Stevin. Geschiedenis van de natuurwetenschap in Nederland 1580–1940* (Boom: Meppel, 1985), pp. 82–3, www.dbnl.org/tekst/berk003voet01_01/colofon.htm (accessed September 27, 2012).

received recognition from its officialdom only in the 1750s.[37] If we contrast this pattern with natural philosophical teaching in the British or Dutch universities, or even in the provincial Dissenting academies in England by the 1720s, it is clear that a generation or more of French students in more than 400 colleges did not have access to knowledge directly useful to the process of industrialization. In 1735, perhaps with a bit of exaggeration, Voltaire claimed that there were not twenty people in France who understood Newton. One was his mistress, Madame du Châtelet.[38]

Particularly in the colleges they controlled, the Jesuits fought the introduction of Newtonianism into the 1740s and beyond – although by then the failure of Cartesian explanations was too obvious to be successfully ignored. Where the formal, clerically controlled educational institutions resisted or ignored Newtonian mechanics, the diffusion of industrially useful knowledge generally occurred a full generation or more after its British acceptance, largely after 1760 rather than before 1740. Put another way, it was possible to learn more about applied mechanics at a London coffeehouse lecture series than in any French *collège de plein exercise* prior to the late 1740s. Only then did the curriculum of the nearly 400 French colleges begin to shift decisively away from Cartesian metaphysics toward both a theoretical and applied Newtonianism. Focusing on the most backward of the colleges, the historian who has studied the curriculum of all of them concludes: "If Newton finally triumphed in France it was probably over the corpse of the Jesuit Order."[39] The Jesuits were only expelled in 1762.

Ten years earlier they had sought to censor the greatest project of the Enlightenment – in terms of scope, size, and personnel – Diderot's *Encyclopedia*, volumes of which began to appear in 1751.[40] Probably

[37] L. W. B. Brockliss, "Aristotle, Descartes and the New Science: Natural Philosophy at the University of Paris, 1600–1740," *Annals of Science*, 38, 1981, pp. 57–8, 67–8; for a good general discussion, see H. Guerlac, *Newton on the Continent* (Ithaca, NY: Cornell University Press, 1981).

[38] See also B. D. Steele, "Military 'Progress' and Newtonian Science in the Age of Enlightenment," in B. D. Steele and T. Dorland, *The Heirs of Archimedes: Science and the Art of War through the Age of Enlightenment* (Cambridge, MA: MIT Press, 2005), pp. 361–90. For Voltaire, see J. B. Shank, *The Newton Wars and the Beginning of the French Enlightenment* (University of Chicago Press, 2008), p. 363.

[39] Brockliss, 1987, pp. 353–8, 376–80, and 366 for the quotation. There was still, however, a strong emphasis on mathematical skills in university courses. In terms of the age of pupils, the French colleges are the nearest equivalent to the Dissenting Academies. In the year XI, the first *Bulletin de la société pour l'industrie nationale*, Paris, p. 179 complained that "on s'est peu occupé en France de technologie, et jamais cette étude n'a fait partie de l'instruction publique." Supplied by Jeff Horn.

[40] J. D. Burson, *The Rise and Fall of Theological Enlightenment: Jean-Martin de Prades and Ideological Polarization in Eighteenth-Century France* (Notre Dame, IN: University of Notre Dame Press, 2010), pp. 154–6.

25,000 copies circulated before 1789 and the outbreak of the Revolution. Its pages are filled with drawings and descriptions of mechanical inventions and devices. Its inspiration was Baconian; Diderot and his collaborators adored the new science and the promise it held to transform the human estate. As he put it: "Men struggle against nature, their common mother and their indefatigable enemy." In a utopian work intended to inspire the Russian monarch to establish the most modern of universities, Diderot urged that mechanics be the first science to be studied because it is "the science of the first utility."[41] The revolutionary instructors at *L'École polytechnique* would have agreed heartily.

Never should this account of *ancien régime* French scientific education suggest that prior to the French Revolution there had been a massive backwardness in mechanical knowledge among all segments of the French elite. By far the most scientifically literate of the earlier period were military engineers.[42] The preponderance of the state and the army in the area of technical and mechanical education naturally meant that their interests would be served before those of society. The new mechanical knowledge was most systematically exploited in the service of state projects, not least in the making of war, but also in agricultural improvement.[43] The tendency to bend science in the service of the state may have been further strengthened by the exclusivity of the engineering schools, which prior to the French Revolution consistently chose men of aristocratic birth for places in their classes.[44] Yet increasingly, the abbé Nollet's lectures were the standard text.

One of the earliest textbook explications of Newton's system in French, and intended for the highly literate found in the colleges and academies, Sigorgne's *Institutions Newtoniennes* (1747), relied entirely upon mathematical explanations and never mentioned machines or illustrated local motion mechanically. A few years earlier Madame du Châtelet had presented a sophisticated discussion of Newton and contemporary disputes about aspects of his physics. In *Institutions de physique* (1740), she sought a

[41] D. Diderot, *Plan d'une université pour le gouvernement de Russie*, in *Œuvres complètes*, Vol. III (Paris, 1875), p. 429, for "leur mère commune et leur infatigable ennemie"; and p. 457.

[42] C. C. Gillespie, *Science and Polity in France at the End of the Old Regime* (Princeton University Press, 1980), p. 90.

[43] Rappaport, 1969, pp. 119–36.

[44] C. S. Gillmore, *Coulomb and the Evolution of Physics and Engineering in Eighteenth Century France* (Princeton University Press, 1971), pp. 12–14. In the Netherlands, too, military engineering was much more highly developed than was civil; see H. Lintsen, *Ingenieurs in Nederland in der negentiende eeuw* (The Hague: Nijhoff, 1980), pp. 23–8. For a good illustration of the French "style" of scientific inquiry versus the British, see R. Gillespie, "Ballooning in France and Britain, 1783–1786," *Isis*, 75, 1984, pp. 249–68.

grand synthesis of current science and metaphysics. She laid little emphasis upon mechanics and its applications. Yet as the student notebooks of the DuPont family confirm, many French colleges of the 1770s and 1780s were indeed teaching applied mechanics that had been available a full generation earlier in British universities and academies, but especially in public lectures and in literary and philosophical societies.[45] In the 1780s, when the French academician Charles-Augustin de Coulomb explained the Newcomen engine to his colleagues, he referred back over forty years to the writings of the English mechanist and Huguenot refugee Desaguliers. He then went on to explain in detail the scientific nature of Watt's improvement –the first time this had been done in French.[46]

Textbook knowledge of Newtonian mechanics, although important, was not sufficient. When scientifically and mechanically trained engineers came out of schools, they were overwhelmingly aristocratic in background and their education had been intended to also teach military discipline. They in turn went on generally to become military servants of the state. As occurred in France especially after the reforms of the 1740s, the theoretical and mathematical bent to their science, as well as the aristocratic baggage they carried to an industrial site, worked against successful innovation.[47] French military engineers possessed abundant mechanical knowledge, often learned from the same books available to Smeaton or Jessop, and very occasionally they had worked directly with fire and steam machines. The difference lay in their military affect and their sociology, which were complemented and affirmed by their more mathematical and

45 See the student notebooks of Eleuthère Irénée du Pont (b.1771), Hagley Museum and Library, Delaware, Longwood MSS, Series B Box 10, course notes taken at the Collège Royal in the period 1784–9, on natural history, physics, pneumatics, botany, and notes from books by Desaguliers, Nollet, and Franklin; lesson of February 5, 1789 on simple and complex pumps; copy book for 1787 on specific gravity of water and gravity in general. Compare M. Sigorgne, de la Maison & Société de Sorbonne, Professeur de Philosophie en l'Université de Paris, *Institutions Newtoniennes, ou introduction à la philosophie de M. Newton* (Paris, 1747) with a text later in the century that illustrates the change during the next half-century: M.-J. Brisson, *Traité élémentaire, ou principes de physique*, Paris, An VIII, p. v: "Cet ouvrage, qui est destiné à la jeunesse de l'un et l'autre sexe, comprend toutes les questions relatives à la Physique." It is complete with illustrations that could have been out of Desaguliers and it made physics and mechanics accessible to any highly literate reader.

46 Payen, 1969, p. 129.

47 On the French engineering corps, see A. Blanchard, *Les ingénieurs du "roy" de Louis XIV à Louis XVI* (Montpellier: l'Université Paul-Valéry, 1979), pp. 182–94; note the absence of any machinery or mechanical instrumentation in the description of the curriculum in mathematics, mechanics, and hydraulics. Note also (p. 236) the increasingly noble character of the engineering corps after 1748. She builds upon and confirms the work of Roger Chartier, "Un recrutement scolaire au xviiie siècle. L'école royale du génie de Mézières," *Revue d'Histoire Moderne et Contemporaine*, 20, 1973, pp. 353–75.

theoretical understanding of science, and in their real as well as perceived relationship to the state. All inhibited the industrially successful deployment of their knowledge. By contrast, the British "civil engineer" – a category of professional first named by John Smeaton – had a different, more subservient, relationship to the entrepreneurs and local magistrates who employed him than did his French military counterpart. When French engineers visited Britain in the 1780s they were shocked and impressed by the egalitarian approach taken by civilians toward engineers.[48] The French engineer's self-imagining had included service to state and society, but not direction from, or employment by, the king's subjects.

Thus, when we invoke a cultural setting in eighteenth-century Europe that encouraged applied science, we must include the symbols of birth and authority – the political culture and value system of the *ancien régime* – just as we need to include knowledge systems made available in formal and informal institutions of learning. So pervasive were the military mores of French engineers that when they migrated they seldom became civil engineers in private employment; they sought out other governments, state or local.[49] When they embarked on civil projects, canals, harbors, or the drying of marshes, their first considerations were the military needs of the state; commerce came second. Not in every instance, but in general and because of their educational system, they tended "to scorn the instruments of the nascently industrial."[50]

Revolutionary zeal in science

In imitation of what France thought the British patent system achieved, in 1791 a new system for awarding patents was instituted and within the next few years inventors of everything – a new system for navigating canals (by the American Robert Fulton), one for building better pianos, another for reducing the cost of printing school books, and one for improving the speed of ships – applied for patent protection. The ministers charged with their issuance had a background in science such that they could assess, for example, according to "the theory of affinities," if the patentee's chemical process would indeed produce "soda and sulphate of soda." The chemist Berthollet assessed the viability of the application. The applicant argued plausibly that national benefits in such production would follow and

[48] M. Bradley, "Engineers as Military Spies? French Engineers Come to Britain, 1780–1790," *Annals of Science*, 49, 2, March 1992, pp. 137–61.

[49] Blanchard, 1979, pp. 289–311. [50] Ibid., pp. 453–61, p. 465.

eliminate French dependence on British imports such as Epsom salts.[51] Yet the new patenting law benefitted a class of men who could afford the 1,500 livres needed to secure a patent for fifteen years. It also eliminated the role that used to be played by French scientific academicians who, under the old regime, possessed the bitterly resented power to stop a patent if they thought its device would probably not work. They had not built it (or anything else), but they could veto it.

From the 1790s the ministers of state responsible for granting patents still needed to understand what principles had been applied in the new technology. They received in detail a description of what sort of technical knowledge of mechanics or chemistry had enabled the inventor to create his device. Where such knowledge had been used, patent applicants spelled it out in some detail: "The physical principles of this invention reside in the general law of hydrostatics." Sometimes inventors made it clear that they did not know the physical or chemical principles at work in their process.[52] As the industrial expositions held in Paris from 1798 to 1819 amply illustrate, French industry moved gradually, but quite noticeably, away from manufacturing fine luxury items to manufacturing machines for industry and scientific instrumentation. The change also provoked social tensions. At the first exposition the craft artists refused to be grouped with the manufacturers.[53]

Well into the 1820s the French government awarded prizes at public expositions for innovations that ranged from a new model of a steam engine for use in a Saint-Quentin factory to improvements in solid colors for cottons. Always British practices in science and manufacturing lurked in the government's assessment. In the 1840s, academicians, asked to survey and reform French scientific practices, wanted a vast upgrading of the laboratories for physics and chemistry at the Paris *Académie des sciences* and compared what it currently had to the superior facilities in England and Germany. They further insisted that machines

[51] AN, F12 997, "Mémoire" of M. Carny, May 1789.

[52] Cited from a patent mémoire by one Schmidt from 1799 in Jérôme Baudry: "La technique et le politique: la constitution du régime de brevets moderne pendant la Révolution (1791–1803)" (M.A. thesis, École des Hautes Etudes en Sciences Sociales, Paris, 2008–9). Kindly brought to my attention by the author. He has mined the 215 brevet applications found at the Institut National de la Propriété Industrielle, Paris. On imitating British patent law, see G. Galvez-Behar, "Genèse des droits de l'inventeur et promotion de l'invention sous la Révolution française," 2006, 5–6, to be found at http://halshs.archives-ouvertes.fr/halshs-00010474/en/ (accessed October 2, 2012).

[53] Le Normand and de Moléon, 1824, on the expositions from 1798 to 1819. For the refusal, see L. M. Lomüller, *Guillaume Ternaux 1763–1833. Créateur de la première intégration industrielle française* (Paris: Les Éditions de la Cabro d'Or, 1977), p. 109.

be brought into university instruction just as they were at the University of London.[54]

However useful, scientific education did not ensure employment in private industry. In 1808, the *Manuel du négociant* listed sixty-four "mechanists and machinists" at work in Paris. By contrast, there were still 400 government-employed engineers of bridges and roads and hundreds of others occupied by the state in artillery, the overseeing of fortifications, mines, geography, and the marine.[55] Nevertheless, real efforts were being made to give them knowledge suitable for industry. In 1808, at the *Conservatoire des arts et métiers*, the main training school in applied mechanics established in 1794, leading industrialists held significant positions. The son of the originally British cotton manufacturer Milne was "chief of the practical school of spinning." Skilled machine makers such as J. Montgolfier of ballooning fame joined him.

These efforts were sporadic, however. All mention of machines and application disappeared from the faculty positions at the *Conservatoire* by January 1816. Application reappeared in 1821 when the school hired three professors in "chemistry applied to the arts, mechanics applied to the arts, and industrial economy" and they were paid more than the professors of geometry and design. Clearly, as we shall see in the next chapter, an ambiguity existed over the value of the education originally promoted by republican reformers.[56]

French education in science after 1789

Despite the expense of the patent fee, the post-1789 goal for industrial progress had an egalitarian tendency. By 1792 enlightened visionaries such as the Marquis de Condorcet, now in positions of authority in government, proposed the reorganization of traditional secondary education.

[54] Le Normand and de Moléon, 1824, pp. 25–35. For the comparison with London, see Académie des sciences, Paris, MSS 18, enclosure with letter of June 18, 1845 from the Minister of Public Instruction to Dumas, dean of the faculty of sciences, Paris, and printed for the author, J. B. Dumas, *Rapports addressés a M. Le Ministre de l'Instruction publiques*, June 20, 1846.

[55] Guillerme, 2007, pp. 317–18. For the new patents, see the whole of AN, F12 998. See the brevet awarded on 24 Messidor, year 7 to Henry-Joseph Girard, Paris, for a new machine to increase the speed of boats, complete with mathematical explanation.

[56] AN, F 1b I, 34, Appointements du Mois de Frimaire an. 14, salaries and employees listed for 1808–9, among other dates. Milne's name, present in 1806, no longer appears after September 1814, and he was among the most highly paid at 4,000 francs per year. For January 1816 list of faculty and salaries, see No. 41. Gaultier, the professor of geometry, remained. A position appears for "Du dessin de la Mécanique." Salaries, with the exception of the director, are now lower than those before 1815. The new professors are Clement, Dupin, and Say.

They placed the mechanical arts and the practical elements of commerce front and center in the curriculum of the secondary schools.[57] Condorcet even believed that all new science-oriented faculties could be found to staff this grand experiment in progressive education intended to create a new democratic citizen. Increasingly in the 1790s a working assumption gained traction: English industrial prowess depended upon their superior machines, and education in physics, mechanics, and mathematics would promote innovation.[58]

Amid all the jealous looking-over-the-shoulder across the Channel, Boulton was one of the few commentators before 1790, either French or English, who mentioned the state of mathematical and scientific education in either place. In this regard there is growing evidence suggesting that the British were further ahead in such education by the middle of the eighteenth century.[59] Whatever the case then, after 1789, the French reformers and revolutionaries who were brought to power made education a centerpiece of the new mindset they hoped to create. At the heart of the educational reforms lay the new *écoles centrales*, established, it was hoped, in every province, with teachers drawn mostly from the laity. This bold experiment, inspired by the Enlightenment and undertaken in 1795 amid enormous financial and military distress, laid great emphasis on the teaching of mathematics and science aimed at application. The law establishing the schools even mandated that each have a public library, a natural history cabinet, a cabinet of physics, and a collection of machines or models for *arts et métiers*. Students were to make a dignified progress toward the actual state of human knowledge and "l'esprit philosophique" that characterized the past century.

There were, however, serious gaps between the ideal and the reality. Zealous for the success of the new secondary school curriculum, teachers

57 Condorcet, *Rapport et projet de décret sur l'organisation générale de l'instruction publique (avril 1792–décembre 1792)*, in *Une Éducation pour la Démocratie. Textes et projets de l'époque révolutionnaire*, ed. B. Baczko (Geneva: Droz, 2000), p. 221.

58 AN, F14 4250, 1805 Statistique minéralogique du Département du Léman ... by G. Lelivec, engineer of the mines; entire discussion of all mining of every substance; machines never mentioned. See also 1809, by Miché, chief engineer, *Mémoire sur les Mines de houille et le commerce de ... Jemappes*. Competition with England cited as critical (year 10); their coal is superior and accounts for their preeminence, particularly from the produce of Northumberland; the coals of Jemappes are comparable; "the work of exploitation in England has the advantage over those of this department ... because of the conduct of the operation and the perfection of the machines they employ." Their machines for extraction are more complex than ours (they are also near the sea); we need to develop our navigation system to compete.

59 J. R. Edwards, "Teaching 'Merchants' Accompts' in Britain during the Early Modern Period," A2009/2, www.cardiff.ac.uk/carbs/research/working_papers/accounting_finance/A2009_2.pdf.

from all over the country wrote to Paris to complain that they did not have the demonstration instruments they needed to teach the application of mechanics to real bodies in time and space. Yet they persevered. A similar curriculum that stressed mathematics and physics was put in place for the training of all engineers. Filling the cabinets and the teaching chairs remained a goal with which civil unrest, emigration, and international wars constantly interfered.[60]

The negative assessment of France's educational system made by the revolutionaries, at least when it came to training in applied science, may have been more right than wrong. When in 1800 Chaptal set out to reform science education, his minister of public education, Pierre-Louis Roederer, commissioned a study of British mathematical instruction by someone who seems to have known both systems remarkably well. Certainly the unsigned *mémoire* is detailed about the methods used to teach mathematics and most other subjects, and the distinctive types of English schools are described accurately. Chaptal and Roederer wanted to reform every branch and level of education, and they were particularly interested in mathematics. Their educational spy claimed that in Britain education in mathematics was superior.[61] If this is true – and it may very well be – the fact is significant and must be seen as one part in the complex story of why Britain industrialized first. Roederer was informed that while French penmanship excelled, the teaching of mathematics "has acquired the greatest perfection with the English." The ability to use arithmetic and algebra can even be seen among porters and valets in London, the report concluded. In addition, unlike Chaptal and Roederer, we now know that after 1750 education in British primary and secondary schools for boys – and even girls – rose steadily in numbers and years of attendance.[62]

All this comparative information assisted in the establishment of the elite *lycées*, a national French system of superior secondary education that gave serious attention to science and mathematics, including a "professor of applied mechanics for the arts and crafts and technology."[63] Note that a minority of boys and even fewer girls (in any country) engaged in

[60] For one such school, see C. Pouthas, *L'Instruction publique à Caen pendant la Révolution* (Caen: Louis Jouan, 1912).

[61] AN, Roederer, MS 29 AP 75, f. 395, on the primary schools of England; there is no uniformity, especially in the grammar schools, which as a result of English prosperity have inadvertently improved the level of education and have come to form the students for universities. On the subject of "calcul": "C'est cette partie de l'enseignement qui acquéri la plus de perfection chez les Anglaise."

[62] De Pleijt, 2011, pp. 5–6.

[63] AN, MS 29 AP 75, the private papers of Roederer, ff. 395–9, see article 12. See f. 619 for the structure of the lessons in physics and its application, and f. 666 on the suppression of the *écoles*.

secondary education in this period, and in 1802, when the *lycées* replaced the *écoles centrales*, they were meant to educate a mere 6,400 pupils. After the restoration of the Bourbon monarchy in 1815 the *lycées* became known as royal colleges; before that date they were simply alternative forms of secondary education.[64]

More than mathematics occupied the minds of the Napoleonic administrators. Chaptal and his ministers established new schools to replace the more democratic *écoles centrales*, and these meritocratic *lycées* were to be only in certain towns, favor the children of state bureaucrats, and specifically seek to stimulate industrial development in the region.[65] Vastly expanded, the *lycées* remain to this day one of the best forms of secondary schooling to be found in any Western country. In 1802, the curriculum of the French secondary schools had expanded to include Euclidean geometry, works by Descartes, and especially Newton and the major Newtonians. In 1810 the *lycée* in Rouen mandated the books to be used in physics, most by Newtonians: Haüy, 's Gravesande, Desaguliers, Mussenbroek, Mariotte, Nollet.[66] In effect, the Napoleonic administrators were institutionalizing the best and most progressive scientific education available from the eighteenth century.

After 1795, despite the reforming efforts of the French revolutionaries, only 31 of the approximately 105 new French central schools (for students aged fifteen and older) possessed significant collections of scientific equipment. Professors complained of having to teach without an amphitheater, laboratory, or cabinet of physics, and as a result having "to speak

[64] See Décret impérial concernant le Régime de l'Université, November 15, 1811, found in AN, F17 2504, last folder labeled 1813. See also P. Brenni, "The Evolution of Teaching Instruments and their Use between 1800 and 1930," *Science & Education*, 21, 2012, pp. 196–7.

[65] AN, 29 AP 75, f. 399, in any year the goal is for 6,000 students in the *lycées*, 3,000 chosen by the government from the children of military and functionaries who serve the republic well; the other 3,000 to be chosen by examination. There is to be a six-year course of study; government may distribute its largess unequally. Eventually La Fleche and one other are added and 6,400 pupils becomes the goal, f. 429; "nombre d'élèves que doit avoir chaque lycée doit varier." It must be remembered that the state "ne seul qu'une prime pour former les collèges; et ce système actuel peut eu quelque sorte se comparer au système du manufactures. Un Département n'a t-il point de manufactures? Le Gouvernement y envoie des ouvriers, des matières premières." By age fifteen or sixteen they should be nearly finished and doing mechanics and optics, see f. 645, professors are to use books approved by the government and it consulted Delambre and Cuvier at the Institute. See also M. S. Staum, *Minerva's Message: Stabilizing the French Revolution* (Montreal: McGill-Queen's University Press, 1996).

[66] AN, F 17 1559, "Liste des ouvrages ... approuvés de 1802–1830;" in 1802, works by Newton and Newtonians such as Keill, Gregory, and Maclaurin; also Daniel Bernoulli, Euler,'s Gravesande, LaGrange, Cassini, Monge, Camus, Desaguliers, Musschenbrock, and Haüy, among others. For Rouen, see Archives Départementales de Seine-Maritime, IT 1641 signed by Vitales, March 31, 1810.

metaphysically." Of course, in an average year before 1789 perhaps only 5,000 youth a year may have taken a course in physics. It is not surprising that in all of Continental Europe by 1790 there were fewer civil engineers in the private employment of mechanically knowledgeable entrepreneurs than was the case in Britain. Yet in regions where industrial activity stood as a possibility, for example in the area around Mont Blanc, the professor of physics and chemistry (in this case the same person) addressed the scientific issues raised by chemistry of gases, the density of the coal, and the need to identify specific gravities of various substances found in the region. The professor at Jemappes possessed an interest in "une machine hydropneumatique" for water and coal extraction. In the department of the Tarn the professor of physics and chemistry also offered a course on the dyeing of fabrics.[67]

Very little was added to the scientific reading list devised by Chaptal until the 1830s, although as we are about to see in the next chapter, gradually much was subtracted. During the reign of Napoleon, which ended in 1815, the commitment remained to teach workers of every kind to calculate and to "know descriptive geometry and ... the notions of physics and chemistry [and] to study the mechanism of machines."[68] When we turn to the French occupation of the Low Countries, we will see similar policies put into place in Belgium.

The French revolutionaries believed that prior to 1789 the clergy were responsible for the backwardness of the schools. This belief put them at odds with their own clergy at home, and especially in recently conquered Belgium where Catholicism ran deep and was nearly universal.[69] Whatever the bias of the French revolutionaries, some evidence exists to

[67] R. R. Palmer, "The Central Schools of the First French Republic: A Statistical Survey," in *The Making of Frenchmen: Current Directions in the History of Education in France, 1679–1979*, ed. D. N. Baker and P. J. Harrigan (Waterloo: Historical Reflections Press, 1980), pp. 230–1. For the *ancien régime* he is relying on the figures of Taton; in the 1790s, adults, both men and women, began to seek education in physics, and these schools had pupils ranging from the age of fifteen to thirty. By this time the courses in physics and mechanics are remarkably uniform and employ the textbooks of Brisson, Nollet, and Chaptal or Fourcroy in chemistry. Where there were no machines, professors drew descriptions of them and they sometimes indicated their application in manufacturing; see AN, Paris, 17 1344/1, the entire box, and first treatise by Boisset on the Mont Blanc department and Lemeret writing from Jemappes. Lenormand at the Tarn is also in charge of inspecting manufactures, see letter of 20 fructidor, year 7. On speaking metaphysically, see De Roussel writing from Calvados. In year 7 Brisson was teaching 200 students; most of the other 800 (approx.) respondents are teaching about 25 to 40.

[68] *Exposé de la situation de l'Empire français. 1806 et 1807* (Paris: Imperial Printer, 1807), p. 18. A similar claim is made in the exposé of 1809.

[69] For evidence of this continuing tension, see Algemeen Rijksarchief, Brussels, Binnenlandse Zaken, Zuidelijk Provincien, inv. nr. 3993, October 16, 1815 to March 31, 1818; Gent, College Royal, Bestuur.

suggest that the teaching of science in Catholic schools continued to lag behind what could be found in state-sponsored public schools until well into the nineteenth century.[70]

The Napoleonic administrators had figured out what anecdotal evidence confirms. If a young man was going to make a career in industry, and particularly in the application of machinery and its maintenance, in his youth he had to receive education in geometry and algebra, in basic mechanics of a Newtonian sort, and, of course, he had to be literate and numerate. Many British young men, such as James Watt, or M'Connel and Kennedy, received such an education when they were apprentices; also, as in the case of John Marshall, through self-education they built upon a firm foundation in literacy and numeracy.

Indeed, fully two-thirds of British inventors and improvers in the eighteenth century had been apprenticed. As we saw in the cases we have examined, the content of an apprenticeship is nearly impossible to reconstruct. Yet the claim has also been made for the Low Countries that apprenticeship was the most common experience of education in the early modern period.[71] No comparable figures are available for France. At the same time British formal education was entirely decentralized, and only a school-by-school search can tell us what was being taught. Where we know particular school systems, in the case of those run by Quakers, we can establish linkages between the teaching of natural philosophy, mathematics, and careers in industry. The same can be said of the Dissenting Academies. Yet the teaching of science and mathematics in grammar schools (the English equivalent to *lycées*) was not formally and universally instituted until after 1849. Arguably at the revolutionary *écoles centrales* of the 1790s, pupils received more basic science than they would have in a British grammar school. Certainly the revolutionary inspectors of that decade extolled the schools as offering an education "most striking in the progress of the human spirit in modern centuries," and with its many applications, physics exemplified what can be done for the "glory and happiness of mankind."[72]

70 P. J. Harrigan, "Church, State, and Education in France from Falloux to the Ferry Laws: A Reassessment," *Canadian Journal of History*, 36, 1, 2001, p. 66.

71 B. De Munck, *Technologies of Learning: Apprenticeship in Antwerp Guilds from the 15th Century to the End of the Ancien Régime* (Turnhout: Brepols, 2007), p. 5.

72 Friends Library, Euston Road, London, MS note book for good penmanship of William Sturge 1797, Ackworth School, MS Box G 1/5/1–2; and for the correlation between attendance at Ackworth and a career in industry, see E. Milligan, *Biographical Dictionary of British Quakers in Commerce and Industry, 1775–1920* (York: Sessions Book Trust, 2007), pp. 552–5 for students at Ackworth from 1779. For a similar curriculum, see Friends Library, Minute book of Joseph Sam's School, 1809–1828, at Darlington, County Durham, MS Vol. S.25. On apprentices, see Meisenzahl and Mokyr, "The Rate

This educational vision entirely embraced the secular, and eventually it would provoke a powerful, religious reaction. In the first decade of the nineteenth century, French administrators sought to maintain the secular orientation, and hence they were also clear on another vexed subject. The secondary schools were not to be in the business of teaching religion; that prohibition would be lifted during the reaction that came in the years after 1815 and the restoration of monarchy and church.[73]

With the restoration the secular authorities continued the rhetoric of being committed to the Baconian ideal of utility. They also put in place the Royal Institute, where scientists, among other *savants*, gathered and coveted the distinction of membership. Contemporaries believed the Institute had come to "realize the thought of the celebrated Bacon."[74] After the Napoleonic wars, praise for Baconianism did not, however, absolve the English of their failings. The French said that, unlike their English counterparts, they innovated "for the entire world" while the English "are jealous and envious." French critics complained that some people think that everything coming from across the Channel must be wonderful and are possessed of a foolish "Anglomania."[75] The more the English aspire to supremacy, some said, the more the French realize that all England's achievements originate with the flight of French Protestants after 1685 when Louis XIV revoked their religious liberty. The French, went the complaint, had already initiated those industries from which the English now benefitted. The moral of the story of French industry consisted of never ceasing to contest the preeminence of England in this "war of industry."

Gaps remained. In 1818 the Parisian Conservatory charged with the task of maintaining state-of-the-art mechanical devices possessed sophisticated batteries coming from the work of Volta, machines of every sort for spinning and weaving cotton as well as many other textiles, pneumatic machines, hydraulic machines, and multiple measuring devices, but – curiously and tellingly – not a single steam engine. Had it been state-of-the-art, a steam engine would have been made by Watt or modeled on his

and Direction of Invention," www.nber.org/papers/w16993. On science in the grammar schools, see A. Digby and P. Searby, *Children, School and Society in Nineteenth-Century England* (London: Macmillan, 1981), pp. 29–40. For the opening oration of André-Marie Ampère at the École Central at Bourg, see www.ampere.cnrs.fr/ms-ampere-302-57-1.5.html. Undated but addressed to "citizens" and probably from 1795 or 1796.

73 *Discours prononcé par Roederer, Orateur du Gouvernement sur le projet de loi relative à l'Instruction publique ... 11 floréal an 10*; 1 mai 1802, pp. 12–14 found at f. 681, AN, 29 AP 75. For an overview of the polemics characteristic of the left and right during the Restoration, see M. P. Owre, "United in Division: The Polarized French Nation, 1814–1830" (Ph.D. dissertation, University of North Carolina at Chapel Hill, 2008).

74 *Mémorial universel de l'industrie française* (Paris: Didot, 1821), p. 497.

75 Le Normand and de Moléon, 1824, pp. 48–51.

design.[76] When in 1822–3 an engineer appeared in Paris with the ability to build steam engines, he advertised them as being able "to rival those of England."[77] The neglect in teaching applied mechanics at the main Parisian engineering school may very well have contributed to the malaise into which French mechanical applications appear to have fallen. Certainly after 1830, when educational reform was everywhere discussed, the absence of interest in application at the engineering school figured high on the list of what needed to be addressed. Now, state-of-the-art instruction was to be based upon manuals on English mechanics.[78]

The gap in the application of steam was one of the prime reasons why French commentators said that "the imagination is confounded when contemplating the astonishing impact made on English industry by the genius in mechanics."[79] Perhaps predictably, from 1818 to 1823 more than twenty treatises on industrial mechanics poured from the French presses. In the same period an estimated 6,000 English mechanicians, artisans, millwrights, and master engineers were lured to France. In the 1830s, the tri-weekly newspaper, *L'Europe industrielle*, regularly reported on the number of steam engines and horsepower at work in Birmingham, or the state of English canal building and railroad construction. Generally it also kept its eye on other European countries and their relative industrial progress.[80] The journal documented the gap remaining between British and Belgian industrial development. As we are about to see, something else, not simply the high cost of labor or the absence of coal, had to be at work in deepening the puzzle of French industrial retardation.

[76] [G. Christian], *Catalogue général des collections du Conservatoire Royal des arts et métiers* (Paris: Mme Huzard, 1818).

[77] This is Bresson fils; see C. Malo, *Bazar Parisien, ou tableau raisonné de l'industrie* (Paris: au bureau du Bazar, 1822–3), pp. 66–7.

[78] AN, F14 11057, "Note sur l'organisation de l'École des Ponts et Chaussées par M. Navier, ingénieur en chef Septembre 1830, Rapport sur le cours de Mécanique appliquée de l'école des Ponts et Chaussées, L'ingénieur en chef soussigné a commencé à faire les leçons de mécanique appliqué en 1819. M. Eisenman n'ayant rien écrit sur cette matière, on ne peut dire en quoi consistait l'instruction dans il était chargé avant cette époque. Les Ingénieurs qui cherchent dans leurs souvenirs quelques traces de cette instruction n'en retrouvent presque aucune.... Enfin il serait indispensables de le procurer une ou deux des meilleures encyclopédies anglaises, qui sont des sources précieuses d'instruction. Ces ouvrages existent à la bibliothèque de l'institut, et l'expérience vous apprend chaque jour qu'il est impossible quand on en est privé de l'occuper conversablement des sciences et des arts, et d'en suivre les progrès. Il est inutile d'ajouter qu'outre ces collections, il faudrait que la bibliothèque peut avoir les ouvrages utiles qui paraissent journellement."

[79] Chamber of Commerce, *Enquête faite par ordre du Parlement d'Angleterre pour constater les progrès de l'industrie en France* (Paris: Boudouin, 1825), p. 10 from the preliminary discourse introducing the translation.

[80] Guillerme, *La naissance*, p. 321–2.

6 The puzzle of French retardation II

Restoration and reaction

Late in the reign of Napoleon, around 1812, a reformer within the Ministry that oversaw religion penned an angry treatise on the state of religion and the French clergy. Everything – from celibacy to their education – warranted reform, and the author noted in passing that high among clerical failings stood the complete refusal to undertake study in "les sciences mathématiques et physiques." By comparison to the "rapid march of all the sciences, the general perfection of their methods, theology has remained stationary."[1] Even allowing for bias, there is little evidence to contradict this anonymous assessment of clerical education at the opening of the nineteenth century.

In 1812, the Catholic Church was directed by the university to consolidate its ecclesiastical secondary schools, and then to put them in towns where their students could take courses at a *lycée* or college. Cardinal Joseph Fesch, Archbishop of Lyon, took umbrage at the government's commands. At the height of his power, Fesch had persuaded the Pope to come to Paris and crown Napoleon emperor. Despite receiving many honors, by 1812 Fesch had felt the cold chill that descended from Napoleon's growing disputes with the papacy. Thus Fesch had little to lose when he wrote to the Grand Master of the University and the Ministry of Cults to inform them that philosophy undertaken by students possibly destined for the priesthood had to be under the careful oversight of a bishop.

When it came to the physics taught in the French secondary schools, the archbishop complained bitterly that he would not even speak about physics, in a century where it has been used to efface the name of the Creator and his works, and "the observation of nature serves to destroy revealed Religion; it has never been more essential than today to allow the

[1] AN, Paris, MS f. 19 326, "Mémoire sur l'Etat de la Religion & du clergé en France," document unnumbered, 65 ff., ff. 21–3, "pour les sciences mathématiques & physiques il n'est pas du tout question." It is undated but placed in the files with documents from 1812, followed by documents from 1808.

Figure 10 Cardinal Joseph Fesch, an uncle of Napoleon Bonaparte, 1763–1839

Bishop to direct the study of physics ... to protect the students of the Sanctuary from an insidious philosophy that would oppose the religion of Jesus Christ, the human traditions and the elements of the world itself." Similar sentiments remained current in conservative Catholic circles well into the 1830s.[2]

[2] AN 19 4062, letter of January 10, 1812. And for his response to individual cases of possible closure, see his letter of December 10, 1811 in AN F 19 4062 and the response, where Fesch is told that the decree does not permit any exceptions, December 23, 1811; the same

Archbishop Fesch and his many followers spoke for much of the clerical leadership of the Church and its attitude toward science. Such views did not stop the Napoleonic administrators in their quest to add secular elements to the education offered in the ecclesiastical secondary schools. After 1812 the reorganization led to the closing of a number of ecclesiastical secondary schools, or their removal to more remote towns where there was no college or *lycée*. The University wanted to give the clergy knowledge of the human sciences so that they might better understand "the actual state of society . . . [and] acquire the right to speak with knowledge of the cause that made the glory of the century and forcefully leave behind the abuse of science."[3] Yet despite being relocated nearer to training in science or mathematics, the clerical schools leave little evidence that they broadened the training of future priests to subjects other than philosophy, theology, and the humanities. Certainly in 1828, when assessing the need for special new schools for more and better-educated priests, no mention is made of mathematics or science in a proposal to improve the curriculum.[4] Eleven years later the superior of the College of

letter of January 10, 1812 is also sent to the Ministry of Cults: "Je ne parle point de l'étude de la physique dans un Siècle où on semble prendre à tache d'effacer le nom du Créateur de dessus ses ouvres et de se servir de l'observation de la nature pour détruire la Religion révélé: il n'a jamais été plus essential qu'aujourd'hui de laisser aux Evêque la direction de l'étude de la physique, affine qui suivant le précepte de l'Apôtre ils puissant prémunir les Elèves du Sanctuaire d'une philosophie insidieuse qui voudront oppose à la Religion de Jésus Christ, les traditions humaines et les éléments même du monde. Videte ne quis vos decipiate per philosophiam et inanem fallaciam secundum traditionem hominum, secundum elementa mundi, et non secundum Christum." Underlining in the original. Such sentiments could also be found among British right-wing Tories: T. Whiting, *Mathematical, Geometrical, and Philosophical Delights . . . A Eulogium on the Newtonian Philosophy* (London: T.N. Longman, 1798), p. 19, "the Democratic school would make us believe, that particles, of inert, matter, from their most chaotic state, could dance, into form and order." See also *Œuvrés complètes de F Delamennais* (Paris: Paul Daubree et Cailleux, 1836–7), Vol. 7, "De la Religion considérée dans ses rapports avec l'ordre politique et civil," p. 104, "La science véritable, car il en est une, la science qui vient de Dieu et qui conduit a Dieu, à qui la doit-on, si ce n'est au clergé? Transmise par lui d'âge en âge, il la conservera fidèlement: mais il repousse sans doute, et ne cessera de repousser avec horreur, la fausse science, les trompeuses lumières qu'admirent quelques insensés." The April/June 2000 issue of *Annales Historiques de la Révolution Française* was devoted to the question of scientific inquiry and the French Revolution. Of particular interest, the article by Herve Grau, "L'Enseignement des Sciences Physiques fut-il Révolutionnaire? La Physique Expérimentale à Nantes du Collège Oratorien à L'École Centrale."

[3] AN F 19 4062, letter of response to Fesch, from the Grand Master of the Imperial University, January 23, 1812. See "Décret Impériale, 15 Novembre 1811," article 4, #24, insisting that they teach both letters and science. Found in AN F 17 2504, last folder labeled 1813.

[4] AN, MS F 19 326, "Rapport de l'évêque de Beauvais (Mgr. Feutrier) des affaires ecclésiastiques au Roi, 16 juin 1828." On the reorganization, see AN F 19 4062, "Université Impériale. Etat des écoles secondaires ecclésiastiques actuellement existantes."

Saint-Joseph in Lille proclaimed: "We are resisting with all our strength the forces that are precipitating the University in the direction of the almost exclusive study of the natural sciences, and we are faithful, as far as is possible, to the old traditions of the Schools."[5] He referred to the teaching of scholasticism, the philosophy of Aristotle as Christianized by Thomas Aquinas. Arguably, the whole of the nineteenth century witnessed constant strife between liberal secularists and the Catholic clergy over who would control French education, whether primary or secondary.

The strife began during the reign of Napoleon and was only exacerbated with the restoration of the monarchy and church in 1815. The Restoration brought a renewed emphasis on religious instruction and the moral probity of French students, while the clergy were returned to their preeminent place in primary school education.[6] French clerically controlled schools in the eighteenth century had a spotty but real concern for technical education; in 1815, after a generation of secularization and anticlericalism, when the clergy returned, they threw their considerable educational zeal in the direction of re-Christianization.[7] The new Restoration government embodied a profound reaction against what it regarded as the excesses of the French Revolution, and education now had to be re-reformed. "Religion and love of the King must be made the base of education," inculcated without ceasing, and state inspections in every district were to report back to the Ministry of the Interior that all children in primary schools received religious and moral instruction. It may be hard at this distance to imagine that physics was a cause of the French Revolution, but that is the import of what Archbishop Fesch had to say about it.

Consequently, even when in the service of religious piety, the system of state inspectors inherited from Napoleon did not sit well with the Church. Given that the lay rectors of the regional academies were in charge of overseeing all aspects of education, the Archbishop of Paris pointedly informed the king: "That anywhere the rector of the academy will be an irreligious

[5] Quoted from the archives of the Institution libre du Sacré-Cœur, Tourcoing, in R. Gildea, *Education in Provincial France 1800–1914* (Oxford: Clarendon Press, 1983), p. 195. For the Napoleonic period, see also A. Leon, "Promesses et Ambiguïtés de l'Œuvre d'Enseignement Technique en France, 1800 à 1815," *Revue d'Histoire Moderne et Contemporaine*, 17, 3, 1970, pp. 846–59. T. Shinn, "From Corps to 'Profession': The Emergence and Definition of Industrial Engineering in Modern France," *The Organization of Science and Technology in France, 1808–1914* (Cambridge University Press, 1981).

[6] Archives Départementales, Seine-Maritime, MS 1T 873: Fonds de l'Académie, Administration générale, Lettres ministérielles au recteurs au sujet du personnel, 1823–1826; see letters for 1826 to and from Paris, Ministère des Affaires ecclésiastiques et de l'Instruction publique.

[7] A. Prévot, *L'Enseignement Technique chez les Frères des Écoles Chrétiennes au XVIIIe et aux XIXe siècles* (Paris: Ligel, 1964), pp. 87–100.

man; your people will be without religion." The entire discussion of the academies that regionally oversaw secondary education was framed within the context of what the Archbishop saw as the excesses of the French Revolution when "the rights of man became the universal catechism." In 1818, a test of religious probity was imposed, and a certificate of morality and the profession of the Catholic religion were required of all primary school teachers.[8] As late as the 1840s, even men of science, such as the royalist mathematician A. Cauchy, wrote off the entire eighteenth century as "the source of calamities without number . . . the abuse of talent and science."[9]

Position papers circulating in the Ministry of Ecclesiastical Affairs around 1815 decried how – for a generation – education had bred license and passion. Only a return to teaching morality, respect for king and God, and not least the history of France, will free the young from "the vices of the revolution."[10] In secondary schools the pupils were to be instructed on the abuses introduced by the enlightened "l'esprit philosophique."[11] Needless to say, all the works by the *philosophes*, Voltaire, Diderot, Rousseau, etc., were off school reading lists. In addition, the post-1815 ministers charged with overseeing education were vigilant that books inspiring "in the children of the inferior classes the sentiments of animosity toward the more elevated classes" were also banned. A pupil acting out became a sign of republican and even revolutionary tendencies.[12]

The school inspections from 1817 to 1820 tell an important story about the reaction against science, and reveal the lack of scientific education in the French secondary schools. At the academy in Clermont-Ferrand, the academy at Metz, at Pau, at the relatively new colleges in Corsica, in the north at Caen (where mathematics was taught), the inspectors evince little, if any, interest in the teaching of either physics or chemistry – even, as in Metz, where the faculty possessed one teacher of physics. At least in Lyon, the academy had a zealous teacher of physics who had no instruments, no minerals, plants, or acids. No such instructor appears in the documentation

[8] Archives historiques de diocèse de Paris, 4 rue de l'Asile Popincourt, Paris 11, letter of 1816, n.d. from the archbishop addressed to "Sire." For the certificates, see AN F/17/10172/180, letter of April 17, 1818 from the rector of the Academy of Lyon.

[9] A. Cauchy, "Sur la recherché de la vérité," *Bulletin de l'Institut Catholique*, second installment, April 14, 1842, p. 21. Reference kindly supplied by Amir Alexander.

[10] AN, MS F 19 326, ff. 425–30.

[11] AN, Paris, F17 11752, Commission de l'instruction publique, 27 juin 1816. On the approval of books hostile to the Enlightenment, see "Liste générale des ouvrages qui ont été adoptés. . . . pour l'usage des Collèges . . . depuis 1802," #258, a work by de Portalis.

[12] AN, F 17 23396, book #244, "Commission charge de la révision des livres," 1831. For impact of the reactionary discipline, see M. Pickering, *Auguste Comte: An Intellectual Biography, Volume 1* (Cambridge University Press, 1993), pp. 27–31.

about Marseilles where none of the professors has time for, or interest in mathematics. The academy at Toulouse insisted that it must have mathematics and science, in part because of the local medical school, and saw to it that physics and chemistry were taught in the early 1820s. It also taught pure and applied mathematics and lacked only someone sufficiently qualified to occupy the chair of physics. At Dijon, physics was promoted at the academy, but at the Royal College (the colleges were roughly on the level of *lycées*) the chairs of physics and mathematics were vacant, but the subjects were taught nonetheless. Rectors of the academies instructed that physics and chemistry be taught in the commercial towns and cities, but it is unclear how many followed their instructions.[13]

During this period of drought for the sciences, the distinguished French scientist J.-M. Ampère was an inspector of the royal colleges, and after 1815 his papers contain scathing attacks on the teaching of science and mathematics. He described it right up to 1828 as nothing less than "deplorable."[14] Although the various inspection reports of the circumstances into which scientific education had succumbed were clear, there was no real interest in anything other than the religious devotion of the students and the state of the humanities. One exception can be seen in the reports of Ampère. Case by case, he decried the condition into which the academy at Dijon had fallen, but then praised the teaching of science at Caen. Other inspectors evince no burning love of the clergy, and first and foremost wanted them to submit to the will of the University, the administrative body (not a teaching institution) charged with the task of overseeing primary and secondary education for the nation. When combined with a clergy submissive to lay authority, the inspectors in turn were clear that devotion to religion was all part of order and obedience.[15]

[13] AN F 17 6809/1, ff. 189–355, and f. 356 for the conditions at Lyon; f. 327 for mathematics at Marseilles; f. 378 for Toulouse, report of July 14, 1817; Dijon f. 163 but placed after f. 210 and between f. 209 which are out of order. For Toulouse, see F 17 6810, f. 493, filed out of order and dated 1823. For the near absence of scientific education in the colleges of the Côte d'Or, see ff. 165, with mathematics present in about half of the schools. The majority of the faculty was, by far, lay. See Archives départementales, Seine-Maritime, IT 864: Fonds de l'Académie, Instruction ministérielles et correspondance diverse adressées au recteur, 1819–1822, Commission de l'Instruction Publique, Division du Personnel, Bureau de Coll. Roy, Paris, le 30 novembre 1819 Monsieur le Recteur, la Commission a senti la nécessité de donner dans tous les Collèges Royaux, une direction fixé et un forme aux cours de sciences physiques, qui malgré le zèle et le talent de Professeurs, n'ont eu jusque à ce jour faute de d'unité, que des résultats incomplète.

[14] www.ampere.cnrs.fr/ms-ampere-302-81-1.5.html image 81; MSS, André-Marie Ampère, Chemises 302 et 302bis [carton 20], 1775–1836. Accessed December 15, 2012.

[15] AN 17 6809/1, f. 406. Ampère insists that the physics course must be experimental. His report on Caen is in AN F 17 6810, June 16, 1829. See AN F 17 6810 for the instructions to the inspectors of studies, 1823, where there is no mention of science.

Dessiné d'après nature en 1825, et Gravé par Ambroise Tardieu.
ANDRÉ MARIE AMPÈRE
(Mathématicien et Physicien),
Membre de l'Académie des Sciences,
Professeur au Collège royal de France et à
l'Ecole polytechnique, des sociétés d'Edimbourg,
de Cambridge, de Genève, Helvétique, etc.
Né à Lyon (Dépt. du Rhône) le 20 Janvier 1775.

Figure 11 André-Marie Ampère (1775–1836)

In 1818, a popular work, receiving the prize for the best book from the *Société pour l'instruction élémentaire*, presented a young man, a small-time buyer and seller of goods, who travels about the countryside accompanied by a priest, and sheds light and joy wherever he goes. He praises religion and the king – many times – and extols the merits of everything from mutual education (where children teach one another), the National Guard, the payment of taxes and the metric system, to vaccination. Primly he preaches against the insolence of servants toward their masters, the perils of over-eating and drinking, and the indolence and laziness of the locals. He ends by proclaiming that a general prosperity will come, and that all men must dedicate themselves to France. In this way they will demonstrate to other nations their superiority.[16]

The prize book went through multiple editions over the next fifty or more years. Yet the enduring smugness of the little boy, Simon, belied an under-the-surface anxiety. As had their pre-1815 predecessors, the French authorities nervously looked at instructional methods in Holland and England and sought to imitate them. Students were mutually to instruct one another, in imitation of the method known as Lancasterian; reading, writing, and arithmetic remained at the core of primary education, but the local curé and a committee of the district were to maintain "the order of morals and religious instruction." Protestants and Jews had to be educated separately. Conservative clerics bitterly opposed mutual instruction, regarding it as a subversion of priestly authority. Even in 1816, when the Lancasterian method was new and introduced by some Christian Brothers, the leadership of the Church viewed it with suspicion, and eventually it largely disappeared from the schools.[17]

Liberal reformers fought back against the reactionary climate, but to little avail – until the Revolution of 1830. Most took the position that nothing they advocated for the advance of industry need threaten the necessity for a moral and religious education. They argued that science and industry can be ameliorated by rapid progress, and that "general notions of physics, chemistry, natural history, physiology, botany, agriculture, and the principals of hygiene . . . the principal laws of mechanics"

[16] L. P. de Jussieu, *Simon de Nantua, ou le Marchand Forain* (Paris: chez L. Colas, 1818), passim.

[17] AN F 17 23396, Enseignement mutuel, École des Lisieux, 7 Novembre, 1819. See the correspondence of the Archbishop of Paris for 1816, Archives historiques de diocèse de Paris, Paris 9, letter of February 9, 1816 from Archbishop Alex. Ang. Duc de Reims to Comte de Vaublanc, Minister of the Interior.

offer an everyday utility. None of their arguments seemed to impress the ultra-royalists or the hierarchy of the Church.[18]

In general the restored Catholic Church could only have been pleased, despite the persistent complaining of its ultra-royalist right-wing. The state subsidized novitiates for the training of orders of Christian brothers, while religious books were being diligently distributed in the re-Christianized schools.[19] In the further reaction of 1822, when the nobleman and bishop of Paris, Denis Frayssinous, became Grand Master of the University, he made clear that pupils must have "their eyes on sacred objects; they are the true way to give them religious habits."[20] As early as 1808, when new guidelines were issued for education, he believed "in the uniformity of education, the fidelity to the Emperor and that . . . the pupils be attached to their Religion . . . education will be based on the precepts of the Catholic Church."[21] Therein lay his single-minded concern.

In multiple orations, many centered on the horrors of the French Revolution, Bishop Frayssinous made clear his belief that the *philosophes* of the eighteenth century had planted the seeds of revolution. They had exaggerated the advantages of the sciences, letters, and arts – all became more commonplace than ever before. Their popularity coincided with the Revolution, one of the greatest calamities that ever afflicted the earth.[22] While the good bishop could acknowledge the achievements of science, he did so only as an afterthought.[23] Given his attitude toward secular learning and the French Revolution, we cannot be surprised when we observe the downward course of scientific and technical education after the Restoration. To start the process, efforts were made to remove Ampère as a school inspector; other scientists came to his defense. Indeed, after police reports in 1826, the Royal Academic Society of the Sciences, an originally non-royal and republican body, was prohibited, and its members left to protest that they had never spoken a word about "politics or religion." Deep suspicion shaped the Church's response, especially to any

[18] A. C. Renouard, *Considérations sur les lacunes de l'éducation secondaire en France* (Paris: Antoine-Augustin Renouard, 1824), pp. 6, 78–80.

[19] L. P. de Jussieu, *Simon de Nantua, ou le Marchand Forain*, Paris, January 6, 1820, "Rapport" presented to the secretary of state for the ministry of the interior on religious books being distributed in the schools. See the entire folder, F17 12451 for the payment of expenses for educating the Brothers of Christian Doctrine and the Brothers of Christian Schools.

[20] *Circulaire de Mgr Frayssinous*, June 1822; BFM, Fol-R Pièce-205.

[21] AN, AB xix 514, letter of September 3, 1818, underlining in the original.

[22] M. D. Frayssinous, *Conférences et discours inédits* (Paris: Adrien Le Clere, 1843), pp. 39–40. For a secondary work that contains the same sentiments, see A. Chevalier, *Les frères des écoles chrétiennes et l'enseignement primaire après la révolution, 1787–1830* (Paris: Libraire Poussielgne Frères, 1887).

[23] Ibid., p. 601.

curriculum heavily dominated by science and its application. A leading, although controversial, Catholic intellectual of the 1820s and 1830s wrote: "*L'école polytechnique* furnishes an example of the sad reforms that take from religion a part of its influence over man."[24]

At the same time, and at the height of the reaction, the police spied on the free and public lectures given by Parisian professors at the *Conservatoire des arts et métiers* and found that they contained eulogies "to liberty and equality ... and that a King is more often an ignorant and unjust man." Among the greatest offenders, M. Dupin, a teacher of geometry and applied mechanics, also had accomplices teaching literature, chemistry, and economics, when, the police said, they were not teaching sedition. Whenever Dupin lectured, the amphitheatre was packed with attentive young men preparing for careers in manufacturing or commerce, and students of mathematics – or so the spies reported. Particular surveillance also had to be placed on the courses in chemistry and industrial economy. Perhaps all learning intended for industrial development had become inherently suspect. Certainly such applied instruction was described consistently as anti-monarchical and irreligious. In the minds of the police authorities, such liberal groups sought "to exploit all types of industry, all human knowledge in the interest of the revolution." The three great "powers of modern time ... the financial aristocracy, the scientific and the industrial" would prepare the triumph of a new liberal and revolutionary order.[25] In addition, industrialists and merchants, at least in Rouen, had become suspect because of "the

[24] AN, F 17 3038, pamphlet dated December 27, 1826, "Les membres de la commission administrative, charge de réclamer après du Ministre de l'intérieur, contre son arête du 31 janvier 1826." For the reports, see AN F 7 6689, from the prefecture of police to the Ministry of the Interior, January 30, 1826, it had become associated with certain Masonic lodges. For the attack on the Polytechnique, see *Œuvres complètes de F. Delamennais*, Vol. 7, p. 347, "Education publique." See also www.ampere.cnrs.fr/amp-corr677.html and www.ampere.cnrs.fr/ms-ampere-306-2-1.5.html

[25] AN, F 7 6965, #12,391 Paris, January 14, 1825, to the Prefect of Police. There is particular concern over M. Dupin. For his teaching of geometry and applied mechanics, see first item in this dossier, dated October 13, 1828. For Clement teaching chemistry and Say on the industrial economy, see #12, 391, Paris, December 17, 1824, labeled confidential; #12391 on filled lecture halls. See #12, 395 for a teacher of mathematics with liberal opinions, and May 4, 1827 for liberals meeting in the room of a Masonic lodge; #12394 for another "vénérable" of a lodge. See also AN F 76915 letter of March 8, 1826, in #8351 on a literary society in Paris, L'Athènée. For a *mémoire* that ties all these projects, science, industry, and finance, the conservatory, the lectures of Dupin, under the banner of revolution and liberalism, see Prefecture de police, Paris 26 mars 1825, in AN F 7 6689/23 and in the same box, March 26, 1825. For Dupin's teaching at the *Conservatoire*, see K. Chatzis, "Theory and Practice in the Education of French Engineers from the Middle of the 18th Century to the Present," *Archives internationals d'histoire des sciences*, Vol. 60, June 2010, 1 3, p. 54n.

violence of the revolutionary opinion." This premier industrial city, according to the police, had become "the theatre of intrigue." It was also seen to be the case that certain industrialists forged ties with secret societies of liberals in search of a way to return to the principles of the French Revolution. A cloud of liberal conspiracy hung over the 1820s.[26]

Such police reports fed the extreme reaction of the decade. Then and thereafter, during the first half of the nineteenth century, the Church engaged in a massive, encyclopedic effort to undo the damage done by Diderot and the *philosophes* and to initiate "une science catholique."[27] This French Catholic reaction to the culture of the Enlightenment, given the role of the clergy in primary and secondary education, had consequences for the training of a new generation of engineers and industrialists. Certainly in 1830, when another revolution brought in a more liberal monarch, clerical supporters thought that during the past fifteen years the bishops had followed an "absurd theology," and "one of them had told me it is dangerous that the people would be instructed." They were better off working the soil or pursuing a craft – for the laity that was enough.[28]

One other element must be reckoned into the general malaise into which scientific education after 1815 had fallen. Science depends upon open communication, and in this period live demonstrations of its principles, particularly in mechanics, were deemed essential. Ampère made the point in multiple reports where he insisted that physics had to be taught experimentally. In this same period all voluntary associations had

[26] S. Neely, *Lafayette and the Liberal Ideal 1814–1824: Politics and Conspiracy in the Age of Reaction* (Carbondale, IL: Southern Illinois University Press, 1991), in particular Chapter 7, and G. Malandain, *L'introuvable complot. Attentat enquête et rumeur dans la France de la Restauration* (Paris: EHESS, 2011). See also AN F 7 6689/ 26, letter of January 8, 1821 from Prefecture de la Seine-Inférieure, about the secret Society of Reformers. There are reports in the dossier from various cities, Calvados, Marseille, Besançon, including a report on the Masonic lodges in Paris, June 1, 1825 from the prefecture of the police, and one from Poitiers on a society "prétendue maçonnique." In the same box, ff. 307–19, information about a Masonic group with the name of Misraim, September 8, 1822, from Montpellier, also Paris, May 7, 1825, ff. 503–22; 362; much of this box is devoted to this group. On freemasonry in the politics of the Restoration, see A. B. Spitzer, *Old Hatreds and Young Hopes: The French Carbonari against the Bourbon Restoration* (Cambridge, MA: Harvard University Press, 1971), pp. 219–24. The link between industrialists and the Charbonnerie is made in J.-N. Tardy, "Le flambeau et le poignard. Les contradictions de l'organisation clandestine des libéraux français, 1821–1827," *Revue d'histoire moderne & contemporaine*, 57–1, 2010, p. 73.

[27] S. Dord-Crouslé, "Les entreprises encyclopédiques catholiques au XIXe siècle: quelques aspects liés à la construction du savoir littéraire," in L. Andries, ed., *La Construction des savoirs XVIIIe–XIXe siècles* (Lyon: Presses Universitaires, 2009), pp. 177–210.

[28] AN F 19, 860, Poulard, the bishop of Autun to the Minister of Public Instruction and Religion, not dated, but from 1830 as seen by the other letters in the dossier.

to be approved by the government, and its ministers did not hesitate to deny authorization even to a literary society if they thought it could become a "center ... for democratic principles and associations."[29] All discussions of religion or politics were prohibited at any authorized gathering, and at least one provincial scientific and literary society conducted its proceedings in secret.[30] This climate could hardly be described as nurturing for science.

After the Revolution of 1830 the state changed the agenda for public education, and while religion remained important, school inspectors were told to pay particular attention "to the diverse parts of commercial and industrial" education, to "this necessity of our age."[31] But arguably, the damage had been done. The change in direction came after nearly twenty years – a generation of young people – when the educational ideals of the French Revolution were systematically undermined. In 1831, inspectors reported that "the colleges had fallen under the empire of the clergy" and urged that at least one inspector always be a mathematician. That said, the record also shows that in some colleges, Montpellier and Caen for example, a high degree of scientific education could be found by the late 1820s. In places like Grenoble, where mathematics and chemistry were needed for mining and commerce, the courses were available. By very late in the 1820s the University had begun inspections specifically aimed at the state of the sciences in the various academies and colleges. Some of the pressure for scientific teaching may have come from the general public that, it was said, crowded around open windows and doors to hear the courses on physics and chemistry.[32]

In 1828, the University of France, which oversaw all secondary education, concluded that a special course of commercial instruction needed to be established at the Royal College in Rouen. By that date the guidelines tell what French educators thought had to be possessed by the successful businessman. First, for students no older than fourteen, a foundation had to be laid in elementary mathematics, including the operation of banking, double-entry bookkeeping, and geometry. Grammar and rhetoric

[29] AN, F 7 6697, confidential letter of October 10, 1828 to the Minister of the Interior from Chaumont, Haute-Marne, the prefect, Louis de St. Gene. The discussion is about a possible refusal to allow a literary circle in Chaumont, and another in Langres.

[30] AN F 7 6697, dated 1827, see statutes in folder "Valognes Société scientifique et Littéraire." Many dossiers in this box devoted to masonic lodges.

[31] AN F 17 6810, f. 224, "Instructions à M.M. les Inspecteurs génereraux ... de 1832."

[32] For the academy at Montpellier, see AN F 17 6810, f. 416 report on the faculty of science, July 22, 1828; same box f. 549 for Grenoble, 1826; for Toulouse, 1827, f. 450, where chemistry for industrial arts is taught, as is physics, which has a following among young army officers; f. 263, 1831 on the academy at Rennes and the need for a mathematician; the crowds can be found in 1830 in Toulouse, f. 290, July 25, 1830.

remained important, followed by study of the English language, French history, and industrial geography around the globe. Thereafter came the principles of statics and mechanics, the construction and operation of major machines, in particular steam engines and water wheels – all to be capped by visits of professors and students to the principal industrial establishments of Rouen. Physics and chemistry remained important, with particular attention paid to their industrial applications. In short, by 1830 the commercial had come to mean the industrial.[33]

Science in the industrial heartland: the Department of the North

If we take the Department of the North and the area around Calais, close to what was (then and now) Belgium, it is possible to observe the revolutionary curriculum at its birth after 1789 – and at its eventual demise after 1815. The North is not just any province from the perspective of industrial development. Just south of the department of Jemappes, seized from the Austrians in 1795, this northern region of France was its most populous, had access to Belgian and French coal, and its engineers could witness the advanced state of machine technology found at the Austrian/Belgian coal mines. By contrast, at the famous French mine owned by the Anzin Company, Newcomen engines had been installed late in the eighteenth century but little was done to maintain them in good working order. The department offers another remarkable advantage: all the reports about the state of education in 1790–1, requested by the new revolutionary government, have been preserved.[34]

From the perspective of education in mathematics and the sciences, the reports make for grim reading. The vast majority of the colleges, aimed at male children generally from twelve to eighteen years of age, offered no mathematics or science. In the 1780s, the situation for mathematics improved and it was generally lumped with architecture. Nowhere in the records of finances or endowments does money appear for experimental equipment or laboratories. In the universities and colleges of Lille, at least forty students worked with one professor of mathematics, and that figure was down because of the political instability in the north. In the colleges near the university of Douai, deference had to be given to its teaching of

[33] Archives Départementales de Seine-Maritime, IT 1657, Décembre 23, 1828.

[34] Reed G. Geiger, *The Anzin Coal Company. Big Business in the Early Stages of the French Industrial Revolution* (Newark, DE: University of Delaware Press, 1974), pp. 58, 86–7. For the reports, see P. Marchand, *Écoles et Collèges dans le Nord à l'aube de la Révolution. L'enquête du directoire du département du Nord sur les établissements destinés à l'instruction de la jeunesse (1790–91)* (Lille: Université Charles de Gaulle, 1988).

mathematics and the sciences at the higher level. It is not clear what was being taught at Douai under the rubric "dialectics, philosophy, and mathematics," nor is it clear how students at the lower levels prepared to take in what the university had to offer.[35]

After 1795 the schooling for French students aged at least fourteen in the Department of the North paid new attention to mathematics, especially as it applied to actual bodies. Even, calculus was introduced, although scientific instruction came more slowly.[36] In 1795, the decree went out throughout the department that the new schools were to have four new classrooms, for mathematics, physics, chemistry, and natural history.[37] The following year further uniformity was added to the science curriculum and the professors were instructed about the order in which the science topics should be taught.[38] The directives coming out of Paris remained completely silent on the subject of religious education or the traditional classical education, although by 1807 the Ministry of the Interior demanded that the lay faculty not spend its time teaching the catechism, devoted as it was to dogma. Much to the annoyance of the local ecclesiastics, that was to be done by priests in a separate place outside of the school. All secondary schools were to follow the directive. Undeterred by the law, the clergy in the department struck back and took to ringing church bells and holding public processions.[39] As in many other places in revolutionary France, the practice of religion had become deeply vexed.

The secondary school curriculum could also be filled easily with secular subjects. In some places, such as Douai, such a dramatic turn away from

35 Marchand, 1988, p. 49.

36 Archives départementales du Nord (ADN), Lille, Séries L 4840, printed circular, Programme d'exercices publics, qui auront lieu a le école centrale du département du nord, établie a Lille, les 28 et 29 Fructidor, an VI de la République (Lille: chez Jacquez). See AN F 19 456, Cambrai, January 19, 1807, the secondary school in Cambrai had two professors of mathematics out of five faculty. See also N. Hulin, "La place des sciences naturelles au sein de l'enseignement scientifique au XIXe siècle/The place of natural science within the 19th-century science curriculum," *Revue d'histoire des sciences*, 51 4, 1998, pp. 409–34.

37 Ibid., Séries L 4840, Extrait des registres du comité d'instruction publique, règlement de police pour les écoles centrales ... 8 ventôse, l'an 3 de la république; circular printed at Douai.

38 Ibid., *Extrait des registres des délibérations de l'administration centrale du département de la Moselle, 25 Prairial 4th year* (1796). Here the guidelines call for math and physics and experimental chemistry; article 5, "la physique sera enseignée pendant les sept premiers mois de l'année, et la chimie, pendant les cinq autres. Le professeur enseignera la premiere science dans l'ordre suivant, proprieties des corps, mouvement, statique, hydrostatique ... feu, lumière electricité." This circular is printed in Metz and to be sent to the Department of the North. See also *Avis du jury d'instruction nommé ... pour la formation de l'école centrale de Maubeuge*.

39 Series L 4840. For annoyance, see letter of February 10, 1807 to the Minister of the Interior, February 9, 1807.

religion and theology constituted a significant departure from what had been taught right up to 1790. In Douai, famous for its many seminaries and colleges, the vast majority taught no science and little mathematics, but by 1804, if not before, the new *lycée* (originally the *école centrale*) offered mathematics and physics and the Royal College possessed a "cabinet of physics, rich in instruments." By 1800 schools in Lille, as well as Namur (now being within a department of France), had added electricity, gases, and air pressure to the curriculum.[40] In less than ten years the city of Lille demanded a public course in physics, with salaries and instruments for demonstrations paid for by the Ministry of the Interior.[41] Its industrial prowess was honored during a royal visit in 1827. Two years earlier the city had requested public courses in geometry and applied mechanics.[42]

After 1815 something happened to scientific education in the secondary schools of the Department of the North. In most cases mathematical instruction continued, but physical and chemical science largely disappeared. In 1816, physics was still being taught at the Royal College but only four students elected to take it. The curriculum had returned to being overwhelmingly classical.[43] In 1822, at the Collège de Cambrai, mathematics, including geometry, was being taught, but neither physics nor mechanics. In the same year the Collège d'Armentières was teaching no mathematics or science, but the following year it instituted the teaching of arithmetic, the metric system, and the fundamentals of algebra. So, too, the Collège du Quesnoy in 1823 taught neither math nor science. The Collège de Tourcoing taught commercial arithmetic; the Collège de Baillaud and the Collège de Lille offered mathematics only. In 1824, at the Collège de Valenciennes, the inspector complained about the math exercises and problems being too easy. In 1822, the inspection of the secondary schools in the region overseen by the Academy of Douai found

[40] Archives Municipales de Douai, 1R 8: Lycée an XIII–XIV, Lycée de Douai, *Programme des Exercices Publics, qui auront lieu sous la Présidence de MM. Les Membres du Bureau d'Administration*, printed brochure; 1R, 18 (printed brochure), Université de Douai, Collège Royal de Douai; *Programme d'exercices publics, qui auront lieu a l'école centrale ... Lille, year 8*, p. 6, where gases and air pressure are being taught, also electricity. For teaching the catechism outside the school, see AN, F 19 456, Cambrai, January 19, 1807, from the prefect of the Department of the North. For the colleges at 1790, see Marchand, 1988, pp. 105–28.

[41] ADN, Lille Box 1 T /19/1–4, minister of interior in 1809 has received a request to set up a free course in experimental physics and giving money for salary and instruments; course of chemistry in place in the 1820s.

[42] [Anon.] *Relation du séjour du Roi a Lille ... Le 7 et 8 Septembre 1827* (Lille: Reboux-Leroy), pp. 47–51; 95–100. For the courses in applied mechanics, see ADN, IT 158 Paris, November 11, 1825, letter from the Ministry of the Interior to the Prefect, circular No. 56.

[43] ADN, MS 2 T 1712 Report on the Royal College of 1816.

geometry – but no science. In 1825, its cabinet of physics had deteriorated woefully. By 1840 the situation with physics in the secondary schools under the direction of the departmental academy had changed somewhat, and at least one possessed a "cabinet de physique" and the teaching was under the direction of a layman. In other places it still left much to be desired.[44]

In addition, the ecclesiastical secondary schools – for young men who might become priests – displayed neglect for science, thus suggesting that if their graduates became clergy and went into teaching they would be forced to stay away from those subjects or work awfully hard to catch up. If one of them then went on to the seminary in the region he would have received little help. A letter of 1828 to the Ministry of Education reported that the seminary in Cambrai taught neither mathematics nor science.[45] These deficiencies were noted by liberal critics, who were convinced that the teaching of mathematics and mechanics, particularly in the North, would result in further industrial development and wealth for the state.[46]

The Department of the North should not be uniquely faulted. If we take the Department of the Eure in Normandy, its secondary schools also overseen by the Imperial University and the Academy of Rouen, the situation appears not very different. Rouen was a major center for the production of cotton cloth, and from the 1790s onward we can document a concentrated

[44] Archives Municipales, Douai, 1R 24: Académie de Douai, ..., 1821–1830, Douai, le 2 mai 1825, "A Monsieur le Proviseur du Collège Royal de Douai, Monsieur le Proviseur, Depuis que j'ai l'honneur d'appartenir au Collège Royal, j'ai souvent et inutilement présenté des observations sur la détérioration progressive des instruments de Physique, et sur la nécessité d'y porter un prompt remède. Aujourd'hui le mal a pris un tel accroissement, qui, tous nos instruments sont menacés d'une destruction complète." See Archives Municipales, Douai, 4M 21, where 7,000 francs will be needed for repair and renewal; for the sophisticated contents of the local museum's cabinet, see Archives Municipales, Douai, 8A64, *Explication divers objets en Peinture, Histoire naturelle, Antiquités, Médailles et Instruments de Physiques, qui composait le Muséum de la Ville de Douai, Publiée par la Société d'Agriculture, Sciences, et Arts du Département du Nord*, Juillet, 1807, A Douai. De l'Imprimerie de Villette, Rue du Clocher St. Pierre, No. 71 (208) Cinquième Division, Instruments de Physique et de Chimie; AN F 17 8838, letter of February 5, 1840 from the inspector Vincent to the Inspection extraordinaire des Institutions et pensions on the school of the abbé Haffreingue in Boulogne sur Mer, in folder labeled Douai. In this region a number of students also took lessons at the Royal College. See also in same place, "Exposé sommaire de la situation des établissements privés d'instruction secondaire du ressort de l'Académie de Douai."

[45] All these examples are drawn from Archives Départementales du Nord, MS 1 T /19/1–4; AN F17 10384, letter of September 20, 1823 from Douai to the Grand Master of the University on the suppression of "clandestine" primary schools and the new ones now authorized by the state.

[46] C. Dupin, *Effets des l'enseignement populaire de la lecture, de l'écriture et de l'arithmétique, de la géométrie et de la mécanique* (Paris: Bachelier, 1826), pp. 25–57.

interest in the acquisition of steam engines.[47] Even before 1815, its colleges by and large taught mathematics but very little science. Exceptions were duly noted in the reports to the academy. At the college of Evreux, the principal "was professor of mathematics at *l'école centrale*, and as a result many of his students have gone on to attend *l'école polytechnique*." Throughout the country, the *écoles centrales* had been abandoned in 1802 and renamed as secondary schools known as *lycées*. In 1814, a teacher at one of them in Rennes requested that he be allowed to set up a course of instruction in mechanics. The local principal wrote to ask whether it would be permitted under the laws and statutes of the University. We do not know what answer he received, although the principal noted that it would be more suitable for persons of an advanced age. At Toulouse the academicians taught a significant number of students; they received instruction in mathematics but not in science.[48] Only in 1826 did the royal council on public instruction, now a part of the Ministry of Ecclesiastical Affairs, mandate that more complex mathematics and physics be taught in the colleges. It is not clear that much changed in the wake of that decree. It had been preceded by one of 1821 that had little or no effect, and in 1828 the ministry noted "the repugnance of the students" for mathematical studies. The following year the university demanded that each academy report on the morals, religion, and politics of every faculty member. In sum, from 1805 to 1826, where physics was taught at all, it was given as a single, very general course in the *lycées*.[49]

Paris and elsewhere

In the mid 1830s, the University was still struggling with the professors in Paris to push them to teach mathematics in its complexity. It may have been unwittingly assisted by a new school established to teach "English youth apparently from industrial families," intended to occupy places in industry. Living languages (as opposed to Latin), history, geography, physics, chemistry, and mathematics were the main focus of the school. There was also an emphasis on application. Around the same time in Paris students could also attend "an industrial institution" and it appears to

[47] AN F12 997, Dossier #73, from the Département de La Seine-inférieure, for many applications to patent steam engines.

[48] AN F17 8837, folio size dossier "Université Impériale, Académie de Toulouse, Département de la haute Garonne, Etat des chefs d'établissement," c. 1820.

[49] See the dossier assembled under June 9, 1829 from the Ministry of Public Instruction to all the rectors; AN F 17 8858. See N. Hulin, "Le problème de physique aux xix et xxe siècles," in P. Caspard, ed., *Travaux d'élèves pour une histoire des performances scolaires et de leur évaluation XIXe–XXe siècles*, 54, 1992, pp. 48–9.

have been recently established.[50] At the Royal College of Saint Louis in Paris students wanting to make their way to the polytechnic gravitated to a particular professor. Indeed, it would seem that in the late 1830s the students were now eager to receive the best possible education for a scientific or engineering career.[51] Predictably, the professors of physics were demanding an end to their "shocking inequality" and requesting equal pay and status with those in the humanities.[52] Also in this decade natural history and chemistry were introduced into the curriculum. In 1838–40 the list of books upon which the pupils were to be examined included the ancient classics, mathematics – from arithmetic to trigonometry – plenty of geography and history, but next to nothing in physics and chemistry. Yet the 1830s constituted a watershed, and in the provincial colleges extra funds had to be allocated to augment the cabinet of physics and the chemistry laboratory.[53]

By 1842 students in the fourth to ninth districts of central Paris could receive their scientific education by also attending the Royal College, or by going to one of a number of secondary schools dedicated to the sciences and functioning as a pathway to the *École Centrale des Arts et Manufactures*. By this date it became possible to choose a course of education for "professions properly described as industrial," although not many students opted for it, and it was predominantly scientific. In such schools students learned also about the design of machines, but in general the inspectors took a dim view of their morals and behavior. Two schools were evidently dedicated to the study of commerce and elementary industry. Graduates were able to apply to the *école polytechnique*, or to one of the special schools that emphasized practical application. All could avail themselves of instruction at one of the colleges in the vicinity, such as the Collège St. Louis.[54]

[50] AN F17/6894, dated September 1826; F17 6894, letter dated November 20, 1828; see in the same box letter of October 8, 1833 on Paris. For the school for English pupils, see AN F 17 8838, school of M. Houseal, described in letter of May 14, 1833; and under Mr. Gignoux see mention of the industrial institution in the same letter.

[51] AN, F17 8837, folder labeled "Collèges, Institutions, et Pensions 1812–1813," within that report labeled "Rapport sur les établissements d'instruction publique du Dept. de l'Eure pour l'année 1811." The entire box is relevant. See AN f 17 6894, letter of November 19, 1838 from the College to the inspector general.

[52] AN F17, 6894, letter of August 16, 1839 signed by the professors and addressed to the Ministry. For "shocking inequality," see letter of May 2, 1742 from Paris to the Ministry.

[53] AN F 17 8838, rector of the Academy of Angers, December 21, 1835.

[54] AN, F/17/1557, "Liste de MM les Examinateurs des Livres Classiques," the first list of 1840 containing no books on physics or chemistry, but the second list "presented for university adoption" introduced only in 1839, Deguin, *Cours Élémentaire de Physique*, 2nd edn., and P. Isidore, *Exercises sur la physique*. Later in the same year Olivier, *Mécanique usuelle* and Pinaud, *Programme d'un cours Élémentaire de Physique* were suggested. In 1840, chemistry made its appearance in a work by Burnouf. For the behavior of students in the

In 1840, national examiners specifically in mathematics and science were appointed, and throughout the 1840s books in every field became more numerous and more sophisticated. Assessing the condition of primary and secondary education in 1840, inspectors still found the greatest weaknesses to be in the fields of mathematics and the sciences. A survey of the Department of the Vosges found that "various notions in physics and chemistry are badly taught." At a school for boys aged eight to fifteen in Colmar, natural history, physics, and chemistry were not taught at all. At another school in the district mathematics, physics, and chemistry were taught "as [far as] possible without instruments or laboratory." The inspector noted the need to improve the education in "physical and industrial sciences" and that in manufacturing towns more scientific and less literary education had been attempted. When reporting on a school run by the Brothers of the Christian Retreat, the inspectors found that, while the instruction followed "le mode universitaire," the exception appeared in the total neglect of the sciences. In Rouen, by 1840 students in need of courses in mathematics and science received them at the local college.[55] In the 1850s, the Paris *lycée* requested that mechanics become mandated in the curriculum as it was directly relevant to "the industrial life." The race was on to find, and buy, the necessary machines for an education in mechanics.[56]

Rightfully, we may ask, what happened to the scientific education of the generation between 1810 and 1840? If we assume that a set of discrete decisions, made as always within the limits imposed by budgetary constraints, downgraded math and science and favored religious and classical subjects, then it is possible to postulate a cause. Not everyone approved of the educational innovation that came with the French Revolution. The Church initiated a clerically led assault against a secular educational establishment that, it claimed, valued moral instruction less than the culture of the sciences.[57]

school dedicated to the sciences, see F 17 8838, entire folder (40ff.) about Paris, report of November 1842; not least, the science students smoked. For the school dedicated to commerce and industry, see Pension Chalamet and it cost 25 fr. a month. For education suited to the industrial professions, see F 17 8838, letter of December 9 on the tenth and eleventh arrondisements.

[55] AN F 17 8838, Rector of the University of France to the Ministry of Public Instruction, January 30, 1840; letter of February 20, 1840 from Strasbourg from the inspector discussing a school in the arrondisement of Colmar; letter of February 19, 1840 discussing the absence of the laboratory; for education under the brothers, see letter of 1840 (without month or date), Academy of Aix, concerning Sainte Croix. For Rouen see AN F 17 8838, letter of January 10, 1840 to the Academy of Rouen from the rector (at bottom of box).

[56] Ibid., letter of March 16, 1857 to the head of the Ministry of Public Instruction.

[57] *L'ami de la religion et du roi, Sur l'éducation publique et sur les lycées*, pp. 1–5, Vol. 5, 1814.

As early as 1815 the restored monarchy initiated a renewed emphasis upon Catholic religious instruction, and the clergy got the right to oversee all Catholic religious instruction in the schools. Both primary and secondary schools saw an influx of clerical educators. By 1824 the Ministry of Ecclesiastical Affairs and Instruction had an overall budget of 25 million francs a year for clerical salaries versus one of 1.8 million francs for the staffing of the royal colleges and the primary schools. Even if we assume that only a small portion of the first actually taught, and every one of the second were lay, the ratio is a remarkable one.[58]

Although overall civilian control through the Ministry of the Interior was maintained, the clergy were directly involved in curricular oversight. If the Church had had its way, the clergy would have had their power-sharing further enhanced by royal decree. As even one of the liberal leaders of primary school education put it, "the foundation of instruction with us as in all Christian schools is religious morality."[59] There were ideological nuances in the Catholic vision of education, but no faction embraced science wholeheartedly. Note, however, as late as the 1820s inspectors of localities all over the country reported to their academies that clandestine primary schools continued to exist. They were deemed to be irreligious, and their existence suggests that not every family endorsed the project of re-Christianization.[60]

It had zealous and impassioned advocates. At one extreme, the ultra-royalist supporters of king and church believed that the previous century had rendered multiple injustices against educational institutions, all in the name of "what called itself philosophy."[61] The suspicions roused by enlightened philosophies extended all the way to science itself. Materialism lurked in those precincts, and science had fostered its rise. The ultra-royalists believed it impossible "to open a book of science without finding there the principles subversive of all religion, all morality [;] education, and instead of being a benefit, it has become a true danger." Societies that exist "with erroneous systems in chemistry or in physics" exhibit a form of moral corruption; science can be ignored, "a people are able to

[58] For a summary of this legislation, see M. Chatillon, *Almanach du clergé de France* (Paris: Guyot, 1824), pp. 525–39. For salaries, see dossier, AN F 19 1340/A.

[59] See the appeal of 1828 from the minister, the secretary of state for public instruction, to increase the role of the local bishops in the committees that oversee the instruction of children, *Journal d'Education*, vii, April, 1828, pp. 181–6; the quote comes from an oration by the titular head of the society for mutual education, p. 383, same journal, August, 1828.

[60] AN, F17 10384, reports on primary schools during the early 1820s.

[61] *La Foudre*, October 15, 1823, p. 54. In the following year this journal is bought up secretly by the moderate right-wing government.

attain a very high degree of civilization without knowing the true causes of gravitation."[62]

Such anti-science ideas circulated widely. A liberal satire aimed against the ultra-royalist assault on science – one that came to the attention of the police – put words in the mouth of the inspector of public education in Marseille: "Physics, mathematics, chemistry, finally, all the sciences that you are taught are only pernicious to the sociability of men. Our King has no need of savants, he wants monarchist and religious men, and oh I made a mistake, religious and monarchical men." The authorities found the satire particularly sinister because it insinuated that all students would be treated like seminarians and their "classes in mathematics, physics and chemistry would be suppressed."[63] Parents would justifiably be alarmed. Curiously, the satire actually said nothing about seminarians; the authorities made the linkage and in the process tell us what other sources confirm: science had no place in a clerical education. When the Marseille inspector, the former Spanish exile the abbé Eliçagaray, made his way to the medical college at Montpellier and began to lecture on the virtues and orders of the government, some students started to murmur – much to the annoyance of the abbé, who would go on during the Catholic reaction to become Grand Master of the University.[64]

When first lecturing to the professors and students at the Royal College in Marseille, the abbé Eliçagaray had said nothing about science. Instead he ignored all secular subjects in the interest of insisting that first and foremost the collegians needed to realize that "politics and religion can never be separated." Liberals are rebels, factious, revolutionary, and Jacobin. Furthermore, he did say: "We have no need of *savans* ... we want subjects faithful and devout. Make *savans* if you want; it is your affair, but have all the men [possess] a royalism pure and ardent."[65] The satire had put into print words that in fact had not been said, but such sentiments had been implied. The ultra-royalist reactionaries were convinced that the schools had become hotbeds of irreligion and atheism.[66]

[62] Ibid, #48, n.d., but 1822–3, pp. 6–7.

[63] AN F 7, 6915, #8314, printed journal, *Le Caducée*, dated June 18, 1821, supposedly spoken by the inspector on his first visit to the college in Marseille. For the letter describing the damage done, see Marseille, June 23, 1821 from the Prefect of Bouches-du-Rhône.

[64] J. J. Oechslin, *Le mouvement ultra-royaliste sous la Restauration. Son idéologie et son action politique (1814–1830)* (Paris: R. Pichon & R. Durand-Auzias, 1960), p. 162; on his Spanish exile, see G. Weill, *Histoire de l'enseignement secondaire en France* (Paris: Payot, 1921), p. 30.

[65] AN F 7 6915, #8310, "Discours de Mr Eliçagaray aux Professeurs du Collège Royal de Marseille."

[66] Oechslin, 1960, Chapter 3; pp. 162–70.

Reactionary forces had become deeply involved in the educational system and they were in open revolt against the Enlightenment and its errant stepchildren, science and the French Revolution. They were convinced that a philosophical education, as found in England, must be a liberal one.[67] In the post-1815 ideological wars it would appear that in some places science and mathematics suffered collateral damage. If the national granting of doctorates in science and mathematics may be taken as indicative, then in the period from 1811 to 1816, eleven highest degrees were awarded, and the situation remained at one or two a year until the 1830s.[68]

Once removed from the extreme views of the ultra-royalists, less radical royalists displayed little overt hostility toward science *per se*, but they also evinced not even a passing interest in its advance or application. The Enlightenment did not get off as lightly. The hostility toward "le siècle des lumières" found among ultra-conservatives also prevailed among the less radical conservatives, suggesting one reason why they displayed so little interest in matters scientific or, for that matter, industrial. The leading right-wing daily of the 1820s looked upon English affairs and saw only disorder, worker unrest, and the abuses of child labor – nothing of an industrial or economic nature penetrated its gaze. Nor were scientific lectures in Paris advertised in most of its pages.[69]

Yet more moderate conservatives followed the science of the day and reported on it in the pages of their daily newspaper. They recommended books on astronomy, and urged parents and teachers to present them to their children and students, to call attention to "the universal providence that reigns in the world."[70] But Restoration Catholic ambivalence toward science meant that when a new professor of medicine gave his inaugural address he had to assure his audience that doubt about the truths of religion is not the fault of science but rather of "false knowing (*faux savoir*)" which judges, without actually knowing.[71] Even at the Royal University, charged with overseeing education throughout the country, the topic of science in relation to religion produced nervousness. Just a few years earlier in 1820, at a time of student unrest, moderate conservatives thought the university professors were responsible for "the atheism that

67 *La Foudre*, #42, 1821, p. 415.
68 AN, F17 5577 for the years from 1811 to the 1860s where the numbers steadily increased decade by decade.
69 For example, see *Le Drapeau Blanc*, June 30, 1819, #15, and *inter alia* for the period 1819–28. On November 16, 1819 #154 and #158 a notice appears for "the spectacle of experimental and amusing physics" by M. Rossi.
70 *La Quotidienne*, January 4, 1823, 4, p. 4; January 9, 1823, 9, p. 4.
71 Ibid., March 11, 1823, #70, p. 2.

hides itself in our schools under the veil of indifference."[72] Similar sentiments prevailed in Catholic circles well into the 1850s.

The 1820s were precarious for the educational fortunes of French science, and in this intimidating environment liberal but anonymous critics decried its avoidance. They noted the penchant for Aquinas and scholasticism found among the clergy.[73] In the period from 1809 into the 1840s the books approved for use in the secondary school curriculum featured basic physics, and only in the 1830s turned toward industrial application.[74] By that decade, when the political wind shifted somewhat toward the left, school reform was once again on the agenda.

In Lille, the Society for the Sciences, Agriculture and the Arts issued a report in 1829 calling for a new Central School for Arts and Manufacturing that would put in place "the diverse elements in industrial instruction." Located in Paris, but intended to serve, among others, pupils from the Department of the North, the school would form civil engineers, manufacturers, directors of factories, and captains of industry. The Society was quite explicit about what needed to be taught to the next generation of industrial leaders: descriptive geometry, industrial physics, industrial mechanics, chemistry – general and applied – the exploitation of mines, industrial natural history, construction, design, and industrial statistics and economics. Such an education would bring rapid industrial success and "this establishment [would be] the most important of its genre that had been formed in our country."[75]

Such plans surfaced in many places and settings. A new society founded in Paris in 1831 offered a renewed educational agenda that called for physical and moral education to be sure, but also "scientifique et industrielle" education.[76] Predictably, in the 1830s we find curricula and books introduced into French primary schools that addressed geometry and applied mechanics.[77] By that decade, however, mature industrial leaders of the new generation, particularly if educated in the region of the North, lacked a basic familiarity with applied mechanics. It is reasonable to argue that knowledge-not-present has consequences for industrial development.

72 Ibid., July 1, 1820, #183, p. 4.
73 [Par un Professeur] Nouveau plan d'éducation, épitre adressée à tous les membres du corps enseignant et aux pères de famille (Paris: chez tous les marchands de nouveautés, 1828).
74 AN 17 1559, "Liste générale des livres qui on l'été autorisés pour l'enseignement des sciences," from 1809–45.
75 Archives départementales du Nord, IT 158, Lille, July 3, 1829.
76 AN, F17 3038 dossier "Société des Méthodes d'enseignement."
77 AN F17 1559, ff. 36–41; "Liste des ouvrages" dated 1843, f. 43, one work dates from 1828 and concerns the application of geometry to industry.

In 1843, one of the largest cotton manufacturers in the Department of the North decided to modernize his factory and introduce state-of-the-art equipment. Mr. Motte of Motte, Bossuet et Cie arranged to have all the equipment shipped from Britain, installed by English workers, and, more to the point, he bragged that they did all of this, despite import taxes, more cheaply than if he had used French equipment and workers.[78]

We know that British workers were not underpaid relative to their French counterparts. What the cost differential reveals is the relative scarcity of equipment and skilled French workers compared with what could be obtained in Britain at less cost, even taking into account international shipping of men and machines, in addition to import taxes. A critical mass of skill, of mechanical knowledge and know-how, made a difference. It created a knowledge gap in available power technology between Britain and the rest of the world, for which French industry, somewhat unfairly, has had to carry the burden of proof. The gap would be closed only in the half-century after 1850, and then slowly.

The evidence continues to mount that the era of the Industrial Revolution also witnessed the first knowledge economy in the world. No single causal explanation should be advanced for why parts of Western Europe, then America, industrialized first. For decades economic history has been written as if culture and knowledge were irrelevant. All that mattered, economic historians claimed, were high wages, or low fuel costs, or secure titles to land, low taxation – but now, belatedly, a few people are adding scientific culture to the mix. Surely the point here is that it all mattered.[79] *Homo economicus* possessed in some places, and not others, certain culturally transmitted information that could be used to

[78] Archives du Monde du Travail, Roubaix, MS 1988007–0016 Motte MSS, a memoir of 1943 by Gaston Motte says that his grandfather introduced equipment of English origin in 1843. There is a report by Kuhmann, given to the Jury départemental du Nord, found in folder labeled 1830–1845; "les ateliers de construction tous les métiers sans exception sont venus de l'Angleterre, la levée de la prohibition a la sortie avant permis aux constructeurs anglais ... en France a des prix bien inferieurs a ceux auxquels nous pouvons construire" typed script toward bottom of the box. For an overview of cotton manufacturing in the region, see M. Kasdi and F. G. Krajewski, "L'industrie textile entre campagnes et villes. Deux filières textiles en Flandres du xviii siècle au milieu du XIXe siècle," *Revue du Nord*, 375–6, 2008, pp. 497–530. Between 1805 and 1843, 12 percent of all cotton manufactures in the country came from this department. The centers were Lille, Roubaix, and Tourcoing (p. 515). On Motte, see also M. S. Smith, *The Emergence of Modern Business Enterprise in France, 1800–1930* (Cambridge, MA: Harvard University Press, 2006), pp. 143–4.

[79] Here endorsing the sentiments found in J. Appleby, *The Relentless Revolution: A History of Capitalism* (New York: W.W. Norton, 2010), pp. 155–62. For a refreshing approach to the problem of French retardation, see Kelly *et al.*, "Precocious Albion: Factor Prices, Technological Change and the British Industrial Revolution," unpublished paper, circulated UCLA, May 6, 2011.

an industrial advantage. French industrial retardation had many roots, to be sure, but deficiencies in scientific education for boys (the situation was even worse for girls) must now be added to the story. That said, the French must be given their due. In the area of chemical dyeing and bleaching of fabrics, they led the way and in the process carved out an area of expertise that would make French fashion the envy of the world.[80]

Arguably, in the period from 1750 to 1850 France was the most centralized state in Western Europe. Educational policies and values originating in Paris had consequences throughout the country. The only other region in north-west Europe where state-fostered industrial development might have leapt forward lay in the Low Countries. Belgium had coal, as did a few of the very southern areas of the Dutch Republic. The Dutch had capital and up to 1800 enjoyed a per capita income that rivaled the British. But industrial development occurred in Belgium at a much faster rate than in the northern Netherlands.

Why? In the period from roughly the 1580s to 1700 the Dutch had led in technological advances. After 1700 that position of dominance gradually collapsed. As we shall see, joined at the hip geographically, the Austrian Netherlands – what we will call, after its post-1830 name, Belgium – and the Dutch Republic became after 1815 the Kingdom of the Netherlands. By the time both were united and before, each took separate paths toward industrial application.[81] Scientific culture must now be factoring into the story of industrial development in the Low Countries.

[80] Guillerme, *La naissance*, pp. 343–75.

[81] K. Davids, *The Rise and Decline of Dutch Technological Leadership: Technology, Economy and Culture in the Netherlands, 1350–1800* (Leiden: Brill, 2008), Vol. Two, p. 533, citing J. de Vries, "Dutch economic growth in comparative-historical perspective, 1500–2000," *De Economist*, 148 (2000), pp. 433–66.

7 Education and the inculcation of industrial knowledge

The Low Countries, 1750–1830

> "Vous connaissez trop bien, Messieurs, l'utilité d'un cours de chimie et de minéralogie pour le progrès des arts chimiques et manufactures en ce département."[1] Letter of April 2, 1808 from the professor of mathematics and physics in Liège, Vanderheyden, to the Bureau of Administration in Paris requesting money for a laboratory, chemical samples and a small mineralogical collection – all in the service of the "chemical arts and manufacturing."[1]

From at least 1600 three countries led in the overall prosperity of Europe: the Netherlands, Britain, and Belgium. Sometimes first in wealth, other times third, by common consent Belgium became the first nation state in Continental Europe to experience sustained industrial development, that is, to systematically apply power technology to mining and manufacturing. An equally known commonplace, and a perpetually puzzling one, is the Dutch failure to industrialize until decades after the British and the Belgians. Yet unlike Belgium, throughout much of the eighteenth century the Dutch Republic enjoyed a remarkably free press; a habit of religious toleration born of necessity, openness to immigrants and their skills; and not least, abundant capital. Like Belgium, the Dutch Republic was also highly urbanized, but it possessed a gross domestic product per head of the population better than both

[1] Research for this chapter, a great deal of it done by Dorothee Sturkenboom, post-doctoral fellow, and the extensive travel it required throughout the Low Countries and France, were made possible by the National Science Foundation, grant No. 9906044. Letter of 1808 comes from Archives d'Etat, Liège, Fonds Françaises Prefecture, inv. nr. 452–4. In the period in question the Austrian Netherlands became French in 1795, then legally a part of the Kingdom of the Netherlands in 1815, and finally in 1831 the independent state of Belgium. For background on the subject of Belgian education, see M. de Vroede, "Onderwijs en opvoeding in de Zuidelijke Nederlanden 1815-circa 1840," *Algemene Geschiedenis der Nederlanden*, Vol. 2 (Weesp, Fibula-Van Dishoeck, 1983). For the laws governing education, see T. Charmasson and A.-M. Le Lorrain, *L'Enseignement technique de la Revolution* (Paris, 1987), pp. 75–139, law of October 25, 1795 is the first of the series. For the rules governing the *école centrale* in Liège, see Archives Nationales (AN), Paris, F 17/1344/23.

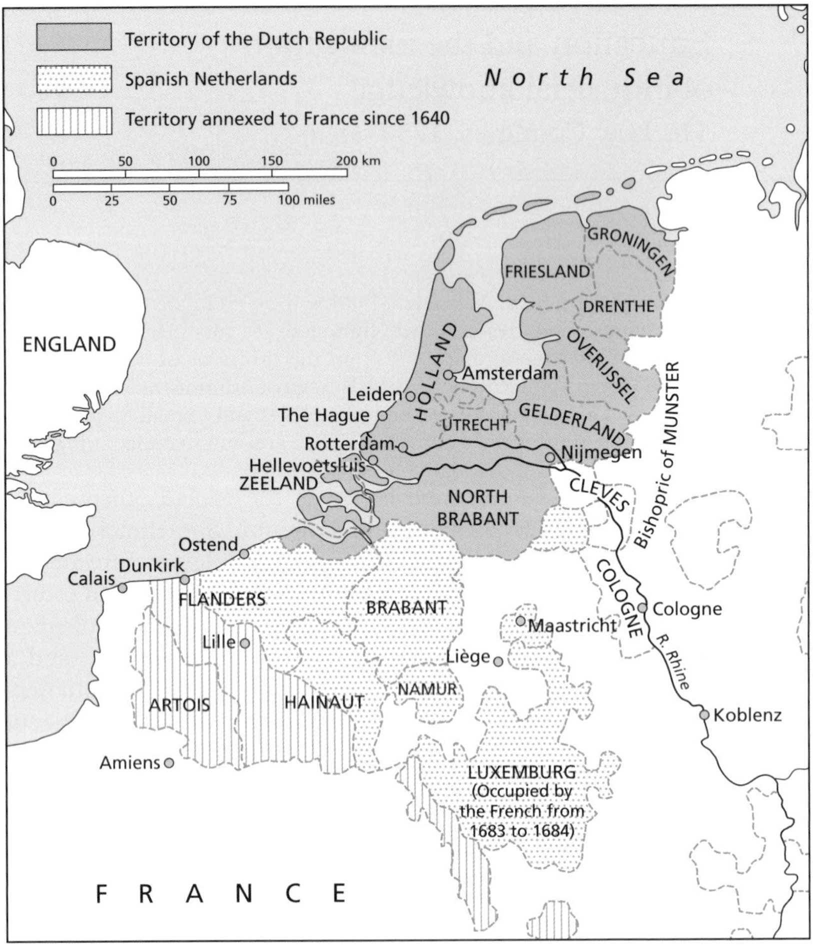

Map 1 The Low Countries and France before 1715 when the Austrian Netherlands were still Spanish

Britain and Belgium. By 1725 wages in both Britain and Belgium were comparable; they were even higher in the Dutch Republic.[2] In addition, assuming that adult height bears relation to nutritional levels and economic development, in 1800 the male population of the Dutch Republic

[2] For a good summary of the British case with an eye to the Dutch situation, see C. Macleod, "The European Origins of British Technological Predominance," in L. P. de la Escosura, ed., *Exceptionalism and Industrialisation: Britain and Its European Rivals, 1688–1815* (Cambridge University Press, 2004), pp. 111–26; and in the same collection of essays, see R. C. Allen for wages and gross domestic product (GDP), "Britain's Economic Ascendancy in a European Context," pp. 15–34.

Map 2 The Low Countries after 1815 when unified as the Kingdom of the Netherlands and before Belgium revolted in 1830–1

was significantly taller than their French counterparts, an advantage that disappeared in the 1830s and returned only in the 1860s.[3]

[3] Floud *et al.*, *The Changing Body: Health, Nutrition, and Human Development in the Western World since 1700* (Cambridge University Press, 2011), pp. 228–9. On censorship, see G. J. C. Piot, *Le Règne de Marie-Thérèse dans les Pays-Bas autrichiens* (Louvain: Vve Charles Fonteyn, 1874), Chapter 9.

We asked in previous chapters – however unfashionably – about the causes of French retardation; so, too, the different patterns of industrial development evident in the Low Countries after 1750 require attention. In France, scientific education occurred in fits and starts: renewed and strengthened in the 1790s by French revolutionaries, only then to experience significant stagnation from the second decade of the nineteenth century until well into the 1830s. It seems entirely reasonable to ask whether comparable trends in scientific culture relating to education can be seen in the Low Countries, both north and south.

In 1808, when Vanderheyden wrote, yet again, from Liège to Paris – Belgium now being incorporated into the French government – this professor of physics and experimental chemistry (who opens the chapter) expressed a truism dear to the hearts of the French administrators. Their revolutionary vision of science in the service of manufacturing first came to dominance in the 1790s. The ideology about the need for education in applied science as the key to industrial development survived into the next decade and the administrators under Napoleon. The program of educational reforms instituted in France in 1795 was extended northward after the formal annexation of the Low Countries. The Austrian Netherlands and the Bishopric of Liège became the Scheldedepartement of France. The Dutch Republic remained conquered, but unincorporated into France until after 1810. Its control over education, still largely a local matter, remained intact right up to 1810.

Labeling the old Belgian colleges an "absurd mess," the revolutionaries tied educational reform directly to republican beliefs and ceremonies. Remarkably, they instructed the Belgians to conclude revolutionary fêtes with lessons in physics, geography, agriculture, and other useful arts. Those who wanted to stay behind for such lessons would learn about "the flower of scientific objects." The republican temples should also be decorated with "celestial spheres." Indeed, the establishment of the national fêtes had the distinctive purpose of addressing the need for an education in physics, "too long neglected." The Belgians were told that revolutionary festivals teach science, and its utility would serve the needs of industrial development.[4]

[4] Rijksarchief Liège, Maastricht, 03. 01, Frans Archief (1794–1814, inv. nr. 2449, from François de Neufchâteau to the professors and librarians of the *écoles centrales*, 17 vendémiaire, year VII; "la loi qui vous appelle ainsi que vos élèves aux solemnité décadaire et aux fêtes nationales, vous présente une occasion de manifester votre zèle . . . A les cérémonies on pourrait faire succéder de leçon de physique ou de géographie des cours d'agriculture ou d'autre arts utiles. . . . Vous pourriez, par exemple, essaÿer de faire comprendre le système du monde, explique la diversité des climats, des saisons, des

The French-instituted *écoles centrales* in Belgium went on to reinforce scientific learning. Departments that contain "factories and manufactures" for the most part "require knowledge of a superior order." Yet as late as 1808 the head of the school system in Liège thought that none of the schools, apart from the *école centrale*, was up to the task.[5] Clearly, the new schools and their masters had their work cut out for them.

At the Liège school an eager young instructor like Vanderheyden, despite his frustration at the lack of instruments and equipment, spent two hours in every school day, for two years, trying to bring his pupils, generally aged fifteen to nineteen, up to an acceptable level of knowledge in physics and chemistry. In an area rich with coal deposits, the curriculum included a heavy dose of mechanics, with particular attention paid to "the machines and manufactures of the Department of the Outré, also to the theory and practice of fire pumps, simple and double in effect." In 1813, the academy in Liège wrote to the Grand Master of the Imperial University in Paris to inform him how "the varied industry that enriches the four Departments, of which this city is the most important, makes the courses in Chemistry, physics and natural history an education of the first necessity." Amid the Napoleonic wars, the rector of the academy also made clear that the shortage of money and the conscription of young men into the army was harming the quality of what could be taught. Yet even in the face of such obstacles, courses in public education in science commenced in a number of Belgian towns.[6]

The inculcation of science occurred despite the tensions provoked by war and revolution. The professors insisted on the necessity of educational reform, and the equipment to teach the new curriculum, in the face of "enemies of the republican constitution" who were trying to lure the young people of the school in the name of "aristocracy, fanaticism ... and hypocrisy." If the administrators of the school were indifferent to reform, would this not play into the hands of their enemies? The professors wrote

phénomènes naturels, Ils [?] pour cet effet, il conviendrait d'orner les temples décadaires d'une sphère céleste et d'un globe terrestre. Enfin, vous pourrie ÿ donner des notions sur la Chimie et sur l'histoire naturelle. Ces sciences comportent des démonstrations et des expériences curieuses et attrayantes. Vous feriez figurer dans ces jeux instructifs, les plus avancés des élèves dont vous séries contiens; et qu'el bonheur pour leurs parents. ... Sur les fêtes nationales, je dois vous faire encore un remarquer intéressante l'embellissement de ces fêtes exige qu'on donne des soins à l'éducation physique, trop longtemps négligées."

5 Report from the Prefect to the Ministry in Paris, AN, Paris F 17/8106.

6 AN, Paris, F 17 1344/1, for his responses to questions sent to Vanderheyden by the Minister of the Interior, year 7, 1799. Archives d'Etat, Liège (hereafter AEL), Fonds Français Préfecture, inv. nr. 448–2, *Programme de l'École centrale du département de l'Ourte* (Liège: Desoer, 1799) p. 22. For the 1813 document, see AN F 17 1581. For the new courses in science for the public, see AN, Paris, F 17 6635, for courses in Brussels, Liège, Leuven; ARA, BiZa, 2.04.01 inv. nr. 3988 for Verviers.

urgently to the authorities about the need for proper buildings, a room for instruction, modest lodging for themselves, and the need for a professor of natural history who knew the environment around Liège and understood coal and the problems of combustion. In addition, they needed a professor of design who could instruct "young workers who come in search of instruction relative to the profession that they will exercise."[7]

Never before in European history had science been allied so closely with any economic and secular ideology. When forced to explain what the French revolutionary ideology and its attendant institutions entailed, the leaders of a now stabilized revolution made scientific education a centerpiece of their goals for economic progress. Upon their arrival in Belgium, the French administrators and their Belgian sympathizers also insisted that in the primary schools both boys and girls be taught about the rights of man and citizen, and they condemned the "conservators of religion" for their ancient prejudices and absolute hostility toward republican institutions.[8]

Thus re-educated, the best and brightest among the young Belgian republicans would then go on to the new *école centrale*. There they would find instructors who believed that the man of science should destroy "the enchanted world" preached by fanaticism. A new generation of faculty in the sciences could be trained and go on to staff the *lycées* of the Napoleonic period.[9]

Slowly, the Ministry in Paris sought to address and rectify the multiple needs of the new schools, sending books and instruments as finances permitted. The Belgian schools also benefitted from collections left behind by the religious orders as they were disbanded, and by *émigrés* fleeing in opposition to the revolution.[10] Eventually, by 1802 in France and Belgium, Chaptal and his ministers established new schools to replace the more democratic *écoles centrales* and these meritocratic *lycées* were to be

[7] AEL, Fonds Français Préfecture, inv. nr. 448–2, year 7.

[8] Archives d'Etat, Mons, Fonds Français et Hollandais, Province Hainaut, nrs. 761, year 6.

[9] AEL, Fonds Français Préfecture, inv. nr. 448–6, Paris, year 6, complaining about the absence of equipment for teaching science: "le Bureau Central m'a autorisé â donner un Cours de Phantasmagorie; science qui traite de tous les moyens physiques dont on a pu abuser dans tous les tems dans tous les lieux et chez tous les Peuples pour faire croire à la Résurrection et à l'apparition des Morts. Le Gouvernement protège cet établissement . . . il a senti de besoin d'encourager le physicien Philosophe dont les travaux et la Morale tendent à Detruire le monde enchanté qui ni doit son existence qu'a la Baquette du fanatisme." For the next generation of teachers, first trained in the *écoles centrales*, see "Note sur Mr. Thiry," Professeur de Mathématiques et de Physique en Lycée de Bruxelles, AN F 17 1563, March 22, 1808.

[10] AEL, Fonds Français Préfecture, inv. nr. 448, list of items now possessed by the school in year 9, signed by Vanderheyden. In the same archive inv. nr. 458–22 on books confiscated, 1813.

only in certain towns, favor the children of state bureaucrats, and specifically seek to stimulate industrial development in the region.[11] Vastly expanded, the *lycées* became sound platforms for secondary schooling.

Also after 1800 the status of theory over practice was reasserted in the salary structure of the *lycées*, where the professor of physics was paid 2,000 francs a year, while the professors of chemistry, French literature, and mechanics got 1,500 each.[12] Religion had been dethroned forever – so they hoped – in the curriculum of French and Belgian state schools, and science, pure and applied, had been elevated even over the teaching of French literature. The negative assessment of the educational system of the old order, at least when it came to training in applied science, may have been more right than wrong. After 1795 the French system of education dominated Belgian schools, and unlike after 1815 in France, continued long after the French, defeated in battle, left the Low Countries.

Throughout the newly conquered territories, it was believed by the French, an enhanced education for the new citizenry would in turn foster innovation. The educated public had to be enlisted to support the task of increasing industrial development. A voluntary society was established precisely for the purpose of furthering the invention of machines and the useful arts in general. In the newly occupied territories, from Turin to Brussels and Amsterdam, men were sought to join *la Société d'encouragement pour l'industrie nationale*. Its tasks included the collection and distribution of foreign devises and the construction of machine models "to form the students in all the branches of useful industry to naturalize or spread in France."[13]

[11] 29 AP 75 AN, f. 399, in any year the goal for France was for 6,000 students in the *lycées*, 3,000 chosen by the government from the children of military and functionaries who served the republic well; the other 3,000 to be chosen by examination. There was to be a six-year course of study; government might distribute its largess unequally. Eventually La Fleche and one other are added and 6,400 pupils becomes the goal, f. 429; "nombre d'élèves que doit avoir chaque lycée doit varier." It must be remembered that the state "ne seul qu'une prime pour former les collèges; et ce système actuel peut eu quelque sorte se comparer au système du manufactures. Un Département n'a't-il point de manufactures? Le Gouvernement y envoie des ouvriers, des matières premières." By age fifteen or sixteen they should be nearly finished and doing mechanics and optics, see f. 645, Profs are to use books approved by the government and it consulted Delambre and Cuvier at the Institute. See also M. S. Staum, *Minerva's Message. Stabilizing the French Revolution* (Montreal: McGill-Queen's University Press, 1996).

[12] AN, MS F 17 4559, n.f. At least in Belgium as late as 1800 all teachers received the same 3,000 francs per year; MS 17 1344 14, 14 Nivoise an X.

[13] Rijksarchief Limburg (RAL), Maastricht, 03. 01 inv. Nr. 2523, 2624; year 10 for rules of the Society.

In 1803, a list of all the books that must occupy a place in the library of any *lycée* received wide circulation. It began with mathematics, proceeded through the sciences, and ended with history. Not a single religious work appeared on the list.[14] In 1815, when the new Dutch government surveyed the schools in Liège, it found a gymnasium, two colleges, elementary Latin schools, and in the colleges mathematics and the natural sciences were taught in all years, and religion did appear in the curriculum.[15]

In Ghent, as early as 1796 the Society for Public Instruction and the Arts also had the purpose of supplying "a salutary counter poison to the aristocratic that corrupts opinion ... [and] to compose by their publicity [an antidote] to the influence of the libels of Royalism." Within ten years the political edge had largely disappeared from the various new societies that were to concern themselves solely with "the sciences and culture." A society "for the physical and medical sciences" of 1806 had as its founders two professors, one in physics, the other in mathematics, and almost entirely local doctors, botanists, and pharmacists. It had the blessings of the Ministry of the Interior, the mayor, and the bishop. Its records make oblique reference to the passing of the "revolutionary turbulence" and make clear its entirely utilitarian direction. Out of it, in Liège in 1810, came the "Société d'Émulation établie à Liège pour les Sciences et les Arts." It built upon an earlier society founded in 1779, an instantiation of enlightened sociability. Within the year its attention turned toward industry, the prosperity of agriculture, a free school to teach design, and not least, the application of steam engines to coal mining. Similar societies sprang up in Antwerp in 1801 and in Mons in 1808.[16]

Such Belgian societies legitimated and enhanced the respectability of science, in the process obscuring its revolutionary and republican associations. They also provided networks where skills learned on the shop floor were passed along. Some technical processes such as dyeing could be learned only through hands-on experience. Knowing how to work systematically could also be learned early and well at the new schools with their

[14] Stadsarchief, Ghent, series U, inv. nr. 870, "Catalogue des Livres doivent composer la Bibliothèque d'un Lycée conformément à l'article 27 de l'Arrêté du 19 Primaire an XI."

[15] See ARA, Binnenlandse Zaken, 2.04.01, inv. nr. 3988.

[16] www.gedhs.ulg.ac.be/ebibliotheque/articles/opsomer/emulation.html for a discussion of this society. The work of Carmelia Opsomer is basic; see also *Règlement de la Société Libre d'Emulation ... à Liège* (Liège: Desoer, 1812). For a discussion of the 1806 society, see Archives d'état, Liège, Fonds Français Prefecture, inv. nr. 458–21; 458–20; 458–12. For an account of the societies in the town before 1789, see AEL, Fonds Français Prefecture, inv. nr. 458–12. For steam, see Bibliothèque General, Liège, 23323 B, *Procès Verbal de la Séance de la Société Libre d'Emulation* (Liège: Latour, 1812), p. 81. For the issues that concerned the society in the 1780s, see R. Malherbe, *Société Libre d'Emulation de Liège, Liber Memorialis 1779–1879* (Liège: L. de Their, 1879).

technical orientation.[17] The French-inspired voluntary societies for improvement became habitual and flourished long after the French occupation ended in 1815.

In 1817, in Ghent the Société Philomatique took up the "propagation of the exact sciences," especially those suitable for industry. In the same year its activities were complemented by another society, for the improvement of industry and manufacturing.[18] There is nothing surprising in the choice of Ghent as the site for a national exhibition of industry, held in 1820. In 1816, the new Dutch government had decreed that the town would have one of the three new "high schools" – more like universities – set up also in Louvain and Liège. The southern Netherlands had leapt ahead of the north in both technical education and industrial development. From the perspective of useful knowledge, we need to address the causes of this growing disparity between Belgium and the Dutch Republic.[19]

After the independence of Belgium, further development occurred in the educational infrastructure that encouraged industry. First in Ghent, then in Liège, schools of industry appeared in the 1830s and they were intended to teach arts and crafts, design especially for the tracing of machines, the knowledge necessary for the overseers of workshops and mechanical engineers. All the subjects that began under the French occupation appeared in the curriculum, with one new element, "the moral of industry demonstrated, the influence of good habits," the intelligence needed for industrial life. Aimed at boys from twelve to twenty, these free schools sought to instill knowledge, but just as importantly the discipline of work, and to offer advancement in the trades but also in engineering, with attention to manufacturing and mining.

At almost the same time the Newcastle mining engineer John Buddle was assisting Durham University in its course in mining. So, too, across the Channel the Belgians established a specifically industrial education,

[17] See R. Fox, "Science, Practice and Innovation in the Age of Natural Dyes, 1750–1860," in M. Berg and K. Bruland, eds., *Technological Revolutions in Europe* (Northampton, MA: Edward Elgar, 1998), pp. 86–95. For the rules of the Society for Public Instruction, see Rijksarchief, Ghent (hereafter RAG), Scheldedepartement, inv. nr. 3085/1, dated 1796.

[18] For the societies, see Stads Archief Gent (SAG), reeks T (14), inv. nr. 501 and RAG, Hollands Fonds inv. nr. 766/25. And for yet another society founded in 1827, see RAG, Gent, Hollands Fonds, inv. nr. 78/6.

[19] For the documents relevant to the exhibition, see RAG, Gent, Hollands Fonds, inv. nrs. 30/1–10 and 611/1–2; 30/10 where the lists show goods from the North, i.e. the Netherlands, in a minority. For the high schools, see Algemeen Rijksarchief, Brussels (hereafter ARA), Biza, 2.04.01, inv. nr. 3986, folio 309, "Reglement op de inrigting van het Hooger Onderwys in de Zuidlyke Provincien," signed A. R. Falck.

with mathematics, mechanics, physics and chemistry, design, natural history, and not least, political economy – all needed for a new generation of industrialists. Industrial mechanics had come into its own within the setting provided at two Belgian universities. The university course in Liège included a program of outreach by its faculty, which also set up a special School of Arts, Manufactures, and Mines in imitation of one at Ghent. It included courses in "the exploitation of mines, metallurgy, descriptive geometry with special applications for the construction of machines." The first two years were to be theoretical, the second two applied. Under the category of application came "mechanics applied to the arts, physics, geology and mineralogy applied to the arts ... industrial constructions ... visits to the principal industrials in the city and its environs."[20] Detailed notes left by the professors show how thorough these courses were and how oriented toward industry they had become.[21]

All of these initiatives in the direction of industrial education had their roots in the period of Dutch governance, 1815 to 1831. Among the founders of special schools were engineers and mathematicians such as Germinal-Pierre Dandelin, who also traveled to England on behalf of the government to discover what was being done there industrially. Those who deny that industrial development possessed a basic knowledge component might be tempted to ignore these Belgian and British educational initiatives. We cannot.

Disaggregating the Low Countries

The very phrase "the low countries," meant to include the Dutch Republic and Belgium, obscures more than it illuminates. After 1609 the Dutch Republic had effectively freed itself from Spanish domination, and in the process established a system of national governance, from Zeeland in the south to Friesland in the far north, that was, nevertheless, the most decentralized in Western Europe. By contrast, to the south, the Spanish Netherlands, after 1713 the Austrian Netherlands (after 1831 Belgium; here described as Belgium throughout), was ruled by

[20] For founding documents, curriculum, etc., see Stadsarchief, Ghent, series U, inv. nr. 1424 and 1427 for both Ghent and Liège. For a lengthier discussion of these special schools, see A. Le Roy, *L'Université de Liège depuis sa Fondation* (Liège: J. G. Carmanne, 1869), pp. 1013–48. On Dandelin, see pp. 126–39.

[21] University of Liège, Central Library, MS 1310, Course in mineralogy, 1829–30, by Mr. Levy; lessons in physics by Mr. Delvaux, no date but circa 1817–30, MS 4028 C to 4042 C, lessons given by M. A. Lesoinne.

representatives of Hapsburg monarchs, receiving orders first from Madrid, then, after 1713, from Vienna. In the period up to the French invasion of 1794 and within Belgium, the tiny principality of Liège belonged to its largely absentee bishop, and its independence from him was abolished only by the invasion.

Two monarchs in Vienna dominated the eighteenth century in Belgium. Empress Maria Theresa (d. 1780) and her son, Joseph II, held together a disparate empire of some 26 million people, in which the southern Netherlands was but a minuscule portion. Maria Theresa and Joseph also pursued different policies toward the church and modernization in general.[22] Maria Theresa allowed the Catholic Church and its censorship laws to dominate the Austrian Netherlands until the 1760s. Then the desire to modernize and improve its colony to the far West led the Austrian administrators, notably Patrice François de Nény, to seek secular allies in the Belgian cities. The reformers also eventually adopted scientific education, particularly in experimental Newtonianism, as a goal for the Belgian colleges and its one university at Louvain. They also set up a new national academy for the arts and sciences. As a weapon to reform secondary education, the academy was critical in freeing science from the Procrustean bed of scholasticism.[23]

Before de Nény, Cobenzl, beginning in the 1750s, made allies even north of the border, in Dutch radical and free-thinking circles, and initiated the reforms. As a freemason, Cobenzl found collaborators among his brothers in the Dutch Republic, and they entertained a particular animus against the Jesuits. Thus, in contrast to the Dutch Republic, the Enlightenment came late to the Austrian Netherlands. When it did, the agenda of the Austrians included reform in education and a promotion of economic development. Yet a city like Liège, under the control of its bishop during most of the eighteenth century, possessed no academy or society dedicated to the arts or literature, no school of design, no cabinet of physics, mathematics, or natural history until organized in 1779 by its new bishop and freemason, F.-C. de Velbruck. Promptly, and as early as 1781 and 1788, artistic and mechanical expositions were held in Liège, sponsored by the voluntary society that he founded. In the 1780s, however, it turned against the enlightened absolutism of the next bishop and in

[22] H. Hasquin, *Joseph II. Catholique anticlérical et réformateur impatient* (Brussels: Racine, 2007), pp. 115–22.

[23] See G. de Boom, *Les Ministres Plénipotentiaires dans les Pays-Bas autrichiens principalement Cobenzl*, in *Académie Royale de Belgique, Mémoires*, Tenth Series, Vol. 31, 1932, pp. 59–61, 235–6. And Piot, 1874, pp. 145–8. See essay by Geert Vanpaemel in R. Halleux, ed., *Histoire des sciences en Belgique de l'Antiquité à 1815* (Brussels: Crédit Communal, 1998), pp. 333–7.

1789 sided with the patriots and the French Revolution. Austrian successes at reform may be seen as too little, too late.[24]

Correctly or not, the administrators in Vienna who pushed reform regarded Belgium as dirty, poor, and intolerant by comparison with the Dutch Republic. In addition, like many other Catholic monarchical states, the Austrians distrusted the Jesuits as giving loyalty first to the Papacy, and as a force for retardation, particularly in education. In 1773, following the example of the French and the Spanish, they expelled them from the Hapsburg territories.[25] As in the French case, the expulsion of the Jesuits offered an opportunity to bring the teaching of natural philosophy up to date and to embrace notions of its application. Various other teaching and clerical orders continued to oversee a majority of the Belgian colleges, what we would call secondary schools.

The Austrian reformers, who expelled the Jesuits, were straightforward about their teaching philosophy, and remarkably prescient. They vowed to scrap the habit of student dispositions and compositions preparatory to the study of scholastic theology, and to substitute "the elements of a number of useful sciences particularly in experimental physics." In the Austrian Netherlands, science was reserved for the faculty of its university, Louvain, and there the reforms were to begin. This reform would introduce "decency and cleanliness among the scholars."

By far the most important reform, preliminary to correcting the current defects in education, "is ... to give young men the first principles of different sciences, in this way to impose the use of their minds to develop ... the relations, the utility of principles and their application."[26] First came logic, geometry, both speculative and practical, and then algebra. These were seen to be necessary for the study of mechanics. The principles of mechanics and astronomy were then to be taught, and "the scholars will observe the different machines and utensils that serve the arts, in effect the application of the principles of mechanics" – the

[24] On Cobenzl, see M. Galand, *Charles de Lorraine, gouverneur général des Pays-Bas autrichiens (1744–1780)* (Brussels: Éditions de l'Université de Bruxelles, 1993), pp. 109–46. On Cobenzl and the radicals, see M. C. Jacob, *The Radical Enlightenment: Pantheists, Freemasons and Republicans* (London: George Allen & Unwin, 1981; 2nd edn., 2004), pp. 111, 232. See also letters of Rousset de Missy to Cobenzl, Archives générales du Royaume, Brussels, MS T 100, 1210, ff. 1–63, hereafter AGR. Rousset assures him of his loyalty by saying that he is "un frère maître" and then adding the Masonic sign ⊲. For a contemporary account of Velbruck, see AEL, Fonds Français Prefecture, inv. nr. 458–12, dated 1806, written by the town's librarian to the mayor.

[25] F. A. J. Szabo, *Kaunitz and Enlightened Absolutism 1753–1780* (Cambridge University Press, 1994), pp. 241–7.

[26] AGR, Comité Jésuitique, MS T 083/01, box 6, Protocole des Délibérations du Comité établi pour les affaires résultant de la suppression de la Société des Jésuites des Pays Bas, February 28, 1774 to June 6, 1774, ff. 102–3.

science of the possible. After mechanics came marine astronomy, geography, overseas voyages, finally experimental physics, which led to metaphysics. New books were to be created and purchased for all these subjects. By 1780 geometry or arithmetic was being taught in many of the colleges for which visitation records survive, but Latin and the humanities continued to occupy pride of place. The reforms remained largely on paper only.

By end of the 1770s experimental physics was alive and well in Louvain, and both physics and mathematics remained university based. Although there were plans to reform all the colleges that narrowly fed Louvain, nothing came of them – they were just too expensive. What the thinking of these Austrian reformers demonstrates is not a particularly industrial vision – that would come twenty years later with the French conquest – but an enlightened one that could easily be put in the service of an industrial enlightenment. Industry and economic development never are mentioned. The Austrians wanted to repudiate the scholastic philosophy, and the "ultramontane opinions," the pro-papal attitudes, promulgated by the Jesuits, and to create subjects loyal to the state who would apply the mind "to things and not words."[27]

Belgian application of power technology to mining and manufacturing appeared in the eighteenth century. Steam engines were employed in mining from at least 1725, but their numbers grew very slowly. In Liège, the first engine for raising water was erected in 1723, but only four were in operation in 1767. By 1800 estimates place sixty-seven steam engines in all of Belgium, and a mere five in the Netherlands. The overwhelming majority of the Belgian engines were used in mines. It should not surprise us to find that after 1760 a self-conscious identification with the Austrian reforms also appeared among Belgian literate elites.[28]

The rich coal veins in Belgium had begun to be tapped, and a few steam engines had been introduced in manufacturing. Many of these innovations came from British entrepreneurs such as William Cockerill (d. 1832), who mechanized wool spinning and introduced steam engines in Liège. Indeed, by the 1770s English engineers and pumps were easily observed at various Belgian sites. So, too, English machines for cotton spinning (jennies) could be found in Brussels. The leading cotton

[27] Ibid., ff. 100–16.

[28] For the number of engines, see H. Lintsen and R. Steenaard, "Steam and Polders. Belgium and the Netherlands, 1790–1850," *Tractrix. Yearbook for History of Science, Medicine, Technology and Mathematics*, Vol. 3, 1991, p. 126. In the mid nineteenth century there were 2,000 engines in Belgium and 300 in the Netherlands. In 1812, a Liège coal mine purchased a steam engine from the Périers for 20,000 French francs; see Bibliothèque d'histoire de ville de Paris, N. A. MS 147, dated June 6, 1812.

manufacturer of Ghent, Lieven Bauwens, whom we met in the introduction, displayed a keen interest in English machines and made use of the services of a Manchester-trained mechanist. He also imported English workers and possessed a working knowledge of English.[29] Late in the 1790s, employing steam engines, Bauwens made considerable profit supplying the French army with uniforms. He kept at his factory a collection of books on matters commercial, but included writings by Rousseau and Montesquieu.[30]

Yet some of the new industrial initiatives were government-inspired. The beginnings of the Belgian chemical industry can be traced to the efforts of the Austrian-led reformers. Similarly, the teaching of Newtonian mechanics appeared in the main college of Brussels, put there by the Austrian-appointed professor of mathematics, who was a practicing engineer.[31] By the 1830s more men were employed in coal mining in Belgium, population 4 million, than in France with more than 30 million.[32]

Despite the best efforts of the Austrian reformers, the forces for philosophical and religious orthodoxy did not go quietly. As late as 1777 a plan for reforming Belgian education, clerically proposed, wanted the secondary education of adolescents to be primarily religious. Of the books recommended in science, none contained Newtonian mechanics.[33] By the same token, nothing that the Austrians sought to accomplish clashed with the ideal of the virtuous citizen, properly educated in humanistic studies dominated by Latin.[34] The goal became the revitalization of education through new handbooks and translations of the classics – not

[29] For machines in Brussels, see AN, Paris, F 12 1556, year 3; on Bauwens, see Stadsarchief, Ghent, Fonds Napoleon de Pauw, MS 3235, letters of François d'Arripe, 1807–14, on his business dealings; MS 3248, January 18, 1799 about English machines; MS 3356, letter from an English worker, John Jepson, no date, complaining about his lodging. See MS 3286 letters of D. Clark to L. Bauwens, October 14, 1804, in English.

[30] Ibid. MS 3699 for the library; MS 3629 on making uniforms in 1798.

[31] E. Mailly, *Notice sur Rombaut Bournons, membre de l'Académie Impériale et Royale*, found in *Mémoire couronnés et autres mémoires* (Brussels: Hayez, imprimeur de l'Académie royale, 1877), Vol. 27, pp. 19, 28–9.

[32] Dunn, 1844, pp. 162–3. France employed 23,751 workmen and Belgium employed 37,171. For English engineers and devises, see Archives nationales, Paris, MS Marine G 106, f. 42,1734, for an English engineer with a certificate from Desaguliers; f. 69, 1736, a pump is described as being able to elevate water "in the manner of the English."

[33] H. Hasquin, ed., *La vie culturelle dans nos provinces au XVIIIe siècle* (Brussels: Crédit Communal, 1983), pp. 132–3, discussing the journal *Vlaemschen Indicateur*. A. André-Felix, *Les débuts de l'industrie chimique dans les Pays-Bas autrichiens* (Brussels: Université libre de Bruxelles, 1971). A copy of the 1777 plan can be seen at Rijksarchief Limburg, archief Kloosterrade, in the papers of S. P. Ernst, No. 2061, Film 51.

[34] For Latin poetry from 1779 and all the colleges, see AGR, Commission Royale des études, MS 33A.

some abstract ideal of "modernization."[35] By and large, in most of these French- and Flemish-speaking schools, boys of fifteen – to take one year – received far less science than did their counterparts in the college at Glasgow or in the British Dissenting academies.

Nationally, the best laid plans of the Austrians, including a new academy of science, probably stirred as much unrest as they rattled traditional elites. Beginning in 1780, Joseph II (d. 1791) tried to continue the reforms put in place from the 1760s onward, but his reign lasted only ten years, and by 1786 he was alarmed by the restiveness evident in his far Western colony. The previous administration of his mother, Maria Theresa, had been bitterly, yet perhaps wisely, divided about how much reform and economic development should or could be imposed on the Belgians. Administrators bent upon centralization, and with it reform, sought economic development in everything from coal to textiles and canal building. They certainly had a hand in the removal of the Jesuits from education. Joseph II in turn sought to go further and to achieve a thorough reform of the royal and private colleges. He encountered stiff opposition, largely clerically led. There was also a shortage of trained personnel, a situation similar to that faced by the French after their Jesuits had been expelled ten years earlier. Complex politics would intervene to render Joseph's plans moot and the Austrians, like the bishop in Liège, found themselves opposed alike by liberals, who favored reform but wanted to be consulted, and conservatives, who sided with the old aristocracy and the traditional clergy.

Revolution in 1787 in Brussels and a French invasion in 1792 led to the military defeat of the Austrians in 1794, and, in passing, sealed the fate of Belgian education. In 1773, the Jesuits had been forced to leave a large gap into which, after 1795, the French now rushed. The French revolutionaries were able to impose their vision of education: anti-clerical, deeply indebted to the Enlightenment, and committed to science for industrial application.[36]

In every Belgian town occupied by the French, dedication to science accompanied republican ideology. In Ghent, public societies for the promotion of science, for public instruction leading to "progress in the sciences, letters and the arts," combined their vision with the defeat of

[35] See D. Leyder, *Pour le bien des lettres et de la chose publique. Maria-Theresia, Jozef II en de humanioa in hun Nederlandse Provincies* (Brussels: Paleis der Academiën, 2010), Chapter 2; my thanks to the author for bringing this excellent study to my attention. On the practicing engineer, Rombaut Bournons, see p. 87.

[36] See H. Hasquin, ed., *L'Académie Impériale et Royale de Bruxelles ses Académiciens et leurs réseaux intellectuels au XVIIIe siècle* (Brussels: Académie Royale de Belgique, 2009), essays by Bruno Bernard.

royalism and "aristocratic poisons"; "the passion for *les belles lettres* and the sciences entails the love of the Republic and liberty." The societies mixed learning with discussions of politics and the French Constitution.[37]

Nothing about Belgian reform would prove easy. In 1797, the University of Louvain was dissolved and its cabinet of physics distributed to the new *écoles centrales*. But, as in the French case, the new Belgian schools experienced a massive shortage, not only of teachers but also of books. Like their colleagues in Liège, the professors in Mons wrote to the French minister in charge of education about "the impossibility [of students reading for their lessons] without having elementary books in the sciences that they must teach."[38] The clear implication casts doubt on the quality of much of eighteenth-century scientific education.

Not everything bad educationally should be blamed on the Jesuits, however. In historical writing they enjoy a bad press, being seen as curmudgeonly scholastics with little interest in mathematics and science, especially if detached from Thomistic philosophy. While it is true that scholasticism ruled in all their colleges and secondary schools, the Jesuits did pioneer a Renaissance-style curriculum that privileged eloquence, rhetoric, and grammar, and their work with scientific texts and instruments in China is well known.[39] In Europe they were no more uninterested in the new mechanical science than was the Dutch elite of the eighteenth century.[40] The latter, let the record show, were overwhelmingly Protestant, but with intellectual interests very different from their British counterparts in the commercialized urban gentry and landed aristocracy. The Belgian landed aristocracy and Catholic clergy were not alone in their disinterest in science for application, and a revitalized humanism, shorn of Jesuitical pedantry, remained the ideal among Belgian educational reformers right into the 1780s. At that same moment

[37] Rijksarchief, Ghent, inv. nr. 3085/1, in 1796 (7 pluviose, year 4).

[38] M.-T. Isaac and C. Sorgeloos, "La diffusion des sciences dans les Écoles Centrales," in R. Halleux, ed., *Histoire des sciences en Belgique de l'Antiquité à 1815* (Brussels: Crédit Communal, 1998), pp. 385–414. M. Galand, *Charles de Lorraine, gouverneur général des Pays-Bas autrichiens (1744–1780)* (Brussels: Éditions de l'Université de Bruxelles, 1993), pp. 124–55. For the book situation in Mons, see B. Lux, ed., *Sciences et Lumières à Mons 1792–1802* (Brussels: Académie Royale de Belgique, 2004), p. 30 in M.-T. Isaac and C. Sorgeloos, "Livres et Lumières à l'école centrale du département de Jemappes 1797–1802."

[39] N. Golvers, "L'œuvre des jésuites en Chine et l'exportation de la 'science belge,'" in Halleux, ed., *Histoire des sciences en Belgique*, pp. 273–95.

[40] M. Prak, *Gezeten Burgers. De Elite in een Hollandse Stad, Leiden 1700–1780* (Leiden: De Bataafsche Leeuw, 1985), p. 208–11, 223. On Jesuit education, see J. P. Lodewijk Spekkens, *L'École centrale du département de la Meuse-Inférieure Maëstricht 1798–1804* (Maastricht: Ernest van Aelst, 1951), pp. 12–15.

Orangist reformers in the Dutch Republic recommended science to young orphans as a way of making them into good and loyal citizens. Science could serve many purposes, not all of them industrial, and that particular focus informed some elites in some places in Northern and Western Europe.[41]

Note while neither Belgium nor the Dutch Republic was homogeneous in religion, the Dutch were predominantly Protestant and the Belgians overwhelmingly Catholic. Small pockets of French and German remained spoken in the Dutch Republic, but it was largely Dutch-speaking, while its southern equivalent spoke Flemish (essentially Dutch) north of Brussels, and French in the southern provinces bordering on France. Amid all these distinctions, the vastly different systems of governance, highly localized in the Republic, centralized in Belgium, probably had the greatest effect on the scientific education and industrial development that emerged in both countries.[42]

The Kingdom of the Netherlands, 1813–1831

After unification as the Kingdom of the Two Netherlands in 1813, officially in 1815, the contrast became even starker: between the mechanization of mining and manufacturing in Belgium that began slowly in the 1760s and the industrial retardation found in the Netherlands. Less than twenty years after unification, in 1830 a revolution that began in Brussels led to independence for Belgium. With partition in 1831, the Dutch lost their industrial heartland to the south and with it the educational infrastructure that after 1795 and the French invasion successive governments had worked to instill.

By contrast, a pattern of educational reform in Belgium begun fitfully by the Austrians was continued by the French revolutionaries after 1795, then after 1800 by Napoleon, and finally by the central government of the Kingdom of the Netherlands, located in The Hague. Among and between them, they created Belgian secondary schools and universities capable of meeting the challenge of industrial development. Indeed, their curricula

[41] L. L. Roberts, "Instruments of Science and Citizenship: Science Education for Dutch Orphans during the Late Eighteenth Century," *Science and Education*, 21, 2, 2012, pp. 157–77.

[42] J. Mokyr, "The Industrial Revolution and the Netherlands: Why did it not happen?" Departments of Economics and History, Northwestern University, j-mokyr@nwu.edu, December 1999. Prepared for the 150th Anniversary Conference organized by the Royal Dutch Economic Association, Amsterdam, December 10–11, 1999. For a response to Mokyr's early work on this topic, see J. C. Riley, *International Government Finance and the Amsterdam Capital Market, 1740–1815* (Cambridge University Press, 1980, reissued, 2008), pp. 224–49.

aimed to promote it, even to the point, by 1810, of introducing courses in mineralogy for mining and in the 1820s on steam engines.[43] The French introduced academies in most Belgian cities and while once intended only to oversee secondary education as they did in France, they were gradually transformed into centers for training in the natural sciences, first by the French and then by the Dutch government operating from The Hague. By contrast, the French made few inroads into the localized system of education entrenched in the Dutch schools.[44]

In 1815, the Kingdom of the Netherlands legally consolidated under an absolutist monarch, Willem I. His policies re-enforced the economic gains of the previous half-century, and established new corporations to assist in the enactment of royal policies. One of the most important of these was the General Netherlands Society for the Patronage of Industry (most commonly known as the *Société Générale*), which Willem utilized to foster the industrial development of Belgium. This bank was, at the time, almost unique in Europe precisely because it financed industrial projects, not commercial exchange. It is one of many tangible signs that the newly restored monarchy meant for Belgium to take the lead in industrial development.

By the autumn of 1815 the new administration was sufficiently established that it undertook a survey of education in all the colleges of the southern provinces.[45] The new Dutch government suppressed the academy and *lycée* established by the French in Liège and replaced them with a "gymnasium," a "collège inférieur" and also a "collège supérieur." The reform claimed to be in the interest of a more orderly curriculum and a response to discontent among both parents and teachers, but the gymnasium was actually a *lycée* under a different name. The model was intended for all the provinces in the kingdom, which meant, in the context of education, the southern provinces. Schools for girls were also established, but these had a new, industrial element. Always girls were trained to be wives and mothers, with physical exercise added along with moral and

[43] AN, Paris, F 17 1098, on mineralogy in Liège and on steam, see Archives d'état Mons, Fonds Français et Hollandaise, Province Hainaut, inv. nr. 756, letter of March 1822. See also *Bibliothèque des Instituteurs, Ouvrage utile à tous ceux qui sont chargés directement ou indirectement de l'éducation de la jeunesse* (Mons: Hoyois, 1819–32, 1833–41), Vols. 1–12, with attention paid to the education of girls – but not in science.

[44] On the academies, see AN, Paris, F 17 1428, 1812–14, describing the academy in Liège; and AN F 17 1580–5, and see Archives d'état, Liège, Fonds Français Prefecture, inv. nr. 456-1 to 456-3, 456-5.

[45] Albert Schrauwers, "'Regenten' (Gentlemanly) Capitalism: Saint-Simonian Technocracy and the Emergence of the 'Industrialist Great Club' in mid-nineteenth century Netherlands," *Enterprise & Society*, 11, 4, December 2010, pp. 753–5. For the educational survey, see ARA, Binnenlandse Zaken, 2.04.01, inv. nr. 3988.

religious education, language, arithmetic for commercial application, and music. The novel industrial education for girls focused now on cloth, the making of garments, embroidery – "a branch of industry entirely profitable to those who exercise it in a great manufacturing and commercial city" – and also on bread making and the "theory and practice" of making syrups, liqueurs, and the conservation and drying of fruit. Children might also be educated in these arts provided they were strictly overseen.[46]

The utilitarian thinking about industry and education brought to the Low Countries by the French remained in place and was only strengthened during the period of the Kingdom. Governmental commissions endorsed the view, often promoted by scientists involved in higher education, that English power depended upon its invention of new instruments and machines and the future lay with such inventiveness in industrial mechanics. The professor of physics at Namur put the issue straightforwardly: "The principal source of public prosperity is industry . . . it is certain that the study of rational mechanics was carried out nowhere better than in [France]. Meanwhile industrial mechanics was there in its infancy . . . while this science became popular in England and marched from conquest to conquest."[47] The secondary schools were to foster public education in science aimed at industrial advance.

However well meaning, orders taken from The Hague never sat well in Willem's southern provinces. His absolutist attempt to impose the Dutch language – and reform in the Catholic seminaries – stirred up resentment that led to revolt in 1830. Nothing remotely like such a national effort in educational reform can be seen in the seven Dutch provinces where local rule managed to thwart French intentions – then those of King Willem I – to reform the inherently localized system of Dutch governance. This pattern of local control held in educational matters. Even those Dutch scientists who favored the French approach to education in applied

[46] ARA, Binnenlandse Zaken (1813–64), 2.04.01, inv. nr. 3993, letter of November 16, 1815; and 3992 on the education of girls, and children, in the industrial arts, dated September 1816.

[47] ARA, 2.02.01 inv. nr. 2227, "Rapport van den Administrateur voor het onderwijs, de kunsten en wetenschappen." May, 1825, "l'influence qu'exercent depuis la fin du siècle dernier, les sciences positives et surtout la mécanique et la chimie qui en sont devenir les guides indispensables? . . . L'Angleterre qui a étonné le continent, aussitôt qu'elle a pü s'en faire connaître, par le spectacle imposant de ses machines et qui dominera par suite." See also in the same folder, mémoire van Cauchy, February 2, 1825, ARA, sentences in the report come from Cauchy's letter, as does the material in the text: "Il est certain que l'étude de la mécanique rationnelle n'a été portée nulle part aussi loin que dans la seconde de ces contrées. . . . Cependant la mécanique industrielle y'était, pour ainsi dire, encore dans l'enfance, il y a dix ans, tandis que cette science devenue populaire en Angleterre y marchait incessamment de conquête en conquête."

science found themselves thwarted by local patriarchs who had little interest in industry or the social application of scientific knowledge.

Basically, unlike the Belgians, the Dutch retained a degree of local autonomy exercised by the same political elite that in 1787 revolted against the stadholder, William V. Despite many setbacks (not least a British-supported Prussian invasion), the Patriots who led the revolt, aided by the invading French army, managed to reassert control in 1795. By and large, at that moment the Dutch welcomed the French with open arms and saw them as partners in a process of reform and modernization. The resulting constitution of 1798 – the first in the Republic's history – encountered opposition but was eventually passed. Education remained firmly Christian, either Protestant or Catholic, with Jews also being permitted their own schools. The curriculum was overwhelmingly humanistic, and its content was only reaffirmed in 1806 when the Republic became the Kingdom of Holland under the rule of Lewis Napoleon, brother of the French emperor. The laws of 1806 did free public education from the grip of the religious authorities but did not alter the content of the curriculum significantly.[48]

Despite the 1806 installation of Napoleon's brother as ruler of the Netherlands (formerly the Dutch Republic), and hence a supposed reinvigoration of French authority, no real progress was made in establishing technical and applied science education. At the same time the Dutch universities were put into disarray by an attempt to bring them under the authority of the new Imperial University in Paris. All these efforts were short-lived. In 1813 and with the landing of the exiled Prince of Orange in The Hague, the French occupation was essentially over, and by mid 1814 the ministers in Paris had lost their power to govern. Fatefully, the Dutch universities reinstituted education in Latin; very little innovation in science or its application can be associated with them. In 1825, King Willem decreed that the universities must institute technical training on the "application of chemistry and mechanics to the useful arts," but the decree was honored more by breach than by execution.[49] By contrast, the king and his ministers intervened directly in the choice of a new professor of mineralogy in Liège and insisted that he have practical experience in mines and

[48] J. F. A. Braster, "The schoolwet van 1806: Blauwdruk voor een onderwijsbestel," in H. Hallebeerk and A. J. B. Sirks, eds., *Nederland in Franse schaduw. Recht en bestuur in het Koninkrijk Holland (1806–1810)* (Hilversum: Verloren, 2006), pp. 147–64.

[49] K. van Berkel *et al.*, *A History of Science in the Netherlands: Survey, Themes, and Reference* (Leiden: Brill, 1999), Chapter 4.

factories, even that he should undertake a trip to England.[50] By the second decade of the nineteenth century public courses in the sciences appeared with state approval in Brussels, Liège, Ghent, and Louvain.[51]

Clearly, scientific education is part of the story of the divergence in industrial development between the two Low Countries. Yet curricula and education in general have been neglected in favor of solely economic arguments that have dominated any attempt at explanation. Every conceivable economic argument has been offered to account for the differing rates of industrial development between the two countries. It is worth bearing in mind that, within countries, industrialization was usually regional in character. In Britain, the prosperity of the north-east ultimately led to declining industrial development in the agriculturally rich area of East Anglia. In Belgium, urban centers near coal mines generally led the way, and iron forging had flourished in the area around Namur from the fifteenth century. Demonstrating such regional differences does not, however, solve the problem: why Britain, why Belgium, and why not the Netherlands? These questions pertain to the period from the 1780s to the 1830s when for most of it, political instability or constant warfare drained both Dutch and Flemish resources.

Dutch decline

There is general agreement in the historiography that by the 1730s the Republic experienced a decline in prosperity and international influence. Many factors have to be weighed in when assessing why this happened, but largely economic explanations, and not political or cultural ones, have until recently dominated the discussion. The Dutch had no coal (technically not true, but hardly abundant) and the Belgians did. That reality, it is said, holds the key to Dutch stagnation and Belgian development. Others argue that Dutch wages were the highest in Europe and they held back economic development (notice that the same argument in reverse has been used to explain British industrial prowess and the need to mechanize). The power of the Dutch guilds to control wages also figures in these sorts of economic models. Other economic arguments point to the high rate of return still available from investment in overseas trade, a disincentive for merchants to branch out into manufacturing or embrace

[50] ARA, Brussels, Staatssecretarie, 2.02.01, inv. nr. 227, May 13, 1825. In Belgium, some curricular questions and propositions continued to be published in Latin, see *Annales Academiae Leondiensis, 1818–1819*, ed. J. M. Vanderheyden (Liège: P. J. Collardin, 1821). The use of Latin in the official publications continued into the late 1820s.

[51] AN, Paris, F 17 6635, letter from Louvain dated December 16, 1811.

technological innovation. Still others argue that a nation of barely two million people had to continue with international trade and commerce if only to compete with the level of consumption and capital exchange witnessed in its larger rivals.

Some of these economic factors were undoubtedly important, but then so, too, was the devastating political turmoil in the Dutch Republic from the early 1780s to the revolt against the stadholder in 1787, and well beyond. A Prussian invasion stopped the revolution in its tracks, and many of its leaders, known as Patriots, fled south to Brussels or Paris. In less than two years Paris became the Mecca of European revolutionaries and many Dutch exiles learned from the experience. In 1795, the French army, accompanied by various Patriots, triumphantly entered Amsterdam. Thus began a period of French occupation and domination that lasted until 1813. More onerous on the Dutch than the Belgians, over a period of nearly twenty years the French extracted more than 200,000 million guilders in retribution and left the Republic virtually bankrupt after their defeat at Waterloo.

The pattern of Dutch political and economic decline visible in the eighteenth century was accompanied by a cultural component. The "golden age" of the seventeenth century witnessed Dutch technological prowess in agriculture, ship building, water engineering, and tool making – and then came a slow but dramatic change. After 1750 the Dutch largely played catch-up with their French and British neighbors. Innovations from each increasingly guided Dutch economic development. As early as the Dutch Revolution of 1747 reformers angrily pointed to the absence of the elite's interest in science and manufacturing. Where we find evidence of sophisticated scientific education for the aristocracy, no mention is made of mechanical devices for manufacturing.[52]

More recently, explanations for Dutch decline have begun to think beyond population size, or coal deposits, etc. They have focused on education and rightly noted that the Republic failed "to make further

52 [Anon.], *Aanspraak gedann aan de Goede Burgeren, die tot Welzyn van stad en land, op den 9 Augustus 1748, op den Kloveniers Doelen Vergadert zyn geweest* (Amsterdam, 1748), p. 1: "de Konsten en Wetenschappen zyn onbeloond van ons gevlooden; de Koophandel is haare Stief-Vaders ontvlugt; de Fabriquen, die onuitputbaare Goudmynen der Volkeren, en waarop STAAT met regt zig voormaals dorft beroemen, en waarop dezelve is gevest, zyn naar andere Natien overgegaan." For such lecturing, see University Library, Amsterdam, MS. X.B.1, "Leçons de physique de Mr le Prof. Koening." The Hague 1751–2, 348 pp. Intended for French-speaking supporters of William IV, thus probably for the circle around Willem Bentinck. See also http://words.fromoldbooks.org/Chalmers-Biography/k/koenig-samuel.html. And see Royal Library, The Hague, MS 75 and J. 63 on lessons given to the Prince of Orange in arithmetic and algebra, May 1759, 34 ff.

advance along the very route of technological learning that did not suffer diminishing returns, namely the route of formal learning."[53] Certainly foreign contemporaries were aware of the considerable unrest that had replaced the seemingly effortless prosperity available two generations earlier. Indeed, they contrasted the learning visible in Edinburgh's social scene to the elite drinking and eating clubs in Amsterdam.[54]

It has been known for some time that Dutch popular scientific learning in the eighteenth century was nowhere near as vibrant as what could be observed in Britain. So, too, Dutch institutions of higher learning, in Harderwijk, Deventer, and Gelderland, evinced little interest in the latest developments in mechanics; the same was true for the main Dutch scientific society, *De Hollandsche Maatschappij der Wetenschappen*. Only in the late 1780s did the Holland Society for Science concern itself with the application of scientific knowledge to industry, but by then far more pressing concerns gripped the political nation. As late as 1813, French administrators found the library of Leiden University too small and deficient in books on physics.[55]

In the French and as we shall see after 1795 in the Belgian case, the state moved aggressively in the area of education with an industrial focus. The Dutch, by contrast resisted all such efforts and only in 1806 did the French assert monarchical control over Dutch institutions such as water management, taxes, and the organization of the major religions. Without state intervention, generally elites get the kind of education they desire, and Dutch oligarchs, as well as merchants, evinced little interest in scientific education in the period after the 1730s. The curricula of their academies, the contents of school libraries, the proceedings of scientific societies reveal the same story: little interest in cutting-edge mechanics or their application, although some regents did see the value of scientific education for promoting good citizenship.[56]

Recent nationalist efforts to argue that the Dutch universities of the eighteenth century retained the vibrancy of the seventeenth century rest on little evidence, and their insularity was only reinforced by the use of Latin well into the nineteenth century. Their cabinets of physics existed not to train the next generation of engineers and have been described as

53 Davids, 2008, p. 526.

54 Dr. Williams's Library, London, Wodrow–Kenrick correspondence, MS 24, f. 41, dated 1760. For the contrast, see British Library, MSS ADD 6858, f. 35, Elizabeth Montagu to A. Mitchell in Berlin, March 6, 1767.

55 AN, Paris, F 17 1098, July 22, 1813, letter from Leiden.

56 A summary of the account in my *The Cultural Meaning of the Scientific Revolution* (New York: Alfred Knopf, 1987), pp. 182–98, but as modified by the recent work of Lissa Roberts.

"dilettantish."[57] With one or two notable exceptions, technological innovators and reformers tended to come from the Patriot wing of Dutch politics – the same people who in 1795 welcomed the French as liberators. With a newly written Constitution that left much power in the hands of the localities and oligarchs, the Patriots managed only fitful success against the entrenched power of local elites. Before the 1830s, where we see pioneering efforts at installing power technology, the steam engines were as much for Dutch gardens as for land reclamation.

Maastricht

The city leading in Dutch industrialization after 1830 was Maastricht and until that date it had been Belgian, not Dutch. Located in the far north of Belgium – after 1831, legally after 1839, located in the far south of the Netherlands – it had been the only city to experience the educational reforms first of the Austrians and then of the French. During the eighteenth century the elite of Maastricht were no more or less interested in science than their Leiden or Amsterdam counterparts, but unlike them, after 1795 they did not control secondary education.

There is some information about the educational system in the autumn of 1795 when the French conquerors arrived. Reporting back to Paris, the administrator found no books remaining "that treat the sciences and the arts" other than theology. There was no cabinet of natural science in Maastricht, although a citizen in the town had been identified as possessing "various instruments of physics … [such as] a pneumatic pump, electricity complete with the conductors and batteries, a microscope … two barometers and a thermometer, with different pieces relative to the laws of movement and a hydrostatics." These were purchased and were deemed essential, as was all the equipment needed to teach design and architecture. Various marble reliefs were to be taken from the churches for a museum that would give students "a high idea of the sciences and the arts … excite their imagination and contribute to their success." Just as importantly, students were to be shown the "devises and ingenious machines" useful for the arts and manufactures, and, administrators

[57] Davids, 2008, pp. 490–4; Allamand's miniature steam engine could not be made to work sufficiently for his demonstrations, see L. Roberts, "Mapping steam engines and skill in eighteenth-century Holland," in L. Roberts, S. Schaffer, and P. Dear, eds., *The Mindful Hand: Inquiry and Invention from the Late Renaissance to Early Industrialisation* (Amsterdam: Koninklijke Nederlandse Akademie van Wetenschappen, 2007), pp. 205–6 for the engine and the cabinets of physics; Roberts would like to detach the installation of steam engines from a Newtonian or scientific culture, see pp. 216–17.

argued, only by having examples of such devises could they understand their merits.[58]

By 1806, when the central school in Maastricht was converted to a *lycée*, a list was provided of all the physical and chemical equipment. It contained hundreds of items, among them devises to illustrate the weight of the air, various items to be placed in a void, a small table from 's Gravesande's text to show the "composition of forces," gravitational attraction, another of his to illustrate the pressure of liquids, on and on into hundreds of items for physics and chemistry, and not least a library of more than 5,600 items. It still had a plurality of books on theology, but nearly 300 in physics, chemistry, mathematics, and medicine. In physics, Desaguliers' text, from which two generations earlier Watt had educated himself, led the list.

The ministerial correspondence makes clear the overwhelming interest in promoting the sciences, from book buying to prize giving, and in the promulgation of technological innovation. All these books and cabinets remained in place long after the French had departed Belgium, and Maastricht in particular. When the new government inspected the schools in 1815 it found chemistry and physics alive and well in the curriculum.[59] The Dutch administration steadily built on this foundation and by 1825 recommended education in machines and chemistry in direct imitation of what could be seen in England and France.[60]

[58] AN, Paris, F 17 1088, document 174, Letter of 27 brumaire, year 7, from M. Van Heijlerhoffee; on machines in the schools, see Rijksarchief, Limburg (hereafter RAL), 03.01, inv. nr. 2449, document 246 signed by the Minister of the Interior, year 7.

[59] AN, Paris, F 17 1088, dossier 18, document 212 and in the same dossier, document 209. These lists are confirmed and augmented by RAL, 03.01, Frans Archief, inv. nr. 2456, compiled by Van Minckelers. He has doubts about the loyalty of many citizens to the French republic, year 9, and in 03b a list of the main books in theology, jurisprudence, philosophy, economy, politics and commerce, metaphysics, physics, natural history, agriculture and botany, mathematics, astronomy, astrology, optics, hydrography, hydraulics, arts, design, painting and sculpture, military arts, "belles lettres," chemistry, etc. There were also books on mineralogy; exploitation of mines, and 1,173 livres had been spent on physics alone. In year 11 Newton's *Principia* led the physics list, followed by D'Alembert, Euler, Bouguer, Lalande, Lagrange, etc. For prizes given, see RAL, 03. 01, inv. nrs. 2449–2550; inv. nr. 2450, document 19, for an outline of curriculum, and document 222 on the contents of the *Annales des arts et manufactures, ou Recueil de mémoires technologiques sur les Découvertes modernes*, beginning in year 8. In year 12 they were still buying, see documents 205–6. These remarkable lists are further confirmed in Gemeente Archief, Maastricht, inv. nr. 334 and 336, in same, Athenaeum, inv. nr. 336. For the December 1, 1815 inspection by the new Dutch government, see ARA, Binnenlandse Zaken, 2.04.01, inv. nr. 3988, from the governor of Limburg, signed by the general secretary, W. A. Pillena.

[60] ARA, Staatssecretarie, 2.02.01, inv. nr. 2227, KB, 13 May 1825: "It is after all generally well-known, and is upon all occasions by the English Government

Maastricht remained a part of Belgian territory until 1839 when, led by its garrison, the town demanded to leave the newly independent country and join the Netherlands. Its *école centrale* has been richly documented, and the curriculum in science and secular subjects predictably resembled that to be found in Mons, or Liège, or south of the Belgian border, in Amiens or Paris. The school gradually evolved in the same building into a college or athenaeum where studies in the humanities were complemented by mathematics, physics, and chemistry, and the professor of physics and chemistry was the highest paid member of the faculty. Grammar, the study of the Bible, and design rounded out the curriculum.

Records of the athenaeum in the 1820s, and into the 1830s after independence, show the steady purchase of mechanical and electrical equipment and a strong science presence in the curriculum. The classes concentrated on the physics of simple machines, latent heat, atmospheric air and its pressure, and of course the specific gravity of various elements. By the late 1830s the library's catalogue filled 416 handwritten folio pages and it was state-of-the-art in the sciences. By that decade classes were given in what was explicitly called mechanics, hydrostatics, and pneumatics; machines were introduced into the classroom. Gradually, more attention was focused on electricity.[61]

All the formal education in science had its analogue in Maastricht's civil society where, in 1824, the Society of Friends of the Sciences, Letters and Arts formed around several of the professors at the athenaeum as well as merchants, entrepreneurs, doctors, architects, clergy, pharmacists, lawyers, and military officers. They devoted themselves to everything from the history of the town, its buildings, and monuments, to astronomy, a

acknowledged, that to the inventors of the new tools thanks must be expressed, re the astonishing expansion of the diligence of the working people, and as a result the welfare and fortune (riches) to which England has gotten in the most recent years." The government is taking advice from Prof. Cauchy, professor of mineralogy and metallurgy in Namur.

61 Rijsarchief, Limburg, Maastricht 04.01, inv. nr. 9113, Archief van het Provinciaal Bestuur, 1814–1913. Circa 1814 he was paid 1,500 guilders and others generally received 1,200 guilders. For the purchase of equipment in the 1830s, see Gemeente Archief, Maastricht (1804–64), inv. nr. 243–6, and nr. 294 for the curriculum in the 1820s (hereafter GAM). For the library catalogue, see GAM, Athenaeum Maastricht (1804–64) and for the curriculum in 1831–2 see inv. nr. 249, *Programma der lessen, welke gegeven worden op het koninklijk Athenaeum van Maastricht gedurende het school jaar 1831–32.* In physics the classes used Biot and in chemistry, Thenard. Both Dutch and French were taught by that year. For the classes throughout the 1820s, see inv. nr. 280–92. For courses in mechanics, see inv. nr. 334. For the rules governing the athenaea and colleges, see GAM, inv. nr. 78.

machine constructed "to demonstrate centrifugal force," and a discussion of what causes the explosion of steam engines. The Society particularly applied itself to promoting industrial development in the region and offered courses in a variety of subjects, from geometry to the building of fire pumps. Its library gave access to journals and books in the sciences, and by the 1840s offered a wide range of free industrial courses intended for workers.[62]

Perhaps it is not accidental that Maastricht became one of the first Dutch cities to industrialize. In 1836, Petrus Regout (b. 1801), who may be described as the Wedgwood of Holland, installed a mechanized earthenware factory in the city, complete with steam engine. Regout had been educated at the local college, the heir to the *école*.[63] Other ceramics and paper makers followed suit. Industrialization spread throughout other Dutch towns, but more slowly.

Scientific education in Belgium

The argument about political turmoil from the 1780s onward also applies to the Belgian situation. In 1787, revolution against the Austrians was followed by French invasion and occupation from 1794 until 1813. Church lands were confiscated, aristocratic privileges revoked, and wealth taxed, while all young men were conscripted into the French army. The Low Countries, perhaps more than any other part of Europe, were affected by the French Revolution, but not always in ways that were detrimental.

Indeed, contemporary thinking on the Dutch–Belgian experience of the French Revolution now lays emphasis upon the modernizing effects of French rule, particularly in matters educational and scientific.[64] It was during the Napoleonic period that Belgian publications on scientific matters increased, and the manufacturing of arms and the use of steam engines significantly expanded in Liège. The Belgian *Académie des sciences* was re-established and science rendered central to the curriculum of the

[62] Stadsbibliotheek, Maastricht, SB Br. LC 1492: *Règlement de la Société des Amis des Sciences, Lettres et Arts établie à Maastricht* (Maastricht: L. Th. Nypels, 1828), and for the 1820s see CB T 1225 (1824–31). Also at the same city library, see *Rapport sur les travaux le la Société des Amis des Sciences . . . 1842 jusqu'à 1850.*

[63] Spekkens, *L'École centrale du département de la Meuse-Inférieure Maëstricht 1798–1804*, pp. 58–60, 153, section 2. See also A.J. Fr. Maenen, *Petrus Regout (1801–1878)* (Nijmegen: N.V. Centrale Drukkerij, 1959), pp. 20–1, 84. For the role of science and mathematics in 1815 when Maastricht was a part of Belgium, see ARA, Binnenlandse Zaken, 2.04.01, inv. nr. 3988.

[64] J. C. Baudot, *Histoire des sciences et de l'industrie en Belgique* (Brussels: Jourdan, 2007).

universities or academies at Louvain, Ghent, Maastricht, and Liège. Not least, Napoleon granted the Belgians a monopoly on zinc production.[65]

At their heart the reforms put in by the French laid emphasis upon science, broadly conceived as experimental, tactile, both theoretical and applied. It is essential to realize that our definitions of science that basically split it off from engineering are not what the reformist French educators and their Belgian supporters had in mind. At the *école centrale* in Liège from 1797 to 1804, "Citizen" Vanderheyden, whom we met earlier, gave "an exposition on the general properties of bodies, explicated the elements of 'Phoronomie,'" that is mechanics, treated air, gases, electricity, magnetism and galvanics, while chemistry followed a popular manual of the day.[66] Emphasis was supposed to be based upon hands-on experience. A few years earlier his predecessor had quit in frustration because he did not have the necessary instruments for the lessons.[67] Vanderheyden complained bitterly of the same problem and the complaining continued throughout the French occupation.

However abstract we may imagine the scientific discipline as being, it was brought down to earth, sometimes literally. The professor of mathematics taught calculus and trigonometry but also devoted two months to lessons on terrain and the measurement of elevation for use in maps, while his colleague, also in mathematics, taught arithmetic "relative to commerce and to mathematics, the new system of weights and measures," and decimalization. In Ghent, the professor of chemistry and experimental physics in the second year of the course taught about the properties of water, about thermometers, optics, theory of colors, etc., and then paid considerable attention to the metals that appear in mines, the extraction of minerals, the use of specific gravity to identify substances, and an examination of the principal element found in the region. "He also gave a course particularly for commercial students."[68] By 1820 Ghent held an industrial exposition at which its metal

[65] Ibid., pp. 33–46. The periodicals include *Journal de chimie et de physique, ou recueil périodique des découvertes dans les sciences chimiques* (edited by J. B. Van Mons). See also the writings of G. J. Christian, *Vues sur le système générale des opérations industrielles ou plan de technonomie* (1819) and his *Traité de mécanique industrielle* (3 vols.), and *Annales générales des sciences physiques* (Brussels: Weissenbrush, 1822–5). In 1822, Willem I founded the Société générale des pays bas.

[66] Archives d'État, Liège, Fonds Français Préfecture, inv. nr. 448. The manual being followed is by Bouillon-la-Grange. Foronomie is "Bewegingsleer, leer van de beweging van vaste en vloeibare lichamen," that is mechanics in English.

[67] Ibid., inv. nr. 448–6.

[68] The printed *Programme des cours de L'École Centrale du département de l'Escaut, qui s'ouvriront le premier brumaire an XII*, Ghent, 1802, pp. 6–7, and found in Archives nationales, Paris, F17 1344 14.

industries figured prominently, and thanks to its cotton industry it had become known as "Manchester on the Continent."[69]

Between 1795 and 1815 – all years when war raged either on land or at sea – the French educational system made a significant impact on Belgium. We want to know whether it bore relation to industrial developments in the region. In effect, we want to know whether Vanderheyden's assumption about science broadly conceived and the encouragement it gave to manufacturing, was right. We will probably never be able to show former students as entrepreneurs on the shop floor, applying what they had learned, although it has been possible, in Manchester for instance, to show entrepreneurs in steam and cotton using the mechanical knowledge they possessed.[70] The best we can do in the Belgian case is show a correlation between areas of industrial development and educational innovation in science broadly conceived.

The town of Ghent is a good place to start as it would emerge by the 1820s as a center for cotton manufacturing. In the aftermath of the French takeover, Ghent got a state-of-the-art curriculum in science as well as other subjects. Teachers were hired in design, natural history, ancient languages, mathematics, physics and chemistry, grammar, and literature, and a new library was established.[71] Up-to-date textbooks were specified by the author's name. In the course on physics, everything from the properties of water, including steam, to magnetism and electricity alternated with chemistry, where emphasis was placed on metallic substances found in mines, the production of ammonia, and nitric acid. In this Flemish-speaking part of Belgium, instruction was to be in French because "France and Belgium are today governed by the same head and laws . . . as it was made in the time of Charlemagne."

Added to the expense of the Ghent school were a public library, botanical garden, cabinets of natural history, physics, and chemistry. More than 26,000 books and manuscripts made up the new library, and works in natural history and the sciences accounted for over 1,200 of them. In the natural history cabinet, mineralogy samples included various types of coal, zinc, metals, mercury, and iron, and in the cabinet of physics and chemistry could be found the usual levers, weights, and pulleys, but also pneumatic machines and cylinders, and many objects

[69] Rijksarchief Gent, Hollands Fonds, inv. nr. 611/2 for details on the exposition.

[70] Jacob and Reid, 2001, pp. 284–304.

[71] For the faculty, see Archives nationales, Paris, F 17 1425. By 1813 there were fifteen faculty and the professors of physics, and chemistry and mathematics had worked in various French schools and possessed a doctorate. Charles Joseph Bayard was one of these and he was also a priest.

to illustrate electricity.[72] In 1802, Chaptal wrote to the prefect of the department referring to vague plans to establish an "École d'arts mécaniques et de chymie" in Belgium.[73] Apparently Ghent was competing with Brussels as the site for the school in mechanics and chemistry that never happened. Its consolation prize was a school for medicine, surgery, and pharmacology.

At the Ghent *école centrale*, seventeen- to twenty-year-old sons of merchants, jewelers, apothecaries, tailors, a master of music, a surgeon – the vast majority from Ghent, but also Paris, Lille, and Brussels – availed themselves of its courses and took prizes for their work. It was also possible to attend another secondary school in the town as well as a school of commerce – neither taught science, and the secondary school had no books in physics or chemistry in its library. Similarly, the college seminary in the town taught only religion and Latin.

The French administrators were perfectly aware that they were offering "lessons on matters of great interest to society" and cited precisely the sciences and mathematics as subjects that had been lacking before their arrival. The vision of the French administrators was frankly industrial, "[let me observe in passing] that in a country of manufacturers, chemistry must be an essential branch of instruction." To enhance the education in science, more than 2,000 livres was devoted to equipping Ghent with laboratories in everything from "a pneumatic machine" to flasks for conserving different gases. The experimental physics being taught came from the mainstay of Newtonian natural philosophy, the textbook of Desaguliers.[74]

[72] AN, Paris F 17 1344/14, for financial overview of 14 Nivoise year 10. See printed program in the same folder, *Programme des cours de L'École Centrale, du Département de l'Escaut, qui s'ouvriront le premier brumaire an XII* (Ghent: Goesin-Verhaeghe, 1804), which gives a detailed curriculum, and specifies that the Newtonian text by Haüy should be used. In Belgium, the original name of the schools remained and the term "*lycée*" was used after 1804. On the library and cabinet of physics, etc., see AN, Paris F 17 1087. For the books to be used, see AN, Paris, F 17 1087, dossier 9 (should be 10), document 101. For the cabinets and their contents, see AN, F 17 1087 dossier 9, documents 105 and 107. For the cost of physics and chemistry materials, see Rijksarchief Ghent, series J inv. 3738/2.

[73] Rijksarchief Gent, Gent, series J, inv. nr. 3735/2, brief van Chaptal to prefect Faipoult, 17 frimaire an XI; Chaptal is answering an earlier letter from Faipoult in which he has argued that Ghent would be a better place for the school than Brussels. Liège has expressed similar interest.

[74] Rijksarchief, Ghent, series J, 3128/53 for lists of prize winners and the profession of their fathers. The textbook of Brisson was also used in physics and Chaptal in chemistry; see series J 3861/2. For the other secondary school, see its program of exercises and contents of its library, Stadsarchief, Ghent, series U, inv. nr. 865 and 866, and Rijksarchief, Fonds Scheldepartement inv. nr. 3734/6. There were books in physico-theology; and see inv. nr. 3743/5 for the other secondary school and 3743/11 for the seminary. AN, Paris, F 17 2484

From the French point of view, all these improvements must have been seen as money wasted. By 1815 they were forced out of Belgium, and it was united with the Dutch Republic, creating the Kingdom of the Netherlands. Changes were made by the Dutch king ruling from The Hague. Education in Ghent returned to being in Flemish and the teaching of the Catholic religion also resumed. The clergy came out in force, but control over education remained firmly in the hands of the Dutch administrators in The Hague. In 1816, they issued 200 new guidelines to govern higher education in the southern provinces. The teaching of Catholicism was restored to the curriculum, but not at the expense of science and mathematics; if anything they were expanded. Curators of instruments were even instructed to bring into their collections agricultural instruments and machines for manufacturing.[75]

Throughout the 1820s the local secondary schools in Ghent continued to emphasize the usefulness of mathematics and science: "all high schools give lessons in experimental physics." The reasoning behind this education became clearer by the year: "in a city of commerce and industry as Ghent where the arts flourish [it is] daily more and more [necessary] to encourage . . . studies in physical science"; in particular the discoveries of Newton, especially on characteristics of all bodies, have given mankind very useful discoveries.[76] This praise is significantly different from what could be heard in France during the 1820s.

Late in that decade, education for industry – in imitation of two schools in France – came to Ghent and children were offered eight years of

for inspection reports for 1809 showing problems. For what the French saw themselves as doing for society, see AN, F 17 1565 letter to Roederer, 1810; for the industrial vision, see letter of the prefect of the department to Fourcroy, letter of 22 ventose, year 11, when they are trying to get a *lycée* established in the town. For laboratory equipment put in place in 1810 when the central school was replaced by the *lycée*, see Stadsarchief, series U, inv. nr. 869. For the physics and mathematics actually taught, see *Programme des Exercices publics*, 1812, Rijksarchief, Scheldedepartement, inv. nr. 3744/4, and for the number of students in 1810, see inv. nr. 3743/6; and inv. nr. 9011/15 for books in the library, including Desaguliers.

75 ARA, Binnenlandse Zaken (1813–64), 2.04.01, inv. nr. 3986, f. 309, September 25, 1816, see article 15–17, and article 18 for emphasis on usefulness, and article 131 on machines.

76 Stadsarchief, Ghent, series U inv. nr. 906, 1824 letter of Timmermans to the ministry, "in bijna alle athenae geeft men lessen van physique experimentale." He is talking about the athenea, or secondary schools, in the region. In the same folder for usefulness, see letter of 1824 from Merden, "gelooft ist dat het zeer nuttig zou zyn das lessen van natuurkunde ook in die collegian gegeven woerden." For the discussion of Newton, see in the same series from 1828–9, "men heeft hun ook gesproken eeniger ontdekkingen van Newton, en bezonderlijk van de eigenschap die alle ligchamen bezitten, om, door een zekere kracht, naar elkander getrokken te worden, hoe deze wonderbare wet der natuur, de beweging der hemelsche ligchamen regeert, wat nut deze ontdekking heet bygebragt, en hoe zij aanleiding gegeven heeft, tot andere voor het menschdom zeer nuttige ontdekkingen."

instruction that began with basic mathematics, reading, and writing, and continued with geometry, mechanics, geography, and the Dutch language. From this followed training in basic crafts for wood, metal, gold and silver making, ending in the final years with higher mathematics, physics, and chemistry. The purpose of these new schools was clear: "Within a few years the Dutch shall give an exemplar of industry to all the people of Europe."[77] In various cities the Dutch ministers urged the establishment of schools for design and drawing, which "is indispensable for those destined for the arts, mechanics," and so, too, elementary mathematics had to be taught because it was needed by all the professions as well as for understanding scientific demonstrations. In 1826, a school of mines was established at the university in Liège and "courses in applied chemistry for the industrial arts will be opened in the universities."[78] By 1833 the province of Hainaut inaugurated its own society for the study of the sciences, arts, and letters, in which the sciences and industrial applications tended to predominate.[79]

In 1830, the Belgians revolted from the Kingdom and Belgium came into existence. In the following year the curriculum of the colleges was further upgraded and more difficult mathematics was added. So, too, the "first principles of physics and the chemistry of minerals" were added with the intention of bettering what had been taught "in the Holland years."[80] In 1830, public courses in chemistry were given at the Industrial School of Ghent, and like those of the Society of Friends in Maastricht, the courses were intended to illustrate the basic chemical principles needed for manufacturing.[81] Later in the decade 100–150 auditors attended courses in physics and chemistry given in free schools paid for by the municipality. These ranged from practical notions in geometry to the general properties of bodies, the theory of heat, to simple machines, steam engines, and even "a superficial explication of the machines employed in the cotton industry." In attendance were "workers, artisans, foremen, manufacturers, young men . . . destined for industry." The lead that Ghent took in cotton manufacturing cannot be understood without a sense of the educational

[77] G. A. Le Normant, *Plan ter vestiging van eene school voor handwerkslieden, in welke 400 jongelingen aanhoudend in de kunsten en ambachten zullen onderwezen worden, zonder iets aan den staat te kosten* (Ghent: J. N. Houdin, 1826), p. 23.

[78] Archives d'Etat, Mons, Fonds Français et Hollandais, Province Hainault, inv. Nr. 768–1, 768–5, 768–6.

[79] Société des sciences, arts, lettres du Hainaut, *Table des Publications 1839–1924* (Tournay: Grande imprimerie-Litho Tournaisienne, S.C., 1937).

[80] Stadsarchief, Ghent, inv. nr. 903.

[81] SAG, reeks U, inv. nrs. 2354, 2356, 2358, 2359, 2361, February 1830.

infrastructure available to anyone who might wind up on the factory floor.[82]

None of the industrial prowess of Ghent would have been possible without the coal to run the steam engines that powered the cotton factories. One source of that coal lay in the town of Mons, about fifty miles away, with a population of about 18,000. By the early nineteenth century its coal industry required new canals as shipping by water was far cheaper than over land. Occupying French engineers were deployed, and one of them wrote at length about the fumes and coal dust that pervaded the Mons air. It was so foul as to render parts of the town, in his opinion, uninhabitable.[83]

This French engineer also examined Mons' secondary school and praised the courses that were given in physics, chemistry, and mathematics. He noted with approval a school for design, and the uniformity of the education organized by the government. The town records give a valuable portrait of what had to be done to bring the new, secular education to Mons, just as it had been brought to the other towns that became industrial centers in the nineteenth century. First the actual *école centrale* had to be established, and then came the need to acquire the necessary books and equipment.

The Parisian administrators had definite views about what such a library should contain, and by the early nineteenth century they actually made a list. It began with mathematics with multiple volumes, went on to mechanics and physics dominated by the texts of the major Newtonians, and ended with natural history, chemistry, and human history. Nothing was mandated in religion or literature.[84]

The ministry in Paris queried the administrators in Mons as to how many books they had at their disposal. A promising "over 30,000" came back as the answer. They had been seized from the religious houses and abbeys suppressed in the department. The promise soon faded; the Parisian officials learned from the librarian "that 7/8th of those belong

[82] SAG, reeks U, inv. nr. 1428, letter of September 5, 1837 from Prof. E. Jacquemyns, the secretary of the Council of Professors at the School. See also Library, SAG, code GSA 1 3 GE 14, *Règlement organique de L'École industrielle de Gand* (Ghent: L. de Busscher-Brarckman, 1833).

[83] Archives nationales, Paris, MS AP/147, letters of Jacques François Piou, largely in 1805. He is in charge of building a canal from Mons to Charleroi and then from Charleroi to Brussels. On population, see AN, F 17 9105, in 1813.

[84] For a copy of the list, see Stadsarchief, Ghent, series U, inv. nr. 870, dated 1803. In the interests of space I list only surnames in the order in which they appear; under physics, 's Gravesande, Desaguliers, Musschembroek (three works), Segaud La Fond, Boyle (three works), Franklin, Nollet, Priestley, Libes, Brisson, *Dictionnaire raisonné de physiques*; Alpini, Haüy, Jacotat, Cotes.

under the hammer, or fit only for dregs of the monastic libraries."[85] There was little to be found in civil history, the sciences, and the arts, nothing of the modern, and in consequence nothing any good in natural history, chemistry, experimental physics, and analytic philosophy.

Asked to say whether there were copies of Diderot's great encyclopedia, the librarian answered in the affirmative, and then began a set of questions and answers that revealed what the French administrators and their counterpart in Mons thought was necessary for a proper secondary education. The most straightforward description belongs to the category, the Enlightenment; all of its major works, and some minor, were deemed essential. Did Mons have a copy of the *Encyclopédie méthodique*? No. What about works by Buffon, Voltaire? No. What do you and your colleagues think is essential for education?

The answers tell us much about the knowledge deemed vital for Belgian development: works on painting, sculpture, engraving, architecture, and mechanics – spelled out in some detail – plus a huge library in natural history including mineralogy, botany, and agriculture – the most modern works in medicine and veterinary, and works on ancient languages. In mathematics and mechanics, everyone important in the eighteenth century appears on the list: Clairaut, Mazéas, Lasaille, Rivard, Bossuet, Euler, Laplace, Bion, Cousin, all of Newton, Leibniz, Pascal de l'Hôpital, Maupertuis, D'Alembert, Bernoulli, Diderot, Leclerc, Sauri, Lemoine, Faucher, Lamÿ, etc. The abbé Nollet was deemed essential to the teaching of experimental physics, as were Brisson, Sigaud de la Fond, B. Franklin, the abbé Bertholan, Paulian, Lavoisier, Priestley, and the Dutch Newtonian Musschenbroek. In language and literature, Locke led the list, followed by Leibniz, C. Wolf, Gassendi, Helvetius, Malebranche, Rousseau, Condorcet, and Mirabeau. The complete Buffon was urgently needed for teaching, as well as many books in natural history. Books to teach the ancient languages were high on the list, as was almost every book in mathematics.

So, too, history. The abbé Raynal's philosophical history of the two Indies as well as works from the Scottish Enlightenment came high on the list, as did the vast travel literature about every part of the known world. The librarian noted that they were lucky to get from the Estates of Hainaut books "essential in a public library," such as Diderot's *Encyclopedia*,

[85] AN, Paris, F 17 1088, dossier 10, document 87, 1799, "Ce qu'on a trouvé dans les diverses maisons religieuses et abbaÿes supprimées de ce département, non compris Tournay, dont les livres ne sont pas encore arrivés, monte à 30254 volumes, dont les sept huitièmes, environ, sont à rebuter et méritent d'aller au pilon. Ce n'étoit plus que la lie des bibliothèques monastiques." He was asked to make a list of the pre-1500 titles (incunabulae) and gave seventy-seven of them. He also listed ten of the Church fathers.

Bayle's *Dictionary*, and not least, the Parisian edition of Picart's even-handed and non-judgmental *Ceremonies and Religious Customs of all the People of the World.*[86] *Belles lettres* required many of the classics by Horace and Cicero, or Aristotle, and then works from the eighteenth century by Gibbon, Mercier, D'Alembert, Voltaire, Fénelon, and Fontenelle. Legislation and morals began with Montesquieu and Rousseau, Filangheri (the Italian theorist of reform and free trade), Beccaria (against torture), Locke, and Mablÿ (on government), rounded off by Blackstone, Millar, Hume, D'Holbach, and Franklin.

The educational reforms initiated by the French revolutionaries sought to create a cultivated, literate citizen who knew ancient languages, literature, mathematics, experimental physics, and chemistry. The books on these subjects were routinely given to prize-winning pupils.[87] This was the Enlightenment brought to education, used as a beckon, a harbinger of the secular and the modern. Perhaps understanding the educational ideals of the French revolutionaries helps to explain the clerical reaction against them in 1815. In Belgium, the reaction never got off the ground because the Dutch state and monarch in The Hague would not countenance it. This is not to say that the Belgian religious authorities did not attempt to reassert their educational role after 1815. Indeed, they complained bitterly that the French regime had neglected the humanities and in general put people off educating their children, in part because there were so few ecclesiastical positions available.[88] The reports to the new government make clear that religion had crept back into the curriculum, but not to the exclusion of the sciences and mathematics.

[86] Ibid. Also listed in the category of essential books are those by Trévoux, de Moreri, La Martiniere, Ducange, *La bibliothèque de l'homme d'état et du citoyen*, *Les monuments de la monarchie française*; *L'antiquité expliquée* by Montfaucon, the history of voyages of Prévôt, treatises on public law and diplomacy, histories of the provinces of Belgium, etc.

[87] For what was taught in the school in 1800, see J. Becker, *Un établissement d'enseignement moyen à Mons depuis 1545* (Mons: Léon Dequesne, 1913), pp. 335–9. For a complete list of the books held in the library in 1801, see Archives d'Etat, Mons, Fonds Ville de Mons, inv. nr. 1999, 514pp. handwritten folios, "Minute du Catalogue des Livres de la Bibliothèque près l'École Central du Département de Jemappes." Mons was in this department. Cf AN, Paris, F 17 1343–44/1. By 1804 there are two secondary schools in Mons. For the prize books, see the list from Liège, AEL, Fonds Français Prefecture, inv. nr. 449–4, year 7.

[88] For the complaints, see the mayor of Louvain to the new *sous-intendant*, ARA, Binnenlanden Zaken, 2.04.01 inv. nr. 3988, September 26, 1815. See the entire folder for the curriculum in colleges all over the country in 1815.

Conclusion

Explanations about economic change are still bedeviled by unspoken philosophical assumptions. When talking about work and prosperity, or lack thereof, or about the production of goods and machines, we assume that the forces at play must be material – money being foremost among them. They have to be countable, movable, and capable of mathematical expression. Being truly scientific when studying economic change means that the historian, whenever possible, must use equations and numbers to express change over time. What a disruption to introduce something as vague as knowledge or education – that is, culture which, it is assumed, must be immaterial.

The unspoken assumptions rest on the old matter/spirit, body/mind dichotomy, with its roots deep in Western thought, both classical and Christian. Seen in this manner, one-dimensional *homo economicus* responds to material stimuli, rushes to make profit, invents technology when it is needed, and prides himself on the rationality of his choices. For example, when faced with an exorbitant cost of wage labor (even when he does not know, comparatively, that it is exorbitant), he seeks to develop other sources of energy, and in an effort to reduce his wage bill, turns to coal. To caricature the argument, he comes upon the right knowledge that just happens to be there when he needs it. In the eighteenth century, whether engaged in manufacturing or mining, the best means of achieving profitability meant accessing the new, coal-driven steam engine, among other mechanical devices.

When thousands of economic actors find the same solutions in response to economic stimuli, deep changes can occur in the direction of increased productivity and profit. The historical macrocosm of Western Europe from roughly 1750 to 1850 witnessed just such an increase, and a phenomenon took hold with which we are still very much familiar. The expectation of continuous economic expansion – with ups and downs to be sure – is now fundamental to our material lives. It is a direct by-product of what has been described as the First Industrial Revolution. Knowing about the solutions that produced industrial development does not, however, in the first instance tell us how or why they were found. For that we need access to the lived history of the human beings who made the decisions.

This book presents a series of microcosms, largely urban, centered on innovative entrepreneurs and engineers and what they knew, or what they might have learned, as they sought to make sense out of the world around them, and not least to make a profit while living in it. Their minds are imbedded in material circumstances, to be sure, but also in sets of values, beliefs, interests, and knowledge systems. They are not simply bodies set in motion by collision with material reality, their trajectory imagined as predetermined by cost–benefit analysis. Their skilled hands matched minds steeped in the knowledge systems new to the eighteenth century.

Knowledge of the physical universe gave entrepreneurs a singular advantage when economic decisions were being made. Their participation in the scientific culture of the day meant they could approach coal mining, or cotton and linen production, or spindle making and engine construction, armed with knowledge once assumed to be irrelevant to *homo economicus* as classically formulated. They understood in systematic ways phenomena such as air pressure, the force of a lever, the problem of friction – all but a small part of the relatively new science of applied mechanics.

With mechanics in the Newtonian tradition came experimental method, and early industrialists worked on machines, or problems of weight and motion, in ways that invoked laboratory practices learned at school, or from a tutor, or from skilled engineers who plied their trade in factories, or engine houses, at mine shafts, or canals. By the mid eighteenth century there were more such people in Britain than on the Continent, but the Continent was catching up fast. Where we see mechanical knowledge systematically taught – as was the case in Belgium – we find entrepreneurs capable of deploying it. Where contemporaries knew that the knowledge mattered for industry, they sought to bring it into lecture rooms and classrooms. After 1795 the French revolutionaries reformed the entire mathematics and science curricula of their secondary schools in order to make mechanical and experimental knowledge available to all.

Nothing succeeds like success. Possessed of new human capital, the Boultons, Watts, M'Connels, Kennedys, Marshalls, Bauwens and Mottes became innovative entrepreneurs to be imitated. In hindsight, most histories have dwelt on their wealth and decision making in business and assigned importance to their ledger books, their accounting skills and profit margins, their efforts to control wages and minimize their risks in the marketplace. Perhaps we even once imagined their minds as blank except for the occasions when they ventured into the marketplace armed with facts and figures generated by their business. In this book we have stopped to ask, Could they have done what they did without – what the French called – industrial mechanics? The evidence suggests they could not. Perhaps the applied scientific knowledge even drew them to industry in the first place; they knew the principles upon which machines worked and they were eager to try them out or improve upon them. They seized the opportunity that their mechanical knowledge provided.

The core of the Industrial Revolution rested on technological innovation. The shift to power technology, to inorganic rather than organic energy, depended in the first instance on the power of steam engines. Many innovations also involved skillful handwork, to be sure, but without the knowledge base upon which the engine rested it becomes very difficult to imagine the new industrial power clearly visible in Britain by 1800. No amount of counting, no graphs or charts that track economic growth over decades, can explain the sources of industrial innovation. Knowledge was critical, and this book examines it and its deployment. We have sought out the lecture halls, factory floors, and schoolrooms where mechanics could be learned and cultivated. Unapologetically, we have focused on the human capital in minds that grappled with industrial problems.

Our understanding of the mind has advanced far beyond the Lockean model of the blank slate. Neuroscience and related disciplines present pictures of the brain as interactive with its environment, absorbing information as well as applying categories, connected to the world in a holistic fashion. In ways mysterious, the mind follows suit. The environment made possible by machines was strikingly new and called forth innovative responses. Remember John Marshall on his factory floor applying Newtonian mechanics to the friction of bobbins. Or think of Mr. Clark trying to convince Lieven Bauwens to invest in his new mathematical spindles. We have followed Matthew Boulton to Paris, and found him searching for what he deemed important: evidence of science being taught in the capital. All these economic actors believed that their knowledge, if properly applied, could bring success.

In a previous book I described committees of the House of Lords in the 1790s querying engineers about water power lost or gained from the building of canals. Both peers and engineers referenced hydrostatics and dynamics. There were plenty of other settings outside of London where knowledge was also critical. Think of what Northumberland coal viewers had to know in order to install a profit-making engine and access coal never before imagined as usable. Remember M'Connel and Kennedy in Manchester, on a steep learning curve that took them from knowledge of spindles and weaving to correcting the engineering plans supplied by Boulton and Watt for the new steam-driven cotton factories. Then there is the education of Watt himself. While cutting out the numbers for the faces of clocks, he spent his evenings mastering the most complex Newtonian textbooks of his day.

Mechanical knowledge did not exist in a vacuum, and in some historical settings it proved to be controversial. Contemporaries understood the power that could be extracted from those textbooks on mechanics, and some of them had grave misgivings about the effect on religion. After 1815 French religious authorities feared the implications of what they called "physics," and the teaching of math and science declined in French schools. The situation was not remedied until late in the 1830s, and indeed the hostility between men of science and the French clergy was endemic throughout much of the nineteenth century.[1] Nothing about that atmosphere encouraged industrial development.

Knowledge relevant to industrial innovation depended upon access. In various countries the educational infrastructure, where it can be known, has been examined for what sort of scientific knowledge was actually taught. In Britain, the search for curricula is a virtually impossible undertaking; every school was essentially independent. Thus, while we cannot always know how youthful British engineers or entrepreneurs acquired their knowledge, we can show its presence in their maturity. By contrast, on the Continent the French state left an invaluable set of records of what it allowed to be taught before 1789 and, most importantly, after it.

The French revolutionaries were the preeminent modernizers of education in every field, but nowhere more so than in the teaching of all branches of the sciences and their application. Perhaps the greatest beneficiaries of those efforts were the Belgian schools. Even after the French departed in 1815, the Belgians kept their commitment to scientific education largely because the country came under the control of the Dutch King Willem I. After that year, as we saw, the French schools succumbed to either a disdain for science or its demise for lack of clerical interest. At the same time French curricula made little impact in the Dutch Republic where, although controlled by France from 1795 to 1814, local government and systems of education remained largely intact.

Relentlessly this book resists any explanation of how or why the Industrial Revolution happened first in Western Europe, from roughly 1750 to 1850, that does not make applied scientific learning a major part of the story. Its evidence comes from many sites, from cotton and linen factories, coal mines, informal and formal settings for education, and not least from the observations of contemporaries. It adds to what we know

[1] See T. Verhoeven, "The Satyriasis Diagnosis: Anti-Clerical Doctors and Celibate Priests in Nineteenth-Century France," *French History*, 26, 4, 2012, pp. 504–23.

about the deployment of industrial mechanics through interrogations of engineers conducted by peers of the House of Lords, or through the correspondence of lead miners, coal viewers, and factory owners, or by the testimony of engineers themselves. At every turn this book asks the reader to observe knowledge at work in minds responding to a new environment never before witnessed in the Western world.

Currently we know too little about the innovative entrepreneur except that we acknowledge his importance.[2] The human face of industrial innovation has been obscured by the material conditions deemed to be sufficient to explain economic progress. Put human capital back into the story and suddenly minds, books, lectures, school curricula become central to the story of Western economic development. We have missed them for far too long, and without human actors the vitality, creativity, relentless questioning, and experimental reasoning of trial and error disappear. Why would we want to so impoverish our histories and make them so much less interesting? Why turn something as complex as industrial development into an abstraction?

[2] W. J. Baumol, *The Microtheory of Innovative Entrepreneurship* (Princeton University Press, 2010).

Bibliography

Académie des sciences, Paris, MSS 18
Algemeen Rijksarchief, Brussels (hereafter ARA), Biza, 2.04.01, inv. nr. 3986; Conseil privé; MS T 100, 1210, ff. 1–63, letters of Rousset de Missy; Comité Jésuitique, MS T 083/01, box 6; Binnenlandse Zaken, 2.04.01, inv. nr. 3988
American Philosophical Society, Philadelphia, MS B/M 291
Archives d'état, Brussels MS A.E.M., Charbonnages Bois du Luc, ff. 51–87;
Archives d'Etat, Liège (hereafter AEL), Fonds Français Préfecture, inv. Nr. 448–2
Archives d'Etat, Mons, Fonds Français et Hollandais, Province Hainaut, nrs. 761, year 6
Archives Départementales, Loire Atlantique, Nantes, Loire L 930
Archives Départementales Seine, Amiens, MS 80003
Archives Départementales, Seine-Maritime, MS 1T 873: Fonds de l'Académie
Archives historiques de diocèse de Paris, 4 rue de l'Asile Popincourt, Paris 11e
Archives Nationales, Paris, series F 12, F14, F 17; F7; Marine MS G 110; E 2660 2a (AN)
Bibliothèque Générale, Liège, 23323 B
Bibliothèque historique de la ville de Paris, MS 772; N.A. MS 147
Bibliothèque nationale de France (BFM)
Birmingham Central Library, James Watt Papers, 3/18, 69; 4/4, 11, 53, 69, 76; 6/14–20, 46; C1/15, 20; C2/12, 15; C4/A7, C18A; W/6, 11, 13; MS LB/1 (BCL), Boulton and Watt Papers, Letter Books; Matthew Boulton Papers, Box 357; MS 3782/12/107/28, ff. 15–16; MS 3782/12/108/14, 17, 49
Bristol Record Office, White MS, No. 08158
British Library, London; 936 f. 9/61; 1607/3837; MSS 44, 799, f. 136; MSS ADD 6858; MSS ADD 38355, f. 169
The Brotherton Library, Leeds, Special Collections, MS 18; The Marshall MSS, fully searchable at http://industrialization.ucla.ats.edu; Gott MSS; Marriner MS 65/1; MS 194/14; MS Dep. 1975/1/6
Centre national de la recherche scientifique, Paris, Manuscrits d'André-Marie Ampère, Chemises 302 et 302bis [carton 20], 1775–1836 www.ampere.cnrs.fr/ms-ampere-302-89-1.5.html
Charles E. Young Research Library, University of California, Los Angeles, Bound Manuscripts Collection, Collection 170/587; the papers of John Bowring.
Cornish Mining World Heritage, Boulton and Watt Papers www.cornishmining.net/story/bwpapers.htm, now housed at the Cornish Record Office
Dr. Williams's Library, London, Wodrow–Kenrick correspondence, MS 24
East Riding of Yorkshire Archive Service, MS DDCC/150/276
École des Ponts et Chaussées (EPC), Paris, MS 3013
Fitzwilliam Museum, Cambridge, MS 48–1947

Friends Library, Euston Road, London, MS note book, William Sturge 1797, Ackworth School, MS Box G 1/5/1–2
Gemeente Archief, Maastricht, inv. Nr. 334 and 336, in same, Athenaeum, inv. nr. 336
Hagley Museum and Library, Delaware, Longwood MSS, Series B Box 10
Harper Collection of Private Bills, 1695–1814
An Act for Vesting, for a certain Term therein mentioned, in John Tuite, his Executors, Administrators and Assigns, the Sole Property of a Water Engine by him invented 1695–1814, House of Commons. Parliamentary Papers at http://parlipapers.chadwyck.com/fulltext.do?id=harper-001066&DurUrl=Yes
House of Lords Record Office, London, Main Papers, Canal Bill records
The Institution of Civil Engineers, London, MS Society of Civil Engineers, Treasurer's minutes and accounts, 1793–1821, meeting record of "Smeatonians"
John Rylands Library, Manchester, J Benson MSS; John Seddon MSS; Botfield Papers (1758–1873); M'Connel and Kennedy, all letters sent and received
National Library, Ireland, MS 13176(4)
North of England Institute of Mining and Mechanical Engineers (NEIMME); Buddle MSS; MS GA/2; Forster MSS; Brown MSS; MS East/3a/3b; NCBI/JB/2261–2271; Bell/3/265, 327–333, 337, 387; DX 840/2; John MSS; Weeks MSS; "History of Coal Mining," #125, ff. 5–64
Northumberland Record Office, SANT/DRA/2/9/2/14, A and B; SANT/BEQ/18/11/13/ff. 175–80, 187–93, 197–229, 286–98
Rijksarchief Liège, Maastricht, 03. 01, Frans Archief (1794–1814, inv. nr. 2449)
Rijksarchief Limburg (RAL), Maastricht, 03. 01 inv. nr 2523, 2624
Royal Library, The Hague, MS 75, and J. 63
Sheffield City Library, Bagshawe Collection, MS 494, John Barker's Letter Book, 1765–1811
Society of Merchant Venturers, Bristol, MS Letter Book
Stadsarchief, Ghent, Fonds Napoleon de Pauw, MS 3285; series U, inv. nr. 870; reeks T (14)
Stadsbibliotheek, Maastricht, SB Br. LC 1492
Tyne and Wear Archives, Newcastle, MS DX198/1, MS GU/MA/2/2
University Library, Amsterdam, MS. X.B.1, "Leçons de physique de Mr le Prof. Koening"
University of Liège, Central Library, MS 1310, Course in mineralogy, 1829–30
West Yorkshire Archive Service, Wakefield, MS C482/1
Whitby Literary and Philosophical Society Library, Pannett Park, Whitby, UK
Wolverhampton Archives, Edward Short's notebook, MS DX-840/2, ff. 4, 59

SECONDARY SOURCES

Acemoglu, D., and J. A. Robinson. *Why Nations Fail: The Origins of Power, Prosperity and Poverty*. New York: Crown, 2012.
Allen, R. C. "Britain's Economic Ascendancy in a European Context." In *Exceptionalism and Industrialisation: Britain and Its European Rivals,*

1688–1815, ed. Leandro Prados de la Escosura, pp. 15–34. Cambridge University Press, 2004.

Allen, R. C. *Industrial Revolution in Global Perspective*. Cambridge University Press, 2009.

André-Felix, A. *Les débuts de l'industrie chimique dans les Pays-Bas autrichiens*. Brussels: Université libre de Bruxelles, 1971.

Appleby, J. *The Relentless Revolution: A History of Capitalism*. New York: W.W. Norton, 2010.

Archaeologia Aeliana, 3rd series, Vol. III, 1907.

Ashton, T. S. *An Eighteenth Century Industrialist: Peter Stubs of Warrington 1756–1806*. Manchester University Press, 1939.

Ashworth, W. J. "The Intersection of Industry and the State in Eighteenth-Century Britain." In *The Mindful Hand: Inquiry and Invention from the Late Renaissance to Early Industrialisation*, ed. L. Roberts, S. Schaffer, and P. Dear, pp. 349–78. Amsterdam: Koninklijke Nederlandse Akademie van Wetenschappen, 2007.

Ashworth, W. J. "Quality and the Roots of Manufacturing 'Expertise' in Eighteenth-Century Britain." In *Expertise: Practical Knowledge and the Early Modern State*, ed. E. H. Ash, Vol. 25, *Osiris*, 2nd series. University of Chicago Press, 2010.

Baker, K. *Condorcet*. University of Chicago Press, 1975.

Barker, H. "'Smoke Cities': Northern Industrial Towns in Late Georgian England." *Urban History* 31 (2004), 175–90.

Barnes, B. "Elusive Memories of Techno-science." *Perspectives on Science* 13 (2005), 156–7.

Barrell, J. *Imagining the King's Death: Figurative Treason, Fantasies of Regicide 1793–96*. Oxford University Press, 2000.

Baudot, J. C. *Histoire des sciences et de l'industrie en Belgique*. Brussels: Jourdan, 2007.

Baudry, J. "La technique et le politique: la constitution du régime de brevets moderne pendant la Révolution (1791–1803)." M.A. thesis, École des Hautes Etudes en Sciences Sociales, Paris, 2008–9.

Becker, J. *Un établissement d'enseignement moyen à Mons depuis 1545*. Mons: Léon Dequesne, 1913.

Becker, S., E. Hornung, and L. Woessmann. "Catch Me If You Can: Education and Catch-up in the Industrial Revolution." *Stirling Economics Discussion Paper 2009–19*, Stirling Online Research Repository, http://d.repec.org/n?u=RePEc:stl:stledp:2009–19&r=his. Accessed December 17, 2012.

Bensaude-Vincent, B., and C. Blondel, eds. *Science and Spectacle in the European Enlightenment*. Aldershot: Ashgate, 2008.

Berg, M. "Product Innovation in Core Consumer Industries in Eighteenth-Century Britain." In *Technological Revolutions in Europe: Historical Perspectives*, ed. M. Berg and K. Bruland. Cheltenham: Edward Elgar, 1998.

Bernard, B. *Essays* in *L'Académie Impériale et Royale de Bruxelles ses Académiciens et leurs réseaux intellectuels au XVIIIe siècle*, ed. H. Hasquin. Brussels: Académie Royale de Belgique, 2009.

Bertuglia, C. S., S. Lombardo, and P. Nijkamp, eds. *Innovative Behavior in Space and Time*. Berlin: Springer, 2000.

Blanchard, A. *Les ingénieurs du "roy" de Louis XIV à Louis XVI*. Montpellier: l'Université Paul-Valéry, 1979.

Bradley, M. "Engineers as Military Spies? French Engineers Come to Britain, 1780–1790." *Annals of Science* 49, 2 (March 1992), 137–61.

Brand, J. *The History and Antiquities of . . . Newcastle upon Tyne*. Vol. II. London: B. White and Son, 1789.

Braster, J. F. A. "The schoolwet van 1806: Blauwdruk voor een onderwijsbestel." In *Nederland in Franse schaduw. Recht en bestuur in het Koninkrijk Holland (1806–1810)*, ed. H. Hallebeerk and A. J. B. Sirks, pp. 147–64. Hilversum: Verloren, 2006.

Brenner, R., and C. Isett. "England's Divergence from China's Yangzi Delta: Property Relations, Microeconomics, and Patterns of Development." *The Journal of Asian Studies* 61 (May 2002), 609–62.

Brenni, P. "The Evolution of Teaching Instruments and Their Use between 1800 and 1930." *Science & Education* 21 (2012), 191–226.

Brockett, J. T. *A Glossary of North Country Words*. 2 vols. In one, 3rd edn. Newcastle upon Tyne: Emerson Charnley, 1846.

Brockliss, L. W. B. "Aristotle, Descartes and the New Science: Natural Philosophy at the University of Paris, 1600–1740." *Annals of Science* 38 (1981), 33–69

Brockliss, L. W. B. *French Higher Education in the Seventeenth and Eighteenth Centuries: A Cultural History*. Oxford: Clarendon Press, 1987.

Burns, D. Thorburn. "The Lunar Society and Midland Chemists." *Analytical Proceedings* 28 (December 1991).

Burson, J. D. *The Rise and Fall of Theological Enlightenment: Jean-Martin de Prades and Ideological Polarization in Eighteenth-Century France*. Notre Dame, IN: University of Notre Dame Press, 2010.

Cantoni, D., and N. Yuchtman. "Educational Content, Educational Institutions and Economic Development: Lessons from History." Munich Discussion Paper 2012–2, Department of Economics, University of Munich. http://ideas.repec.org/p/lmu/muenec/12691.html Accessed, December 2012.

Cardwell, D. S. L. "Power Technologies and the Advance of Science, 1700–1825." *Technology and Culture* 6 (1965), 188–207.

Carlson, R. E. *The Liverpool and Manchester Railway Project, 1821–1831*. Newton Abbot: David & Charles, 1969.

Carpenter, A. T. *John Theophilus Desaguliers: A Natural Philosopher, Engineer and Freemason in Newtonian England*. London: Continuum, 2011.

Chapman, S. D. *The Cotton Industry in the Industrial Revolution*. Houndmills: Macmillan Education, 1987.

Charmasson, T., and A.-M. Le Lorrain. *L'Enseignement technique de la Révolution*. Paris: Economica INRP, 1987.

Chartier, R. "Un recrutement scolaire au xviiie siècle. L'école royale du génie de Mézières." *Revue d'Histoire Moderne et Contemporaine* 20 (1973), 353–75.

Chatzis, K. "Theory and Practice in the Education of French Engineers from the Middle of the 18th Century to the Present." *Archives internationals d'histoire des sciences* 60 (June 2010), 43–78.

Cherry, G. E. *Birmingham: A Study in Geography, History and Planning*. New York: Wiley & Sons, 1994.

Chevalier, A. *Les frères des écoles chrétiennes: et l'enseignement primaire après la révolution, 1787–1830*. Paris: Libraire Poussielgne Frères, 1887.

Christie, I. R. *Wars and Revolutions: Britain, 1760–1815*. Cambridge, MA: Harvard University Press, 1982.

Clark, G. N. *The Wealth of England from 1496 to 1760*. New York: Oxford University Press, 1946.

Clavering, E. "The Coal Mills of Northeast England: The Use of Waterwheels for Draining Coal Mines, 1600–1750." *Technology and Culture* 36 (1995), 211–41.

Cohen, H. F. "Inside Newcomen's Fire Engine, or: The Scientific Revolution and the Rise of the Modern World." *History of Technology* 25 (2004), 111–32.

Colls, R. *The Pitmen of the Northern Coalfield: Work, Culture and Protest, 1790–1850*. Manchester University Press, 1987.

Colls, R. "Remembering George Stephenson." In *Newcastle upon Tyne: A Modern History*, ed. R. Colls and B. Lancaster, pp. 272–5. Chichester: Phillimore & Co., 2001.

Connell, E. J., and M. Ward. "Industrial Development, 1780–1914." In *A History of Modern Leeds*, ed. Derek Fraser, Manchester University Press, 1980, 142–76.

Cookson, G. "The West Yorkshire Textile Engineering Industry, 1780–1850." Submitted for the degree of D. Phil., University of York, Department of Economics and Related Studies (July 1994).

Cookson, G. "Family Firms and Business Networks: Textile Engineering in Yorkshire, 1780–1830." *Business History* 39 (1997), 1–20.

Corfield, P. J., and C. Evans. *Youth and Revolution in the 1790s: Letters of William Pattison, Thomas Amyot and Henry Crabb Robinson*. Gloucestershire: Alan Sutton Publishing, 1996.

Court, W. H. B. "A Warwickshire Colliery in the Eighteenth Century." *The Economic History Review* 7 (May 1937), 221–8.

Davidoff, L., and C. Hall. *Family Fortunes: Men and Women of the English Middle Class, 1780–1850*. London: Hutchinson, 1987.

Davids, K. "Apprenticeship and Guild Control in the Netherlands, c. 1450–1800." In *Learning on the Shop Floor*, ed. B. De Munck, S. L. Kaplan, and H. Soly, pp. 65–84. New York: Berghahn Books, 2007.

Davids, K. *The Rise and Decline of Dutch Technological Leadership: Technology, Economy and Culture in the Netherlands, 1350–1800*. Vol. II. Leiden: Brill, 2008.

de Boom, G. *Les Ministres Plénipotentiaires dans les Pays-Bas autrichiens principalement Cobenzl*. In *Académie Royale de Belgique. Mémoires*, 10th Series, Vol. XXXI. Brussels: Lamertin, 1932.

De Munck, B. *Technologies of Learning: Apprenticeship in Antwerp Guilds from the 15th Century to the End of the Ancien Régime*. Turnhout: Brepols, 2007.

De Munck, B., S. L. Kaplan, and H. Soly, eds. *Learning on the Shop Floor: Historical Perspectives on Apprenticeship*. New York: Berghahn Books, 2007.

de Pleijt, A. M. "The Role of Human Capital in the Process of Economic Development: The Case of England, 1307–1900." *CGEH Working Paper* No. 21. Utrecht University: November 2011, www.cgeh.nl/working-paper-series/.

de Selincourt, E., ed. *The Letters of William and Dorothy Wordsworth*, 2nd edn., rev. by Chester L. Shaver. *Vol. I, The Early Years, 1787–1805*. Oxford: Clarendon Press, 1967.

de Vries, J. "Dutch Economic Growth in Comparative-Historical Perspective, 1500–2000." *De Economist* 148 (2000), 433–66.

de Vroede, M. "Onderwijs en opvoeding in de Zuidelijke Nederlanden 1815–circa 1840." Vol. II. Algemene Geschiedenis der Nederlanden (Weesp: Fibula-Van Dishoeck, 1983).

Delbourgo, J. *A Most Amazing Scene of Wonders: Electricity and Enlightenment in Early America*. Cambridge, MA: Harvard University Press, 2006.

Désert, G. *et al. De l'hydraulique à la vapeur XVIIIe–XIXe siècles*. Caen: Cahier des Annales de Normandie, No. 25, 1993.

d'Hérouville, H. A. de Ricouart. "Le desséchement des Moëres." *Revue de la Société Dunkerquoise d'Histoire et d'Archéologie* 2 (November 1985), 13–28.

Dhombres, J. "L'enseignement des mathématiques par la 'méthode révolutionnaire.' Les leçons de Laplace à l'École normale de l'an III." *Revue d'histoire des sciences* 33 (1980), 315–48.

Digby, A., and P. Searby. *Children, School and Society in Nineteenth-Century England*. London: Macmillan, 1981.

Dord-Crouslé, S. "Les entreprises encyclopédiques catholiques au XIXe siècle: quelques aspects lies à la construction du savoir littéraire." In *La Construction des savoirs XVIIIe–XIXe siècles*, ed. L. Andries. Lyon: Presses Universitaires, 2009.

Drew, D. E. *Stem the Tide: Reforming Science, Technology, Engineering, and Math Education in America*. Baltimore, MD: The Johns Hopkins University Press, 2011.

Duckham, B. F. "The Emergence of the Professional Manager in the Scottish Coal Industry, 1760–1815." *Business History Review* 43, 1 (1969), 21–38.

Dunn, M. *An Historical, Geological, and Descriptive View of the Coal Trade of the North of England; Comprehending its Rise, Progress, Present State, and Future Prospects*. Newcastle upon Tyne: Pattison and Ross, 1844.

Earle, P. *The Making of the English Middle Class: Business, Society and Family Life in London, 1660–1730*. London: Methuen, 1989.

Eckersley, R. "The Drum Major of Sedition: The Life and Political Career of John Cartwright, 1740–1824," Ph.D. dissertation, University of Manchester, 1999.

Edgerton, D. "'The Linear Model' Did Not Exist: Reflections on the History and Historiography of Science and Research in Industry in the Twentieth Century." In *The Science–Industry Nexus: History, Policy, and Implications*, ed. K. Grandin and N. Wormbs, pp. 1–36. New York: Watson, 2004.

Edwards, J. R. "Teaching 'Merchants' Accompts' in Britain during the Early Modern Period." A2009/2, www.cardiff.ac.uk/carbs/research/working_papers/accounting_finance/A2009_2.pdf.

Elliott, P. "The Birth of Public Science in the English Provinces: Natural Philosophy in Derby, 1690–1760." *Annals of Science* 57 (2000), 61–100.

Ellis, H. "'A Manly and Generous Discipline?': Classical Studies and Generational Conflict in Eighteenth and Early Nineteenth Century Oxford." *History of Universities* 25, 2 (2011), 143–72.

Farrar, W. V. *Chemistry and the Chemical Industry in the 19th Century: The Henrys of Manchester and Other Studies*, ed. R. L. Hills and W. H. Brock. Aldershot: Variorum, 1997.

Ferguson, N. *Civilization: The West and the Rest*. New York: Penguin, 2011.

Flinn, M. W. *The Origins of the Industrial Revolution*. London: Longman, 1966.

Floud, R., R. W. Fogel, B. Harris, and S. C. Hong. *The Changing Body: Health, Nutrition, and Human Development in the Western World since 1700*. Cambridge University Press, 2011.

Fox, C. *The Arts of Industry in the Age of Enlightenment*. New Haven, CT: Yale University Press, 2009.

Fox, R., ed. *Technological Change: Methods and Themes in the History of Technology*. Amsterdam: Harwood Academic Publishers, 1996.

Fox, R. "Science, Practice and Innovation in the Age of Natural Dyes, 1750–1860." In *Technological Revolutions in Europe*, ed. M. Berg and K. Bruland, pp. 86–95. Northampton, MA: Edward Elgar, 1998.

Fox, R., and A. Guagnini. *Laboratories, Workshops, and Sites: Concepts and Practices of Research in Industrial Europe, 1800–1914*. Berkeley Papers in the History of Science, Vol. XVIII. Berkeley, CA: The Regents of the University of California, 1999.

Fraser, D., ed. *Municipal Reform and the Industrial City*. Leicester University Press, 1982.

Galand, M. *Charles de Lorraine, gouverneur général des Pays-Bas autrichiens (1744–1780)*. Brussels: Éditions de l'Université de Bruxelles, 1993.

Galloway, R. L. *A History of Coal Mining in Great Britain*. Vol. I. Newton Abbot: David and Charles, 1969. Reprint of the edition of 1882.

Galvez-Behar, G. "Genèse des droits de l'inventeur et promotion de l'invention sous la Révolution française," 2006, 5–6, Institut de Recherches Historiques du Septentrion (IRHIS); CNRS, Université Charles de Gaulle, Lille, III, http://halshs.archives-ouvertes.fr/halshs-00010474/en/.

Gascoigne, J. *Joseph Banks and the English Enlightenment: Useful Knowledge and Polite Culture*. New York: Cambridge University Press, 1994.

Geiger, R. G. *The Anzin Coal Company: Big Business in the Early Stages of the French Industrial Revolution*. Newark, DE: University of Delaware Press, 1974.

Gildea, R. *Education in Provincial France 1800–1914*. Oxford: Clarendon Press, 1983.

Gillespie, C. C. *Science and Polity in France at the End of the Old Regime*. Princeton University Press, 1980.

Gillespie, R. "Ballooning in France and Britain, 1783–1786," *Isis* 75 (1984), 249–68.

Gillmore, C. S. *Coulomb and the Evolution of Physics and Engineering in Eighteenth Century France*. Princeton University Press, 1971.

Goldstone, J. A. "Efflorescences and Economic Growth in World History: Rethinking the 'Rise of the West' and the Industrial Revolution." *Journal of World History* 13 (2002), 323–89.

Goldstone, J. *The Happy Chance: The Rise of the West in Global Context, 1500–1800*. Cambridge, MA: Harvard University Press, 2004.

Golinski, J. *Science as Public Culture: Chemistry and Enlightenment in Britain, 1760–1820*. New York: Cambridge University Press, 1992.

Golvers, N. "L'œuvre des jésuites en Chine et l'exportation de la 'science belge.'" In *Histoire des sciences en Belgique de l'Antiquité à 1815*, ed. R. Halleux, pp. 273–95. Brussels: Crédit Communal, 1998.

Goodman, D. "Science and the Clergy in the Spanish Enlightenment." *History of Science* 21 (1983), 111–40.

Gordon, R. B. "Who Turned the Mechanical Ideal into Mechanical Reality?" *Technology and Culture* 29 (October 1988), 744–78.

Goring, J. "The Breakup of Old Dissent." In *The English Presbyterians: From Elizabethan Puritanism to Modern Unitarianism*, ed. C. G. Bolam, J. Goring, H. L. Short, and R. Thomas, pp. 175–218. London: George Allen & Unwin Ltd., 1968.

Graham, J. A., and B. A. Phythian, eds. *The Manchester Grammar School, 1515–1965*. Manchester University Press, 1965.

Grau, H. "L'Enseignement des Sciences Physiques fut-il Révolutionnaire? La Physique Expérimentale à Nantes du Collège Oratorien à L'École Centrale." *Annales Historiques de la Révolution Française* (April/June 2000), 149–58.

Grevet, R. *L'avènement de l'école contemporaine en France, 1789–1835*. Villeneuve-d'Ascq [Nord]: Presses universitaires du Septentrion, 2001.

Griffin, C., and I. Inkster, eds. *The Golden Age: Essays in British Social and Economic History, 1850–1870*. Aldershot: Ashgate, 2000.

Guerlac, H. *Newton on the Continent*. Ithaca, NY: Cornell University Press, 1981.

Guillerme, A. *La naissance de l'industrie à Paris. Entre sueurs et vapeurs: 1780–1830*. Seyssel: Champ Vallon, 2007.

Harrigan, P. J. "Church, State, and Education in France from Falloux to the Ferry Laws: A Reassessment." *Canadian Journal of History* 36 (2001), 51–83.

Hasquin, H., ed. *La vie culturelle dans nos provinces au XVIIIe siècle*. Brussels: Crédit Communal, 1983.

Hasquin, H. *Joseph II. Catholique anticlérical et réformateur impatient*. Brussels: Racine, 2007.

Heaton, H. "Benjamin Gott and the Industrial Revolution in Yorkshire." *The Economic History Review* 3 (1931–2), 45–66.

Heilbron, J. L. *Electricity in the 17th and 18th Centuries: A Study of Early Modern Physics*, Berkeley, CA: University of California Press, 1979.

Hellyer, M. *Catholic Physics: Jesuit Natural Philosophy in Early Modern Germany*. Notre Dame, IN: University of Notre Dame Press, 2005.

Hilaire-Pérez, L. "Invention and the State in 18th-Century France." *Technology and Culture* 32, 4 (1991), 911–31.

Hills, Rev. Dr. R. L. *James Watt*. Vols. I and II. Ashbourne: Landmark Publishing, 2002–5.

Hinchliffe, G. *A History of King James's Grammar School in Almondbury*. Huddersfield: The Advertiser Press Ltd., 1963.

Hiskey, C. E. "John Buddle (1773–1843): Agent and Entrepreneur in the North-East Coal Trade." Thesis for the degree of M. Litt., University of Durham, 1978.

Hopkins, E. "Boulton before Watt: The Earlier Career Re-considered." *Midland History* 9 (1984), 43–58.

Horn, J. "Machine-breaking in England and France during the Age of Revolution." *Labour/Le Travail* 55 (spring 2005), 143–66.

Horn, J. *The Path Not Taken: French Industrialization in the Age of Revolution 1750–1830*. Cambridge, MA: MIT Press, 2006.

Houston, R. H. "Literacy, Education and the Culture of Print in Enlightenment Edinburgh." *History* 78 (October 1993), 373–92.

Howe, A. *The Cotton Masters, 1830–1860*. Oxford: Clarendon Press, 1984.

Hudson, P. *The Industrial Revolution*. London: Edward Arnold, 1992.

Hughes, E. "The First Steam Engines in the Durham Coalfield." *Archaeologia Aeliana or Miscellaneous Tracts Relating to Antiquity*, 4th Series, No. 27, pp. 29–45. Newcastle, 1949.

Hughson, I. *et al. The Auchenharvie Colliery: An Early History*. Ochiltree: Shenlake, 1996.

Hulin, N. "La place des sciences naturelles au sein de l'enseignement scientifique au XIXe siècle/The place of natural science within the 19th-Century science curriculum." *Revue d'histoire des sciences* 51, 4 (1998), 401–26.

Humphries, J. "The Lure of Aggregates and the Pitfalls of the Patriarchal Perspective: A Critique of the High Wage Economy Interpretation of the British Industrial Revolution." Nuffield College, Oxford, July 2011, http://d.repec.org/n?u=RePEc:nuf:esohwp:_091&r=his.

Hunt, B. J. *Pursuing Power and Light: Technology and Physics from James Watt to Albert Einstein*. Baltimore, MD: The Johns Hopkins University Press, 2010.

Hunt, C. J. *The Book Trade in Northumberland and Durham to 1860: A Biographical Dictionary of Printers, Engravers ... Booksellers, Publishers*. Newcastle upon Tyne: Thorne's Students' Bookshop, 1975.

Hunt, L., and M. Jacob. "The Affective Revolution in 1790s Britain." *Eighteenth Century Studies* 34 (2001), 491–521.

Inkster, I. "The Social Context of an Educational Movement: A Revisionist Approach to the English Mechanics' Institutes, 1820–1850." In *Scientific Culture and Urbanisation in Industrialising Britain*. Aldershot: Ashgate, Variorum, 1997.

Insley, J. "James Watt's Cookbook Chemistry." *Notes and Records of the Royal Society* 65 (20 September 2011).

Isaac, M.-T., and C. Sorgeloos. "La diffusion des sciences dans les Écoles Centrales." In *Histoire des sciences en Belgique de l'Antiquité à 1815*, ed. R. Halleux, pp. 385–414. Brussels: Crédit Communal, 1998.

Isaac, M.-T., and C. Sorgeloos. "Livres et Lumières à l'école centrale du département de Jemappes 1797–1802." In *Sciences et Lumières à Mons 1792–1802*, ed. B. Lux. Brussels: Académie Royale de Belgique, 2004.

Jacob, M. C. *The Radical Enlightenment: Pantheists, Freemasons and Republicans*. London: George Allen & Unwin, 1981; 2nd edn. 2004.

Jacob, M. C. *The Cultural Meaning of the Scientific Revolution*. New York: Alfred Knopf, 1987.

Jacob, M. C. *Living the Enlightenment: Freemasonry and Politics in Eighteenth Century Europe*. New York: Oxford University Press, 1991.

Jacob, M. C. *Scientific Culture and the Making of the Industrial West*. New York: Oxford University Press, 1997.

Jacob, M. C. "Commerce, Industry and the Laws of Newtonian Science: Weber Revisited and Revised." *Canadian Journal of History* 35 (August 2000), 275–92.

Jacob, M. C. "Scientific Culture and the Origins of the First Industrial Revolution." *História e Economia – Revista Interdisciplinar* 2, 1–2 (2006), 55–70.

Jacob, M. C. "Mechanical Science on the Factory Floor: The Early Industrial Revolution in Leeds." *History of Science* 45 (2007), 197–221. Also found at http://industrialization.ats.ucla.edu/

Jacob, M., and M. Kadane. "Missing Now Found in the Eighteenth Century: Weber's Protestant Capitalist." *American Historical Review* 108, 1 (February 2003), 20–49.

Jacob, M. C., and D. Reid. "Technical Knowledge and the Mental Universe of Manchester's Cotton Manufacturers." *Canadian Journal of History* 36 (2001), 283–304.

In French translation: "Culture et culture technique des premiers fabricants de coton de Manchester." *Revue d'histoire moderne et contemporaine* 50 (2003), 133–55.

Jacob, M. C., and L. Stewart. *Practical Matter: Newton's Science in the Service of Industry and Empire, 1687 to 1851.* Cambridge, MA: Harvard University Press, 2004.

Jenkins, D. T. *The West Riding Wool Textile Industry 1770–1835.* Edington: Pasold Research Fund Ltd., 1975.

Jones, E. L. "Culture and its Relationship to Economic Change." *Journal of Institutional and Theoretical Economics* 151 (June 1995), 269–85.

Jonsson, F. A. "The Industrial Revolution in the Anthropocene." *The Journal of Modern History* 84 (September 2012), 679–96.

Kasdi, M., and F. Ghesquier Krajewski. "L'industrie textile entre campagnes et villes. Deux filières textiles en Flandres du xviii siècle au milieu du XIXe siècle." *Revue du Nord* 375–6 (2008), 497–530.

Kelly, M., J. Mokyr, and C. Ó Gráda. "Precocious Albion: Factor Prices, Technological Change and the British Industrial Revolution." Unpublished paper, circulated University of California, Los Angeles May 6, 2011.

Kirkham, Dr. N. "Steam Engines in Derbyshire Lead Mines." *Transactions of the Newcomen Society* 38 (1965–6), 69–88.

Klein, U. "Techno-science avant la lettre." *Perspectives on Science* 13 (2005), 226–66.

Landes, D. S. *Introduction to Favorites of Fortune: Technology, Growth, and Economic Development since the Industrial Revolution*, ed. P. Higonnet, D. S. Landes, and H. Rosovsky. Cambridge, MA: Harvard University Press, 1991.

Langford, P. *Public Life and Propertied Englishmen 1689–1798.* New York: Oxford University Press, 1991.

Langford, P., and C. Harvie. *The Eighteenth Century and the Age of Industry.* Vol. IV in *The Oxford History of Britain.* New York: Oxford University Press, 1992.

Langins, J. "Sur la première organisation de l'École polytechnique. Texte de arrêté du 6 frimaire an III." *Revue d'histoire des sciences* 33 (1980), 289–313.

Laudan, R. "Natural Alliance or Forced Marriage? Changing Relations between the Histories of Science and Technology." *Technology and Culture* 36, 2 (1995), Supplement, pp. S19–22.

Lee, C. H. *A Cotton Enterprise: 1795–1840: A History of M'Connel & Kennedy, Fine Cotton Spinners.* Manchester University Press, 1972.

Lefèvre, W. "Science as Labor." *Perspectives on Science* 13 (2005), 194–225.

Leon, A. "Promesses et ambiguïtés de l'œuvre d'enseignement technique en France, 1800 à 1815." *Revue d'Histoire Moderne et Contemporaine* 17, 3 (1970), 846–59.

Lesger, C. "Merchants in Charge: The Self-Perception of Amsterdam Merchants, ca. 1550–1700." In *The Self-Perception of Early Modern Capitalists*, ed. M. C. Jacob and C. Secretan, Chapter 3. New York: Palgrave-Macmillan, 2006.

Levere, T., and G. L'E. Turner, with contributions from Jan Golinski and Larry Stewart. *Discussing Chemistry and Steam: The Minutes of a Coffee House Philosophical Society, 1780–1787*. New York: Oxford University Press, 2002.

Leyder, D. *Pour le bien des lettres et de la chose publique. Maria-Theresia, Jozef II en de humanioa in hun Nederlandse Provincies*. Brussels: Paleis der Academiën, 2010.

Lintsen, H. *Ingenieurs in Nederland in der negentiende eeuw*. The Hague: Nijhoff, 1980.

Lintsen, H. W. "De vuurmachine van het droogdok in Hellevoetsluis." In *Wonderen der Techniek: Nederlandse ingenieurs en hun Kunstwerken*, ed. M. L. ten Horn-van Nispen, H. W. Lintsen, and A. J. Veenendaal Jr. Zutphen: Walburg Pers, 1994, 21–3.

Lintsen, H., and R. Steenaard. "Steam and Polders. Belgium and the Netherlands, 1790–1850." In *Tractrix: Yearbook for History of Science, Medicine, Technology and Mathematics*, Vol. III (1991), 121–47.

Lipsey, R. G., K. I. Carlaw, and C. T. Bekar. *Economic Transformations: General Purpose Technologies and Long Term Economic Growth*. New York: Oxford University Press, 2005.

Litton, P. M., ed. "The Journals of Sarah Mayo Parkes, 1815 and 1818." *Publications of the Thoresby Society*, Second Series, Vol. XIII (Miscellany), 2003.

Lok, M., and N. Scholz. "The Return of the Loving Father: Masculinity, Legitimacy and the French and Dutch Restoration." *Low Countries Historical Review* 127, 1 (2012), 19–44.

Lomüller, L. M. *Guillaume Ternaux 1763–1833. Créateur de la première intégration industrielle française*. Paris: Les Éditions de la Cabro d'Or, 1977.

Lord, P. "History of Education in Oldham." M.Ed. thesis, University of Manchester, 1938.

Lourens, P., and J. Lucassen. "Ambachtsgilden in Nederland: een eerste inventarisatie." *NEHA-JAARBOEK voor economische, bedrijfs- en techniekgeschiedenis* 57 (1994), 34–62.

Lourens, P., and J. Lucassen. "Ambachtsgilden binnen een handelskapitalistische stad: aanzetten voor een analyse van Amsterdam circa 1700." *NEHA-JAARBOEK voor economische, bedrijfs- en techniekgeschiedenis* 61 (1998), 121–62.

Machlup, F. *The Economics of Information and Human Capital. Vol. III, Knowledge: Its Creation, Distribution, and Economic Significance*. Princeton University Press, 1984.

Mackintosh, M., J. Chataway, and M. Wuyts. "Promoting Innovation, Productivity and Industrial Growth and Reducing Poverty: Bridging the Policy Gap." Special issue, *The European Journal of Development Research* 19, 1 (2007).

MacLeod, C. *Inventing the Industrial Revolution: The English Patent System, 1660–1800*. New York: Cambridge University Press, 1988.

MacLeod, C. "The European Origins of British Technological Predominance." In *Exceptionalism and Industrialisation: Britain and Its European Rivals, 1688–1815*, ed. L. Prados de la Escosura, pp. 111–26. Cambridge University Press, 2004.

Maenen, A. J. Fr. *Petrus Regout (1801–1878)*. Nijmegen: N. V. Centrale Drukkerij, 1959.

Mailly, E. *Notice sur Rombaut Bournons, membre de l'Académie Impériale et Royale*. In *Mémoire couronnés et autres mémoires*, Vol. XXVII. Brussels: Hayez, imprimeur de l'Académie royale, 1877.

Malandain, G. *L'introuvable complot. Attentat enquête et rumeur dans la France de la Restauration*. Paris: EHESS, 2011.

Marchand, P. *Écoles et collèges dans le Nord à l'aube de la Révolution. L'enquête du directoire du département du Nord "sur les établissements destinés à l'instruction de la jeunesse" (1790–91)*. Lille: Université Charles de Gaulle, 1988.

Marsden, B., and C. Smith. *Engineering Empires: A Cultural History of Technology in Nineteenth-Century Britain*. New York: Palgrave, 2005.

Mason, S., ed. *Matthew Boulton: Selling What All the World Desires*. Birmingham City Council in association with Yale University Press, 2009.

McCants, A. E. C. *Civic Charity in a Golden Age: Orphan Care in Early Modern Amsterdam*. Chicago: University of Illinois Press, 1997.

McClellan, J. E. "Un Manuscrit inédit de Condorcet: Sur l'utilité des académies." *Revue d'histoire des sciences* 30 (1977), 241–53.

McClellan, J. III. *Science Reorganized: Scientific Societies in the Eighteenth Century*. New York: Columbia University Press, 1985.

McCloy, S. J. *French Inventions of the Eighteenth Century*. Lexington: University of Kentucky Press, 1952.

Meisenzahl, R., and J. Mokyr. "The Rate and Direction of Invention in the British Industrial Revolution." National Bureau of Economic Research Working Paper 16993. Cambridge, MA: April 2011, www.nber.org/papers/w16993

Milligan, E. *Biographical Dictionary of British Quakers in Commerce and Industry, 1775–1920*. York: Sessions Book Trust, 2007.

Minard, P. "L'inspection des manufactures en France, de Colbert à la Révolution". Thèse de doctorat, Université de Paris-I, 1994.

Mishra, C. S., and R. K. Zachary. "Revisiting, Reexamining and Reinterpreting Schumpeter's Original Theory of Entrepreneurship." *Entrepreneurship Research Journal* 1 (2011), Article 2, www.bepress.com/erj/vol1/iss1/2.

Mitch, D. "The Role of Education and Skill in the British Industrial Revolution." In *The British Industrial Revolution: An Economic Perspective*, 2nd edn, ed. J. Mokyr, pp. 241–79. Boulder, CO: Westview Press, 1999.

Mitchell, B. R. *Economic Development of the British Coal Industry 1800–1914*. Cambridge University Press, 1984.

Mokyr, J. *Industrialization in the Low Countries, 1795–1850*. New Haven, CT: Yale University Press, 1976.

Mokyr, J. "The Industrial Revolution and the Netherlands: Why did it not happen?" Departments of Economics and History, Northwestern University, December 1999. Prepared for the 150th Anniversary Conference Organized by the Royal Dutch Economic Association, Amsterdam, December 10–11, 1999.

Mokyr, J. *The Gifts of Athena: Historical Origins of the Knowledge Economy*. New York: Oxford University Press, 2002.

Mokyr, J. *The Enlightened Economy: An Economic History of Britain 1700–1850*. New Haven, CT: Yale University Press, 2009.

Mokyr, J. "Entrepreneurship and the Industrial Revolution in Britain." In *The Invention of Enterprise: Entrepreneurship from Ancient Mesopotamia to Modern Times*, ed. D. S. Landes, J. Mokyr, and W. J. Baumol. Princeton University Press, 2010.

Morris, R. J. "The Rise of James Kitson: Trades Union and Mechanics Institution, Leeds, 1826–1851." *Publications of the Thoresby Society*, Vol. XV, 1972.

Morus, I. R. *Frankenstein's Children: Electricity, Exhibition, and Experiment in Early-Nineteenth-Century London*. Princeton University Press, 1998.

Muldrew, C. *Food, Energy and the Creation of Industriousness: Work and Material Culture in Agrarian England, 1550–1780*. Cambridge University Press, 2011.

Munford, A. A. *The Manchester Grammar School, 1515–1915: A Regional Study of the Advancement of Learning in Manchester since the Reformation*. London: Longmans and Green, 1919.

Musson, A. E., and E. Robinson. *Science and Technology in the Industrial Revolution* (with Foreword to the Second Printing by M. C. Jacob). Reading: Gordon and Breach, 1989 (first printing 1969).

Neely, S. *Lafayette and the Liberal Ideal 1814–1824: Politics and Conspiracy in the Age of Reaction*. Carbondale, IL: Southern Illinois University Press, 1991.

Nixon, F. "The Early Steam Engine in Derbyshire." *Transactions of the Newcomen Society* 31 (1957–8 and 1958–9), 1–28.

Nuvolari, A., B. Verspagen, and N. von Tunzelmann. "The Early Diffusion of the Steam Engine in Britain, 1700–1800: A Reappraisal." Working Paper Series, January 2011/03, 1–35, www.lem.sssup.it/

Oechslin, J. J. *Le mouvement ultra-royaliste sous la Restauration. Son idéologie et son action politique, 1814–1830*. Paris: R. Pichon & R. Durand-Auzias, 1960.

Outram, D. "The Ordeal of Vocation: The Paris Academy of Sciences and the Terror, 1793–95." *History of Science* 21 (1983), 251–74.

Owre, M. P. "United in Division: The Polarized French Nation, 1814–1830." Ph.D. dissertation, University of North Carolina at Chapel Hill, 2008.

Palmer, R. R. "The Central Schools of the First French Republic: A Statistical Survey." In *The Making of Frenchmen: Current Directions in the History of Education in France, 1679–1979*, ed. D. N. Baker and P. J. Harrigan. Waterloo, Canada: Historical Reflections Press, 1980.

Parker, H. T. *An Administrative Bureau during the Old Regime: The Bureau of Commerce and Its Relations to French Industry from May 1781 to November 1783*. Newark, NJ: University of Delaware Press, 1993.

Parthasarathi, P. *Why Europe Grew Rich and Asia Did Not: Global Economic Divergence, 1600–1850*. Cambridge University Press, 2011.

Passeron, J.-C., and J. Revel, eds. *Penser par cas*. Paris: École des Hautes Études en Sciences Sociales, 2005.

Payen, J. *Capital et machine à vapeur au XVIIIe siècle. Les frères Périer et l'introduction en France de la machine à vapeur de Watt*. Paris: Mouton & Co., 1969.

Perez, L. "Silk Fabrics in Eighteenth-Century Lyon." In *Guilds, Innovation and the European Economy, 1400–1800*, ed. S. R. Epstein and M. Prak, pp. 232–63. Cambridge University Press, 2008.

Périer, J.-C. *Brevet d'invention. Établi par la loi du 7 Janvier 1791. Machine à vapeur, propre à monter le charbon des mines*. Paris: Baudouin, 1791.

Pickering, M. *Auguste Comte: An Intellectual Biography, Volume 1*. Cambridge University Press, 1993.

Piot, G. J. C. *Le Règne de Marie-Thérèse dans les Pays-Bas autrichiens*. Louvain: Vve Charles Fonteyn, 1874.

Pomeranz, K. *The Great Divergence: Europe, China, and the Making of the Modern World Economy*. Princeton University Press, 2002.

Pouthas, C. *L'Instruction publique à Caen pendant la Révolution*. Caen: Louis Jouan, 1912.

Prak, M. *Gezeten Burgers. De Elite in een Hollandse Stad, Leiden 1700–1780*. Leiden: De Bataafsche Leeuw, 1985.

Prévot, A. *L'Enseignement Technique chez les Frères des Écoles Chrétiennes au XVIIIe et aux XIXe siècles*. Paris: Ligel, 1964.

Pursell, C. W., Jr. *Early Stationary Engines in America: A Study in the Migration of a Technology*. Washington, DC: Smithsonian Institution Press, 1969.

Rappaport, R. "Government Patronage of Science in Eighteenth Century France." *History of Science* 8 (1969), 119–36.

Raymond, J., and J. V. Pickstone. "The Natural Sciences and the Learning of the English Unitarians." In *Truth, Liberty, Religion: Essays Celebrating Two Hundred Years of Manchester College*, ed. B. Smith. Oxford: Manchester College Oxford, 1986.

Reid, D. "A Science for Polite Society: British Dissent and the Teaching of Natural Philosophy in the Eighteenth Century." *History of Universities* 21, 2 (2006), 117–58.

Riley, J. C. *International Government Finance and the Amsterdam Capital Market, 1740–1815*. Cambridge University Press, 1980, reissued 2008.

Rimmer, W. G. *Marshalls of Leeds: Flax-Spinners 1788–1886*. Cambridge University Press, 1960.

Rimmer, W. G. "The Industrial Profile of Leeds, 1740–1840." *Publications of the Thoresby Society, Miscellany*, Vol. 14, Part 2, 1967.

Roberts, L. "Mapping Steam Engines and Skill in Eighteenth-century Holland." In *The Mindful Hand: Inquiry and Invention from the Late Renaissance to Early Industrialisation*, ed. L. Roberts, S. Schaffer, and P. Dear. Amsterdam: Koninklijke Nederlandse Akademie van Wetenschappen, 2007.

Roberts, L. "Instruments of Science and Citizenship: Science Education for Dutch Orphans during the Late Eighteenth Century." *Science and Education* 21 (2012), 157–77.

Robinson, E. "An English Jacobin: James Watt, Junior, 1769–1848." *Cambridge Historical Journal* 11, 3 (1955), 354–5.

Roche, D. *Le Siècle des lumières en province. Vol. I*. Paris: Mouton, 1978.

Rose, M. B. *The Gregs of Quarry Bank Mill: The Rise and Decline of a Family Firm, 1750–1914*. Cambridge University Press, 1986.

Roundtable on "Historians and the Question of 'Modernity.'" *American Historical Review* 116 (June 2011), 631–751.

Sanders, J. G. M., ed. *Revolutionair in Brabant, royalist in Holland*. Hilversum: Verloren, 2011.

Scherer, F. M. *New Perspectives on Economic Growth and Technological Innovation.* Washington, D.C.: Brookings Institution Press, 1999.
Schofield, R. E. *The Enlightenment of Joseph Priestley: A Study of His Life and Work from 1733 to 1773.* University Park, PA: The Pennsylvania State University Press, 1997.
Schofield, R. E. *The Enlightened Joseph Priestley: A Study of His Life and Work from 1773 to 1804.* University Park, PA: The Pennsylvania State University Press, 2004.
Schrauwers, A. "'Regenten' (Gentlemanly) Capitalism: Saint-Simonian Technocracy and the Emergence of the 'Industrialist Great Club' in mid-nineteenth century Netherlands." *Enterprise & Society* 11, 4 (December 2010), 753–5.
Seed, J. "Unitarianism, Political Economy, and the Antinomies of Liberal Culture in Manchester, 1830–50." *Social History* 7 (1982), 1–25.
Shank, J. B. *The Newton Wars and the Beginning of the French Enlightenment.* University of Chicago Press, 2008.
Shinn, T. "From Corps to 'Profession': The Emergence and Definition of Industrial Engineering in Modern France." In *The Organization of Science and Technology in France, 1808 –1914*, ed. R. Fox and G. Weisz. Cambridge University Press, 1981.
Smail, J. "Innovation and Invention in the Yorkshire Wool Textile Industry: A Miller's Tale." *In Les chemins de la nouveauté: innover, inventer au regard de d'histoire*, ed. Liliane Hilaire-Pérez and Anne-Françoise Garçon, pp. 313–29. Paris: Éditions du CTHS, 2003.
Smith, A. "'Engines Moved by Fire and Water' – The Contributions of Fellows of the Royal Society to the Development of Steam Power." *The Newcomen Society for the Study of the History of Engineering and Technology. Transactions* 63 (1991–2), 229–30.
Smith, J. "George Stephenson and the Miner's Lamp Controversy." *North East History* 34 (2001), 113–36.
Smith, K. J., ed. *Warwickshire Apprentices and Their Masters, 1710–1760.* Oxford: Dugdale Society, 1975.
Smith, M. S. *The Emergence of Modern Business Enterprise in France, 1800–1930.* Cambridge, MA: Harvard University Press, 2006.
Smith, R. S. *Early Coal-Mining around Nottingham 1500–1650.* University of Nottingham, 1989.
Spekkens, J. P. Lodewijk. *L'École centrale du département de la Meuse-Inférieure Maëstricht 1798–1804.* Maastricht: Ernest van Aelst, 1951.
Spitzer, A. B. *Old Hatreds and Young Hopes: The French Carbonari against the Bourbon Restoration.* Cambridge, MA: Harvard University Press, 1971.
Stapleton, D. H. *The Transfer of Early Industrial Technologies to America.* Philadelphia: American Philosophical Society, 1987.
Staum, M. S. *Minerva's Message: Stabilizing the French Revolution.* Montreal: McGill-Queen's University Press, 1996.
Steele, B. D. "Muskets and Pendulums: Benjamin Robins, Leonhard Euler, and the Ballistics Revolution." *Technology and Culture* 35 (April 1994), 348–82.
Steele, B. D. "Military 'Progress' and Newtonian Science in the Age of Enlightenment," in *The Heirs of Archimedes: Science and the Art of War through the Age of Enlightenment*, ed. B. D. Steele and T. Dorland. Cambridge, MA: MIT Press, 2005.

Stephens, W. B. *Education in Britain, 1750–1914*. New York: St. Martin's, 1998.

Stevens, E. W., Jr. *The Grammar of the Machine: Technical Literacy and Early Industrial Expansion in the United States*. New Haven, CT: Yale University Press, 1995.

Stewart, L. "Samuel Clarke, Newtonianism, and the Factions of Post-Revolutionary England." *Journal of the History of Ideas* 42, 1 (1981), 53–72.

Stewart, L. *The Rise of Public Science: Rhetoric, Technology, and Natural Philosophy in Newtonian Britain, 1660–1750*. Cambridge University Press, 1992.

Stewart, L. "A Meaning for Machines: Modernity, Utility, and the Eighteenth-Century British Public." *Journal of Modern History* 70 (June 1998), 259–94. Also found at http://industrialization.ats.ucla.edu/

Stewart, L. "The Boast of Matthew Boulton: Invention, Innovation and Projectors in the Industrial Revolution." *Economia e energia secc. XIII–XVIII*. Istituto Internazionale di Storia Economica "F. Datini" (Prato: Le Monnier, 2003), pp. 993–1010.

Stewart, L. "Science and the Eighteenth-century Public." In *The Enlightenment World*, ed. M. Fitzpatrick, P. Jones, C. Knellwolf, and I. McCalman. New York: Routledge, 2004.

Stott, A. "Evangelicalism and Enlightenment: The Educational Agenda of Hannah More." In *Educating the Child in Enlightenment Britain: Beliefs, Cultures, Practices*. ed. M. Hilton and J. Shefrin, pp. 41–55. Aldershot: Ashgate, 2009.

Szabo, F. A. J. *Kaunitz and Enlightened Absolutism 1753–1780*. Cambridge University Press, 1994.

Tann, J. "Fixed Capital Formation in Steam Power 1775–1825: A Case Study of the Boulton and Watt Engine." In *Studies in Capital Formation in the United Kingdom 1750–1920*, ed. C. H. Feinstein and S. Pollard. Oxford: Clarendon Press, 1988.

Tardy, J.-N. "Le flambeau et le poignard. Les contradictions de l'organisation clandestine des libéraux français, 1821–1827." *Revue d'histoire moderne & contemporaine* 57, 1 (2010), 69–90.

Thackray, A. *John Dalton: Critical Assessments of His Life and Science*. Cambridge, MA: Harvard University Press, 1972.

Thackray, A. "Natural Knowledge in Cultural Context: The Manchester Model." *American Historical Review* 79 (1974), 672–709.

Thomson, R. *Structures of Change in the Mechanical Age: Technological Innovation in the United States 1790–1865*. Baltimore, MD: The Johns Hopkins University Press, 2009.

Thornton, D. "Edward Baines, Senior (1774–1848), Provincial Journalism and Political Philosophy in Early-Nineteenth-Century England." *Northern History* 40 (September 2003), 277–97.

Timmins, G. "Technological Change." In *The Lancashire Cotton Industry: A History since 1700*, ed. M. B. Rose, pp. 29–62. Preston: Lancashire County Books, 1996.

Timmons, G. "Education and Technology in the Industrial Revolution." *History of Technology* 8 (1983), 135–49.

Tomory, L. "Building the First Gas Network, 1812–1820." *Technology and Culture* 52 (January 2011), 75–102.

Topham, J. R. "Publishing 'Popular Science' in Early Nineteenth-Century Britain." In *Science in the Marketplace: Nineteenth-Century Sites and Experiences*, ed. A. Fyfe and B. Lightman, pp. 139–52. University of Chicago Press, 2007.

Trebilcock, C. *The Industrialization of the Continental Powers, 1780–1914*. London: Longman, 1981.

Uglow, J. "Vase Mania." In *Luxury in the Eighteenth Century: Debates, Desires and Delectable Goods*, ed. M. Berg and E. Eger, pp. 156–8. New York: Palgrave, 2003.

United Nations Conference on Trade and Development. *The Least Developed Countries Report 2007: Knowledge, Technological Learning and Innovation for Development*. New York and Geneva: United Nations, Autumn 2007.

United Nations Conference on Trade and Development. *The Least Developed Countries Report 2009: The State and Development Governance*. New York and Geneva: United Nations, 2009.

Usher, A. P. "The Industrialization of Modern Britain." *Technology and Culture* 1 (1960), 109–27.

van Berkel, K. *In het voetspoor van Stevin. Geschiedenis van de natuurwetenschap in Nederland 1580–1940*. Boom: Meppel, 1985. www.dbnl.org/tekst/berk003-voet01_01/colofon.htm (accessed September 27, 2012).

van Berkel, K., A. Van Helden, and L. C. Palm, eds. *A History of Science in the Netherlands: Survey, Themes, and Reference*. Leiden: Brill, 1999.

van Deursen, A. T. "A Great Power in Decline (1702–1751)." In *History of the Low Countries*, ed. J. C. H. Blom and E. Lamberts, trans. J. Kennedy. New York: Berghahn Books, 1999.

Vanpaemel, G. In *Histoire des sciences en Belgique de l'Antiquité à 1815*, ed. R. Halleux, pp. 333–7. Brussels: Crédit Communal, 1998.

Vincent, D. "The End of Literacy: The Growth and Measurement of British Public Education since the Early Nineteenth Century." In *History, Historians and Development Policy: A Necessary Dialogue*, ed. C. A. Bayly, V. Rao, S. Szreter, and M. Woolcock. Manchester University Press, 2011.

Vogel, H. U. "The Mining Industry in Traditional China: Intra- and Intercultural Comparisons." In *Cultures of Technology and the Quest for Innovation*, ed. H. Nowotny, pp. 167–90. New York: Berghahn Books, 2006.

Wach, H. W. "Religion and Social Morality." *Journal of Modern History* 63 (1991), 425–56.

Wade, R. *The Rise of Nonconformity in Manchester with a Brief Sketch of the History of Cross Street Chapel*. Manchester: Johnson and Rawson, 1880.

Warde, P. "Energy and Natural Resource Dependency in Europe, 1600–1900." In *History, Historians and Development Policy: A Necessary Dialogue*, ed. C. A. Bayly, V. Rao, S. Szreter, and M. Woolcock. Manchester University Press, 2011.

Watson, R. S. *The History of the Literary and Philosophical Society of Newcastle upon Tyne (1793–1896)*. London: Walter Scott, 1897.

Watts, M. R. *The Dissenters. Vol. I, From the Reformation to the French Revolution*. Oxford: Clarendon Press, 1986.

Watts, M. R. *The Dissenters. Vol. II, The Expansion of Evangelical Nonconformity*. Oxford University Press, 1995.

Webb, R. K. "The Emergence of Rational Dissent." In *Enlightenment and Religion: Rational Dissent in Eighteenth-Century Britain*, ed. K. Haakonssen, pp. 12–41. Cambridge University Press, 1996.

Weber, M. *The Protestant Ethic and the Spirit of Capitalism*. New York: Scribner's, 1953 [originally published in German in 1904–5].

Weill, G. *Histoire de l'enseignement secondaire en France*. Paris: Payot, 1921.

Weiss, J.H. *The Making of Technological Man: The Social Origins of French Engineering Education*. Cambridge, MA: MIT Press, 1982.

Wilson, K. "A Dissident Legacy: Eighteenth Century Popular Politics and the Glorious Revolution." In *Liberty Secured? Britain before and after 1688*, ed. J. R. Jones, pp. 299–334. Stanford University Press, 1992.

Wood, O. "A Cumberland Colliery during the Napoleonic War." *Economica* (New Series) 21, 8 (1954).

Wrigley, E. A. "In Quest for the Industrial Revolution." *Proceedings of the British Academy* 121 (2003), 168–70.

Wrigley, E. A. *Energy and the English Industrial Revolution*. Cambridge University Press, 2010.

PRIMARY SOURCES

Adkin, J. *Evenings at Home; Or, the Juvenile Budget Opened. Consisting of a Variety of Miscellaneous Pieces, for the Instruction and Amusement of Young Persons*. London: J. Johnson, 1794–8, Vol. VI out of VI.

Allen, Z. *The Science of Mechanics*. Providence, RI: Hutchens and Cory, 1829.

Annales Academiae Leondiensis, 1818–1819, ed. J. M. Vanderheyden. Liège: P. J. Collardin, 1821.

Annales des mines, second series. Vol. I. Paris: Treuttel et Wurtz, 1827.

Anon. *Aanspraak gedann aan de Goede Burgeren, die tot Welzyn van stad en land, op den 9 Augustus 1748, op den Cloveriers Doelen Vergadert zyn geweest*. Amsterdam: 1748.

Anon. *Observations on Woollen Machinery*. Leeds: Edward Baines, 1803. Reproduced in *The Spread of Machinery: Five Pamphlets, 1793–1806*. New York: Arno Press, 1972.

Anon. *Provincial words used in Teesdale in the County of Durham*. London: J. R. Smith, 1849.

Anon. *Relation du séjour du Roi à Lille ... Le 7 et 8 Septembre 1827*. Lille: Reboux-Leroy.

Baines, E. Jr. *History of the Cotton Manufacture in Great Britain*. London: Fisher, Fisher & Jackson, 1835.

Beatson, R. *An Essay on the Comparative Advantages of Vertical and Horizontal Windmills: Containing a Description of a Horizontal Windmill and Water Mill, upon a New Construction*. London and Edinburgh: 1798.

Bibliothèque des Instituteurs, Ouvrage utile à tous ceux qui sont chargés directement ou indirectement de l'education de la jeunesse. Vols. I–XII. Mons: Hoyois, 1819–32, 1833–41.

A Catalogue of Optical, Mathematical, and Philosophical Instruments, Made and Sold by W. and S. Jones, Lower Holborn, London, 1837.

A Catalogue of R. Fisher's Circulating Library, in the High-Bridge, Newcastle. Newcastle upon Tyne: M. Angus, 1791.

Bosma, B. *Redenvoering over de Orde en derzelver zigtbaarheid onder de Schepselen*. Second Treatise. Amsterdam: 1765.

Brisson, M.-J. *Traité élémentaire, ou principes de physique*. Paris: 1789.

Catlow, S. *Observations on a Course of Instruction for Young Persons in the Middle Classes of Life*. Sheffield: J. Gales for J. Johnson and T. Knott, 1793.

Cauchy, A. "Sur la recherché de la vérité." *Bulletin de l'Institut Catholique*, 2nd Installment, April 14, 1842.

Chalmers, A. "Samuel Koenig" in *The General Biographical Dictionary*. London: 1812–17, http://words.fromoldbooks.org/Chalmers-Biography/k/koenig-samuel.html.

Chamber of Commerce. *Enquête faite par ordre du Parlement d'Angleterre pour constater les progrès de l'industrie en France*. Paris: Boudouin, 1825.

Chapman, W. *Address to the Subscribers to the Canal from Carlisle to Fisher's Cross*. Newcastle: Edward Walker, 1823.

Chatillon, M. *Almanach du clergé de France*. Paris: Guyot, 1824.

Christian, G. *Catalogue général des collections du Conservatoire Royal des arts et métiers*. Paris: Mme Huzard, 1818.

Christian, G. J. *Vues sur le système générale des opérations industrielles ou plan de technonomie*. Paris: 1819.

Christian, G. J. *Annales générales des sciences physiques*. Brussels: Weissenbrush, 1822–5.

Christian, G. J. *Traité de mécanique industrielle*. 3 vols.

Condorcet, *Rapport et projet de décret sur l'organisation générale de l'instruction publique (avril 1792–décembre 1792)*. In *Une Éducation pour la Démocratie. Textes et projets de l'époque révolutionnaire*, ed. B. Baczko. Geneva: Droz, 2000.

Conyers, J. *The Complete Collier: or the Whole Art of Sinking, Getting, and Working Coal-Mines etc. as is Now Used in the Northern Parts especially about Sunderland and Newcastle*. London: G. Conyers, 1708; reprinted Newcastle, 1846.

Daily Courant, Thursday, January 11, 1705.

Davy, Sir H. *On the Fire-Damp of Coal Mines: From the Philosophical Transactions of the Royal Society*. London: 1816.

de Jussieu, L. P. *Simon de Nantua, ou le Marchand Forain*. Paris: Chez L. Colas, 1818.

Delamennais, F. *Œuvrés complètes de F. Delamennais*. Vol. VII, "De la Religion considérée dans ses rapports avec l'ordre politique et civil." Paris: Paul Daubree et Cailleux, 1836–7.

Desaguliers, J. *A Course of Experimental Philosophy*. Vol. II. London: 1744.

Desaguliers, J. *A Course of Experimental Philosophy*, 2nd edn, Vol. I. London: 1745 (1st edn, London 1734).

Diderot, D. *Plan d'une université pour le gouvernement de Russie*. In *Œuvres complètes*, Vol. III. Paris: 1875.

Drake, D. *An Anniversary Discourse on the State and Prospects of the Western Museum Society*. Cincinnati, OH: 1820.

Dunn, M. *An Historical, Geological, and Descriptive View of the Coal Trade of the North of England . . . and also a General Description of the Coal Mines of Belgium Drawn from Actual Inspection*. Newcastle upon Tyne: Pattison and Ross, 1844.

Dupin, Charles. *Effets des l'enseignement populaire de la lecture, de l'écriture et de l'arithmétique, de la géométrie et de la mécanique*. Paris: Bachelier, 1826.

Edgeworth, M., and R. L. Edgeworth. *Practical Education.* 3 vols. London, 1801: reprint, Poole: Woodstock Books, 1996.

Exposé de la situation de l'Empire français. 1806 et 1807. Paris: Imperial Printer, 1807.

Fairbairn, W. *A Brief Memoir of the Late John Kennedy, Esq.* Manchester: Charles Simms & Co., 1861.

Fenwick, T. *Four Essays on Practical Mechanics*, 2nd edn. Newcastle upon Tyne: printed for the author by S. Hodgson, 1802, second essay.

Frayssinous, M. D. *Conférences et discours inédits.* Paris: Adrien Le Clere, 1843.

Greenwell, G. C. *A Glossary of Terms Used in the Coal Trade of Northumberland and Durham.* Newcastle upon Tyne: John Bell, 1849.

Grundy, J. Sr. *Chester Navigation Consider'd.* N.d., ca. 1736.

Guest, R. *A Compendious History of the Cotton Manufacture.* 1823; reprint, London: Frank Cass & Co. Ltd., 1968.

Hair, T. H. *A Series of Views of the Collieries in the Counties of Northumberland and Durham.* London: James Madden, 1844.

Hardie, F. *Syllabus of a Course of Lectures . . . at his Experimental Philosophic Lecture Room and Theatre of Rational Amusement, Pantheon, Oxford St., London.* London: W. Burton, 1800.

Henry, W. C. "A Biographical Notice of the Late Peter Ewart, Esq." *Memoirs of the Manchester Literary and Philosophical Society*, 2nd Series, No. 7 (1846), pp. 113–36.

Hill, F. *National Education: Its Present State and Prospects.* Vol. II. London: 1836.

Hodgkinson, E. "Some Account of the Late Mr. Ewart's Paper on the Measure of Moving Forces; and on the Recent Applications of the Principles of Living Forces to Estimate the Effects of Machines and Movers." *Memoirs of the Literary and Philosophical Society of Manchester*, 2nd Series, No. 7 (1846): 137–56.

Hooson, W. *The Miners Dictionary. Explaining Not Only the Terms Used by Miners But Also Containing the Theory and Practice of that Most Useful Art of Mineing, More Especially of Lead-Mines.* A facsimile of the edition published at Wrexham in 1747. Ilkley: Scolar Press, 1979.

Huberman, M. "Industrial Relations and the Industrial Revolution: Evidence from M'Connel and Kennedy, 1810–1840." *The Business History Review* 65 (Summer 1991), 345–78.

Hulin, N. "Le problème de physique aux xixe et xxe siècles." In *Travaux d'élèves pour une histoire des performances scolaires et de leur évaluation XIXe–XXe siècles*, ed. P. Caspard, No. 54, 1992.

Journal d'Education, vii (April 1828).

Joyce, J. *Scientific Dialogues*, London: Baldwin, Cradock, and Joy, etc., multiple editions and volumes, beginning in 1802.

Kennedy, J. *On the Exportation of Machinery: A Letter Addressed to the Hon. E.G. Stanley, M.P.* London: Hurst & Co., 1824.

Kennedy, J. *A Brief Memoir of Samuel Crompton; With a Description of His Machine Called the Mule, and of the Subsequent Improvement of the Machine by Others.* Manchester: Printed by Henry Smith, 1830.

Kennedy, J. "Brief Notice of My Early Recollections, in a Letter to My Children." In J. Kennedy, *Miscellaneous Papers on Subjects Connected with the Manufactures of Lancashire reprinted from the Memoirs of the Literary and Philosophical Society of Manchester*. Privately printed, 1849, pp. 1–18.

Kennedy, J. *Miscellaneous Papers on Subjects Connected with the Manufactures of Lancashire reprinted from the Memoirs of the Literary and Philosophical Society of Manchester*. Privately printed, 1849.

Kennedy, J. *Observations on the Rise and Progress of the Cotton Trade in Great Britain, Particularly in Lancashire and the Adjoining Counties*. Manchester: The Executors of the Late S. Russell, 1818.

La Foudre, October 15, 1823.

L'ami de la religion et du roi, Sur l'éducation publique et sur les lycées. Vol. 5, 1814.

Le Normand, L., and J. G. V. de Moléon. *Description des expositions des produits de l'industrie française, faites à Paris depuis leur Origine jusqu'a celle de 1819 inclusivement*. Vol. I. Paris: Bachelier, 1824.

Le Normant, G. A. *Plan ter vestiging van eene school voor handwerkslieden, in welke 400 jongelingen aanhoudend in de kunsten en ambachten zullen onderwezen worden, zonder iets aan den staat te kosten*. Ghent: J. N. Houdin, 1826.

Le Roy, A. *L'Université de Liège depuis sa Fondation*. Liège: J. G. Carmanne, 1869.

Leeds Intelligencer, Vol. 38, 1894, December 14, 1790.

Leeds Mercury, January 3, 1769, January 16, 1770.

Mackenzie E. *A Historical and Descriptive View of the County of Northumberland and of the Town and County of Newcastle upon Tyne*. Vol. I. Newcastle upon Tyne: Mackenzie & Dent, 1811.

Malherbe, R. *Société Libre d'Emulation de Liège, Liber Memorialis 1779–1879*. Liège: L. de Their, 1879.

Malo, C. *Bazar Parisien, ou tableau raisonné de l'industrie*. Paris: au bureau du Bazar, 1822–23.

M'Connel, D. C. *Facts and Traditions Collected for a Family Record*. Edinburgh: Printed by Ballantine and Co. for private circulation, 1861.

Mémorial universel de l'industrie française. Paris: Didot, 1821.

The Newcastle Memorandum-Book or a Methodical Pocket-Journal for the year MDCCCVII. Newcastle upon Tyne: S. Hodgson, 1806.

Nicholson, W. *A Dictionary of Chemistry*. London: G. G. and J. Robinson, 1795.

Nicholson, W. E. *A Glossary of Terms Used in the Coal Trade of Northumberland and Durham*. Newcastle on Tyne: 1888.

Nollet, A. *Leçons de Physique expérimentale*. Vol. I. Amsterdam and Leipzig: Arksteé & Merkus, 1754.

[Par un Professeur]. *Nouveau plan d'éducation, épitre adressée à tous les membres du corps enseignant et aux pères de famille*. Paris: chez tous les marchands de nouveautés, 1828.

Procès Verbal de la Séance de la Société Libre d'Emulation. Liège: Latour, 1812.

Pryce, W. *Mineralogia cornubiensis, a treatise on minerals, mines, and mining: containing the theory and natural history of strata, fissures, and lodes. To which is added, an explanation of the terms and idioms of miners*. London: printed for the author, 1778.

Règlement de la Société des Amis des Sciences, Lettres et Arts établie à Maastricht. Maastricht: L.Th. Nypels, 1828.

Règlement de la Société Libre d'Emulation ... à Liège. Liège: Desoer, 1812.

Renouard, A. C. *Considérations sur les lacunes de l'éducation secondaire en France.* Paris: Antoine-Augustin Renouard, 1824.

Report of the Committee of the Birmingham Mechanics' Institution, Read at the Ninth Anniversary Meeting, Held Friday, January 2, 1835, in the Lecture Room, Cannon-Street. Birmingham: Printed by J. W. Showell, 1835.

Report of the Directors of the Manchester Mechanics' Institution, May 1828, with the Rules and Regulations of the Institution. Manchester: Printed by R. Robinson, St. Ann's Place, 1828.

Rutt, J. T., ed. *The Theological and Miscellaneous Works of Joseph Priestley. Vol. II, Institutes of Natural and Revealed Religion.* London: Smallfield, 1817.

Sigorgne, M. *Institutions Newtoniennes, ou introduction à la philosophie de M. Newton.* Paris: 1747.

Société des sciences, arts, lettres du Hainaut. *Table des Publications 1839–1924.* Tournay: Grande imprimerie-Litho Tournaisienne, S.C., 1937.

The Tenth Report of the Keighley Mechanics' Institution, for the year ending April 4th, 1836 with a list of the members, a catalogue of the books and apparatus. Keighley: R. Aken, 1836.

Thackrah, C. Turner. *An Introductory Discourse. Delivered to the Leeds Philosophical and Literary Society, April 6, 1821.* Leeds: printed for the Philosophical and Literary Society by W. Gawtress, 1821.

Vince, Rev. S. *A Plan of a Course of Lectures on the Principles of Natural Philosophy.* Cambridge: J. Archdeacon, 1793.

Walker, A. *Analysis of a Course of Lectures in Natural and Experimental Philosophy,* 11th edn. London: William Thorne, 1799.

Whiting, T. *Mathematical, Geometrical, and Philosophical Delights ... A Eulogium on the Newtonian Philosophy.* London: T. N. Longman, 1798.

Wilkinson, C. H. *An Analysis of a Course of Lectures on the Principles of Natural Philosophy.* London: 1799.

Young, T. *A Course of Lectures on Natural Philosophy and the Mechanical Arts.* London: Joseph Johnson, 1807.

Index